The Original
Pets
Welcome!

2011

- *57th Edition*

- **Guide to Pet Friendly Pubs**
- **Holidays with Horses**
- **Preparing your cat or dog for travelling abroad**
- **Dog-friendly walks around Britain**

YASSKO HAS A COOL SUMMER DIP
Wendy Halling, Bedford

GW00641739

Foreword

We are delighted to introduce this 57th edition of **Pets Welcome!** with its varied selection of holidays for pets and their owners. The choice of accommodation includes not only self-catering properties and caravans as one might expect, but also many hotels, guest houses and B&B establishments.

As in previous issues, we urge owners to behave responsibly and to ensure their pet does not jump on furniture or beds, and they should not be left unattended for long periods. In this climate of environmental awareness and concern about pollution on our beaches and elsewhere, pet owners should abide by the relevant local authority rules regarding 'doggy' access to beaches and other areas. But for many of us enjoying a country holiday means taking the dog on scenic walks and you'll find a useful selection of especially recommended walks on **pages 24-35.**

Most of our entries are of long standing and are tried and tested favourites with animal lovers. However as publishers we do not inspect the accommodation advertised in Pets Welcome! and an entry does not imply our recommendation. Some proprietors offer fuller facilities for pets than others, and in the classified entry which we give each advertiser we try to indicate by symbols whether or not there are any special facilities and if additional charges are involved. However, we suggest that you raise any queries or particular requirements when you make enquiries and bookings.

If you have any problems or complaints, please raise them on the spot with the owner or his representative in the first place. We will follow up complaints if necessary, but we regret that we cannot act as intermediaries nor can we accept responsibility for details of accommodation and/or services described here. Happily, serious complaints are few. Finally, if you have to cancel or postpone a holiday booking, please give as much notice as possible. This courtesy will be appreciated and it could save later difficulties.

Preparing your Dogs and Cats for Travel Abroad (Page 10), Holidays with Horses (Page 444), and The Guide to Pet Friendly Pubs (Page 448) are now regular features. Our latest selection of Pets Pictures starts on page 18.

We would be happy to receive readers' suggestions on any other useful features. Please also let us know if you have had any unusual or humorous experiences with your pet on holiday. This always makes interesting reading! And we hope that you will mention **Pets Welcome!** when you make your holiday inquiries or bookings.

Contents

©MAPS IN MINUTES™ / Collins Bartholomew (2009)

Tailwagging holidays...
with your best friend

Lodges • Holiday Parks • Cottages • Boating

On many of our holidays you can take your best friend with you, whether it is a cottage, lodge, holiday park or boating break you are looking for.

BOOK NOW or request a brochure
Call **0844 847 1103** QUOTE GA150
Click **www.hoseasons.co.uk/fhgpets**

Before you go anywhere, take a trip to Pets at Home

We know you love to spend quality time with your pet.

So when it's holiday time, we have a huge choice of travel accessories to choose from, including pet carriers, car harnesses and even fans to keep your pets cool on those hot summer days.

Plus, our highly trained advisors in every store can offer you free expert advice and top tips to ensure both you and your pet have a smooth journey.

Wherever you're heading, head for Pets at Home first!

There are over 270 stores nationwide, to find your nearest store log on to: petsathome.com/storelocator

pets at home   where pets come first

UK, Ireland and France 2011

welcome cottages
Make yourself at home

Pets stay **FREE**[†]

Cottage ref: W40741

Pets stay free![†]

We know your pet is one of the family, so they should come with you too...

That's why 1 or more pets can stay **FREE**[†] at a great selection of UK, Ireland and France properties. Discover the perfect holiday cottage **EVERYONE** can enjoy – pond dipping, stick finding and beach bounding. Relax and enjoy being together.

Cottage ref: W41655

Call **0845 268 6982** for your 2011 brochure now or go online at **www.welcomecottages.com** to view our full collection.

ABTA
ABTA No.Y0662
See booking conditions for full details

[†]At selected properties. Booking conditions apply, see main brochure or website

Pet-Friendly
Pubs, Inns & Hotels
on pages 448-453

These establishments may not feature in the main section of the book

Preparing your Pet for travel abroad

How can my pet travel? Because of stringent requirements, dogs and cats travelling under the so-called pet passport scheme cannot make last minute reservations; in general, six-month advance planning is required. Veterinarians must implant a microchip in the animal, inoculate it against rabies, have a laboratory recognized by the Department for Environment, Food and Rural Affairs (DEFRA) confirm by blood sample that the vaccine is active, and issue a PETS certificate. Certificates are valid from six months after obtaining the blood sample results until the date of the animal's next rabies booster shot. (Dogs and cats resident in Britain whose blood sample was drawn before Feb 29, 2000 are exempt from this six month rule). Dogs and cats must also be treated against ticks and tapeworms no less than 24 nor more than 48 hours before check-in (when the animal enters carrier's custody). Animals travelling by air are placed in containers bearing an official seal (the number of which is also inscribed on the PETS certificate) to ensure animals are not exposed to disease en route. Sealing requirements do not apply to Cyprus or Malta. Owners must also sign a certificate attesting that the animal has not been outside participating territories in the last six months. Travellers are cautioned that Britain will enforce its rules rigorously.

Your pet must be injected with a harmless identification ISO (International Standards Organisation) approved microchip. This chip will be read by a handheld scanning device.

From and back to the UK ●●●●●●●●●●●●●●●●●●●●●●●●●●●●●

Ask your vet to implant an ISO (International Standards Organisation) approved microchip - then to vaccinate against rabies recording the batch number of the vaccine on a veterinary certificate together with the microchip number.

Approximately 30 days later your vet should take a blood sample and send it to one of the DEFRA approved laboratories to check that the vaccine has provided the correct level of protection.

Your vet will then issue you with a certificate confirming all the above – in the UK this is called The Pet Travel Scheme Re-Entry Certificate. It is valid for the life of the rabies vaccine, so keep your rabies vaccine up to date and a new certificate will be issued without the need for further blood tests.

Six months from the taking of a successful blood test you will be able to enter or re-enter the UK from Western Europe and 28 other countries including Australia, Japan and Singapore.

Pets must be treated for ticks and for the echinococcus parasite by a qualified vet who will record this on an official UK certificate not less than 24 hours and not more than 48 hours before entry into the UK.

On entering the UK you must therefore have two official certificates; one for the microchip, rabies vaccine and blood test; the second for treatment against ticks and parasites. You will also have to sign a residence declaration form - provided by the travel operator who is carrying out the checking. It simply confirms that the pet has not been outside the approved countries in the previous six months.

From Europe to the UK ●●●●●●●●●●●●●●●●●●●●●●●●●●●●●

As above, you must microchip your pet, vaccinate against rabies and approximately 30 days later your vet will take a blood test sending it to one of the laboratories from the list of those approved by MAFF. SIX MONTHS after a successful blood test your pet will be allowed to travel to the UK providing it has been treated against ticks and worms.

Providing the rabies vaccination is kept up to date the blood test will not have to be repeated. Should there be a break between rabies vaccines a further blood test would have to be taken and then a period of 6 months allowed before re-entry to the UK would be permitted.

Contact your local vet for an indication of the costs involved in preparing your pet for travel abroad. You are responsible for ensuring your pet meets all the rules of the Pet Travel Scheme. If you do not have the procedures carried out in the correct order, and have documentation correctly completed, your pet may not be able to enter the country, or have to go into quarantine.

More information can be obtained from
defra Department for Environment Food and Rural Affairs

Department of Environment, Food and Rural Affairs PETS
website: *ww2.defra.gov.uk/wildlife-pets/*

Pet Travel Scheme Helpline: Tel: 0870 241 1710
Monday to Friday - 8am to 6pm UK time (closed Bank Holidays).

E-mail: quarantine@animalhealth.gsi.gov.uk
(enclose your postal address and a day time telephone number).

Pet Travel Scheme

Holidays in France

For you and your pets

Taking a holiday abroad with a pet use to be inconvenient and hard to arrange, but the increase in pet-friendly accommodation and a change in regulations for travelling with animals means that a holiday with your 'best friend' is a much more realistic prospect.

France is a popular choice, not only because of the relatively short travel time, but also because ease of access through the Channel Tunnel or on a ferry means that there is no need for the extra expense and stress (for you and your pet!) involved in air travel.

See below, or check out our website **www.holidayguides.com** for other options.

Maison Renard

South-facing Charentaise house, set in a quiet hamlet near to the market town of La Rochefoucauld, with its chateau, restaurants, shops etc only a few minutes' drive away. This area of South West France is famous for its rolling countryside, lakes, and rivers, and for the production of wine, cognac and pineau, all to be tasted!! and explored.

The house sleeps up to 6 people, with two bathrooms, fully equipped kitchen, lounge and dining room.

British satellite TV, Wi-Fi internet connection, and phone are provided. The indoor pool is seasonally heated and leads on to the patio and BBQ areas.

WELL BEHAVED PETS ARE WELCOME.

Contact: *John & Sally Fox,*
Tel: 01724 720384 or 00 33 54 521 73 87
e-mail: foxjns@aol.com
or enquiries@maisonrenard.co.uk

Visit our website: www.maisonrenard.co.uk

La Rochefoucauld (Charente Lakes)

Quiet hamlet, surrounded by lakes and beautiful countryside, in the heart of the Charente. Restaurant bars and shops a few minutes away. Ideal for walking, cycling, birdwatching, golf, fishing and water sports in the Charente Lakes.

MAISON RENARD. Tastefully restored Charentaise house in quiet hamlet. Sleeps 6. Fully equipped kitchen, BBQ, indoor pool. South-facing garden. Contact: JOHN & SALLY FOX (01724 720384 or 00 33 54 521 73 87). [🐕]
e-mail: foxjns@aol.com or enquiries@maisonrenard.co.uk   website: www.maisonrenard.co.uk

SINCE 1927

iron for vitality & protein for muscles

WINALOT® WALKS IS BACK!

Winalot® Walks is back and it is bigger and better than ever!

On our simple new Walks page you can quickly and easily find walks to suit

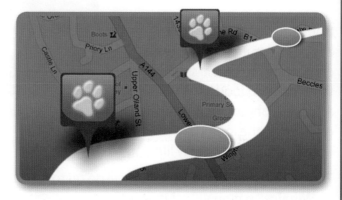

you or help other **Winalot®** families enjoy a great day out by marking your own favourite walking routes.

Visit the website today!
www.winalot-dog.co.uk

® Reg. Trademark of Sociétié des Produits Nestlé S.A.

PURINA
Your Pet, Our Passion.®

SINCE 1927

MEET OUR WINNING WINALOT FAMILY!

Blade the dog, from Walsall, has beaten hundreds of canine competitors to be the star of **Winalot**® dog food, after winning a national photograph competition celebrating the important role dogs play in British family life.

The overall winner and his family will go on to feature on packs of **Winalot**® nationwide this year.

To view the 25 finalists' and other entrants' pictures and their stories, go t

www.winalot-dog.co.uk

® Reg. Trademark of Sociétié des Produits Nestl

PURINA
Your Pet, Our Passion.®

WINALOT® FAMILY MOMENTS COMPETITION EVENT

The **Winalot®** Family Moments campaign, which ran throughout the UK, asked owners to share a picture of themselves with their dog, and describe why their dog is so special to their family.

The 25 finalist families and their four-legged best friends have taken part in a once-in-a-lifetime photo shoot with award winning wildlife photographer, Andy Rouse. Their best picture hung in the Getty Gallery on 12nd-13th December.

At the opening night of the exhibition celebrity dog lover and TV personality, en Fogle, announced the overall winner.

For more pictures and information, go to

www.winalot-dog.co.uk

PURINA
Your Pet, Our Passion.®

Dogs**Trust** : A Dog is For Life

Are you thinking of going on holiday in the UK with your dog?

If so, the Dogs Trust has a free factsheet which will be of particular interest.

"Safe travel and happy holidays with your hound in the UK"

For this and any other of our free Dogs Trust factsheets please contact us at:

**Dogs Trust,
17 Wakley St. London EC1V 7RQ.
Tel: 020 7837 0006**

**Website: www.dogstrust.org.uk
or e-mail us, info@dogstrust.org.uk**

Last year Dogs Trust cared for over 16,000 stray and abandoned dogs at our network of 18 Rehoming Centres. So if you are looking for a companion for your dog or you have a friend who might like a dog, just contact your nearest Dogs Trust Rehoming Centre.

We care for around 1,600 dogs on any given day, so we are sure we will be able to find your perfect partner. The Dogs Trust never destroys a healthy dog.

For details of our Sponsor-a-Dog scheme please call **020 7837 0006**
or visit **www.sponsoradog.org.uk**

Dogs Trust Rehoming Centres

LONDON

Dogs Trust Harefield
0845 076 3647

ENGLAND

Dogs Trust Canterbury
01227 792 505

Dogs Trust Darlington
01325 333 114

Dogs Trust Evesham
01386 830 613

Dogs Trust Ilfracombe
01271 812 709

Dogs Trust Kenilworth
01926 484 398

Dogs Trust Leeds
01132 613 194

Dogs Trust Merseyside
0151 480 0660

Dogs Trust Newbury
01488 658 391

Dogs Trust Roden
01952 770 225

Dogs Trust Salisbury
01980 629 634

Dogs Trust Shoreham
01273 452 576

Dogs Trust Snetterton
01953 498 377

WALES

Dogs Trust Bridgend
01656 725 219

SCOTLAND

Dogs Trust Glasgow
0141 773 5130

Dogs Trust West Calder
01506 873 459

NORTHERN IRELAND

Dogs Trust Ballymena
028 2565 2977

IRELAND

Dogs trust Dublin
enquiries@dogstrust.ie

Registered Charity No. 227523

Donate £1 to your favourite Pets Charity

FHG has agreed to donate £1 from the price of this Pets Welcome! Guide to EITHER
The Royal Society For The Prevention of Cruelty to Animals,
Dogs Trust,
The Kennel Club,
or the Scottish Society for the Prevention of Cruelty to Animals

To allow the Charity of your choice to receive this donation simply complete the slip below and return to FHG at

FHG Guides Ltd, Abbey Mill Business Centre Seedhill, Paisley PA1 1TJ
Closing date end October 2011

Note: Original forms only please, do not send photocopies.

✂---

Please donate £1 from the price of this Pets Welcome! guide to:

RSPCA ☐   DOGS TRUST ☐   KENNEL CLUB ☐   SSPCA ☐

Name ....

Address ....

....

Postcode ....Date ....

HG Guides may send readers details of discount offers for our holiday guides.
⸰ you do not wish to receive this information please tick here ☐
ʼour details will not be passed on to any other organisation.

Readers' Pets Pictures

Send us your favourite Pet Photo!

On the following pages are a selection of pets photos sent in by readers of **Pets Welcome!** If you would like to have a photo of your pet included in the next edition (published in OCTOBER 2011), send it along with a brief note of the pet's name and a few details such as age, breed etc.

Please remember to include your own name and address and let us know if you would like the pictures returned.

FHG will give a FREE copy of the guide in which the picture appears.

We will be happy to receive prints, or pictures by e-mail to

TESS
*Madeleine Thomson &
Tim Neville, Enfield*

editorial@fhguides.co.uk

All pictures should be forwarded by the middle of July 2011.

Thanks to everyone who sent in pictures of their pets and regret that we were unable to include all of them. Pictures not included in this edition will be considered for use in the future. See the following pages for this year's selection.

Send your Pet photo to:
FHG Guides, Abbey Mill Business Centre,
Seedhill, Paisley PA1 1TJ

POPPY
Alison McLelland, Paisley

TIA
Julie Allen, Alvaston

KIKI
Anita Kelsey, London

CRUACH
Elizabeth & David McGregor, Birkhill

PRINCESS JYNX
Julie Allen, Alvaston

STANLEY
Robert Ion, Johnstone

OBAN, SHADOW
Elizabeth Walker-Parker
Grantown-on-Spey

SHYLA
Margaret Thomson, Louth

ROXY
Lynn Gorman, Paisley

TREVOR
Lesley Walding,
Frampton Cotterell

YAYA
Monica Azzali, London

PADDY
Sharon Symons, Bude

CERYS
Wendy Halling, Bedford

MISHKA
Meryl & Mark Dewolfreys, Newquay

HUGO
Jennifer & Victor Gibbons, New Mills

STITCH
Jessica Print, Alcester

CHLOE
Gillian Caldwell, Glasgow

TOBY
Joanne Stenning, Wrexham

KELSEA
Julie Davies, Luton

BLUE
Jean Williamson, Paisley

IF YOU LOVE DOGS
YOU'LL LOVE YOUR DO[G]

BRITAIN'S BEST-SELLING DOG MAGAZI[NE]

116 pages

9 771355 738092

10 >

October 2010
R40
£3.40

your dog

DOG ANSWERS
22 PAGES OF
Qs & As
Solving your problems on
health, training,
behaviour and more

**Share some
magic moments**
Try an activity
holiday with your pet

10
**big mistakes
we make
with our dogs**
And how to
avoid them!

Over
£1,200-worth
of giveaways
– inside
UK only

**Undying
devotion**
The clever,
complicated
Akita

**Health – a
top priority**
Get your
puppy
checked

Living with...
Cruciate
ligament
problems

Wake up
and smell
the dog!

15 years of
your favourite mag
And how the world of dogs has changed

Tested! *Interactive toys *Waterless shampoo *Bowls for greedy dogs
*Country wear for dog and owner *Products to prevent lawn stains
long-term test result

Your Dog is Britain's **best-selling dog magazine,** a monthly read that's packed with tips and advice on how to get the best out of life with your pet.

Every issue contains in-depth features on your dog's health, behaviour, and training, and looks at subjects such as how to pick the perfect puppy for your lifestyle.

Breeds

Facts, figures, and practical advice on all your favourite breeds of dog.

Dog Answers

Twenty-two pages of your problems solved by our panel of experts — everything from training, health, behaviour, feeding, breeds, grooming, legal, and homeopathy.

Tested!

...ong and short-term testing of a range of dog-related products — everything from tough toys to wellies.

And lots, lots more...

...ur Dog Magazine is available from your newsagent, priced at £3.40. Alternatively, why not take out a subscription? To find out more, call the subscriptions hotline on 01858 438854 and quote ref PW10.

A dog-friendly walk in...

Loch Lomond and The Trossachs

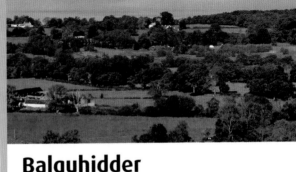

The first beauty spot we are stopping off at on our dog-friendly tour of the UK is Loch Lomond and The Trossachs.

Balquhidder

This walk, which begins in Balquhidder, takes you along pine-scented forest paths where you will be able to enjoy fine views of Kirkton Glen and the surrounding scenery.
By Mary Welsh.

Crianlarich
Lochearnhead
Loch Lomond and The Trossachs National Park
Callander
Aberfoyle
Helensburgh
Balloch
Dunoon
Greenock
Glasgow

The lovely view of Loch Voil.

Majestic Loch Lomond is not far from Balquhidder.

Pic: Loch Lomond and The Trossachs National Park Authority.

Fact file

Distance: 9km/ 5½ miles.
Time: 3 hours.
Map: Explorer 365.
Start/parking: In Balquhidder; grid reference 536209.
Terrain: Good tracks throughout, may be muddy after rain.
Nearest town: Callander.
Refreshments: Kings House Hotel, Balquhidder; Monachyle Mhor, Balquhidder.
Public toilets: None en route.
Public transport: Call Traveline on 0871 200 2233.
Stiles: One.
Suitable for: All the family. Dogs should be on leads if there is livestock about.

These walks have been reproduced from Your Dog Magazine, Britain's best-selling dog magazine, available from all good newsagents from the seventh of every month. Your Dog is priced at £3.40 and is packed with practical advice on every aspect of caring for and enjoying your pet. For more information, call the editorial department on 01780 766199; for subscription details call 01858 438854 or visit www.yourdog.co.uk

1 Wind left of the new church (built in 1853) to take [t]ree-lined gravelled [tra]ck, directing you [to]wards a waterfall. [Beside] you hurries the [Kirk]ton Burn. Ignore [th]e path to the right, [wh]ich is your onward [ro]ute, to walk to a [foo]tbridge from where [yo]u have a fine view [of] the delectable fall. [Re]turn to the path [yo]u ignored earlier, [no]w on your left, and [sig]nposted 'Creag an [Tui]rc and Kirkton Glen'. [Th]e pleasing path [cli]mbs uphill, through [tre]es, to go over an [eas]y stile, and then [lea]ds steadily through [the] conifers. Watch [out] for the sign on the [righ]t directing you to [Cre]ag an Tuirc. After

0.5km go through a hurdle gate on the right, descend steps to cross a stream and climb up the other side. Ascend to a cairn and a seat on the top of a crag, with a lovely view of Loch Voil below.

2 Return from the crag and on through the hurdle. Continue left, down the path to the main track, where you turn right along a way that leads through Kirkton Glen. Go past a track coming in on the left and then another on the right. Go ahead into the glen to walk through an area where young conifers have been planted. Stride on through a fine stand of Scots pine and carry

on. Now that much of the forest has been felled it is possible to see the shape of the glen.

3 Follow the track to the head of the glen to reach a signpost. Bear right, still on the forestry track, and return down the glen. Because the

track is at a higher altitude you are able to see the glen stretching down below you. About a mile along you have another fine view of Loch Voil. Follow the track as it winds right and joins your outward route. Turn left and follow back to Balquhidder church and the parking area.

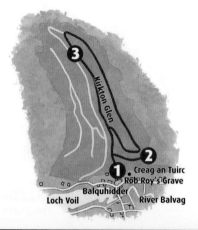

A dog-friendly walk in...
The North York Moors National P

The North York Moors National Park, with its wild and wonderful dales and hills, is a fantastic place to visit.

The White Horse above the village of Kilburn.

Kilburn White Horse

igh on the edge of the Hambleton Hills a giant white horse keeps watch over the village of Kilburn. Standing below it all you can see is a mass of white. From the village the rather oddly shaped large horse with a small head, stubby legs and a long tail, stand out stark against the deciduous woodland all about it. **By Mary Welsh.**

Staithes ○   Whitby
Robin Hood's Bay ○
North York Moors National Park
○   ○   Scarborough
Thirsk   Pickering

The church in Kilburn village.

The cottage of carpenter Robert Thompson — otherwise known as the Mouseman of Kilburn.

Watch out for falling tow lines as you go and keep to the path — gliders approach from any direction and are silent, so you will have no warning to get out of the way. Follow the path as it continues above the White Horse. When you reach the top of the tail, take the railed steps down the steep hillside to arrive in a small car park.

3 Here you have a choice. If you wish to visit Kilburn village on foot, join the narrow road (known locally as the Mare's Tail) and turn right to walk for a mile. In summer this can be quite busy but there are several verges you can walk on. Remember that you will have to return up the road (for a mile). To continue with the walk, if you decide not to visit Kilburn, turn right at the bottom of the steps (left through the car park if you have walked from Kilburn), go through the car park and then a gate on to a track into the forest. Where the track divides take the signposted right fork and follow the path below the limestone cliffs of Roulston Scar.

4 When the way forks again, take the right branch, known as the Thief's

Highway, and strike steeply uphill through the fine woodland. At the top of the slope, join the path along the escarpment, turning left to walk your outward route.

From the car park at Sutton Bank visitor centre, with dogs on the lead, cross the main road, the A170, with care. Turn left along the signposted level footpath to walk along the edge of the escarpment. From here you can see the Vale of York with the Pennines as a backdrop, considered by James Herriot as the 'best view in Yorkshire'. To your left is Kilburn Moor Plantation. Carry on ahead along this delightful way, ignoring the path descending right.

2 Stroll on, now with the Yorkshire Gliding Club's airfield to your left.

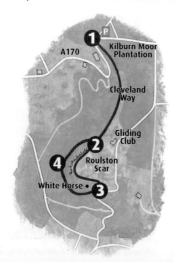

Fact file

Distance: 5km/3 miles or 8km/5 miles.
Time: 2 hours or 4 hours.
Map: Explorer OL26.
Start/parking: Sutton Bank National Park centre; grid reference 516831.
Terrain: Mostly on level paths and tracks with a steepish descent of many steps and steepish return ascent to the scarp edge.
Nearest towns: Thirsk and Helmsley.
Refreshments: Sutton Bank National Park centre cafe and Kilburn village.
Public toilets: Sutton Bank centre.
Public transport: Moors Bus network. For information call 01845 597000.
Suitable for: All the family. Dogs on leads to Kilburn.

A dog-friendly walk in...
The Brecon Beaco

The Brecon Beacons stretch from Llandeilo in the west to Hay-on-Wye in the east, and is one of three national parks in Wales. This stunning area is a popular destination for visitors who enjoy the freedom and remoteness of the Welsh countryside.

Enjoy the views at Blaen Llia.

Blaen Llia & Sarn Helen

The main sandstone mass of the Brecon Beacons meets a narrow strip of limestone just north of Ystradfellte, on the southern edge of Fforest Fawr (the Great Forest). This open-country walk cuts across these contrasting landscape on moorland tracks, past a small Iron Age hill fort, and finally along a section of Roman road. **By Evelyne Sansot.**

Along the Roman road with Fan Llia in the background.

A derelict limekiln on the route.

As you leave the car park, turn left on to the road and ▢low it for 0.8km ▢ mile). At a sharp ▢nd to the left, ▢ntinue straight on to ▢valled track. After ▢ate, take the right ▢k as waymarked.

2 After the next gate take the ▢ left fork across ▢ pasture, heading ▢ the right of a ▢estone crag. Pass ▢erelict limekiln just ▢ow the crag and ▢ntinue along the ▢ne path as it makes ▢urve to the left ▢tween the limestone ▢arpments of ▢nau Gwynion. About ▢m into the next ▢d keep along this ▢in track, ignoring another one shooting off to the right.

3 Make an elbow turn to the right in front of the gate in the bottom corner (at an angle between the wall and the track you have just followed). The path is not clearly defined at this point as it cuts across the rough pasture. Keep heading towards some scraggy hawthorn trees in the distance then, as you reach the brink of the field, aim for a small circular wire fence enclosure around a swallow-hole, cross a track and continue straight up the slope to a gate in the wall.

4 Bear left past the remains of an Iron Age hill fort on the crest on your right, suddenly emerging above the valley of Nedd Fechan, with views to the north over some of Fforest Fawr's sandstone summits (from right to left, Fan Nedd and Fan Gyhirych). Go through a gate and walk down several fields along the clearly waymarked footpath to the bottom of the valley.

5 Turn right on to the narrow road and enter Blaen-nedd-Isaf Farm. Walk past the farmhouse then turn immediately left across the farmyard to walk round the left-hand side of the barn. Cross the river over a footbridge and walk straight up a small wooded area, then a pasture.

6 Turn right at the top, on to Sarn Helen, the Roman road, thereby joining the Beacons Way. Cross the river again over a footbridge and continue straight up the other bank, later to pass the Maen Madoc standing stone.

7 Turn right on to the road to rejoin the car park on your left.

Fact file

Distance: 8km (5 miles).
Time: Allow 3 hours.
Map: Explorer OL12 Brecon Beacons National Park, West and Central.
Start/parking: Blaen Llia car park; grid reference SN927166.
Terrain: Mainly good tracks and footpaths across pastures with gentle ascents and descents.
Nearest towns: Glyn-Neath, Merthyr Tydfil, Brecon.
Refreshments: None.
Public toilets: None.
Public transport: None.
Stiles: None.
Suitable for: All.

A dog-friendly walk in...
The Norfolk Broad

The Norfolk Broads National Park has rich history and unique wildlife. Restored windmills, medieval churches, charming villages, and peaceful waterways are just a few of the delights that visitors discover when they explore the Broads.

Horsey Windpump

Recognised as an internationally important wildlife site, the Horsey Estate is also a superb destination for anyone who enjoys birdwatching. This route allows visitors to enjoy the peace and tranquillity of the area along with the chance to walk by the sea.
By Anita Delf.

North sea

Norfolk Broads

Caister-on-sea

Norwich

Great Yarmouth

NORFOLK

Lowestoft

SUFFOLK

The 'big Norfolk skies' at Horsey Beach.

Pic: The Broads Authority.

The Broads offers visitors a peaceful and tranquil holiday destination.

and the end of the path. Turn right, climb the stile and walk on the field edge to the houses ahead. Climb the stile at the end of the path to reach a lane. If you wish to take the shorter walk turn right by the footpath sign and follow the lane round to the church and main road. The Nelson Head public house is then directly opposite on the main road or you can turn right to return to the car park. Otherwise at the lane turn left and walk to the main road. Turn right along this road walking with care as it can be busy.

3 At the sharp bend turn left down the gravel track taking you back into the Horsey Estate, to reach a small car parking area. There is a choice of route here, you can turn right going through the kissing gate and along the path by the dunes or, if you prefer, you can continue ahead through Horsey Gap to reach the sea and turn right to walk along the beach.

1 From the car park at the Horsey Windpump walk to e steps and footpath n and then turn right ong the towpath. llow the path and ardwalk until it aches a gate. To e left are wonderful ws of Horsey Mere. om here on dogs will ed to be kept on ad as sometimes re is livestock in e fields. Go through e gate and cross e field diagonally t to a further gate. ss through this and ntinue along the h and boardwalk to ch the cut.

Continue alongside the water's edge to the ruined dpump ahead

Horsey Mill is owned by The National Trust.

4 Turn right at the next concrete gap on to a wide fenced track. If you choose the beach walk then you will need to turn right away from the beach, climbing the short sand hill. The track is then directly ahead of you. Continue on this track to arrive at the Nelson Head pub. From the Nelson Head turn right to the road, then turn left along it, following it back to the car park. This road is busy and must be walked with care, using the grass verge as much as possible.

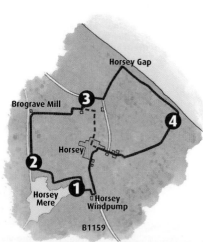

Horsey Gap
Brograve Mill
3
Horsey
2
4
1
Horsey Mere
Horsey Windpump
B1159

Fact file

Distance: 8 km (5 miles) or 4.8 km (3 miles).
Time: Allow 2½ hours.
Map: Explorer OL 40, The Broads.
Start/parking: The National Trust car park at Horsey Windpump on the B1159. It costs 30p per hour; grid reference TQ457224.
Terrain: Good paths; flat except for the climb through the sand dunes to the beach.
Nearest town: Great Yarmouth.
Refreshments: Nelson Head pub — dogs welcome inside on a lead. Seasonal shop/tea room at Horsey Mill, open Wednesday to Sunday, 10am – 4.30pm, with outside tables.
Public toilets: Horsey Mill car park — seasonal only.
Public transport: None.
Stiles: Two low wooden stiles — dogs may need to be lifted over.
Suitable for: All the family.

A dog-friendly walk on...
The South Downs

Stop off at the South Downs, with its chalk hills that afford beautiful views of the coast and nearby beaches. Designated as an Area of Outstanding Natural Beauty, the South Downs extends through the counties of East Sussex, West Sussex and part of Hampshire.

The view over the downs from Chanctonbury.

Chanctonbury Ring

Take the opportunity to explore one of the most mysterious and magical sites on the South Downs. The ring is a fascinating place at any time of year and in any weather. Don't be deterred if the top is shrouded in low cloud as this only adds to the atmosphere. On a clear day the views are second to none and a camera can do them justice. **By Sylvie Dobson.**

Trees frame the view from Chanctonbury H

HAMPSHIRE

WEST SUSSEX

Winchester

The South Downs National Park

Burgess Hill

Southampton

EAST SUSSEX

Chichester

Eastbourne

Brighton

Portsmouth

Littlehampton

Worthing

Bognor Regis

Isle of Wight

to the right for a short while before turning and looking back. In the distance you will see Cissbury Ring and beyond that the sea. Ahead the imposing sight of the Chanctonbury Ring comes into view. Pass through a gate and on to access land where you can roam freely.

3 By all means explore the ring but then keep over to the right and aim for the trig point from where you can get an all-round view of the surrounding area. On a clear day you can see the Isle of Wight away to the south-west and far away to the north beyond the Weald you should be able to make out the North Downs. Return to the main track, spending a few minutes by the nearby dew pond, and continue the walk. You may be tempted to use an alternative route through the adjoining access land but be aware that there are likely to be sheep grazing. The track is a safer proposition and just as enjoyable.

4 Keep right at a fork and start a steady descent.

1 Leave the car park and continue ahead along the ›ugh ascending track. ›on you will be in the ›elter of the trees ›vering the flanks of ›e hill. Bear left at ›n apparent fork and ›en just keep climbing ›n the main track. ›om the bottom the ›mb looks daunting ›t once you get ›arted you will ›ickly get into ›hythm and ›fore long will ›nerge from ›e trees to join ›wide crossing ›ck. This is the ›nowned South ›wns Way.

2 From here the views are limited, so walk along

You will pass another gate leading on to the access land and over to your left you will see a short, grassy runway used for the occasional light aircraft. You should look for the track that leads to this airstrip; immediately beyond this take the narrow path on the right following it down the hillside to a stile and on to a road.

5 Turn right and just beyond the turning to St Mary's Church you will see a stile on the right. Pass over the stile and then a short footbridge before climbing some strategically placed steps up the hillside. Continue through open pasture where sheep may be grazing. Keep walking with the hedge to your left but be alert for a fingerpost that may at times be partly hidden by foliage. You are directed diagonally right across open fields and on to a gate at the foot of Chanctonbury Hill — you don't have to climb it again! Turn left along a wide track which contours the lower slopes of the scarp before eventually joining the path you followed from the car park.

Fact file

Distance: 2.5km to 3km (1½ miles).
Time: 2 – 3 hours.
Map: Explorer 121, Arundel and Pulborough.
Start/parking: Chanctonbury Ring car park and picnic area signed from the A283 between Washington and Steyning; grid reference 146123.
Terrain: An initial climb on to the ridge of the downs followed by a less noticeable descent. Paths are well used and clearly defined.
Nearest town: Worthing.
Refreshments: The Frankland Arms in Washington village.
Public toilets: None.
Public transport: Full details from Traveline, call 0871 200 2233. Compass Travel operates a local service that passes the track to the car park, call 01903 690025.
Stiles: Six.
Suitable for: Dogs and owners used to exercise. Lots of off-lead opportunities.

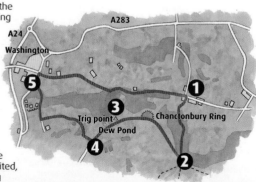

England and Wales · Counties

1. Plymouth
2. Torbay
3. Poole
4. Bournemouth
5. Southampton
6. Portsmouth
7. Brighton & Hove
8. Medway
9. Thurrock
10. Southend
11. Slough
12. Windsor & Maidenhead
13. Bracknell Forest
14. Wokingham
15. Reading
16. West Berkshire
17. Swindon
18. Bath & Northeast Somerset
19. North Somerset
20. Bristol
21. South Gloucestershire
22. Luton
23. Milton Keynes
24. Peterborough
25. Leicester
26. Nottingham
27. Derby
28. Telford & Wrekin
29. Stoke-on-Trent
30. Warrington
31. Halton
32. Merseyside
33. Blackburn with Darwen
34. Blackpool
35. N.E. Lincolnshire
36. North Lincolnshire
37. Kingston-upon-Hull
38. York
39. Redcar & Cleveland
40. Middlesborough
41. Stockton-on-Tees
42. Darlington
43. Hartlepool

NORTH WALES
a. Denbighshire
b. Flintshire
c. Wrexham

SOUTH WALES
d. Swansea
e. Neath & Port Talbot
f. Bridgend
g. Rhondda Cynon Taff
h. Merthyr Tydfil
i. Vale of Glamorgan
j. Cardiff
k. Caerphilly
l. Blaenau Gwent
m. Torfaen
n. Newport
o. Monmouthshire

COTTAGE IN THE COUNTRY COTTAGE HOLIDAYS (01608 646833). Lovely locations with superb walks in some of England's most picturesque countryside. Small friendly company with personal knowledge of the area.
e-mail: enquiries@cottageinthecountry.co.uk   website: www.cottageinthecountry.co.uk

HOSEASONS. Over 200 pet-friendly countryside and seaside locations in the best areas of Britain. Peaceful, stylish lodges and lively holiday parks, some with pools, bars and restaurants. Lowest price guaranteed. Call 0844 847 1103 Quote GA150 or book on-line.
website: www.hoseasons.co.uk

CLAYMOORE NARROWBOATS. Canal Holidays from base in Cheshire. Boats sleep 2-10. Fully equipped. Fuel included in hire. Full instruction. Day and Short Break hire. Car parking. Pets welcome. [🐾]
website: www.claymoore.co.uk

BLUE CHIP HOLIDAYS. Choose from the largest selection of pet-friendly holiday homes in Devon, Cornwall, Dorset, Somerset, Wales and the Isle of Wight with outstanding views the whole family can enjoy. (0844 704 1694).
website: www.bluechipholidays.co.uk/pets

DALES HOLIDAY COTTAGES. Thanks to Dales Holiday Cottages you can get away with the whole family - pets are welcome in more than 350 properties throughout the range. Order your brochure on 0845 266 7633 or see the website for the full range.
website: www.dales-holiday-cottages.com

THE INDEPENDENT TRAVELLER, ORCHARD COTTAGE, THORVERTON, EXETER EX5 5NG (01392 860807). For a wide choice of cottages and apartments throughout England, Scotland & the Isles. Pets welcome in many properties. Quality Cottages in coastal, country and mountain location. Property finding service.
e-mail: help@gowithit.co.uk   website: www.gowithit.co.uk

CAMPING AND CARAVANNING CLUB (0845 130 7632). Visit one of our award-winning UK Club Sites. Most of our sites have dog walking areas for you and your dog to explore. A friendly welcome will be given to you and your pet on our sites, joining is great value for money. [🐾] QUOTE REF NO 3163
website: www.campingandcaravanningclub.co.uk

THE FOUR SEASONS HOTEL, ST FILLANS PH6 2NF (01764 685333). Ideal holiday venue for pets and their owners. Spectacular Highland scenery, walking, fishing, watersports. Wonderful food. Full details on request. STB ★★★ Hotel, AA ★★★ and 2 Red Rosettes, Signpost, Best Loved Hotels. [pw! 🐾]
e-mail: sham@thefourseasonshotel.co.uk   website: www.thefourseasonshotel.co.uk

Bodmin

Bodmin Moor, Bude

Bude, Cawsand, Crackington Haven, Crantock

Crantock, Falmouth

Fowey

CUTKIVE WOOD HOLIDAY LODGES

Nestling in the heart of a peaceful family-owned country estate are six well-equipped comfortable cedar-clad lodges.
Set on the edge of ancient bluebell woods with lovely rural views, you can relax and enjoy yourself in this tranquil and idyllic setting.
Help with the animals, explore the woods and fields, fun play area.
So much for everyone to see and do – memorable beaches, wonderful coasts, walk the moors, inspiring gardens and Eden, theme attractions, historic gems.
Dogs welcome. Ideally situated to enjoy coast and country holidays whatever the time of year.

St Ive, Liskeard, Cornwall PL14 3ND
Tel: 01579 362216
www.cutkivewood.co.uk
e-mail: holidays@cutkivewood.co.uk

Looe

Looe

Looe, Marazion, Mawgan Porth, Mevagissey

FHG Guides publish a large range of well-known
accommodation guides. We will be happy to send you details or
you can use the order form at the back of this book.

Padstow, Penzance, Perranporth, Polruan

Port Gaverne, Porthleven, Port Isaac

St Agnes, St Austell, St Ives

Please mention PETS WELCOME!
when making enquiries about accommodation featured in this guide

Dalswinton House

St. Mawgan-in-Pydar, Cornwall TR8 4EZ. Tel: 01637 860385
www.dalswinton.com • dalswintonhouse@btconnect.com

HOLIDAYS FOR DOGS AND THEIR OWNERS

Overlooking the village of St Mawgan, Dalswinton House stands in
10 acres of gardens and meadowland midway between Padstow and
Newquay with distant views to the sea at dog-friendly Mawgan Porth.

- Dogs free of charge and allowed everywhere except the restaurant
- 8 acre meadow for dog exercise. Nearby local walks. Beach 1.5 miles
- Heated outdoor pool (May-Sep). Off street car parking
- All rooms en suite with tea/coffee fac., digital TV and clock radios
- Wifi access in public rooms and all bedrooms (except the lodge)
- Residents' bar and restaurant serving breakfast and dinner
- Bed and breakfast from £46 per person per night
- Weekly rates available and special offers in Mar/Apr/May/Oct
- Self-catering lodge sleeps 3 adults
- Easy access to Padstow, Eden Project, Newquay Airport & Coastal Path
- Also available: dog-friendly self-catering near Falmouth

Regret no children under 16
Maximum 3 dogs per room at proprietor's discretion

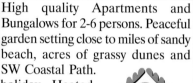

WEST CORNWALL COTTAGE HOLIDAYS, 4 ALBERT STREET, PENZANCE TR18 2LR (01736 368575). Coastal and country cottages, town houses and apartments. Pets with well behaved owners welcome in many of our properties. [🐕]
website: www.westcornwallcottageholidays.com

FARM & COTTAGE HOLIDAYS (01237 459897). An inspiring collection of holiday cottages throughout Cornwall, Devon, Somerset and Dorset in stunning rural and coastal locations. [Pets £20 per week]
website: www.holidaycottages.co.uk

TOAD HALL COTTAGES (01548 853089 24 hrs). Over 250 outstanding, dog friendly coastal, waterside and rural holiday cottages throughout Devon, Cornwall and Exmoor. Some superb beaches await your stroll. Well behaved people welcome too!
e-mail: thc@toadhallcottages.co.uk   website: www.toadhallcottages.co.uk

CORNISH SEAVIEW COTTAGES (01428 723819). Ideal for walking coastal paths and accessing beaches. Pets welcome at most. Furnished and equipped to high standard; all have central heating, dishwashers etc. Visit our website for photos and virtual tours. [Pets £20 per week].
e-mail: enquiries@cornishseaviewcottages.co.uk   website: www.cornishseaviewcottages.co.uk

CORNISH TRADITIONAL COTTAGES. A fine selection of self-catering cottages on both coasts of Cornwall and on Scilly. Pets welcome in many cottages. Free colour brochure: 01208 821666 or visit our website. [Pets £18 per week]
website: www.corncott.com

Bodmin

Quaint county town of Cornwall, standing steeply on the edge of Bodmin Moor. Pretty market town and touring centre. Plymouth 31 miles, Newquay 20, Wadebridge 7.

PENROSE BURDEN, ST BREWARD, BODMIN PL30 4LZ (01208 850277 & 850617; Fax: 01208 850915). Holiday Care Award Winning Cottages featured on TV. Open all year. Outstanding views over wooded valley. Free Salmon and Trout fishing. Superb walking area. Dogs welcome, wheelchair accessible. [Pets £15 per week]
website: www.penroseburden.co.uk

Bodmin Moor

Superb walking area attaining a height of 1375 feet at Brown Willy, the highest point in Cornwall.

DARRYNANE COTTAGES, DARRYNANE, ST BREWARD, BODMIN MOOR PL30 4LZ (Tel & Fax: 01208 850885). Absolutely fabulous detached cottages. Set in private gated gardens. Unique moorland valley setting. Waterfalls, woods, river. Woodburning stoves, four-poster beds, Eden Project and Camel Trail close by. [Pets £15 per week, £7 per short break]
e-mail: enquiries@darrynane.co.uk   website:www.darrynane.co.uk

HENWOOD BARNS HOLIDAY COTTAGES, HENWOOD, LISKEARD PL14 5BP (01579 363576/07956 864263). Three stone barns set around original courtyard on the edge of Bodmin Moor, with stunning views. Tranquil, village location, horse riding two minutes' walk. Woodburning stoves; sleep 2/5; within easy reach of North Cornwall and Devon. [Pets £15 per week]
e-mail: henwoodbarns@tiscali.co.uk   website: www.henwoodbarns.co.uk

Bude

Popular seaside resort overlooking a wide bay of golden sand and flanked by spectacular cliffs. Ideal for surfing; sea water swimming pool for safe bathing.

SANDYMOUTH HOLIDAY PARK, BUDE EX23 9HW (01288 352563; Fax: 01288 354822). A fantastic five star holiday park in Bude, located just minutes from the beach. On-site mini-market. Licensed bar and restaurant. Indoor heated pool. Adventure play area. Mains electricity and waste disposal point. Enjoy England ★★★★★. [Pets £2.50 per night].
e-mail: reception@sandymouthbay.co.uk   website: www.sandymouthbay.co.uk

HEDLEY WOOD CARAVAN & CAMPING PARK, BRIDGERULE, (NR BUDE), HOLSWORTHY EX22 7ED (01288 381404). 16 acre woodland family-run site; children's adventure areas, bar, clubroom, shop, laundry, meals & all amenities. Static caravans for hire, Caravan Storage available. Dog walk nature trail. See main advertisement under Bude. [pw! 🐕]
website: www.hedleywood.co.uk

IVYLEAF BARTON HOLIDAY COTTAGES, NEAR BUDE EX23 9LD. Five cottages sleeping 2-8 in converted stone barns, well equipped with all modern conveniences. Laundry. Tennis court. Certain cottages welcome pets. ★★★★/★★★★★ Contact: ROBERT B. BARRETT (07525 251773). [Pets £20 per week].
e-mail: info@ivyleafbarton.co.uk   website: www.ivyleafbarton.co.uk

GRANARY COTTAGE, ROSECARE, BUDE EX23 0BE. Self- catering ground floor cottage (sleeps 4). Lots of doorstep walking. Good dog and child-friendly pubs and beaches nearby. Short breaks available out of season. Contact: L. HUNT (01384 878287 or 07941 148340). [🐾]
e-mail: lynneh@ethicaltraining.co.uk   website: www.cottagenearbude.com

Cawsand

Quaint fishing village with bathing beach; sand at low tide. Ideal for watersports. Plymouth (car ferry) 11 miles, (foot ferry) 3.

WRINGFORD COTTAGES, HAT LANE, CAWSAND PL10 1LE (01752 822287). Pet-friendly cottages located in Area of Outstanding Natural Beauty on the edge of the Mount Edgcumbe Country Park. Games room. Bar. Heated indoor pool. Tennis court. B&B also available. AA ★★★
e-mail: thecottages@wringford.co.uk   website: www.wringford.co.uk

Crackington Haven

Small coastal village in North Cornwall set amidst fine cliff scenery. Small sandy beach, Launceston 18 miles, Bude 10, Camelford 10.

MINESHOP, CRACKINGTON HAVEN, BUDE EX23 0NR. Cornish Character Cottages, sleep 1 to 8, in tranquil location. Footpath leads through fields/woods to beach/pub. Excellent walking, breathtaking scenery. Open all year. Proud to be inspected and featured in The Good Holiday Cottage Guide. For more details phone CHARLIE or JANE (01840 230338). [£20 per pet per week.]
e-mail: info@mineshop.co.uk   website: www.mineshop.co.uk

Five 18th century converted barns, beamed ceilings, log fires and secluded rural setting. Ideal touring base. Five miles to coast at Crackington Haven. Sleep 2/5. Pets welcome. Open all year. From £100 short breaks, £195 per week. ETC ★★★/★★★★. GOLD AWARD. APPLY: LORRAINE HARRISON, TRENANNICK COTTAGES, WARBSTOW, LAUNCESTON PL15 8RP (01566 781443). [pw! Pets £10 per stay]
e-mail: trenannick–1@tiscali.co.uk   website: www.trenannickcottages.co.ukv

Crantock

Village near the coast 2 miles/3 km SW of Newquay across the River Gannel.

CORNWALL HOLIDAY COTTAGES. Luxury cottages, some with spectacular sea veiws. We have period and modern properties, some with log burners or open fires. Sleeping from 2-10 people in great comfort. Alll equipped to a very high standard. Most have gardens and are within easy reach of a beach. CORNWALL HOLIDAY COTTAGES, PO BOX 24, TRURO TR1 9AG (0845 226 5507) ETC ★★★★/★★★★★ Self Catering. [Pets £30 per week]
e-mail: rentals@cwlcot.com   website: www.cwlcot.com

CRANTOCK BAY HOTEL, WEST PENTIRE, CRANTOCK TR8 5SE (01637 830229; Fax: 01637 831111). Superbly located for a holiday with your dogs; beach 10 minutes' walk. Comfortable bedrooms, quality restaurant, indoor pool, tennis etc. AA ★★★ [Pets £5 per night]
e-mail: stay@crantockbayhotel.co.uk   website: www.crantockbayhotel.co.uk

Falmouth

Well-known port and resort on Fal estuary, ideal for boating, sailing and fishing; safe bathing from sandy beaches. Of interest is Pendennis Castle (18th century). Newquay 26, Penzance 26, Truro 11.

SELF-CATERING BUNGALOW. Sleeps 6. Walking distance of harbour and town. Dogs welcome. For prices and availability contact MRS J.A. SIMMONS (01277 654425) or see our website. ETC ★★★. [Pets £10 per week]
website: www.parklandsbungalow.co.uk

PETER WATSON, CREEKSIDE HOLIDAY HOUSES, RESTRONGUET, FALMOUTH TR11 5ST (01326 372722). Spacious houses sleep 2/4/6/8. Peaceful, picturesque water's edge hamlet. Boating facilities. Use of boat. Own quay, beach. Secluded gardens. Near Pandora Inn. Friday bookings. Dogs welcome. [Pets £15 per week]
website: www.creeksideholidayhouses.co.uk

CORNISH HOLIDAY COTTAGES (01326 250339). Quality, self-catering accommodation in Falmouth and Helford River. Call for a FREE brochure. [Pets £20 per week]
website: www.CornishHolidayCottages.net

SUE & DICK BARRETT, TUDOR COURT, 55 MELVILL ROAD, FALMOUTH TR11 4DF (01326 312807) Strikingly stylish, mock-Tudor family-run guest house, in award-winning gardens. Comfortable, friendly, non-smoking accommodation, a short walk from town and beaches. Open all year incl. Christmas. [Pets £2 per night].
e-mail: enquiries@tudorcourthotel.com   website: www.tudorcourtguesthouse.co.uk

CASTLETON & ENGLETON HOUSE B&B'S, 67/68 KILLIGREW STREET, FALMOUTH TR11 3PR (01326 372644). Two lovely Georgian town houses, next door to each other, two minutes' walk from Falmouth town centre. 7 en suite rooms, 3 twin and 1 single bedrooms. Well behaved dogs by prior arrangement. Enjoy England ★★★
e-mail: DawnEmmerson@aol.com   website: www.falmouth-bandb.co.uk

CREEKSIDE COTTAGES offer a fine selection of individual water's edge, village and rural cottages, sleeping from 2-10. All offer peaceful, comfortable and fully equipped accommodation. Just come and relax. For a colour brochure phone 01326 375972. [Pets £20 per week]
website: www.creeksidecottages.co.uk

PENMORVAH MANOR HOTEL & COURTYARD COTTAGES, BUDOCK WATER, NEAR FALMOUTH TR11 5ED (01326 250277; Fax: 01326 250509). Situated in 6 acres of mature gardens and woodland. Ideal for visiting Cornwall's superb gardens.Close to Falmouth and Coastal Paths. Well behaved dogs welcome. AA ★★★ Hotel, ETC ★★★★ Self-catering. [Pets £7.50 per night.]
e-mail: reception@penmorvah.co.uk   website: www.penmorvah.co.uk

Fowey

Historic town, now a busy harbour, Regatta and Carnival Week in August.

OLD FERRY INN, BODINNICK-BY-FOWEY PL23 1LX (01726 870237; Fax: 01726 870116). Family-run Inn, ideal for many varied walks. Excellent à la carte restaurant; bar meals available. Comfortable bedrooms with colour TV and tea/coffee. Rate £90-£130 per night for two people sharing. ETC ★★★★ Inn [Pets £3.50 per night per pet]
e-mail: royce972@aol.com   website: www.oldferryinn.com

LANCROW BARN, NEAR FOWEY (01726 814263). Quality barn conversion close to sea with spectacular views. Amdega Conservatory, open plan sitting room. Well equipped kitchen. 3 en suite bedrooms.Large enclosed garden with BBQ. Pets welcome. [Pets £20 per week]
e-mail: sarahfurniss@aol.com   website: www.rentahouseincornwall.co.uk

FOWEY HARBOUR COTTAGES. Sleep 2-6. Selection of cottages and flats situated around Fowey Harbour on the South Cornish Coast. All properties registered with VisitBritain and personally vetted. Short breaks and weekend bookings accepted subject to availability Brochure and details from W.J.B. HILL & SON, 3 FORE STREET, FOWEY PL23 1AH (01726 832211; Fax: 01726 832901)
e-mail: hillandson@talk21com   website: www.foweyharbourcottages.co.uk

Helford

Village on inlet South side of Helford River, 6 miles East of Helston.

Enchanting creekside cottages in a timeless and tranquil hamlet. Stunning coastal and riverside walks, country inns, local food, warm and comfortable with cosy log fires. Boat hire, moorings. Short breaks. Open all year. ST ANTHONY HOLIDAYS, MANACCAN, HELSTON TR12 6JW (01326 231 357). [Pets £3 per night, £21 per week].
e-mail: info@stanthony.co.uk   website: www.StAnthony.co.uk

Helston

Ancient Stannary town and excellent touring centre, noted for the annual "Furry Dance". Nearby is Looe Pool, separated from the sea by a bar. Truro 17 miles, St Ives 15, Redruth 11, Falmouth & Penzance 12.

BOSCREGE CARAVAN & CAMPING PARK, ASHTON, HELSTON TR13 9TG (01736 762231) Award-winning, quiet, family park close to beaches and attractions. No bar or clubs. Laundry. Static vans available. Pets welcome. AA Three Pennants. [🐕]
e-mail: enquiries@caravanparkcornwall.com   website: www.caravanparkcornwall.com

SILVER SANDS HOLIDAY PARK, GWENDREATH, KENNACK SANDS, RUAN MINOR, HELSTON TR12 7LZ (Tel/Fax: 01326 290631). Quiet, family-run park. Pets welcome with well-trained owners. Short walk through woodland path to award-winning dog beach. Choice of holiday homes, touring and camping. ETC ★★★★, AA 3 Pennants. [Pets £4 per night, £25 per week]
e-mail: info@silversandsholidaypark.co.uk   website: www.silversandsholidaypark.co.uk

Launceston

Town on hill above River Kensey, 20 miles NW of Plymouth.

SIMON & CLARE HIRSH, BAMHAM FARM COTTAGES, HIGHER BAMHAM, LAUNCESTON PL15 9LD (01566 772141). Eight well equipped cottages in converted 18th century farmhouse and outbuildings. Heated indoor swimming pool with paddling pool. Country location with superb views. Pets welcome. VisitBritain ★★★★[🐕].
e-mail:simon@bamhamfarm.co.uk   website: www.bamhamfarm.co.uk

SWALLOWS & MEADOW COTTAGE. Well equipped cottages with field to the rear. Riverside walks. TV lounge and kitchen. Centrally located for visiting NT houses and gardens, Dartmoor, Bodmin Moor, beaches and harbours. Pets welcome by arrangement. ETC ★★★ Contact: LOWER DUTSON FARM, LAUNCESTON PL15 9SP (01566 776456).
e-mail: holidays@farm-cottage.co.uk   website: www.farm-cottage.co.uk

Liskeard

Pleasant market town and good centre for exploring East Cornwall. Bodmin Moor and the quaint fishing villages of Looe and Polperro are near at hand. Plymouth 19 miles, St Austell 19 miles, Launceston 16, Fowey (via ferry) 15, Bodmin 13, Looe 9.

CUTKIVE WOOD HOLIDAY LODGES, ST IVE, LISKEARD PL14 3ND (01579 362216). Six well-equipped comfortable cedar-clad lodges on country estate with wonderful views. Great for children, dogs welcome. Ideal for coasts, beaches, moors etc. Short breaks. Open all year. [pw! Pets £10 per week].
e-mail: holidays@cutkivewood.co.uk   website: www.cutkivewood.co.uk

SUE JEWELL, BOTURNELL FARM COTTAGES, ST PINNOCK, LISKEARD PL14 4QS (01579 320880). Cosy character cottages set in 25 acres of fields and woodland between Looe and Bodmin. Linen, electricity included. Well equipped. Dog creche. Pets welcome free. [🐕]
e-mail: sue@dogs-holiday.co.uk   website: www.dogs-holiday.co.uk

CLIVE & JULIE FFITCH, REDGATE SMITHY B&B, REDGATE, ST CLEER, LISKEARD PL14 6RU (01579 321578). 200-year-old converted smithy, situated on the southern edge of Bodmin Moor. Extensive and tasty breakfast menu. Excellent pubs and restaurants locally. AA ★★★★ [pw! 🐕]
e-mail: enquiries@redgatesmithy.co.uk   website: www.redgatesmithy.co.uk

BUTTERDON MILL HOLIDAY HOMES, MERRYMEET, LISKEARD PL14 3LS (01579 342636) Two-bedroom detached bungalows on idyllic rural site. Sleep up to six. Games barn; children's play areas. Ideal for touring coasts & moors. Discounts for Senior Citizens/couples Sept to June. Brochure available. [🐕]
e-mail: butterdonmill@btconnect.com   website: www.bmhh.co.uk

---

🐕   Pets are welcome free of charge.

£   A charge is made for pets: nightly or week

pw! Special provision for pets; exercise facility, feeding or accommodation arrangement.

⌂   Separate pets accommodation.

Classified Symbols

LINDA & NEIL HOSKEN, HOPSLAND HOLIDAYS, HOPSLAND COMMONMOOR, LISKEARD, CORNWALL PL14 6EJ (Tel & Fax: 01579 344480). Hi, I'm Ki, an adorable border collie. Come and stay with your pets at my converted barn cottages. Fully equipped, all with DVD. Own field to exercise in or 150 yards from open moorland. [pw! 🐾]
e-mail: hopslandholidays@btinternet.com   website: www.hopslandholidays.co.uk

CELIA HUTCHINSON, CARADON COUNTRY COTTAGES, EAST TAPHOUSE, NEAR LISKEARD PL14 4NH (Tel & Fax: 01579 320355). Luxury cottages in the heart of the Cornish countryside. Ideal centre for exploring Devon and Cornwall, coast and moor and Eden Project. Meadow and paddock (enclosed). Central heating and log burners for cosy off-season breaks. [pw! Pets £15 per week.]
e-mail: celia@caradoncottages.co.uk   website: www.caradoncottages.co.uk

Lizard

The most southerly point in England, with fine coastal scenery and secluded coves. Sandy beach at Housel Bay. Truro 28 miles, Helston 11.

MULLION COVE HOTEL, MULLION COVE, THE LIZARD TR12 7EP (01326 240328). Located on the Cornish Coastal Path in a spectacular position on the Lizard Peninsula. Stunning country and coastal walks. Dog-friendly lounge, comfortable bedrooms, excellent food. AA ★★★ [pw! Pets £7 per night – free in low season]
e-mail: enquiries@mullion-cove.co.uk   website: www.mullion-cove.co.uk

POLURRIAN HOTEL, MULLION, LIZARD PENINSULA TR12 7EN (01326 240421; Fax: 01326 240083). Set in 12 acres with stunning views across Mount's Bay. Two pools, gym, snooker room, tennis court, sun terraces and secluded gardens. Most bedrooms have sea views. VisitBritain/AA ★★★ Hotel [Pets £8 per night.]
e-mail: relax@polurrianhotel.com   website: www.polurrianhotel.com

Longrock

Hamlet to the east of Penzance. Submerged forest to the east.

MRS DOREEN CAPPER, MOUNT VIEW HOTEL, LONGROCK, PENZANCE TR20 8JJ (01736 710416) A family-run pub with comfortable accommodation, situated 100 yards from Mount's Bay in Longrock village. Three en suite rooms and two with shared bathroom. Breakfast in dining room, lunch and dinner available. Dogs welcome by arrangement. Prices from £22 pppn. [🐾]

Looe

Twin towns linked by a bridge over the River Looe. Capital of the shark fishing industry; nearby Monkey Sanctuary is well worth a visit.

WRINGWORTHY COTTAGES, LOOE (01503 240685). 8 luxury stone cottages set in 4 peaceful acres offer you and your pet space for the perfect break. A friendly welcome awaits in our fully equipped, centrally heated cottages, sleeping 2-8. Linen included, walks from our door and more! 7 acre exercise field. ETC ★★★★. [pw! Pets £20 per week, maximum 3 dogs per cottage]
e-mail: holidays@wringworthy.co.uk   website: www.wringworthy.co.uk

TRENANT PARK COTTAGES (01503 263639). Secluded traditional cottages in grounds of country estate. Award-winning gardens and grounds. Open log fires. Open all year, winter short breaks. Well behaved dogs welcome. [Pets £3 per night; £20 per week].
e-mail: Liz@holiday-cottage.com   websites: www.trenantcottages.com
                                          www.trenantcottage.co.uk

MRS BARBIE HIGGINS, TREWITH HOLIDAY COTTAGES, TREWITH, DULOE PL14 4PR (01503 262184; mobile: 07968 262184). Four refurbished cottages in peaceful location with panoramic views near Looe. Fully equipped, 1-3 bedrooms, tastefully furnished. Full central heating. Well behaved dogs welcome. VisitBritain ★★★★ Self-catering. [Pets from £18 per week]
e-mail: info@trewith.co.uk   website: www.trewith.co.uk

TALLAND BAY HOTEL, PORTHALLOW PL13 2JB (01503 272667). At Talland Bay, you'll know you're somewhere special as soon as you arrive. Elegant surroundings, efficient yet discreet service and friendly atmosphere. We are happy to accommodate your four–legged friends too. AA★★★.Two Rosettes. [Pets £7.50 per night].
e-mail: info@tallandbayhotel.co.uk   website: www.tallandbayhotel.co.uk

NEAR LOOE. Peak House is situated overlooking the harbour, with 14 miles sea views, in the picturesque Cornish fishing village of Polperro, between Looe and Fowey on the South Coast. 25 miles city of Plymouth, 12 miles A38, and 15 miles Eden Project. Sleeping 2-8; terraced gardens and private parking; let for 30 years for family holidays, as well as for friends and couples to enjoy. Located in one of the best positions in the village, 3 minutes shops, restaurants, tea rooms, olde worlde pubs, sandy beach, quay, pier and rock fishing, and close to miles of unspoilt National Trust cliff walks, along stunning coastal paths. Prices from £250-£750 per week. Pets and children are very welcome. For brochure, please telephone Graham Wrights offices (01579 344080). [🐾]

TREMAINE GREEN COUNTRY COTTAGES, PELYNT, NEAR LOOE PL13 2LT (01503 220333). A beautiful hamlet of 12 award-winning traditional cosy craftsmen's cottages. Clean, comfortable and well equipped. Set in award-winning grounds with country/coastal walks and The Eden Project nearby. [pw! Pets £20 per week]
e-mail: stay@tremainegreen.co.uk   website: www.tremainegreen.co.uk

VALLEYBROOK, PEAKSWATER, LANSALLOS, LOOE PL13 2QE. Peaceful nine acre site with six superb villas and two delightful cottages, all dog friendly. Individual fenced gardens, dog walks, dog friendly beaches nearby. Short breaks. Open all year. 2 dogs max. ETC ★★★/★★★★. Contact DENISE, KEITH or BRIAN HOLDER (01503 220493). [pw! Pets £3 per night]
website: www.valleybrookholidays.com

NEIL AND THERESA DENNETT, TALEHAY HOLIDAY COTTAGES, PELYNT, NEAR LOOE PL13 2LT (Tel & Fax: 01503 220252). Beautiful, traditional cottages set in four acres of unspoilt countryside offering peace and tranquillity. Breathtaking coastal and country walks. An ideal location for dogs and their owners. Non-smoking. Close to the Eden Project. ETC ★★★★ [Pets £3 per night, £20 per week]
e-mail: infobookings@talehay.co.uk   website: www.talehay.co.uk

Idyllic 18th century country cottages for romantics and animal lovers. Looe three miles. Wonderful walks from your cottage. Cottages warm and cosy in winter. Personal attention from: MRS LAING, TREWORGEY COTTAGES, DULOE, LISKEARD PL14 4PP (01503 262730). VisitBritain ★★★★★ Quality Assurance Scheme. [Pets £21 per week.]
e-mail: stay@cornishdreamcottages.co.uk   website: www.cornishdreamcottages.co.uk

THE OLD RECTORY, LANREATH, LOOE PL13 2NU (01503 220247). Forming part of our Georgian Mansion, six self-catering apartments just 6 miles from Looe and Polperro. One, two or three bedrooms, with lounge, fully equipped kitchen, bathroom. Wi-Fi access. Large and beautifully secluded gardens and heated, open air swimming pool. Children's play area. Pets and families welcome. Enjoy England ★★★ [Pets £20 per week]
e-mail: ask@oldrectory-lanreath.co.uk   website: www.oldrectory-lanreath.co.uk

COLDRINNICK COTTAGES, DULOE, NEAR LOOE. Attractively converted barns set in large secluded gardens. Excellent locality for walking and relaxing. Sleep 2/6 people. Ideal place for families and dogs alike. For a brochure contact BILL AND KAYE CHAPMAN, COLDRINNICK FARM, DULOE, LISKEARD PL14 4QF (01503 220251). [Pets £15 per week, per dog].
website: www.cornishcottage.net

FOX VALLEY COTTAGES, LANLAWREN, TRENEWAN, LOOE PL13 2PZ (01726 870115). Set in beautiful countryside, just three miles from Polperro. Indoor heated pool and spa. Open all year round. Field for dogs to run around. Contact Andy & Linda for details. [pw! Pets £15 per week]
e-mail: info@foxvalleycottages.co.uk   website: www.foxvalleycottages.co.uk

GEOFF & STEPH BOWYER, CARTOLE COTTAGES, PELYNT, LOOE PL13 2QH (01503 220956). Small group of self-catering holiday cottages in a private setting. Large open grounds, children's play area, hot tub and sauna, Wi-Fi. Dogs welcome, field walk. EnjoyEngland ★★★/★★★★
email: info@cartole.co.uk   website: www.cartole.co.uk

BADHAM FARM, ST KEYNE, LISKEARD PL14 4RW (01579 343572). Farmhouse and farm buildings converted to a high standard. Sleep 2-10. All well furnished/equipped; prices include electricity, bed linen and towels. Well behaved dogs welcome (not in high season). Prices from £120 per week. ETC ★★★★. [Pets £4 per night, £20 per week].
e-mail: badhamfarm@yahoo.co.uk   website: www.badhamfarm.co.uk

Marazion

Quaint little village, the oldest town in Britain. Good beach and splendid fishing, sailing waters.

THE GODOLPHIN ARMS, WEST END, MARAZION TR17 0EN (01736 710202) Perched on the edge of the sand, facing St Michael's Mount. Ten en suite bedrooms, most with breathtaking sea views. Relaxing bars. Perfect for exploring coast and coves. AA ★★★★ Inn [Pets £10 per night].
e-mail: enquiries@godolphinarms.co.uk　　　website: www.godolphinarms.co.uk

Mawgan Porth

Modern village on small sandy bay. Good surfing. Inland stretches the beautiful Vale of Lanherne. Rock formation of Bedruthan Steps is nearby. Newquay 6 miles west..

BLUE BAY HOTEL, TRENANCE, MAWGAN PORTH TR8 4DA (01637 860324). Hotel, restaurant and lodges in fantastic location between Padstow and Newquay, overlooking Mawgan Porth beach. ETC ★★ Hotel, ★★★ Self-catering. [pw! Pets £5 per night, max. £20 per visit].
e-mail: hotel@bluebaycornwall.co.uk　　　website: www.bluebaycornwall.co.uk

Mevagissey

Central for touring and walking. Eden Project nearby.

MRS M.R. BULLED, MENAGWINS, GORRAN PL26 6HP (MEVAGISSEY 01726 843517). Traditional cottage, sleeps two to five. Linen, towels, electricity supplied. Beach one mile. Large garden. Central for touring/walking. Near Eden Project and Heligan Gardens. Pets welcome. [🐕]

KILBOL COUNTRY HOUSE HOTEL & COTTAGE, POLMASSICK, MEVAGISSEY PL26 6HA (01726 842481). 'Perfect Peace in Hidden Cornwall'. Small country hotel two miles from the coast. Eight rooms, and one self-catering cottage. No children under 12 years in hotel. [pw! Pets £10 per week].
e-mail: Hotel@kilbol-hotel.co.uk　　　website: www.kilbol-hotel.co.uk

Mousehole

Picturesque fishing village with sand and shingle beach. Penzance 3 miles.

POLVELLAN HOLIDAY FLAT. In Mousehole, a quaint and unspoilt fishing village, a fully equipped self-catering flat with full sea views. Sleeps two. Microwave, cooker, fridge, TV, all bedding and towels provided. Open all year. Apply: MR A.G. WRIGHT, LEAFIELDS FARM, UTTOXETER ROAD, ABBOTS BROMLEY, STAFFS WS15 3EH (01283 840651)[🐕]
e-mail: alang23@hotmail.com

Newquay

Popular family holiday resort surrounded by miles of golden beaches. Semi-tropical gardens, zoo and museum. Ideal for exploring all of Cornwall.

THE GRANARY, RETORRICK MILL, ST MAWGAN, NEWQUAY TR8 4BH (01637 860460). Set in 30 acres, self-catering Retorrick Mill offers two cottages, six chalets, traditional camping and licensed bar. Pets including horses very welcome. For a brochure or further assistance contact Chris Williams.
website: www.retorrickmill.co.uk

QUARRYFIELD CARAVAN & CAMPING PARK, CRANTOCK, NEWQUAY. Fully equipped modern caravans overlooking beautiful Crantock Bay. Separate camping field. Bar, pool, children's play area. Contact: MRS WINN, TRETHERRAS, NEWQUAY TR7 2RE (Tel & Fax: 01637 872792). [Pets £1.50 to £3.50 per night (camping only); £10 to £20 per week in caravan]
e-mail: quarryfield@crantockcaravans.orangehome.co.uk　　　website: www.quarryfield.co.uk

A useful index of towns/counties appears on pages 455-461

TRETHIGGEY TOURING PARK, QUINTRELL DOWNS, NEWQUAY TR8 4QR (01637 877672). Friendly, family-run park minutes from surfing beaches. Touring caravans, tent and campervans welcome. Luxury holiday homes for hire. Shop, off-licence, free showers, electric hook-ups, laundry, children's play area, TV/games room, fishing, licensed bar, Bistro, take-away food in summer. ETC ★★★★ [Pets £2.85 per night]
e-mail: enquiries@trethiggey.co.uk   website: www.Trethiggey.co.uk

MRS DEWOLFREYS, DEWOLF GUEST HOUSE, 100 HENVER ROAD, NEWQUAY TR7 3BL (01637 874746). Single, double or family rooms, two chalets in rear garden. All rooms non-smoking with en suite facilities, colour TV and tea/coffee making facilities. AA ★★★★ [🐾]
e-mail: holidays@dewolfguesthouse.com   website: www.dewolfguesthouse.com

Padstow

Bright little resort with pretty harbour on Camel estuary. Extensive sands. Nearby is Elizabethan Prideaux Place. Newquay 15 miles, Wadebridge 8.

THE METROPOLE HOTEL, STATION ROAD, PADSTOW PL28 8DB (0800 2300365). Here at The Metropole we welcome dogs and their owners. Ideally located near some wonderful coastal walks and stunning beaches. See our website for more details of the hotel and best available rates. [Pets £10 per night]
website: www.the-metropole.co.uk

OLD COTTAGE, TREVONE, PADSTOW PL28 8QN (01904 448933). Sleeps 4. Comfortable character cottage in peaceful village close to beach. Set in designated Area of Outstanding Natural Beauty. Secure garden, parking close by. Stunning walks on doorstep.
e-mail: holidays@trevonecottage.com   website: www.trevonecottage.com

SHANICE, PADSTOW (01473 327479 OR 07973 538670). Modern home, sleeps four (one double, two singles). Wonderful views, patio, barbecue. Short walk to Stein's and Camel Trail. Heating, gas wood-burner, TV+DVD. Open all year. [🐾]
website: www.brookfarm.demon.co.uk

Penzance

Well-known resort and port for Scilly Isles, with sand and shingle beaches. Truro 27 miles, Helston 13, Land's End 10, St Ives 8.

BOLANKAN COTTAGE, CROWS-AN-WRA, ST BURYAN, PENZANCE TR19 6HU (01736 810168). Fully modernised B&B approximately halfway between Penzance and Land's End. Double, twin and family rooms, all en suite with central heating, colour TV, hairdryer and tea/coffee making facilities. Dog-friendly beaches within a short drive. [🐾]
e-mail: bolankancottage@talktalk.net   website: www.bolankan-cottage.co.uk

PENMORVAH GUEST ACCOMMODATION, 61 ALEXANDRA ROAD, PENZANCE TR18 4LZ (01736 363711). A warm welcome awaits pets and owners alike at Penmorvah. We are ideally situated for long coastal walks and exploring, and shops and restaurants are in easy walking distance.
e-mail: penmorvah_penzance@talktalk.net   website: www.penmorvah.net

Perranporth

North Coast resort 6 miles SW of Newquay.

GREENMEADOW COTTAGES, NEAR PERRANPORTH. Spacious, clean luxury cottages. Sleep six. Open all year. Short breaks out of season. Non-smoking. Ample off road parking. Pets welcome in two of the cottages. ETC ★★★ For brochure and bookings: 01872 540483. [Pets £25 per week].
website: www.greenmeadow-cottages.co.uk

Polperro

Picturesque and quaint little fishing village and harbour. Of interest is the "House of the Props". Fowey 9 miles, Looe 5..

POLPERRO. Peak House is situated overlooking the harbour, with 14 miles sea views, in the picturesque Cornish fishing village of Polperro, between Looe and Fowey on the South Coast. 25 miles city of Plymouth, 12 miles A38, and 15 miles Eden Project. Sleeping 2-8; terraced gardens and private parking; let for 30 years for family holidays, as well as for friends and couples to enjoy. Located in one of the best positions in the village, 3 minutes shops, restaurants, tea rooms, olde worlde pubs, sandy beach, quay, pier and rock fishing, and close to miles of unspoilt National Trust cliff walks, along stunning coastal paths. Prices from £250-£750 per week. Pets and children are very welcome. For brochure, please telephone Graham Wrights offices (01579 344080). [🐾]

Polruan

Village at mouth of River Fowey, opposite the town of Fowey.

POLRUAN-BY-FOWEY, Lovely property near quay. Superb views. Parking (for 2 cars). Garden, Sleeps 6/8. Pets. Woodburning stove. Enjoy sailing, fishing, walking or just watching! Pubs and shops. MR T. NEWPORT, POLRUAN HOLIDAY SERVICES LTD, 1 FOWEY VIEW, POLRUAN PL23 1PA (01726 870582)
website: www.polruancottages.co.uk

Port Gaverne

Hamlet on east side of Port Isaac, near Camel Estuary.

GREEN DOOR COTTAGES. PORT GAVERNE. A delightful collection of 18C Cornish buildings built around a sunny enclosed courtyard, and 2 lovely apartments with stunning sea views. Situated in a picturesque, tranquil cove ideal for children. Dogs allowed on the beach year round. Half a mile from Port Isaac, on the Cornish Coastal Path. Traditional pub directly opposite. ETC ★★★★. For brochure: (01208 880293) [🐾]
e-mail: enquiries@greendoorcottages.co.uk　　　　website: www.greendoorcottages.co.uk

Porthleven

Small town with surprisingly big harbour. Grand woodland walks. 2 miles SW of Helston.

PORTHLEVEN. "Kernow agas dynargh" - "Cornwall welcomes you". Fishermen's cottages. Harbour, bay or country views. 3 minutes to beach, coast path, harbourside eating places. Open fires. Pets welcome. Please contact: MRS KERNO (01209 860410). [Pets welcome at a charge]

MRS NEAL, TAMARIND, SHRUBBERIES HILL, PORTHLEVEN, HELSTON TR13 9EA (01326 574303 or 07814 911532). Situated close to beach and coastal path. Five minutes' walk from shops, harbour, restaurants and inns. Garden. Off-road parking. Sea views. Continental and English breakfast served. House also available to let. [🐾]

Port Isaac

Attractive fishing village with harbour. Much of the attractive coastline is protected by the National Trust. Camelford 9 miles. Wadebridge 9.

DAVID AND JENNY OLDHAM, THE GARDEN HOUSE, MICHAELSTOW (01208 850529). Secure garden for dogs. Doggy shower. Lovely far reaching views. Full central heating and electric inc. Bed linen and towels inc. One bedroom with twin or double. Central location in small quiet hamlet. From £188 pw.
e-mail: david.trevella@btconnect.com　　　　website: www.trevellacornwall.co.uk

Homes from home around our peaceful courtyard garden 100 yards from sea in bygone fishing hamlet. Each sleeps six and has full CH, fridge/freezer, washer/dryer, dishwasher, microwave, DVD, video, computer and broadband. £220 (February), £780 (August) weekly. Resident owner. APPLY:- MALCOLM LEE, GULLROCK, PORT GAVERNE, PORT ISAAC PL29 3SQ (01208 880106). [🐾]
e-mail: gullrockportgaverne@btinternet.com　　　　website: www.gullrock-port-gaverne.co.uk

PORT GAVERNE HOTEL, NEAR PORT ISAAC PL29 3SQ (01208 880244; Fax: 01208 880151). Renowned 17th century inn in an unspoilt fishing cove on the rugged North Coast of Cornwall. Beach just 50 yards away. Pets welcome. Self-catering accommodation available. [Pets £3.50 per night].

LONGCROSS HOTEL & VICTORIAN GARDENS, TRELIGHTS, PORT ISAAC PL29 3TF (01208 880243). Lovely Victorian country house hotel with four acres of restored gardens. Close to the area's best beaches, golf courses and other attractions. Newly refurbished en suite bedrooms and suites. [Pets £5.00 per night.]
website: www.longcrosshotel.co.uk

Portreath

Coastal village 4 miles north west of Redruth.

Charming, elegantly furnished, self-catering cottages between Newquay and St Ives. Sleep 2 to 6. Fully equipped including linen. Beautiful beaches. Laundry and games room. Ample parking. Colour brochure – FRIESIAN VALLEY COTTAGES, MAWLA, CORNWALL TR16 5DW (01209 890901) [🐎]

Portwrinkle

Village on Whitsand Bay, 6 miles west of Torpoint.

WHITSAND BAY SELF-CATERING (01579 345688). Twelve cottages sleeping 4-10, all with sea views and situated by an 18-hole clifftop golf course. Children and pet-friendly. [Pets £20 per week].
e-mail: ehwbsc@hotmail.com   website: www.whitsandbayselfcatering.co.uk

Redruth

Market town nine miles west of Truro, 12 miles east of St Ives.

LANYON HOLIDAY PARK, LOSCOMBE LANE, FOUR LANES, REDRUTH TR16 6LP (01209 313474) Superb central location surrounded by beautiful countryside. Indoor heated pool. Games room. Bar/Restaurant/Takeaway/Free entertainment. Play area. Spacious level pitches and short grass. Pets welcome. EnjoyEngland ★★★★. AA Three Pennants.

St Agnes

Patchwork of fields dotted with remains of local mining industry. Watch for grey seals swimming off St Agnes Head.

CHIVERTON PARK, BLACKWATER, TRURO TR4 8HS (01872 560667). Caravan and touring holidays only a short drive from magnificent beaches. Quiet, spacious; exclusive gym, sauna, steamroom; laundry, shop, play area and games room. All amenities. No club, bar or disco. [Dogs £15 per week]
e-mail: info@chivertonpark.co.uk   website: www.chivertonpark.co.uk

DRIFTWOOD SPARS, TREVAUNANCE COVE, ST AGNES TR5 0RT (01872 552428). Take a deep breath of Cornish fresh air at this comfortable B&B ideally situated for a perfect seaside holiday. Dogs on leads allowed on beach. Miles of footpaths for 'walkies'. Children and pets welcome. AA ★★★★ [Pets £3 per night].
e-mail: info@driftwoodspars.co.uk   website: www.driftwoodspars.co.uk

PENKERRIS, PENWINNICK ROAD, ST AGNES TR5 0PA (01872 552202). B&B/Guest House/Hotel with lawned garden, picnic tables, barbeque, ample parking. Comfortable rooms, "real" food. Country/cliff walks, beaches (dog-friendly). B&B £20-£35pppn. Open all year. ETC ★★ [Pets £3 per night.]
e-mail: penkerris@gmail.com   website: www.penkerris.co.uk

🐎   Pets are welcome free of charge.   **Classified Symbols**

£   A charge is made for pets: nightly or weekly.

pw!   Special provision for pets; exercise facility, feeding or accommodation arrangement.

⌂   Separate pets accommodation.

St Austell

Old Cornish town and china clay centre with small port at Charlestown (1½ miles). Excellent touring centre. Newquay 16 miles, Truro 14, Bodmin 12, Fowey 9, Mevagissey 6.

BOSINVER HOLIDAY COTTAGES, ST MEWAN, ST AUSTELL PL26 7DT (01726 72128). Award-winning individual cottages in peaceful garden surroundings. Close to major holiday attractions. Short walk to shop and pub. Phone for brochure. No pets during Summer School holidays. ETC ★★★★ [pw!, Pets £30 per week].
e-mail: reception@bosinver.co.uk   website: www.bosinver.co.uk

St Ives

Picturesque resort, popular with artists, with cobbled streets and intriguing little shops. Wide stretches of sand.

SPACIOUS COTTAGE. Sleeps 7. Near beaches, harbour, shops, Tate Gallery. Terms £390 to £835 per week. Dogs welcome. Available all year. Telephone: Carol Holland (01736 793015). [Pets £10 per week]

BOB & JACKY PONTEFRACT, THE LINKS HOLIDAY FLATS, LELANT, ST IVES TR26 3HY (01736 753326). Magnificent location overlooking golf course and beach. Wonderful spot for walking. Five minutes from beach where dogs allowed all year. Two well-equipped flats open all year. [🐾]
e-mail: bobandjacky@btinternet.com

SANDBANK HOLIDAYS, ST IVES BAY, HAYLE (01736 752594). High quality Apartments and Bungalows for 2-6 persons. Heated, Colour TV, Microwave etc. Dogs welcome. [Pets welcomed at a charge]
website: www.sandbank-holidays.co.uk

St Mawgan

Delightful village in wooded river valley. Ancient church has fine carvings.

DALSWINTON HOUSE, ST MAWGAN TR8 4EZ (01637 860385). Old Cornish house standing in ten acres of secluded grounds. All rooms en suite, colour TV, tea/coffee facilities. Solar heated outdoor swimming pool. Restaurant and bar. Out-of-season breaks. No children under 16. ETC ★★★★ Silver Award. [🐾 pw!]
e-mail: dalswintonhouse@btconnect.com   website: www.dalswinton.com

St Tudy

Village 5 miles north east of Wadebridge.

Comfortable end of terrace cottage in picturesque and friendly village. Enclosed garden and parking. Ideal location for exploring all Cornwall. Short Breaks and brochure available. Contact: MRS R REEVES, POLSTRAUL, TREWALDER, DELABOLE PL33 9ET (Tel & Fax: 01840 213120). [🐾]
e-mail: ruth.reeves@hotmail.co.uk   website: www.maymear.co.uk

Tintagel

Attractively situated amidst fine cliff scenery; small rocky beach. Famous for associations with King Arthur, whose ruined castle on Tintagel Head is of interest. Bude 19 miles, Camelford 6.

MR & MRS N. CAREY, SALUTATIONS, ATLANTIC ROAD, TINTAGEL PL34 0DE (01840 770287). Comfortable, well-equipped, centrally heated cottages sleeping two. Ideal for touring, walking and relaxing. Close to Coastal Path and village amenities. Private parking. Ring for brochure. Pets Free. [🐾]
e-mail: salutations@talktalk.net   website: www.salutationstintagel.co.uk

Tregarne

On the Lizard peninsula, 8 miles east of Helston.

THE HEN HOUSE, TREGARNE, NEAR HELFORD TR12 6EW (01326 280236). Idyllic peaceful country setting a mile from the sea. Superb walks in all directions with year-round dog-friendly beaches Delightful spacious barns each open onto courtyard garden. Wild flower meadow, bird song and complete relaxation. Complimentary Tai-chi. Award Winners for Green Ethos and Quality. AA ★★★★. [Pets £5 per night]
e-mail: henhouseuk@aol.com   website: www.thehenhouse-cornwall.co.uk

Truro

Bustling Cathedral City with something for everyone. Museum and Art Gallery with interesting shop and cafe is well worth a visit.

TRELOAN COASTAL HOLIDAYS, TRELOAN LANE, PORTSCATHO, TRURO TR2 5EF (01872 580989). Seaside holiday camping and caravan park on unspoilt Roseland Peninsula, an Area of Outstanding Natural Beauty. Open all year offering static homes and camping pitches. Close to shops, and dog-friendly pubs and beaches. Truro and Eden Project half an hour. [Pets £1 per night.]
e-mail: info@treloancoastalholidays.co.uk   website: www.treloancoastalholidays.co.uk

HIGHER TREWITHEN, STITHIANS, TRURO TR3 7DR (01209 860863) The ideal centre for your pet and your family. We are surrounded by public footpaths and have 3½ acres of fields. [🐾]
e-mail: trewithen@talk21.com   website: www.trewithen.com

MRS PAMELA CARBIS, TRENONA FARM, RUAN HIGH LANES, TRURO TR2 5JS (01872 501339). Enjoy a relaxing stay on the unspoilt Roseland Peninsula between Truro and St Austell. Self-catering in three renovated barns, B&B in Victorian farmhouse. Children and pets welcome. Brochure available. [Pets £10 per stay, ⌂]
e-mail: info@trenonafarmholidays.co.uk   website: www.trenonafarmholidays.co.uk

KING HARRY COTTAGES, FEOCK, TRURO TR3 6QJ (01872 861917). Two comfortable, well equipped cottages in own charming gardens. Dogs welcome. Beautiful woodland walks. Perfect for fishing and bird watching. Free use of boat. [🐾]
e-mail: beverley@kingharry.net   website: www.kingharrycottages.co.uk

Wadebridge

Town on River Camel, 6 miles north-west of Bodmin

Three barn converted luxury cottage-style self catering homes near Wadebridge. Found along a leafy drive, with wonderful views, beside the lazy twisting Camel River with its "Trail" for walking and cycling. CORNWALL TOURISM AWARDS 2002 - Self Catering Establishment of the Year - "Highly Commended". Sleep 2-7 plus cot. Two dogs per cottage welcome. GARY NEWMAN, COLESENT COTTAGES, ST TUDY, WADEBRIDGE PL30 4QX (Tel & Fax: 01208 850112). [pw! 🐾]
e-mail: relax@colesent.co.uk   website: www.colesent.co.uk

THELMA RIDDLE OR NANCY PHILLIPS, GREAT BODIEVE FARM BARNS, MOLESWORTH HOUSE, WADEBRIDGE PL27 7JE (01208 814916; Fax: 01208 812713). Four spacious, luxury barns furnished and equipped to a very high standard. Wi-Fi. Most bedrooms en suite (king-size beds). Sleep 2-8. Excellent area for sandy beaches, spectacular cliff walks, golf, Camel Trail and surfing. Enjoy England ★★★★★. [🐾]
e-mail: enquiries@great-bodieve.co.uk   website: www.great-bodieve.co.uk

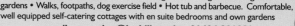

Brixham

Brixham, Broadwoodwidger, Budleigh Salterton, Cheston

Seacove Self-Catering Accommodation

Set of 4 privately owned properties situated on the coastal path. 10 minutes' walk to Brixham town/harbour through Battery Gardens opposite. Dog-friendly beaches. All properties benefit from full gas central heating. Parking. Open all year.

e-mail: seacovebookings@yahoo.co.uk
Tel: 01803 858336 • www.seacove.co.uk

WEST BANBURY FARM COTTAGES

Have it all! Dartmoor tors, coastal paths, water sports, family attractions, fishing, cycling, bird watching, beaches, market towns, castles, cream teas, relaxing, pampering...
West Banbury is ideally located for Dartmoor, North Devon and Cornwall, within easy reach of all of the above and more!

10 charming self-catering cottages, spacious and well-equipped, sleeping 2-8. Heated indoor swimming pool, sauna and games room on site. Children's play area • Grass tennis court • Dogs welcome • Short Breaks available.

e: westbanburyfarmcottages@btconnect.com
w: www.westbanbury.co.uk • t: 01566 780423

Badger's Den

Dalditch Lane, Knowle, Budleigh Salterton EX9 7AH

The cottage is Grade II listed, furnished to a high standard, with three bedrooms, open plan living/ dining room with flat screen TV, DVD player and hi-fi. Fully equipped kitchen leading to a secluded garden and patio. On the back of the lounge there is a sunny conservatory which has access to the downstairs bedroom which has been designed to the highest standards for people with mobility impairments, to include en suite wetroom, large doorways and flat-screen TV.

Pets welcome (not in bedrooms); secure garden, lot of good walks.

01395 443282 • info@holidaycottagedevon.com • www.holidaycottagedevon.com

Cheston is situated in Dartmoor National Park near the village of South Brent. Immaculately maintained, family-run site with all facilities. Cheston is a good base for touring the West Country, perfect for Torquay and Paignton, close to all attractions and 9 miles to the sea. Close by are horse riding, golf, fishing and the cities of Plymouth and Exeter. Children and pets are welcome. Ideal for an inexpensive day walking and exploring Dartmoor with its open spaces for kite flying and swimming in the clear streams.

You can be sure of a warm welcome at Cheston.

Cheston Caravan Park

**Wrangaton Road, Folly Cross,
South Brent, Devon TQ10 9HF • 01364 72586**
www. chestoncaravanpark.co.uk

Visit **www.holidayguides.com**
for pet-friendly accommodation in Britain

Chulmleigh, Colebrooke, Combe Martin

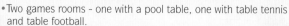
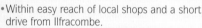

Dartmoor

Dartmouth, Dunsford

East Budleigh, Exeter, Exmoor

Exmoor, Holsworthy, Honiton

Please note...

All the information in this book is given in good faith in the belief that it is correct. However, the publishers cannot guarantee the facts given in these pages, neither are they responsible for changes in policy, ownership or terms that may take place after the date of going to press. Readers should always satisfy themselves that the facilities they require are available and that the terms, if quoted, still apply.

Ilfracombe, King's Nympton, Kingsbridge

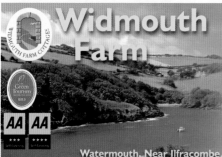

FHG Guides publish a large range of well-known accommodation guides. We will be happy to send you details or you can use the order form at the back of this book.

Sidmouth, South Molton

A useful index of towns/counties appears on pages 455-461

Thurlestone, Tiverton, Torbay, Torquay

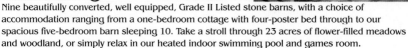

Torquay, Torrington, Totnes

Woolacombe

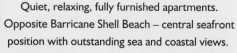

A useful index of towns/counties appears on pages 455-461

Ashburton

Delightful little town on southern fringe of Dartmoor. Centrally placed for touring and the Torbay resorts. Plymouth 24 miles, Exeter 20, Kingsbridge 20, Tavistock 20, Teignmouth 14, Torquay 14, Totnes 8, Newton Abbot 7.

PARKERS FARM COTTAGES & CARAVANS, MEAD, ALSTON CROSS, ASHBURTON TQ13 7LJ (01364 653008). Farm Cottages and Static Caravans to let surrounded by beautiful countryside. Perfect for children and pets. Central for touring; 12 miles Torquay. ETC★★★★ [pw! Pets £17 per week]
e-mail: parkerscottages@btconnect.com   website: www.parkersfarmcottages.co.uk

MRS A. BELL, WOODER MANOR, WIDECOMBE IN THE MOOR, NEAR ASHBURTON TQ13 7TR (Tel & Fax: 01364 621391). Cottages nestled in picturesque valley. Surrounded by unspoilt woodland and moors. Clean and well equipped, colour TV/DVD, central heating, laundry room. Two properties suitable for disabled visitors. Colour brochure available. ETC ★★★ to ★★★★ [pw! £20 per week].
e-mail: angela@woodermanor.com   website: www.woodermanor.com

PARKERS FARM HOLIDAY PARK, HIGHER MEAD FARM, ASHBURTON TQ13 7LJ (01364 654869; Fax: 01364 654004). Static caravans to let, also level touring site with two toilet/shower blocks and electric hook-ups. Central for touring; 12 miles Torquay. ETC ★★★★, AA Four Pennants. [pw! Pets £1.50 per night touring, £17 per week static caravans]
e-mail: parkersfarm@btconnect.com   website: www.parkersfarmholidays.co.uk

Ashwater

Village 6 miles south-east of Holsworthy.

BLAGDON MANOR RESTAURANT WITH ROOMS, ASHWATER, NORTH DEVON EX21 5DF (01409 211224; Fax: 01409 211634). Beautifully restored Grade II Listed building in peaceful location 20 minutes from Bude. 7 en suite bedrooms, three-acre gardens. No children under 12 years. AA Three Red Stars, 2 Rosettes. [pw! Dogs £8 per night]
email: stay@blagdon.com   website: www.blagdon.com

Axminster

Small friendly market town, full of old world charm, set in the beautiful Axe Valley. Excellent centre for touring Devon, Somerset and Dorset. 5 miles from coast.

HAWKCHURCH COUNTRY PARK, HAWKCHURCH, AXMINSTER EX13 5UL (01297 678402). A peaceful and tranquil caravan park situated in beautiful East Devon. Convenience shop. Licensed bar and restaurant. Children's play area. R sally facilities. Mains electricity and waste disposal point. Enjoy England ★★★★. [Pets £2.50 per night]
e-mail: enquiries@hawkchurchpark.co.uk   website: www.hawkchurchpark.co.uk

LILAC COTTAGE. Detached cottage, furnished to a high standard, sleeps six plus cot. Children and pets are welcome. Walled garden and garage. On borders of Devon, Dorset, and Somerset; many seaside towns within 10 miles. Contact: MRS J.M. STUART, 2 SANDFORD HOUSE, KINGSCLERE RG20 4PA (Tel & Fax: 01635 291942; Mobile: 07700 036648). [Pets £10 per week].
e-mail: jm.stuartb@gmail.com

THE FAIRWATER HEAD HOTEL, HAWKCHURCH, NEAR AXMINSTER EX13 5TX (01297 678349; Fax: 01297 678459). Located in the tranquil Devon countryside and close to Lyme Regis, this beautiful Edwardian Country House Hotel has all you and your dog need for a peaceful and relaxing holiday. Dogs most welcome free of charge. Countryside location with panoramic views. AA ★★★, Rosette. [🐾, ⌂]
e-mail: e-mail: stay@fairwaterheadhotel.co.uk   website: www.fairwaterheadhotel.co.uk

LEA HILL, MEMBURY, AXMINSTER EX13 7AQ (01404 881881). Tranquil location. Wonderful scenery. Close to World Heritage Coast. Eight acres of grounds and gardens. Walks, footpaths and exercise fields. Hot tub and barbecue. Comfortable, well equipped self-catering cottages with en suite bedrooms and own gardens. Green Tourism Silver Award, VB ★★★★. [pw! Pets £15 per week]
e-mail: reception@leahill.co.uk   website: www.leahill.co.uk

Bantham

Unspoilt village near market town of Kingsbridge in the South Hams area.

MRS LIBBY SIMMONS, BANTHAM HOLIDAY COTTAGES, 2 THE WATCH, BANTHAM, KINGSBRIDGE TQ7 3AJ (01548 560810). Comfortable, modern, self catering accommodation, with a high standard of furnishings and wonderful views. Cottages 1,2 & 3, sleep 6. No. 4 is ground floor flat sleeping 4. Non-smoking. [🐾]
website: www.banthamholidaycottages.co.uk

Barnstaple

Market town at head of River Taw estuary, 34 miles north west of Exeter.

MARTINHOE CLEAVE COTTAGES, MARTINHOE, PARRACOMBE, BARNSTAPLE EX31 4PZ (01598 763313). Perfect rural tranquillity overlooking the beautiful Heddon valley and close to the Exmoor National Park. Delightful cottages, equipped to a very high standard throughout. Open all year. Sleep 1-2. [🐾].
e-mail: info@exmoorhideaway.co.uk　　　website:www.exmoorhideaway.co.uk

NORTH HILL COTTAGES, NORTH HILL, SHIRWELL, BARNSTAPLE EX31 4LG (01271 850611; mobile: 07834 806434). Sleep 2-6. 17th century farm buildings, sympathetically converted into cottages. Indoor heated swimming pool, jacuzzi, sauna, all-weather tennis court and games room. [Pets £25 per week]
website: www.north-hill.co.uk

LOWER YELLAND FARM GUEST HOUSE, FREMINGTON, BARNSTAPLE EX31 3EN (01271 860101). Delightfully modernised farmhouse accommodation on working farm. Central for North Devon attractions. All rooms en suite, with TV and tea/coffee making. Breakfast includes free-range eggs and home-made bread etc. ETC ★★★★ [Pets £5 per night, £25 per week]
e-mail: peterday@loweryellandfarm.co.uk　　　website: www.loweryellandfarm.co.uk

Bideford

Neat port village overlooking the beautiful Sterridge Valley has a 17th century pub and even older church, and is half-a-mile from the coast road between Combe Martin and Ilfracombe.

THE PINES AT EASTLEIGH, NEAR BIDEFORD EX39 4PA (01271 860561). Luxury B&B and cottages. Log-fires, king-size beds, garden room bar with library, maps and a warm welcome await our guests. B&B from £35pp. No smoking. AA ★★★★ [pw! Pets £5 per night]
e-mail: pirrie@thepinesateastleigh.co.uk　　　website: www.thepinesateastleigh.co.uk

THE HOOPS INN & COUNTRY HOTEL, HORNS CROSS, NEAR CLOVELLY, BIDEFORD EX39 5DL (01237 451222; Fax: 01237 451247). Thatched country inn with open log fires. All bedrooms en suite. Splendid base for touring and outdoor pursuits. Dartmoor and Exmoor within easy reach. AA★★★ and Rosette. [Pets £5 per night]
e-mail: sales@hoopsinn.co.uk　　　website: www.hoopsinn.co.uk

Bigbury-on-Sea

A scattered village overlooking superb coastal scenery and wide expanses of sand.

MR SCARTERFIELD, HENLEY HOTEL, FOLLY HILL, BIGBURY-ON-SEA TQ7 4AR (01548 810240). Edwardian cottage-style hotel, spectacular sea views. Overlooking beach, dog walking. En suite rooms with telephone, tea making, TV etc. No smoking establishment. Licensed. ETC ★★ HOTEL and SILVER AWARD. AA ★★, GOOD HOTEL GUIDE, CESAR AWARD WINNER 2003, "WHICH?" GUIDE, COASTAL CORKER 2003. [Pets £5.00 per night.]

MRS J. TUCKER, MOUNT FOLLY FARM, BIGBURY-ON-SEA, KINGSBRIDGE TQ7 4AR (01548 810267). Cliff top position, with outstanding views of Bigbury Bay. Spacious, self-catering wing of farmhouse, attractively furnished. Farm adjoins golf course and River Avon. Lovely coastal walks, ideal centre for South Hams and Dartmoor. No smoking. Always a warm welcome, pets too! Enjoy England ★★★ [pw! Pets £15 per week]
e-mail: info@bigburyholidays.co.uk　　　website: www.bigburyholidays.co.uk

Bradworthy

Village to the north of Holsworthy. Well placed for North Devon and North Cornish coasts.

PETER & LESLEY LEWIN, LAKE HOUSE COTTAGES AND B&B, LAKE VILLA, BRADWORTHY DEVON EX22 7SQ (01409 241962). Four well equipped cottages sleeping two to five/six. Quiet rural position; one acre gardens and tennis court. Half-a-mile from village shops and pub. Dog-friendly beaches eight miles. Also two lovely en suite B&B rooms with balcony, all facilities, from £31. [🐕]
e-mail: lesley@lakevilla.co.uk   website: www.lakevilla.co.uk

Brixham

Lively resort and fishing port, with quaint houses and narrow winding streets. Ample opportunities for fishing and boat trips.

BRIXHAM HOLIDAY PARK, FISHCOMBE COVE, BRIXHAM TQ5 8RB (01803 853324). Situated on coastal path. Choice of one and two-bedroomed chalets. Indoor heated pool, free club membership, comfortable bar offering meals and takeaway service, launderette. 150 yards from beach with lovely walks through woods beyond. ETC ★★★★. [Pets £30 per week]
e-mail: enquiries@brixhamholpk.fsnet.co.uk   website: www.brixhamholidaypark.co.uk

DEVONCOURT HOLIDAY FLATS, BERRYHEAD ROAD, BRIXHAM TQ5 9AB (01803 853748 or 07802 403289 after office hours). 24 self-contained flats with private balcony, colour television, heating, private car park, all-electric kitchenette, separate bathroom and toilet. Open all year. Pets welcome.
website: www.devoncourt.info

SEACOVE SELF-CATERING ACCOMMODATION (01803 858336). 4 privately owned properties on coastal path, all with full central heating. 10 minutes' walk to harbour and beaches. Open all year.
e-mail: seacovebookings@yahoo.co.uk   website: www.seacove.co.uk

Broadwoodwidger

Village 6 miles north-east of Launceston.

WEST BANBURY FARM COTTAGES, BROADWOODWIDGER (01566 780423). 10 charming cottages, set around two courtyards. Sleep 2-8 (dogs welcome in all). Large indoor pool, sauna, games room etc. Ideal for exploring Devon and Cornwall. [Pets £20 per week]
e-mail: westbanburyfarmcottages@btconnect.com   website: www.westbanbury.co.uk

Budleigh Salterton

South Devon resort of dignified charm. Attractive sea front, shingle beach, pleasant walks in vicinity. Good fishing in sea and River Otter. Taunton 16 miles, Exeter 14, Sidmouth 7, Exmouth 5.

BADGER'S DEN, DALDITCH LANE, KNOWLE, BUDLEIGH SALTERTON EX9 7AH (01395 443282) A thatched, Grade II listed cottage which has been furnished and equipped to a very high standard. Surrounded by coastal paths and countryside. Pets welcome. ETC ★★★★ [Pets £10 per week]
e-mail: info@holidaycottagedevon.com   website: www.holidaycottagedevon.com

Cheston

Hamlet 2 miles South West of South Brent

CHESTON CARAVAN PARK, WRANGATON ROAD, FOLLY CROSS, SOUTH BRENT TQ10 9HF (01364 72586). Situated in Dartmoor National Park this immaculately maintained, family-run site has all facilities and is perfect for touring the West Country and visiting Paignton and Torquay. Children and pets welcome. [Pets £1 per night]
website: www.chestoncaravanpark.co.uk

www.holidayguides.com

Chulmleigh

Mid-Devon village set in lovely countryside, just off A377 Exeter to Barnstaple road. Exeter 23 miles, Tiverton 19, Barnstaple 18.

SANDRA GAY, NORTHCOTT BARTON FARM COTTAGE, NORTHCOTT BARTON, ASHREIGNEY, CHULMLEIGH EX18 7PR (Tel & Fax: 01769 520259). Three bedroom character cottage, large enclosed garden, log fire. Special rates low season, couples and short breaks. Near golf, riding, Tarka Trail and RHS Rosemoor. ETC ★★★★ [🐾]
e-mail: sandra@northcottbarton.co.uk   website: www.northcottbarton.co.uk

Colebrooke

Village 4 miles west of Crediton.

PEARL HOCKRIDGE, THE OYSTER, COLEBROOKE, CREDITON EX17 5JQ (01363 84576). Modern bungalow in pretty, peaceful village. Bedrooms en suite or with private bathroom. Dartmoor and Exmoor a short drive. Children and pets welcome. Open all year. Smoking accepted. [🐾]

Combe Martin

Coastal village with harbour set in sandy bay. Good cliff and rock scenery. Of interest is the Church and "Pack of Cards" Inn. Barnstaple 14 miles, Lynton 12, Ilfracombe 6.

YETLAND FARM COTTAGES, BERRY DOWN, COMBE MARTIN EX34 0NT (01271 883655). 6 well equipped cottages surrounding a pretty paved courtyard. Ideally situated for North Devon beaches, Exmoor, the South West Coastal Path and many tourist and leisure attractions. Linen and towels supplied. Sleep 3-6 plus cot. Well behaved pets welcome. ETC ★★★★ [Pets £15 per week]
e-mail: enquiries@yetlandfarmcottages.co.uk   website: www.yetlandfarmcottages.co.uk

GRASSMERE HOUSE LUXURY HOLIDAY APARTMENT, KING STREET, COMBE MARTIN EX34 0BS (01746 780902 or 07929656239). Luxurious Four Bedroomed Apartment. Sleeps nine, ideal for large families. Air conditioned and non smoking. Small to medium pet dogs welcome. [🐾]
e-mail paulinetaft@msn.com   website: www.grassmerehouse.net

NORTHCOTE MANOR FARM HOLIDAY COTTAGES, NEAR COMBE MARTIN EX31 4NB (01271 882376). Five self-catering holiday cottages grouped around a courtyard. Dogs are warmly welcomed in all of the cottages, three of which have enclosed gardens. 34 acres of fields, woods and rivers to explore. Indoor heated pool, games room and playground. [Pets £25 per week]
e-mail: info@northcotemanorfarm.co.uk   website: www.northcotemanorfarm.co.uk

WATERMOUTH COVE COTTAGES, WATERMOUTH, NEAR COMBE MARTIN EX34 9SJ (0845 029 1958 or 01271 883931). 8 beautiful cottages, most with four-poster and log fire, set beside grounds of Watermouth Castle, 200 yards from harbour/coastal path. Pets welcome. Open all year. [Pets £25 per week]
e-mail: watermouthcove@googlemail.com   website: www.watermouth-cove-cottages.co.uk

Cullompton

Small market town off the main A38 Taunton - Exeter road. Good touring centre. Noted for apple orchards which supply the local cider industry. Taunton 19 miles, Exeter 13, Honiton 11, Tiverton 9.

FOREST GLADE HOLIDAY PARK (PW), KENTISBEARE, CULLOMPTON EX15 2DT (01404 841381; Fax: 01404 841593). Country estate surrounded by forest with modern 6-berth holiday caravans, all well-equipped. Free indoor heated swimming pool. Tents, touring caravans and motor homes welcome. ETC ★★★★, AA 4 Pennants, David Bellamy Gold Award. [Pets £2 per night, pw!]
e-mail: enquiries@forest-glade.co.uk   website: www.forest-glade.co.uk

---

🐾   Pets are welcome free of charge.

£   A charge is made for pets: nightly or weekly.

pw! Special provision for pets; exercise facility, feeding or accommodation arrangement.

⌂   Separate pets accommodation.

Classified Symbols

Dartmoor

365 square miles of National Park with spectacular unspoiled scenery, fringed by picturesque villages.

ILSINGTON COUNTRY HOUSE HOTEL, NEAR HAYTOR, DARTMOOR TQ13 9RR (01364 661452). Don't leave them behind...we welcome your four-legged furry friends too! 10 acres of grounds. Extensive leisure facilities. 2 AA Rosette Restaurant. [pw! Pets £8 per night].
website: www.ilsington.co.uk

DARTMOOR COUNTRY HOLIDAYS, MAGPIE LEISURE PARK, DEPT PW, BEDFORD BRIDGE, HORRABRIDGE, YELVERTON PL20 7RY (01822 852651). Purpose-built pine lodges in peaceful woodland setting. Sleep 2-7. Furnished to very high standard (microwave, dishwasher etc). Easy walk to village and shops. Launderette. Dogs permitted. [Pets £20 per week].
website: www.dartmoorcountryholidays.co.uk

THE EDGEMOOR COUNTRY HOUSE HOTEL, HAYTOR ROAD, LOWERDOWN CROSS, BOVEY TRACEY TQ13 9LE (01626 832466; Fax: 01626 834760). Country House Hotel in peaceful wooded setting adjacent Dartmoor National Park. Many lovely walks close by. All rooms en suite. Dogs welcome. See our website for further details. ETC ★★★ Silver Award [pw! 🐾]
e-mail: reservations@edgemoor.co.uk   website: www.edgemoor.co.uk

CHRIS & JULIE EASTAUGH, THE ROSEMONT, YELVERTON PL20 6DR (01822 852175). Four star quality B&B in village. Open access to moorland. Excellent walking country. Modern, spacious en suite rooms. B&B per room per night: Single £45, Double £65-75. [🐾].
e-mail: office@therosemont.co.uk   website: www.therosemont.co.uk

THE CHERRYBROOK, TWO BRIDGES PL20 6SP (01822 880260). In the middle of Dartmoor National Park with seven comfortable en suite bedrooms. Excellent quality home-made meals. See our website for details, tariff and sample menu. [🐾]
e-mail: info@thecherrybrook.co.uk   website: www.thecherrybrook.co.uk

PRINCE HALL HOTEL, DARTMOOR PL20 6SA (01822 890403). Small, friendly, relaxed country house hotel with glorious views onto open moorland. Walks in all directions. Eight en suite bedrooms. Log fires. Excellent seasonal local food, freshly prepared daily. Fishing, riding, golf nearby. Three-Day Break from £100pppn. [🐾]
e-mail: info@princehall.co.uk   website: www.princehall.co.uk

DEVONSHIRE INN, STICKLEPATH, OKEHAMPTON EX20 2NW (01837 840626) A real country pub! Out the back door onto the north edge of Dartmoor proper. Dogs and horses always welcome, fed and watered.

TWO BRIDGES HOTEL, TWO BRIDGES, DARTMOOR PL20 6SW (01822 890581; Fax: 01822 892306). Famous Olde World riverside Inn. Centre Dartmoor. Log fires, very comfortable, friendly, excellent food. Ideal walking, touring, fishing, riding, golf. Warning – Addictive. ETC/AA ★★★ [🐾]
e-mail: enquiries@twobridges.co.uk   website: www.twobridges.co.uk

COLLAVEN MANOR HOTEL, SOURTON, OKEHAMPTON EX20 4HH (01837 861522). An elegant 15thC manor house set in 4 acres. The nine en suite rooms have glorious views and are individually furnished. Beamed residents' lounge, restaurant featuring local and home-grown produce. AA ★★
[Pets £5 per night]
e-mail: collavenmanor@supanet.com   website: www.collavenmanor.co.uk

Dartmouth

Historic port and resort on the estuary of the River Dart, with sandy coves and pleasure boat trips up the river. Car ferry to Kingswear.

MRS S.R. RIDALLS, THE OLD BAKEHOUSE, 7 BROADSTONE, DARTMOUTH TQ6 9NR (Tel & Fax: 01803 834585). Four cottages (one with four-poster bed). Sleep 2–6. Near river, shops, restaurants. Blackpool Sands 15 minutes' drive. TV/DVD, free wireless internet, linen free. Open all year. Free parking. Non-smoking. ETC ★★★ [🐾]
e-mail: oldbakehousecottages@yahoo.com   website: www.oldbakehousedartmouth.co.uk

WATERMILL COTTAGES, HIGHER NORTH MILL, HANSEL, NEAR SLAPTON, DARTMOUTH TQ6 0LN (01803 770219). Five comfy old stone cottages in 13 acres of unspoilt valley close to dog-friendly beaches and coastal path. Walks from your cottage door, enclosed gardens, log burners. We really welcome pets! [pw!, Pets £25 per week]
e-mail: christine@watermillcottages.co.uk   website: www.watermillcottages.co.uk

DARTSIDE HOLIDAYS, RIVERSIDE COURT, SOUTH EMBANKMENT, DARTMOUTH TQ6 9BH (01803 832093; Fax: 01803 835135). Comfortable holiday apartments with private balconies and superb river and harbour views. Available all year with colour TV, linen and parking. Free Colour Brochure on request. [Pets £50 per week.]
website: www.dartsideholidays.com

Dunsford

Attractive village in upper Teign valley with Dartmoor to the west. Plymouth 35 miles, Okehampton 16, Newton Abbot 13, Crediton 9, Exeter 8.

ROYAL OAK INN, DUNSFORD, NEAR EXETER EX6 7DA (01647 252256). Welcome to our Victorian country inn with real ales and home-made food. All en suite rooms are in a 300-year-old converted barn. Well behaved children and dogs welcome. [🐾]
e-mail: mark@troid.co.uk   website: www.royaloakd.com

East Budleigh

Small village two miles north of Budleigh Salterton.

BROOK COTTAGE. Delightful thatched self-catering cottage. Sleeps 6 in three bedrooms, two en suite shower rooms, bathroom, two living rooms, very well equipped. Wi-Fi. Contact: JO SIMONS, FOXCOTE, NOVERTON LANE, PRESTBURY, CHELTENHAM GL52 5BB (01242 574031; mobile: 0791 094 9926) Enjoy England ★★★★.[Pets £15 per week].
e-mail:josimons@tesco.net   website: www.brookcottagebudleigh.co.uk

Exeter

Chief city of the South-West with a cathedral and university. Ample shopping, sports and leisure facilities.

THORVERTON ARMS, THORVERTON EX5 5NS (01392 860205). Traditional coaching inn just 7 miles north of Exeter. Small, well behaved dogs welcome. 6 en suite bedrooms. Award-winning restaurant. Excellent choice of real ales. Ideal touring base for Dartmoor, Exmoor and Devon's beaches. [Pets £5 per night, pw!]
website: www.thethorvertonarms.co.uk

MRS SALLY GLANVILL, RYDON FARM, WOODBURY, EXETER EX5 1LB (01395 232341). 16th Century Devon Longhouse on working dairy farm. Open all year. 4 Star Silver Award. From £37 to £60pppn. ETC/AA ★★★★ [🐾]
website: www.rydonfarmwoodbury.co.uk

STATION LODGE, DODDISCOMBSLEIGH, EXETER (01647 253104). Comfortably furnished apartment for two people in beautiful Teign River valley. Excellent location for exploring Dartmoor. From £230 per week. For further details contact: IAN WEST, STATION HOUSE, DODDISCOMBSLEIGH, EXETER EX6 7PW. [pw! 🐾]
e-mail: enquiries@station-lodge.co.uk   website: www.station-lodge.co.uk

BEST WESTERN LORD HALDON HOTEL, DUNCHIDEOCK, NEAR EXETER EX6 7YF (01392 832483, Fax: 01392 833765). Standing in extensive gardens/grounds amid miles of rolling Devon countryside. Ideal for getaway break with your pet. ETC ★★★, AA ★★★. [Pets £7.50 per night.]
e-mail: enquiries@lordhaldonhotel.co.uk   website: www.lordhaldonhotel.co.uk

Exmoor

265 square miles of unspoiled heather moorland with deep wooded valleys and rivers, ideal for a walking, pony trekking or fishing holiday

THE STAGHUNTERS INN/HOTEL, BRENDON, EXMOOR EX35 6PS (01598 741222; Fax: 01598 741352). Family-run village inn with river frontage. Beautiful gardens. 12 en suite rooms. Varied menu, log fires, fine wines and cask ales. A walkers' paradise. [Pets £2.50 per night]
e-mail: stay@staghunters.com   website: www.staghunters.com

JAYE JONES AND HELEN ASHER, TWITCHEN FARM, CHALLACOMBE, BARNSTAPLE EX31 4TT (01598 763568). Comfort for country lovers in Exmoor National Park. High quality en suite rooms. Breakfast prepared with local and organic produce. Farm walk through fields to village pub. ETC ★★★★ [One dog free, two dogs £6]
e-mail: holidays@twitchen.co.uk   website: www.twitchen.co.uk

Holsworthy

Town 9 miles east of Bude.

TINNEY WATERS, PYWORTHY. Self-catering. Three beautiful lakes - carp, tench, bream. No day tickets, no close season. Ideal for birdwatching. Contact: J. MASON (01409 271362).
e-mail: jeffmason@freenetname.co.uk   website: www.tinneywaters.co.uk

Honiton

Town on River Otter 16 miles East of Exeter.

COMBE HOUSE DEVON, GITTISHAM, HONITON, NEAR EXETER EX14 3AD (01404 540400). Magical Elizabethan House and Restaurant in 3,500 acres of idyllic countryside. Fabulous food, 15 rooms, one cottage with secure walled garden. Dogs Monthly Petometer 09 "Excellent". Warm welcoming hospitality for owners and their friends. [Pets £9 per night, pw!]
e-mail: stay@combehousedevon.com   website: www.combehousedevon.com

Hope Cove

Attractive fishing village, flat sandy beach and safe bathing. Fine views towards Rame Head; cliffs. Kingsbridge 6 miles.

HOPE BARTON BARNS, HOPE COVE, NEAR SALCOMBE TQ7 3HT (01548 561393). 17 stone barns in two courtyards and four luxury apartments in farmhouse. Farmhouse meals. Free range children and well behaved dogs welcome. For full colour brochure please contact: MELANIE POPE. [pw! Pets £20 per week]
e-mail: info@hopebarton.co.uk   website: www.hopebarton.co.uk

Ilfracombe

This popular seaside resort clusters round a busy harbour. The surrounding area is ideal for coastal walks.

BEACHSIDE HOLIDAY PARK, HELE BAY, ILFRACOMBE EX34 9QZ (01271 863006; Fax: 01271 867296). Breathtaking views from this holiday park in beautiful Hele Bay. Well-appointed static caravans for hire. Superb sea views. Bed linen free of charge. Laundry facilities. Car park. Enjoy England ★★★★★. [Pets £2.50 per night]
e-mail: enquiries@beachsidepark.co.uk   website: www.beachsidepark.co.uk

THE FOXHUNTERS INN, WEST DOWN, NEAR ILFRACOMBE EX34 8NU (01271 863757; Fax: 01271 879313). 300 year-old coaching Inn conveniently situated for beaches and country walks. En suite accommodation. Pets welcome by prior arrangement.[🐕]
website: www.foxhuntersinn.co.uk

Please mention PETS WELCOME!
when making enquiries about accommodation featured in this guide

STRATHMORE, 57 ST BRANNOCKS ROAD, ILFRACOMBE EX34 8EQ (01271 862248) Delightful and friendly Victorian Licensed guest house, 10-minute stroll to both seafront and town centre. 8 individually designed en suite bedrooms. Cosy lounge bar, secluded terraced garden. Children and pets always welcome. AA ★★★★ [Pets £6.50 per night]. Please contact PETE OR HEATHER for more details.
e-mail: info@the-strathmore.co.uk   www.the-strathmore.co.uk

WIDMOUTH FARM, NEAR ILFRACOMBE EX34 9RX (01271 863743). Comfortable, well equipped cottages in 35 acres of gardens, pasture, woodland and private beach. Wonderful scenery. Ideal for birdwatching, painting, sea fishing & golf. Dogs welcome. AA ★★★/★★★★. [pw! Pets £25 per week each].
e-mail: holiday@widmouthfarmcottages.co.uk   website: www.widmouthfarmcottages.co.uk

King's Nympton

3 miles north of Chulmleigh.

COLLACOTT FARM, KING'S NYMPTON, UMBERLEIGH, NORTH DEVON EX37 9TP (01769 572491). Eight Country Cottages sleeping from 2 to 12 in rural area; lovely views, private patios and gardens. Well furnished and equipped. Heated pool, tennis court, BHS approved riding school. Laundry room. Open all year. [pw!, Pets £20 per week]
e-mail: info@collacott.co.uk   website: www.collacott.co.uk

Kingsbridge

Pleasant town at head of picturesque Kingsbridge estuary. Centre for South Hams district with its lush scenery and quiet coves.

DITTISCOMBE HOLIDAY COTTAGES, SLAPTON, NEAR KINGSBRIDGE, SOUTH DEVON TQ7 2QF (01548 521272). Nature trail and 20 acres of open space. Perfect holiday location for dogs and owners. All cottages have gardens and views of surrounding valley. ETC ★★★★ [Pets £20 per week]
e-mail: info@dittiscombe.co.uk   website: www.dittiscombe.co.uk

MRS B. KELLY, BLACKWELL PARK, LODDISWELL, KINGSBRIDGE TQ7 4EA (01548 821230). 17th century Farmhouse, five miles from Kingsbridge. Ideal centre for Dartmoor, Plymouth, Torbay, Dartmouth and many beaches. Some bedrooms en suite. Bed and Breakfast. Evening meal optional. Dogsitting. Pets welcome free of charge. [🐾]

MOUNTS FARM TOURING PARK, THE MOUNTS, NEAR EAST ALLINGTON, KINGSBRIDGE TQ9 7QJ (01548 521591). Family-run site in the heart of South Devon. We welcome tents, touring caravans and motor caravans. Children and pets welcome. Many safe, sandy beaches nearby.
website: www.mountsfarm.co.uk

ASHBURTON ARMS, NEAR KINGSBRIDGE TQ7 2AH (01548 531242). Cosy and welcoming Village Inn, ideal base for exploring beautiful South Hams. Three very comfortable en suite bedrooms. Well behaved pets welcome in bar and as overnight guests. Excellent home-made food.
email: info@ashburtonarms.co.uk   website: www.ashburtonarms.co.uk

Lapford

Village 5 miles south-east of Chulmleigh.

DAVID & MARION MILLS, RUDGE FARM, LAPFORD, CREDITON EX17 6NG (01363 83268). Set in beautiful grounds with pond, orchard and woods. Trout fishing and almost 200 acres to wander in. House very tastefully furnished and fully equipped (sleeps 8). No charge for dogs, linen or fuel. Send for brochure. [🐾]

Lydford

A Dartmoor village of national historical importance, 12 km south of Okehampton and 9km north of Tavistock.

LYDFORD COUNTRY HOUSE, LYDFORD, OKEHAMPTON EX20 4AU (01822 820347; Fax: 01822 820654). Set in 8 acres of beautiful grounds. En suite bedrooms, Italian restaurant. Stables for guests' horses; dog baskets available. Ideal for exploring coastline, Eden Project etc. ETC ★★★★★, Silver Award. [Pets £5 per night].
e-mail: info@lydfordcountryhouse.co.uk   website: www.lydfordcountryhouse.co.uk

Lynton/Lynmouth

Picturesque twin villages joined by a unique cliff railway (vertical height 500 ft). Lynmouth has a quaint harbour and Lynton enjoys superb views over the rugged coastline.

PRIME SPOT CHARACTER COTTAGES. Spectacular area for dog walking and mountain biking. Riverbank cottage for 1-6 at Lynmouth harbour. Romantic thatched cottage for two at Lynton. Seaside cottage for 1-4 at Combe Martin harbour. Available all year. Cosy winter breaks. ★★★/★★★★. Details/ brochures from MRS WOLVERSON (01271 882449).[one pet 🐾]
website: www.primespotcottages.co.uk

RIVER LYN VIEW, 26 WATERSMEET ROAD, LYNMOUTH EX35 6EP (01598 753501). Well presented en suite bedrooms with TV and tea/coffee facilities.Full English breakfast served in the dining area. Comfortable lounge. Exmoor National Park is a short drive away. Pets welcome. [🐾]
website: www.riverlynview.com

CLOONEAVIN HOLIDAY APARTMENTS, CLOONEAVIN PATH, LYNMOUTH EX35 6EE (01598 753334). Eight well equipped self contained apartments and chalet. A short walk to the harbour. Numerous coastal and river walks through idyllic countryside. [Pets £15 per week].
e-mail: relax@clooneavinholidays.co.uk   website: www.clooneavinholidays.co.uk

LYNHURST, LYNTON. Elegant late Victorian country house, retaining many original features, sleeps up to 22 for self-catering. Fully equipped kitchen, 10 bedrooms; linen, towels incl. Dogs welcome. For bookings ring Jane on 01598 753757 or 07807 183814. [🐾, pw!]
website: www.thelynhurst.com

THE NORTH CLIFF HOTEL, NORTH WALK, LYNTON EX35 6HJ (01598 752357). On the South West Coastal Path, the North Cliff is an ideal base for discovering Exmoor and the North Devon Coast. Delicious home cooking. We welcome pets, children and groups. [Pets £4 per night, £20 per week].
e-mail: holidays@northcliffhotel.co.uk   website: www.northcliffhotel.co.uk

JIM AND SUSAN BINGHAM, NEW MILL FARM, BARBROOK, LYNTON EX35 6JR (01598 753341). Exmoor Valley. Two delightful genuine modernised XVII century cottages by stream on 100-acre farm with A.B.R.S. Approved riding stables. Free fishing. ETC ★★★★. [pw! Pets £15 per week.]
e-mail: info@outovercott.co.uk   website: www.outovercott.co.uk

BLUE BALL INN (formerly The Exmoor Sandpiper Inn), COUNTISBURY, LYNMOUTH EX35 6NE (01598 741263). Romantic coaching inn on Exmoor. 16 en suite bedrooms, extensive menus with daily specials, good wines. Horse riding, walking. No charge for dogs. [🐾]
website: www.BlueBallinn.com or www.exmoorsandpiper.com

MOORLANDS. Where countryside and comfort combine. Two self-contained apartments within a family-run guesthouse, within the Exmoor National Park. Hotel amenities available for guests' use. Contact: MR I. CORDEROY, MOORLANDS, WOODY BAY, PARRACOMBE, NEAR LYNTON EX31 4RA (01598 763224). ETC ★★★★ [🐾]
website: www.moorlandshotel.co.uk

MR AND MRS I. RIGBY, BRENDON HOUSE, BRENDON, LYNTON EX35 6PS (01598 741206). Licensed country guesthouse in beautiful Lyn Valley. Ideal walking, fishing, riding. Award winning restaurant serving local food. Weekly discounts and short breaks. VisitBritain ★★★★ [🐾]
email: brendonhouse4u@aol.com   website: www.brendonhouse4u.com

BATH HOTEL, TORS HOTEL, LYNMOUTH, EXMOOR, NORTH DEVON EX35 6EL (01598 752238). Great views of harbour. Quality rooms and service. Ideal for moors. Pets welcome. Off-season discounts available. [🐾]
e-mail: info@bathhotellynmouth.co.uk   website: www.bathhotellynmouth.co.uk

Mortehoe

Adjoining Woolacombe with cliffs and wide sands. Interesting rock scenery beyond Morte Point. Barnstaple 15 miles.

THE SMUGGLERS REST INN, NORTH MORTE ROAD, MORTEHOE EX34 7DR (Tel & Fax: 01271 870891). In the pretty village of Mortehoe. The Smugglers offers luxury accommodation from twin rooms to family suites. En suite rooms, TV, full English breakfast, licensed bar, beer garden, home-cooked meals. Well trained pets welcome. [Pets £5 per week].
e-mail: info@smugglersmortehoe.co.uk   website: www.smugglersmortehoe.co.uk

Noss Mayo

Village 3 miles south west of Yealmpton, on south side of creek running into River Yealm estuary, opposite Newton Ferrers.

CRAB COTTAGE, NOSS MAYO. Charming fisherman's cottage, 50 yards from the quay. Fantastic walks, beaches and dog-friendly pubs on the doorstep. Close to the South Devon Coastal Path. Sleeps 5. Phone 01425 471372 for a brochure. [£25 per pet, per week]
e-mail: 07enquiries@crab-cottage.co.uk　　　　　website: www.crab-cottage.co.uk

Ottery St Mary

Pleasant little town in East Devon, within easy reach of the sea. Many interesting little buildings including 11th century parish church. Birthplace of poet Coleridge.

MRS A. FORTH, FLUXTON FARM, OTTERY ST MARY EX11 1RJ (01404 812818). Charming 16th Century farmhouse. B&B from £30.00. Peace and quiet. Cat lovers' paradise. Masses of dog walks. AA ★★ [🐾 pw!]
website: www.fluxtonfarm.co.uk

Paignton

Popular family resort on Torbay with long, safe sandy beaches and small harbour. Exeter 25 miles, Newton Abbott 9, Torquay 3.

MERRITT HOUSE, 7 QUEENS ROAD, PAIGNTON TQ4 6AT (01803 528959). Traditional Victorian townhouse 5 minutes from town centre and beach. Small dogs welcome in ground floor rooms. En suite shower rooms. Free Wi-Fi. On-site parking. AA ★★★★. [pw!, Pets £3 per night].
e-mail: bookings@merritthouse.co.uk　　　　　website: www.merritthouse.co.uk

BROADSHADE HOLIDAY APARTMENTS, 9 ST ANDREWS ROAD, PAIGNTON, TORBAY TQ4 6HA . An ideal holiday location for families and couples of all ages. All fully equipped for self-catering. Close to Paignton and Goodrington beaches. For bookings and information call 01803 559647. [Pets £15 per week]
e-mail: info@broadshade.co.uk　　　　　website: www.broadshade.co.uk

THE COMMODORE, 14 ESPLANADE ROAD, PAIGNTON TQ4 6EB (01803 553107). Ideally situated on Paignton sea front, sea view rooms. Luxury en suites, refreshments, sea view guest lounge, bar, gift shop. Excellent breakfast. Close to harbour, bus and rail stations. AA ★★★★ [Pets £5 per night, £20 per week].
e-mail: info@commodorepaignton.com　　　　　website: www.commodorepaignton.com

CHRISTINE CLARK & LLOYD HASTIE, AMBER HOUSE, 6 ROUNDHAM ROAD, PAIGNTON TQ4 6EZ (01803 558372). All en suite; ground floor rooms. Good food. Highly recommended. Non-smoking. A warm welcome assured to pets and their families. ETC ★★★★ Silver Award.
e-mail: enquiries@amberhousehotel.co.uk　　　　　website: www.amberhousehotel.co.uk

Plymouth

Historic port and resort, impressively rebuilt after severe war damage. Large naval docks at Devonport. Beach of pebble and sand.

CARSWELL FARM HOLIDAY COTTAGES, HOLBETON, PLYMOUTH PL8 1HH (01752 830020). Five peaceful and individual cottages dotted around our coastal organic dairy farm. Short walk from the sea and beaches. Very well equipped with log fires, private fenced gardens and BBQs. Dogs very welcome. ETC ★★★★ Gold Award. [Pets £20 per week]
e-mail: enquiries@carswellcottages.com　　　　　website: www.carswellcottages.com

CHURCHWOOD VALLEY, WEMBURY BAY, NEAR PLYMOUTH PL9 0DZ (01752 862382). Relax in one of our comfortable log cabins, set in a peaceful wooded valley near the beach. Enjoy wonderful walks in woods and along the coast. Abundance of birds and wildlife. Up to two pets per cabin. [Pets £5 per week each]
e-mail: churchwoodvalley@btconnect.com　　　　　website: www.churchwoodvalley.com

THE CRANBOURNE, 278/282 CITADEL ROAD, THE HOE, PLYMOUTH PL1 2PZ (01752 263858/ 661400/224646; Fax: 01752 263858). Convenient for Ferry Terminal and City Centre. All bedrooms with colour TV and tea/coffee. Licensed bar. Keys provided for access at all times. Free wifi. Under personal supervision. Pets by arrangement. AA ★★★ [🐾]
e-mail: info@cranbournehotel.co.uk　　　　　website: www.cranbournehotel.co.uk

Salcombe

Fishing and sailing centre in sheltered position. Fine beaches and coastal walks nearby.

PORT LIGHT, BOLBERRY DOWN, MALBOROUGH, NEAR SALCOMBE TQ7 3DY (01548 561384 or 07970 859992). A totally unique location set amidst acres of National Trust coastline. Luxury en suite rooms. Superb home-cooked fare, specialising in local seafood. Licensed bar. Pets welcome throughout the hotel. Short Breaks throughout the year. Contact: Sean and Hazel Hassall. [🐾]
e-mail: info@portlight.co.uk   website: www.portlight.co.uk

Seaton

Bright East Devon resort near Axe estuary. Shingle beach and chalk cliffs; good bathing, many lovely walks in vicinity. Exeter 23 miles, Sidmouth 11.

MILKBERE COTTAGE HOLIDAYS, 3 FORE STREET, SEATON EX12 2LE (Brochure: 01297 22925 / Bookings: 01297 20729). Specialising in coast/country holidays on the Devon/Dorset border. Cottages, bungalows, houses, apartments and caravans, ideally situated for walking and exploring the Jurassic Coast. [Pets £20 per week.] VisitBritain ★★★/★★★★★.
e-mail: info@milkberehols.com   website: www.milkberehols.com

AXEVALE CARAVAN PARK, COLYFORD ROAD, SEATON EX12 2DF (0800 0688816). A quiet, family-run park with 68 modern and luxury caravans for hire. Laundry facilities, park shop. All caravans have a shower, toilet, fridge and TV. Wi-Fi is available in every caravan. Relaxing atmosphere.
ETC ★★★★ [Pets £10 per week]
website: www.axevale.co.uk

Sidmouth

Sheltered resort, winner of many awards for its floral displays. Good sands at Jacob's Ladder beach.

SWEETCOMBE COTTAGE HOLIDAYS, ROSEMARY COTTAGE, WESTON, NEAR SIDMOUTH EX10 0PH (01395 512130). Selection of Cottages, Farmhouses and Flats in Sidmouth and East Devon, all personally selected and very well-equipped. Gardens. Pets welcome. Please ask for our colour brochure.
e-mail: enquiries@sweetcombe-ch.co.uk   website: www.sweetcombe-ch.co.uk

OAKDOWN HOLIDAY PARK, WESTON, SIDMOUTH EX10 0PT (01297 680387; Fax: 01297 680541). Devon's multi-award-winning country holiday park. Welcome to Oakdown, set near the "Jurassic Coast" World Heritage Site. Oakdown is level, sheltered and landscaped into groves to give privacy. Our luxurious amenities include aids for the disabled. Enjoy our Field Trail to the famous Donkey Sanctuary. Free colour brochure with pleasure. ETC ★★★★★, 2011 AA South West Campsite of the Year, David Bellamy Gold Award, Loo of the Year Award, Best of British, Excellence in England 2007. [Pets £2.30 per night]
e-mail: enquiries@oakdown.co.uk   website: www.oakdown.co.uk

OTTERFALLS HOLIDAY COTTAGES & LODGES, NEW ROAD, UPOTTERY, HONITON EX14 9QD (01404 861634 ; Fax: 01404 861706). Luxurious fully equipped self-catering cottages and lodges set in 120 acres. Fishing lakes, heated indoor pool. Wonderful walking, including special pet "off-lead" walkways. [pw! Pets £30 per week]
e-mail: hols@otterfalls.co.uk   website: www.otterfalls.co.uk

LEIGH COTTAGES, WESTON, SIDMOUTH EX10 0PH. Cottages and bungalows for couples and families close to SW Coast path, Weston Combe and Donkey Sanctuary. Dog friendly beaches and pubs nearby. Peaceful location. ETC ★★★★ Contact: ALISON CLARKE (01395 516065/514764; Fax: 01395 512662). [pw! Pets £20 per week]
e-mail: Alison@leighcottages.co.uk   website: www.leighcottages.co.uk

South Molton

Busy market town, ideally situated as a base to explore the beautiful countryside of North and Mid Devon, and Exmoor and Dartmoor National Parks

PARTRIDGE ARMS FARM, YEO MILL, WEST ANSTEY, SOUTH MOLTON EX36 3NU (01398 341217; Fax: 01398 341569). Converted, self-catering railway carriage. Situated on the old Taunton to Barnstaple railway line. Fully equipped, sleeps up to 6 people. Children and dogs welcome. Prices start from £490 per week (no hidden extras). Daily rates also available. [🐾]
e-mail: bangermilton@gmail.com

Tavistock

Birthplace of Sir Francis Drake and site of a fine ruined Benedictine Abbey. On edge of Dartmoor, 13 miles north of Plymouth

MRS P.G.C. QUINTON, HIGHER QUITHER, MILTON ABBOT, TAVISTOCK PL19 0PZ (01822 860284). Modern self-contained barn conversion. Own private garden. Terms from £225 inc. linen, coal and logs. Electricity metered. [pw! ⚲]
website: www.higherquither.2day.ws/

THE TROUT & TIPPLE, PARKWOOD ROAD, TAVISTOCK PL19 0JS (01822 618886). Family-friendly traditional pub. Real ales, real food and a real welcome. Dogs welcome.
website: www.troutandtipple.co.uk

LANGSTONE MANOR HOLIDAY PARK, MOORTOWN, TAVISTOCK PL19 9JZ (Tel & Fax 01822 613371). Peaceful Holiday Park, offering camping, cottages, apartment, static caravans. Ideal location outside Tavistock with direct access onto Dartmoor. Bar and evening meals. Excellent location. ETC ★★★★, AA 4 Pennants [Pets £20 per week in self-catering.]
e-mail: jane@langstone-manor.co.uk   website: www.langstone-manor.co.uk

Thurlestone

Village resort above the cliffs to the north of Bolt Tail, 4 miles west of Kingsbridge.

THURLESTONE HOTEL, NEAR KINGSBRIDGE & SALCOMBE TQ7 3NN (01548 560382). Luxury country hotel set in 19 acres of landscaped gardens just five minutes' walk to the sea, offering first class golf, leisure and spa facilities. Superb food and fine dining. Dogs welcome by arrangement. EnjoyEngland/AA ★★★★.
email: enquiries@thurlestone.co.uk   website: www.thurlestone.co.uk

CUTAWAY COTTAGE, THURLESTONE, KINGSBRIDGE TQ7 3NF. Self-catering cottage within a fenced garden in the middle of the village. Private road, 5 minutes to pub and shop, 20 minutes' walk to beaches & sea. Ideal for children, dog walkers and bird watchers. Phone Pat on 01548 560688 [⚲]

Tiverton

Busy market town situated north of Exeter on the A396.

NEWHOUSE FARM COTTAGES, WITHERIDGE, TIVERTON EX16 8QB (01884 860266). Nine well equipped Grade II Listed stone barns, with accommodation ranging from a one bedroom cottage to a 5- bedroom barn. 23 acre grounds, heated indoor pool and games room. [Pets £20 per week, pw!].
website: www.newhousecottages.com

Torbay

An east-facing bay and natural harbour at the western end of Lyme Bay, midway between the cities of Exeter and Plymouth.

J. AND E. BALL, DEPARTMENT P.W., HIGHER WELL FARM HOLIDAY PARK, STOKE GABRIEL, TOTNES TQ9 6RN (01803 782289). Within 4 miles Torbay beaches and one mile of River Dart. Central for touring. Dogs on leads. Tourist Board Graded Park ★★★★. [pw! Pets £2 per night, £15 per week in statics, free in tents and tourers]
website: www.higherwellfarmholidaypark.co.uk

⚲   Pets are welcome free of charge.   **Classified Symbols**

£   A charge is made for pets: nightly or weekly.

pw!   Special provision for pets; exercise facility, feeding or accommodation arrangement.

⌂   Separate pets accommodation.

Torquay

Popular resort on the English Riviera with a wide range of attractions and entertainments. Yachting and watersports centre with 10 superb beaches and coves.

CLIVE MASON AND DIANE SHELTON, AVRON HOUSE, 70 WINDSOR ROAD, TORQUAY TQ1 1SZ (01803 294182). An elegant family-run guesthouse in a quiet residential location. Many local attractions, free on-road parking, a quiet retreat for a relaxing break. EnjoyEngland ★★★★. [Pets £2 per night]
e-mail: avronhouse@blueyonder.co.uk   website: www.avronhouse.co.uk

RED HOUSE HOTEL AND MAXTON LODGE HOLIDAY APARTMENTS, ROUSDOWN ROAD, CHELSTON, TORQUAY TQ2 6PB (01803 607811; Fax: 01803 605357). Choose either the friendly service and facilities of a hotel or the privacy and freedom of self-catering apartments. The best of both worlds! AA/ETC ★★ Hotel & ★★★ Self-catering. [🐕 in flats; £3 per night in hotel]
e-mail: stay@redhouse-hotel.co.uk   website: www.redhouse-hotel.co.uk

THE DOWNS HOTEL, 41-43 BABBACOMBE DOWNS ROAD, TORQUAY TQ1 3LN (01803 328543/ 0845 051 0989). Fully licensed family-run establishment with 12 en suite rooms, eight with private balconies and superb views. Family rooms, reduced rates for under 12s. Dog-friendly. [Pets £5 per night].
website: www.downshotel.co.uk

THE NORWOOD, 60 BELGRAVE ROAD, TORQUAY TQ2 5HY (01803 294236, Fax: 01803 294224). Just a stroll from the seafront, town centre and all local attractions. A quality holiday experience focussing on old-fashioned hospitality, clean comfortable rooms and beautifully presented, home-cooked food. VisitBritain ★★★★.
e-mail: enquiries@norwoodhoteltorquay.co.uk   website: www.norwoodhoteltorquay.co.uk

Torrington

Pleasant market town on River Torridge. Good centre for moors and sea. Exeter 36 miles, Okehampton 20, Barnstaple 12, Bideford 7.

CLOISTER PARK COTTAGES, FRITHELSTOCK, TORRINGTON EX38 8JH (01805 622518). Three recently converted cottages (sleep 6/4/2), all fully equipped, with own patio areas. The attractive market town of Great Torrington is just 2 miles away. Tarka Trail and North Devon beaches close by. ETC ★★★★. [First pet free, additional pets £15 per week]
website: www.cloisterpark.co.uk

RICH AND DIANA JONES, STOWFORD LODGE, LANGTREE, GREAT TORRINGTON EX38 8NU (01805 601487). Sleep 4/6. Picturesque and peaceful. Four delightful cottages and log cabin set within 6 acres of private land with heated indoor pool. Magnificent countryside. Convenient North Devon coast and moors. Phone for brochure. VisitBritain ★★★/★★★★ [Pets £15 per week, pw!]
e-mail: enq@stowfordlodge.co.uk   website: www.stowfordlodge.co.uk

Totnes

Town at tidal estuary of River Dart 7 miles west of Torquay.

THE KINGSTON ESTATE, KINGSTON HOUSE, STAVERTON, TOTNES TQ9 6AR (01803 762235). Luxury holidays in Devon. Self-catering Estate cottages created from restored period outbuildings. Perfect for a family holiday or weekend escape. Leisure facilities. ETC ★★★★★ Self Catering.[pw! Pets £20 per week].
o mail : bookingsenquiries@kingston-estate.co.uk   website: www.kingston-estate.co.uk

MRS ANNE TORR, DOWNE LODGE, BROADHEMPSTON, TOTNES TQ9 6BY (Tel & Fax: 01803 812828; Mobile: 07772318746).) Woodland dog walking on doorstep. Cottage available with one or three bedrooms. Private garden. En suite B&B available. No smoking. Beautiful, quiet position convenient for Dartmoor and the coast. [🐕]
e-mail: info@downelodge.co.uk   website: www.downelodge.co.uk

Please mention PETS WELCOME!
when making enquiries about accommodation featured in this guide

Woolacombe

Favourite resort with long, wide stretches of sand. Barnstaple 15 miles, Ilfracombe 6.

EUROPA PARK, BEACH ROAD, WOOLACOMBE (01271 871425). Static caravans, chalets, camping, surf lodges and surf cabins. Full facilities. Pets welcome. Indoor heated swimming pool, sauna, site shop. [Pets £3 per night]
e-mail: holidays@europapark.co.uk   website: www.europapark.co.uk

SUNNYMEADE COUNTRY HOTEL, WEST DOWN, NEAR WOOLACOMBE EX34 8NT (01271 863668; Fax: 01271 866061). Small country hotel set in beautiful countryside. A few minutes away from Ilfracombe, Exmoor and Woolacombe's Blue Flag Beach. 12 en suite rooms, 4 on the ground floor. Deaf accessible. Pets welcome. [pw!]
e-mail: holidays@sunnymeade.co.uk   website: www.sunnymeade.co.uk

WOOLACOMBE BAY HOLIDAY PARKS (0844 770 0384). Four award-winning Holiday Parks set in delightful surroundings, all beside three miles of golden Blue Flag sandy beach in Devon. Pet-friendly holiday homes with pet pack and "Woof" Guide to Woolacombe.
website: www.woolacombe.com/fpw

WOOLACOMBE COTTAGES, IVYCOTT FARM, WOOLACOMBE EX34 7HL (Tel/Fax: 01271 870846). Holiday breaks in North Devon throughout the year. Seafront Apartments to Farmhouse Cottages, 1-9 Bedrooms. Situated in the heart of North Devon's Gold Coast. Many welcome pets.
e-mail: info@woolacombe-cottages.co.uk   website: www.woolacombe-cottages.co.uk

MRS JOYCE BAGNALL, CHICHESTER HOUSE, THE ESPLANADE, WOOLACOMBE EX34 7DJ (01271 870761). Holiday apartments on sea front. Fully furnished, sea and coastal views. Watch the sun go down from your balcony. Open all year. SAE Resident Proprietor. [pw! Pets £12 per week]
website: www.chichesterhouse.co.uk

Abbotsbury, Bere Regis, Bournemouth

White topps

THE *REALLY* DOG-FRIENDLY PLACE
WHITE TOPPS

Guests enjoying the lounge

Small, friendly and catering only for guests with dogs. In a nice quiet position close to lovely walks on the beach (dogs allowed) and Hengistbury Head. Plus the New Forest isn't far away. There's no charge for pets, of course and the proprietor, MARJORIE TITCHEN, just loves dogs.

We're 100% dog orientated, all our guests bring at least one dog and you're equally welcome whether you have one Yorkie or six Alsatians. Dogs are allowed anywhere - in bedrooms, lounges, even in the dining room should they be unhappy being left alone in the bedroom. Bring your own dog food, we are happy to cook it, free of charge, if required.

We have five bedrooms on the first floor with bathroom and toilets opposite and one room on the ground floor, suitable for elderly or disabled dogs. We do not have any en suite rooms but all have washbasins and tea/coffee making facilities.

- DOG(S) ESSENTIAL - ANY SIZE, ANY NUMBER, ANYWHERE
- GROUND FLOOR ROOM FOR ELDERLY DOGS
- ADULTS ONLY (14yrs +)
- GENEROUS HOME COOKING
- VEGETARIANS WELCOME
- NOT SUITABLE FOR DISABLED
- CAR PARKING

WRITE (SAE APPRECIATED) OR PHONE FOR FACT SHEET.

WHITE TOPPS, 45 CHURCH ROAD, SOUTHBOURNE, BOURNEMOUTH, DORSET BH6 4BB
TEL: 01202 428868
No Credit Cards - Cheque or Cash only

e-mail: thedoghotel@aol.com • www.whitetopps.co.uk
IF YOU DON'T LOVE DOGS YOU WON'T LIKE WHITE TOPPS

Friendly, family-run hotel with parking. Close to beach and shops. Ideal for exploring Bournemouth, Christchurch and the New Forest. Excellent breakfast. En suite rooms, four-poster, double, twin and family room on ground floor, one with wet room suitable for wheelchair disabled. Large adjoining rooms. No smoking.

B&B from £24pn, from £143pp per week. • www.southbournegrovehotel.co.uk

SOUTHBOURNE GROVE HOTEL • 96 Southbourne Road, Southbourne, Bournemouth BH6 3QQ
Tel: 01202 420503 • Fax: 01202 421953 • e-mail: neil@pack1462.freeserve.co.uk

Please mention PETS WELCOME!
when making enquiries about accommodation featured in this guide

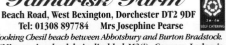

FHG Guides publish a large range of well-known
accommodation guides. We will be happy to send you details or
you can use the order form at the back of this book.

North Perrott, Poole, Portland

A useful index of towns/counties appears at the back of this book

Pet-Friendly
Pubs, Inns & Hotels
on pages 448-453

These establishments may not feature in the main section of the book

Sherborne

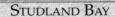

Swanage, Wareham (near Lulworth)

CHURCHFIELD HOLIDAY LETTINGS have the pleasure of offering you all types of quality Self-Catering accommodation in Bournemouth, Poole and surrounding areas within Dorset. Please call Martina Loxton on 01202 779911 or visit our website.
website: www.churchfieldholidaylettings.com

FARM & COTTAGE HOLIDAYS (01237 459897). An inspiring collection of holiday cottages throughout Cornwall, Devon, Somerset and Dorset in stunning rural and coastal locations. [Pets £20 per week]
website: www.holidaycottages.co.uk

ISLAND COTTAGE HOLIDAYS (01929 481555). Pet and dog friendly cottages in beautiful rural and coastal locations on the Isle of Purbeck.
website: www.purbeckcottageholidays.co.uk

DORSET COASTAL COTTAGES (0800 9804070). Carefully selected, traditional cottages in or near villages within ten miles of World Heritage Coast. Many are thatched; open fires or logburners; over half welcome dogs. Available all year. [Pets £15 per week]
website: www.dorsetcoastalcottages.com

DORSET COTTAGE HOLIDAYS. Self-catering cottages, town houses, bungalows and apartments. All within 10 miles of Heritage Coastline and sandy beaches. Excellent walking in idyllic countryside. Short breaks from £95, weekly from £170 (per cottage). Open all year. Free brochure tel: 01929 553443. [🐾]
e-mail: enq@dhcottages.co.uk   website: www.dhcottages.co.uk

Abbotsbury

Village 8 miles NW of Weymouth.

THE OLD COASTGUARDS HOLIDAY COTTAGES, ABBOTSBURY. 17 miles of Chesil Beach at the end of the garden. Outstanding coastal views. Excellent walking. C.H. See our website for availability and details. Tel: 01305 871335. ETC ★★★★. [🐾, pw!]
website: www.oldcoastguards.com

Bere Regis

Village 7 miles north west of Wareham.

MR & MRS R. CARGILL, ROWLANDS WAIT TOURING PARK, RYE HILL, BERE REGIS BH20 7LP (01929 472727). Situated in an Area of Outstanding Natural Beauty. A good base for touring; direct access onto heathland and woodland walks. Ideal for nature lovers, bird watching and quiet family holidays. Tents also welcome. Dogs welcome. David Bellamy Gold Award. ETC ★★★.
website: www.rowlandswait.co.uk

Bournemouth

One of Britain's premier holiday resorts with miles of golden sand, excellent shopping and leisure facilities. .

STOURCLIFFE COURT HOLIDAY APARTMENTS. Two fully furnished apartments, sleep 2/5. Three minutes' walk to beach. Linen provided free. Forecourt parking. Terms from £200. MRS HAMMOND, STOURCLIFFE COURT, 56 STOURCLIFFE AVENUE, SOUTHBOURNE, BOURNEMOUTH BH6 3PX (01202 420698). [Pets £2 per night, £10 weekly]
e-mail: rjhammond1@hotmail.co.uk   website: www.stourcliffecourt.co.uk

ALUM DENE HOTEL, 2 BURNABY ROAD, ALUM CHINE, BOURNEMOUTH BH4 8JF (01202 764011) Renowned for good old fashioned hospitality and friendly service. Come and be spoilt at our licensed hotel. All rooms en suite, colour TV. Some have sea views. 200 metres sea. Parking. Christmas House party. No charge for pets. [🐾]
e-mail: alumdenehotel@hotmail.co.uk   website: www.alumdenehotel.com

BILL AND MARJORIE TITCHEN, WHITE TOPPS HOTEL, 45 CHURCH ROAD, SOUTHBOURNE, BOURNEMOUTH BH6 4BB (01202 428868). Situated in quiet position close to lovely walks and beach. Dogs essential. Free parking. [🐾 pw!]
e-mail: thedoghotel@aol.com   website: www.whitetopps.co.uk

SOUTHBOURNE GROVE HOTEL, 96 SOUTHBOURNE ROAD, SOUTHBOURNE, BOURNEMOUTH BH6 3QQ (01202 420503; Fax: 01202 421953). Friendly, family-run hotel with parking. Close to beach and shops. Excellent breakfast. En suite rooms, four-poster, double, twin and family room on ground floor. B&B from £24pppn. [🐾]
website: www.southbournegrovehotel.co.uk

HOLIDAY FLATS AND FLATLETS a short walk to golden, sandy beaches. Most with private bathrooms. Cleanliness and comfort assured. Dogs welcome. Contact: M DE KMENT, 4 CECIL ROAD, BOURNEMOUTH BH5 1DU (07788 952394). [Pets £30 per week]

MIKE AND LYN LAMBERT, 16 FLORENCE ROAD, BOURNEMOUTH BH5 1HF (01202 304925). Modern Holiday Apartments sleeping up to ten persons, close to sea and shops. Clean, well-equipped flats. Car park. Phone or e-mail for brochure. [Pets from £45 per week]
e-mail: mikelyn_lambert@btinternet.com   website: www.selfcateringbournemouth.co.uk

ANNE & RICHARD REYNOLDS, THE VINE HOTEL, 22 SOUTHERN ROAD, SOUTHBOURNE, BOURNEMOUTH BH6 3SR (01202 428309). A small, family, award-winning non-smoking Hotel only three hundred yards from dog-friendly beach and shops. All rooms en suite with tea/coffee making facilities and colour TV. Residential licence with attractive bar. Full central heating. Forecourt parking. Open all year. FHG Diploma. [🐾]

LANGTRY MANOR, DERBY ROAD, EAST CLIFF, BOURNEMOUTH BH1 3QB (0844 371 3705 - local rate). A rare gem of a hotel where the building, food, service and history blend to form something quite exceptional. Midweek and weekend breaks. Pets welcome by arrangement. Bournemouth Tourism 'Best Small Hotel'. [🐾]
website: www.langtrymanor.co.uk

Bridport

Market town of Saxon origin noted for rope and net making. Harbour at West Bay has sheer cliffs rising from the beach

COGDEN COTTAGES, NEAR BRIDPORT, DORSET. Seven beautifully presented and equipped beachfront sea view cottages all with private sea facing decks or patios. Pets can take advantage of the South West Coastal Path which runs through the property or our private beach. £290-£650. Contact: KIM CONNELLY, OLD COASTGUARD HOLIDAY PARK, BURTON BRADSTOCK, NEAR BRIDPORT DT6 4RL (01308 897223).
website: www.cogdencottages.co.uk

MRS S. NORMAN, FROGMORE FARM, CHIDEOCK, BRIDPORT DT6 6HT (01308 456159). The choice is yours - Bed and Breakfast in charming farmhouse, OR self-catering Cottage equipped for five, pets welcome. Brochure and terms free on request. [1st dog free, 2nd dog £3 per night, £15 per week]
e-mail: bookings@frogmorefarm.com   website: www.frogmorefarm.com

LANCOMBES HOUSE, WEST MILTON, BRIDPORT DT6 3TN (01308 485375). Three cottages and farmhouse, two with enclosed gardens. Set in 9 acres in an area ideal for walking, riding and outdoor pursuits. Children and dogs welcome. Open all year. ETC ★★★★ [Pets £5 per night, £15 per week].
website: www.lancombes-house.co.uk

EYPE HOUSE CARAVAN & CAMPING PARK, EYPE, BRIDPORT DT6 6AL (01308 424903) Small, quiet family-run park lying on the Heritage Coastal Path, 200 yards from the beach. Static vans for hire, tent pitches (all terraced with sea views). Sorry, no touring caravans. Children and dogs welcome. [Pets £2 per night.]
e-mail: enquiries@eypehouse.co.uk   website: www.eypehouse.co.uk

Burton Bradstock

Village near coast, 3 miles SE of Bridport.

MRS JOSEPHINE PEARSE, TAMARISK FARM, BEACH ROAD, WEST BEXINGTON, DORCHESTER DT2 9DF (01308 897784). Self Catering properties sleep 7/12. Overlooking Chesil Beach: three large (MIMOSA FOR WHEELCHAIR DISABLED M3 (1); GRANARY LODGE DISABLED-FRIENDLY M1 and THE MOAT), plus two small Cottages (ETC 3/4 Stars). Part of organic farm with arable, sheep, cattle, horses and market garden with organic vegetables, meat and wholemeal flour available. Good centre for touring, sightseeing, walking. Glorious sea views, very quiet. Lovely place for dogs. Terms from £215 to £995. Please telephone for details. [🐾]
e-mail: holidays@tamariskfarm.com   website: www.tamariskfarm.com/holidays

Charmouth

Small resort on Lyme Bay, 3 miles from Lyme Regis.

MR F. LOOSMORE, MANOR FARM HOLIDAY CENTRE, CHARMOUTH, BRIDPORT DT6 6QL (01297 560226). All units for four to six people. Ten minutes' level walk to beach, many fine local walks. Swimming pools, licensed bar with family room, shop, launderette. Sporting facilities nearby. Children and pets welcome. SAE for colour brochure. [Pets £30 per week]

Dorchester

Busy market town steeped in history. Roman remains include Amphitheatre and villa.

THE BREWERS ARMS, MARTINSTOWN, DORCHESTER DT2 9LB (01305 889361). Country pub with lovely garden. Pub food. Large car park and a large grassed area (which may be suitable for tents). Area in the pub where customers can eat and sit with their dogs.
e-mail: jackie_smith54@hotmail.com   website: www.thebrewersarms.com

GREYGLES, MELCOMBE BINGHAM, NEAR DORCHESTER. Spacious, well-equipped house just 10 miles from Dorchester. Sleep 7. Heating, electricity, linen and towels incl. No smoking. ETC ★★★★ Booking: P. SOMMERFELD, 22 TIVERTON ROAD, LONDON NW10 3HL (020 8969 4830; Fax: 020 8960 0069). [Pets £10 per booking]
e-mail: enquiry@greygles.co.uk   website: www.greygles.co.uk

THE GAGGLE OF GEESE, BUCKLAND NEWTON, DORCHESTER DT2 7BS (01300 345249). Large pub with skittle alley, five acres of land including an orchard. Everything on our menu we make ourselves and as much of it is locally sourced and seasonal as possible. Pets welcome throughout.
website: www.thegaggle.co.uk

CHURCHVIEW GUEST HOUSE, WINTERBOURNE ABBAS, DORCHESTER DT2 9LS (Tel & Fax: 01305 889296). Beautiful 17th Century Licensed Guest House set in the heart of West Dorset, character bedrooms, two lounges, licensed bar and patio garden. Non-smoking. B&B £39–£44pp. Short breaks available. ETC ★★★★ [🐾]
e-mail: stay@churchview.co.uk   website: www.churchview.co.uk

GRACE COTTAGE. Charming cottage with enclosed garden. Lounge/dining room, study/bedroom, two bedrooms, well-equipped kitchen, two bathrooms. Pub nearby. Non-smokers only. Good touring centre. Contact Nicky Willis (01308 863868). [🐾]
e-mail: veronicawillis@tiscali.co.uk   website: www.grace-cottage.com

Evershot

Village 5 miles North of Maiden Newton.

SUMMER LODGE COUNTRY HOUSE HOTEL, RESTAURANT & SPA, FORE STREET, EVERSHOT DT2 0JR (01935 48 2000). Tranquil haven full of Courtesy, Charm, Character, Calm and Cuisine. Individually designed rooms, superb food and wine. Dogs feel at home with towels, dog biscuits, water bowl and basket. AA ★★★★ [Pets £20 per night].
e-mail: summer@relaischateaux.com   website: www.summerlodgehotel.co.uk

Lulworth Cove

Village and Cove on the World Heritage Jurassic Coastline. Good beaches and numerous guided boat trips leaving from the cove showing the highlights of the area.

THE CASTLE INN, LULWORTH COVE BH20 5RN (01929 400311). Family-run, dog-friendly inn with good food, local real ales and B&B accommodation in a wonderful dog walking area. Half a mile from the coast in the heart of the Purbecks. [🐾, pw!]
website: www.lulworthinn.com

Lyme Regis

Picturesque little resort with harbour, once the haunt of smugglers. Shingle beach with sand at low tide. Fishing, sailing and water ski-ing in Lyme Bay. Taunton 28 miles, Dorchester 24, Seaton 8.

LYME BAY HOLIDAYS. Over 200 VisitBritain 3, 4, or 5 Star self catering holiday properties in beautiful country and coastal locations in and around Lyme Regis, many of which welcome pets.
e-mail: email@lymebayholidays.co.uk   website: www.lymebayholidays.co.uk

JON SNOOK AND DEBBY SNOOK, WESTOVER FARM COTTAGES, WOOTTON FITZPAINE, NEAR LYME REGIS DT6 6NE (01297 560451/561395). Within walking distance of the sea. Three beautiful cottages, sleep 6/8, with large secluded gardens. Car parking. Logs available, linen supplied. 3 bedrooms. Well behaved pets welcome. ETC ★★★/★★★★ [Pets £22 per week]
e-mail: wfcottages@aol.com   website: www.westoverfarmcottages.co.uk

North Perrott

Village 2 miles east of Crewkerne.

MRS E NEVILLE, WOOD DAIRY, WOOD LANE, NORTH PERROTT TA18 7TA (Tel & Fax: 01935 891532). Three well-appointed stone holiday cottages set around courtyard in two and a half acres of Somerset/Dorset countryside. Close to Lyme Bay and Jurassic Coast, excellent base for walking, trails and historic properties. Wheelchair friendly. Pets welcome by arrangement. [🐾]
e-mail: liz@acountryretreat.co.uk   website: www.acountryretreat.co.uk

Poole

Flourishing port and market town. Three museums with interesting collections and lively displays.

PEAR TREE HOLIDAY PARK, ORGANFORD ROAD, HOLTON HEATH, POOLE BH16 6LA (01202 622434). A perfect touring caravan park in beautiful Dorset. Convenience shop. Local pub just a short walk away. Children's play area. Mains electricity and waste disposal point. Enjoy England ★★★★. [Pets £2.50 per night]
e-mail: enquiries@peartreepark.co.uk   website: www.peartreepark.co.uk

HARBOUR HOLIDAYS. QUAY COTTAGE in quiet area with sea views. Sky TV and DVD. Dogs welcome. WYCHCOTT - detached bungalow 6 minutes' drive from beaches at Sandbanks. Fenced rear garden. Barbecue. Safe for young children and dogs. Sky TV/DVD. MRS SAUNDERS, 15 WHITE CLIFF ROAD, POOLE BH14 8DU (01202 741637). [🐾]

Portland

Connected to the Dorset mainland by a road bridge. Spectacular cliff views of the World Heritage coastline.

PORTLAND HIDEAWAY (07957 138054 / 01475 689541. Spacious, well-equipped, tastefully decorated and furnished studio accommodation. Sleeps 2. Fully enclosed patio. Off-road parking. Near Portland Bill, an ideal location for coastal holidays and sightseeing.
e-mail: howard@bestlimited.co.uk   website: www.portlandhideaway.co.uk

www.holidayguides.com

Sherborne

Town with abbey and two castles, one of which was built by Sir Walter Raleigh with lakes and gardens by Capability Brown.

WHITE HORSE FARM, MIDDLEMARSH, SHERBORNE DT9 5QN. The Willows sleeps 4/6; Otters Holt sleeps 6/8; Toad Hall sleeps 4; Badger's & Moley's sleep 2; Ratty's sleeps 2/4. Character self-catering holiday cottages in rural location. Well equipped and comfortable. Digital TV, video, free films. 2 acres of paddock, garden and duck pond. Inn 100 yards. ETC ★★★/★★★★. AUDREY & STUART WINTERBOTTOM (01963 210222) [pw!]
e-mail: enquiries@whitehorsefarm.co.uk   website: www.whitehorsefarm.co.uk

FOLKE MANOR FARM COTTAGES. Four comfortable, spacious cottages in converted barns. Sleep 4-8. Peaceful location, outstanding views, walking. Near Sherborne. Open all year. ETC ★★★★. JOHN & CAROL PERRETT, FOLKE MANOR FARM, FOLKE, SHERBORNE DT9 5HP (01963 210731).
e-mail: stay@folkemanorholidays.co.uk   website: www.folkemanorholidays.co.uk

Studland Bay

Unspoilt seaside village at south western end of Poole Bay, 3 miles north of Swanage.

THE MANOR HOUSE HOTEL, STUDLAND BAY BH19 3AU (01929 450288; Fax: 01929 452255). National Trust hotel set in 20 acres on cliffs overlooking Studland Bay. Superb food and accommodation. Log fires and four-posters.Tennis, horse-riding, golf and walking. [Pets £5 per night]
e-mail: info@themanorhousehotel.com   website: www.themanorhousehotel.com

THE KNOLL HOUSE, STUDLAND BH19 3AH (01929 450450). Country house hotel within National Trust reserve. Golden beach. 100 acre grounds. Family suites of connecting rooms. Tennis, golf, swimming, games rooms, health spa. See our Full Page Advertisement under Studland Bay. [Pets £5 per night, including food]
e-mail: info@knollhouse.co.uk   website: www.knollhouse.co.uk

Swanage

Traditional family holiday resort set in a sheltered bay ideal for water sports. Good base for a walking holiday.

THE WHITE SWAN, THE SQUARE 31 HIGH STREET, SWANAGE BH19 2LJ (01929 423804). A pub with warm and friendly atmosphere, three minutes from the beach. Traditional pub food, Sunday roasts. Large beer garden. En suite accommodation. Parking. Free WiFi and internet access. TV and pool table. Children welcome. [Pets £5 per night].
e-mail: info@whiteswanswanage.co.uk   website: www.whiteswanswanage.co.uk

HERSTON LEISURE CARAVAN AND CAMP SITE, WASHPOND LANE, SWANAGE BH19 3DJ (01929 422932) Excellent family camping and caravanning in the beautiful Dorset countryside, close to beaches and to Swanage. Touring pitches, log cabins, park homes and Mongolian Yurts available for hire. Open all year. AA Three Pennants.
e-mail: office@herstonleisure.co.uk   website: www.herstonleisure.co.uk

SWANAGE BAY VIEW HOLIDAY PARK, PANORAMA ROAD, SWANAGE BH19 2QS (01929 422130). A perfect holiday park from which to explore Dorset's stunning coastline. Well-appointed static caravans for hire. Superb sea views. Indoor swimming pool. Bar & restaurant. Take-away facilities. Enjoy England ★★★. [Pets £2.50 per night]
e-mail: enquiries@swanagebayview.co.uk   website: www.swanagebayview.co.uk

THE LIMES, 48 PARK ROAD, SWANAGE BH19 2AE (01929 422664). Informal and friendly, with en suite rooms, TV, tea/coffee making facilities, free Wi-Fi. Children and pets welcome. Car park. Licensed bar. AA ★★★★ [🐾]
e-mail: info@limeshotel.net   website: www.limeshotel.net

🐾   Pets are welcome free of charge.

£   A charge is made for pets: nightly or weekly.

pw!   Special provision for pets; exercise facility, feeding or accommodation arrangement.

⌂   Separate pets accommodation.

Classified Symbols

Wareham (near Lulworth)

Picturesque riverside town almost surrounded by earthworks, considered pre-Roman. Nature reserves of great beauty nearby. Weymouth 19 miles, Bournemouth 14, Swanage 10, Poole 6.

MRS L. S. BARNES, LUCKFORD WOOD FARMHOUSE, EAST STOKE, WAREHAM, NEAR LULWORTH BH20 6AW (01929 463098; Mobile: 07888719002). Peaceful surroundings, delightful scenery. B&B classic farmhouse with style. Breakfast served in conservatory, dining room or garden. All rooms en suite. Free Wi-Fi. Freeview TV. Also our camping and caravanning site nearby includes showers, toilets. Caravan and boat storage available. Near Lulworth Cove, Swanage, Studland, Tank Museum and Monkey World. Open all year. B&B from £40pp per night. Please phone for details. [Pets £6 per night, £40 per week]
e-mail: luckfordleisure@hotmail.co.uk   website: www.luckfordleisure.co.uk

THE SILENT WOMAN INN, BERE ROAD, COLDHARBOUR, WAREHAM BH20 7PA (01929 552909). Traditional country inn nestling in the heart of Wareham Forest. All fresh ingredients, wonderful food. Adults-only inside. Dogs allowed in bar areas and all outside areas except children's play areas.
website: www.thesilentwoman.co.uk

CATRIONA AND ALISTAIR MILLER, CROMWELL HOUSE HOTEL, LULWORTH COVE BH20 5RJ (01929 400253/400332; Fax: 01929 400566). Comfortable family-run hotel, set in secluded gardens with spectacular sea views. Heated swimming pool, 20 en suite bedrooms. Restaurant, bar wine list. Self-catering. Disabled access. ETC/AA ★★ [Pets £2 per night]
website: www.lulworthcove.co.uk

West Bexington

Seaside village with pebble beach. Chesil beach stretches eastwards. Nearby is Abbotsbury with its Benedictine Abbey and famous Swannery. Dorchester 13 miles, Weymouth 13, Bridport 6.

GORSELANDS CARAVAN PARK, DEPT PW, WEST BEXINGTON-ON-SEA DT2 9DJ (01308 897232; Fax: 01308 897239). Holiday Park. Fully serviced and equipped 4/6 berth caravans. Shop and launderette on site. Glorious sea views. Good country and seaside walks. One mile to beach. Holiday apartments with sea views and private garden. Pets most welcome. Colour brochure on request. ETC ★★★★. [🐾]
e-mail: info@gorselands.co.uk   website: www.gorselands.co.uk

Bibury, Bourton-on-the-Water, Chalford, Cheltenham

Forest of Dean, Longhope (near Forest of Dean), Moreton-in-Marsh

Broadclose Cottage Blockley, Near Moreton-in-Marsh GL56 9BA

01386 701570 • e-mail:jf@broadclose.co.uk John & Frances Hoskins (and Toby)

Situated midway between the market town of Moreton-in-Marsh and
Chipping Campden, Blockley is also convenient for Stow on the Wold,
Oxford, Cheltenham and Stratford Upon Avon.
Broadclose, converted from the village dairy, is well furnished and
comfortable.Cosy sitting room, kitchen/diner; upstairs double bedroom
and twin bedroom. CH, towels, linen, electricity inc.
There are splendid dog walks from the front door, and the cottage
garden is safe and enclosed. Off-road parking.

Low Season from £85 per night, £500 per week.
High Season from £105 per night, £600 per week.

www.broadclose.co.uk

The Laurels at Inchbrook

Cow Lane, Inchbrook, Nailsworth GL5 5HA
Tel/Fax: 01453 834021 • e-mail: laurelsinchbrook@tiscali.co.uk
www.laurelsinchbrook.co.uk

A comfortable, rambling house, cottage and garden set beside the Inch Brook and
adjoining fields. Lovely secluded garden, with badgers and bats: the stream is an
otter route, and many birds come to visit us. Pets are most welcome, and there are
dozens of splendid walks and the National Trust's Woodchester Park on our doorstep.

Nailsworth, a fashionable Cotswold town and a centre for excellence when it
comes to eating out, is just under a mile away.

Ideally placed for exploring the West Country, Bath and Forest of Dean as well as
the Cotswolds, our house is perfect for groups and family gatherings. Brochure
on request. Self-catering facilities may be available at certain times of the year.

*Rooms from £35 - £65 per night. Rooms: 4 double (one ground floor accessible),
2 twin, 2 family; all en suite. No smoking. Children and pets welcome. Open all year.*

Hambutt's Mynd

This is the view from all bedrooms

Bed and Breakfast in an old converted
Corn Mill. Very quiet with superb views.
Three minutes to the centre of the village.
Field nearby for exercising dogs.
Central heating. All rooms en suite:
one double, one twin, one single, all with TV.
£36 single, £66 double or twin,
10% discount for 4 nights or more.

MRS E. WARLAND, HAMBUTT'S MYND, EDGE ROAD, PAINSWICK GL6 6UP
Tel: 01452 812352 • e-mail: ewarland@supanet.com
www.accommodation.uk.net/hambutts.htm

AA
★★★
Guest
Accommodation

Stow-on-the-Wold, Stroud

Please mention PETS WELCOME!
when making enquiries about accommodation featured in this guide

Bibury

Village on the River Colne, 7 miles NE of Cirencester.

CAROLINE MANN, HARTWELL FARM COTTAGES, READY TOKEN, NEAR BIBURY, CIRENCESTER GL7 5SY (01285 740210). Two comfortable, fully equipped cottages with country views. Ideally located for touring. Stabling available. Glorious walks, excellent pubs. Non-smoking. Children and well-behaved dogs welcome. ETC ★★★★ [pw! Pets £15 per week]
e-mail: ec.mann@btinternet.com   website: www.selfcateringcotswolds.com

Bourton-on-the-Water

Delightfully situated on the River Windrush which is crossed by miniature stone bridges. Stow-on-the-Wold 4 miles.

CHESTER HOUSE HOTEL, VICTORIA STREET, BOURTON-ON-THE-WATER GL54 2BU (01451 820286). All rooms en suite, all with central heating, colour TV, phone, tea/coffee making facilities. Wheelchair friendly. Ideal for touring Cotswolds. [🐕]
e-mail: info@chesterhousehotel.com   website: www.chesterhousehotel.com

STRATHSPEY, LANSDOWNE, BOURTON-ON-THE-WATER GL54 2AR (01451 810321; mobile: 07889 491993). Tastefully furnished bedrooms with TV, refreshment tray, hairdryer, clock radio. Pleasant tranquil garden. Five minutes' walk from centre of village. Open all year. Terms from £30.00pppn. Pets welcome by prior arrangement. AA ★★★ [Pets £5 per (part of) week]
e-mail: bookings@strathspey.org.uk   website: www.strathspey.org.uk

Chalford

Village 4 miles south east of Stroud.

ROS SMITH, EDGECOMBE HOUSE, TOADSMOOR GL5 2UG (01453 883147). Pretty 18thC cottage in the heart of the Cotswold Hills. Sleeps 2 couples + 1 child in 2 bedrooms. Outdoor heated swimming pool and bubbling hot tub. Free private kennel facilities (optional). Breaks £150-£700. [pw!🐕 ⌂]
e-mail: ros@doggybreaks.co.u k   website: www.doggybreaks.co.uk

Cheltenham

Large residential town, formerly a spa, 8 miles East of Gloucester.

CHARLTON KINGS HOTEL & RESTAURANT, LONDON ROAD, CHELTENHAM GL52 6UU (01242 231061). Ideally located for Cheltenham and the Cotswolds. Close to Cotswold Way. Friendly resident owners. [🐕]
e-mail: enquiries@charltonkingshotel.co.uk   website: www.charltonkingshotel.co.uk

Cirencester

Market town which lies on River Chum, a tributary of the River Thames. Largest town in the Cotswolds, 93 miles from London.

POLLY AND NICK HANDOVER, GLEBE FARM, BARNSLEY ROAD, CIRENCESTER GL7 5DY (01285 659226; Fax: 01285 642622). Restored barn cottages. Fully equipped, some en suite. Patios, communal garden and ample parking. Utility room. Children under 2 years only. Pets welcome by arrangement. Enjoy England ★★★★/★★★★★. [Pets £20 per week]
e-mail: enquiries@glebefarmcottages.co.uk   website: www.glebefarmcottages.co.uk

Clearwell (Forest of Dean)

Village 2 miles south of Coleford in the ancient Forest of Dean.

TUDOR FARMHOUSE HOTEL & RESTAURANT, CLEARWELL, NEAR COLEFORD GL16 8JS (01594 833046; Fax: 01594 837093). Charming 13th Century farmhouse hotel in extensive grounds, ideal for dog walking. 20 en suite bedrooms including Four Posters and Cottage Suite. Award-winning restaurant. AA ★★★ and Two Rosettes. [Pets £5 per night].
e-mail: info@tudorfarmhousehotel.co.uk   website: www.tudorfarmhousehotel.co.uk

Fairford

Small town 8 miles east of Cirencester.

THE BULL HOTEL, MARKET PLACE, FAIRFORD GL7 4AA (01285 712535/712217; Fax: 01285 713782). 15thC family-run coaching inn with 27 fully equipped bedrooms; four-poster beds available. A la carte restaurant. Ideal for touring; many leisure facilities within easy reach. ETC/AA ★★ [Pets £5 per night, £20 per week]
e-mail: info@thebullhotelfairford.co.uk   website: www.thebullhotelfairford.co.uk

Forest of Dean

Formerly a royal hunting ground, this scenic area lies between the rivers Severn and Wye.

DRYSLADE FARM, ENGLISH BICKNOR, COLEFORD GL16 7PA (01594 860259; Mobile: 07766 631988). Daphne & Phil ensure a warm welcome for yourself and your dog. A relaxed, friendly atmosphere awaits you at their farmhouse, which dates back to 1780, on their 184-acre beef farm. In the small village of English Bicknor in the Royal Forest of Dean, with Symonds Yat only 2 miles. AA ★★★★ Highly Commended. [🐾]
e-mail: daphne@drysladefarm.co.uk   website: www.drysladefarm.co.uk

WHARTON LODGE COTTAGES, WESTON-UNDER-PENYARD, NEAR ROSS-ON-WYE HR9 7JX (Tel & Fax: 01989 750140). Two elegantly furnished, fully equipped self-catering retreats overlooking Herefordshire countryside, sleeping 2, 3 or 4 guests. Fully inclusive rates. Dog paradise. Tourist Board ★★★★★ Gold Award. [pw! Pets £4 per night, £20 per week]
e-mail: ncross@whartonlodge.co.uk   website: www.whartonlodge.co.uk

THE SPEECH HOUSE HOTEL, COLEFORD, FOREST OF DEAN GL16 7EL (01594 822607). A friendly Hotel set in the heart of the Forest of Dean. The perfect place for pets. 37 en suite bedrooms. Assorted menus using local produce. AA ★★★. [Pets £10 per night]
e-mail: relax@thespeechhouse.co.uk   website: www.thespeechhouse.co.uk

ANTHONY & INEZ MIDGLEY, HIGHBURY COACH HOUSE, BREAM ROAD, LYDNEY GL15 5JH (01594 842 339 or 07834 408 550). Come and stay in one or more of the three spacious flats in the Coach House of Highbury House, situated on the southern edge of the Royal Forest of Dean. EnjoyEngland ★★★. [pw! 🐾]
e-mail: info@highburycoachhouse.co.uk   website: www.highburycoachhouse.co.uk

THE WYNDHAM ARMS HOTEL, CLEARWELL, NEAR COLEFORD, THE ROYAL FOREST OF DEAN GL16 8JT (01594 833 666; Fax: 01594 836 450). Between the beautiful Wye Valley and the Royal Forest of Dean. Eighteen en suite bedrooms including four poster bedrooms and a sumptuous suite. Pets welcome in bedrooms, bar and hotel grounds. AA ★★★ [Pets £5 per night]
e-mail: res@thewyndhamhotel.co.uk   website: www.thewyndhamhotel.co.uk

Longhope (near Forest of Dean)

Village situated just outside the Forest of Dean. Longhope means 'long, enclosed valley' which describes the aspect of the village.

THE OLD FARM, BARREL LANE, LONGHOPE GL17 0LR (01452 830252) Character-packed, timber framed, converted 450-year-old barns. Set around an old farmyard leading onto paddocks, woodland and play orchard. Dog and babysitting services. Properties sleep 2/3 and 5/6. ETC ★★★★ [pw! 🐕]
e-mail: mattandliza@aol.com   website: www.oldfarmcottages.co.uk

Moreton-in-Marsh

Principal market town in the northern Cotswolds, situated on the Fosse Way.

THE WHITE HART ROYAL HOTEL, MORETON-IN-MARSH GL56 0BA (01608 650731). Historic old coaching inn full of character, quality and comfort. Beautifully furnished throughout to maintain its old world charm while offering 21st century facilities. Wide variety of bedrooms. AA ★★★. [Pets £10 per night]
e-mail: whr@bpcmail.co.uk   website: www.whitehartroyal.co.uk

BROADCLOSE COTTAGE, BLOCKLEY, NEAR MORETON IN MARSH GL56 9BA (01386 701570). Well furnished and comfortable converted cottage mid-way between Moreton in Marsh and Chipping Campden. Ideally situated for visiting Stow on the Wold, Oxford, Cheltenham and Stratford Upon Avon. Sleeps 4. Safe and enclosed garden. [🐕]
e-mail: jf@broadclose.co.uk   website: www.broadclose.co.uk

Nailsworth

Hilly town 4 miles south of Stroud

THE LAURELS, INCHBROOK, NAILSWORTH GL5 5HA (01453 834021; Fax: 01453 835190). A lovely rambling house, cottage and secluded garden where dogs and their owners are encouraged to relax and enjoy. Ideally situated for touring all parts of the Cotswolds and West Country; splendid walks. Brochure. [🐕]
e-mail: laurelsinchbrook@tiscali.co.uk   website: www.laurelsinchbrook.co.uk

Painswick

Beautiful little Cotswold town with characteristic stone-built houses.

MRS E. WARLAND, HAMBUTTS MYND, EDGE ROAD, PAINSWICK GL6 6UP (01452 812352). Bed and Breakfast in an old converted Corn Mill. Very quiet with superb views. Three minutes to the centre of the village. Field nearby for exercising dogs. Central heating. One double room, one twin, one single, all with TV. £36 single, £66 double or twin, 10% discount for 4 nights or more. ALL ROOMS EN SUITE. AA ★★★ [🐕]
e-mail: ewarland@supanet.com   website: www.accommodation.uk.net/hambutts.htm

South Cerney

4 miles from Cirencester in the Cotswold Waterpark, an area of 40 square miles.

ORION HOLIDAYS, COTSWOLDS (01285 801039). A stunning collection of 4/5 ★ lakeside homes. Perfect retreat with pets - Thames Footpath on the doorstep and idyllic countryside to explore. [Pets £15 per week].
e-mail: contact@orionholidays.com   website: www.orionholidays.com/pw

---

🐕 Pets are welcome free of charge.

£   A charge is made for pets: nightly or weekly.

pw! Special provision for pets; exercise facility, feeding or accommodation arrangement.

⌂   Separate pets accommodation.

Classified Symbols

Stow-on-the-Wold

Charming Cotswold hill-top market town with several old inns and interesting buildings. Birmingham 45 miles, Gloucester 26, Stratford-upon-Avon 21, Cheltenham 18, Chipping Norton 9.

THE LIMES, EVESHAM ROAD, STOW-ON-THE-WOLD GL54 1EN (01451 830034/831056). Large Country House. Attractive garden, overlooking fields, 4 minutes town centre. Television lounge. Central heating. Car park. Bed and Breakfast from £27 to £35pppn. Twin, double or family rooms, all en suite. Children and pets welcome. Tourist Board Listed. [Pets £5 per visit]
e-mail: gkeyte@sky.com   website: www.thelimescotswolds.co.uk

THE OLD STOCKS HOTEL, RESTAURANT & BAR, THE SQUARE, STOW-ON-THE-WOLD GL54 1AF (01451 830666; Fax: 01451 870014). Ideal base for touring this beautiful area. Tasteful guest rooms (including three 'garden' rooms) with modern amenities. Mouth-watering menus. Special bargain breaks also available. HETB/AA ★★ [Pets £5 each per stay]
e-mail: fhg@oldstockshotel.co.uk   website: www.oldstockshotel.co.uk

Stroud

Cotswold town on River Frome below picturesque Stroudwater Hills, formerly renowned for cloth making. Bristol 32 miles, Bath 29, Chippenham 25, Cheltenham 14, Gloucester 9.

TOM AND LESLEY WILLIAMS, ORCHARDENE, CASTLE STREET, KINGS STANLEY, STONEHOUSE GL10 3JA (01453 822684; Fax: 01453 821554). Warm welcome at Cotswold Stone cottage. Ideal location to explore undiscovered Cotswolds and Severn Vale. Glorious walks. Evening Meal optional. Local and organic food. Pets welcome.
e-mail: toranda@btconnect.com

MRS A. RHOTON, HYDE CREST, CIRENCESTER ROAD, MINCHINHAMPTON GL6 8PE (01453 731631). Beautiful country house with enclosed acre garden. All rooms on ground floor opening on to patios and lawns. 500 acres of commons, plus country walks nearby. AA ★★★★ [pw! 🐾]
e-mail: stay@hydecrest.co.uk   website: www.hydecrest.co.uk

MRS UNA PEACEY, THE WITHYHOLT GUEST HOUSE, PAUL MEAD, EDGE, NEAR STROUD GL6 6PG (01452 813618: Fax: 01452 812375) Modern guesthouse in Gloucestershire close to Gloucester Cathedral, Tetbury, Stroud. Many lovely country walks. En suite bedrooms, large lounge. Large garden. ETC ★★★★ [🐾]

Symonds Yat

Well known beauty spot on River Wye, 4 miles from Monmouth.

SYMONDS YAT ROCK LODGE, HILLERSLAND, NEAR COLEFORD GL16 7NY (01594 836191). Family-run B&B and Self catering in Forest of Dean near Wye Valley. All rooms en suite, flat screen TV; Freeview, DVD and CD. 4 poster and family rooms. Brochure available on request. Dogs welcome. [🐾]
e-mail: info@rocklodge.co.uk   website: www.rocklodge.co.uk

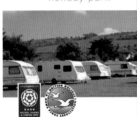

The Hood Arms

a famous 17th century coaching Inn. Situated on the A39 at the foot of the Quantock Hills, close to the spectacular fossil beach at Kilve, a paradise for walkers, mountain bikers, dogs, sporting parties or simply relaxing. The 12 recently refurbished en suite bedrooms include stylish four-posters. Stag Lodge in the courtyard garden has two luxury bedrooms and sitting room. The beamed restaurant offers a relaxed dining experience whilst providing delicious locally sourced food.

A full à la carte menu, chef's specials and bar snacks are available 7 days a week. The bar is full of character and boasts an impressive array of real ales. A warm welcome awaits locals and traveller alike.

Please look at our website for more details and prices.

The Hood Arms, Kilve, Bridgwater, Somerset TA5 1EA
01278 741210 • Fax: 01278 741477
e-mail: info@thehoodarms.com www.thehoodarms.com

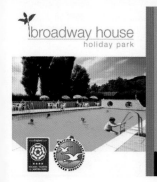

broadway house
holiday park

A fun-filled family holiday caravan park in picturesque Somerset

darwin
holiday parks

- Convenience shop
- Licensed bar & restaurant
- Swimming pool & cafe
- Adventure playground
- Mains electricity
- Waste disposal point

Pet Friendly

To book: 01934 742 610 or www.broadwayhousepark.co.uk

CHEDDAR - SUNGATE HOLIDAY APARTMENTS
Church Street, Cheddar, Somerset BS27 3RA

SELF CATERING

Delightful non-smoking apartments in Cheddar village, each fully equipped. Sleep one/four people. Laundry facilities. Private parking. Family, disabled, and pet friendly.

For full details contact: Mrs. M. M. Fieldhouse (proprietress)

Tel: 01934 842273/742264
enquiries@sungateholidayapartments.co.uk
www.sungateholidayapartments.co.uk

Dunster, Exford, Exmoor

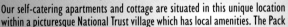

Exmoor, Minehead, Porlock, Quantock Hills

FARM & COTTAGE HOLIDAYS (01237 459897). An inspiring collection of holiday cottages throughout Cornwall, Devon, Somerset and Dorset in stunning rural and coastal locations. [Pets £20 per week] website: www.holidaycottages.co.uk

Bath

The best-preserved Georgian city in Britain, Bath has been famous since Roman times for its mineral springs. It is a noted centre for music and the arts, with a wide range of leisure facilities.

NEWTON MILL HOLIDAY PARK, NEWTON ROAD, BATH BA2 9JF (01225 333909). Tranquil caravan & camping park just 3 miles from the historical city of Bath. Convenience shop. Licensed bar and restaurant. Children's play area. Parking for one car. Mains electricity and waste disposal point. Enjoy England ★★★★. [Pets £2.50 per night]
e-mail: enquiries@newtonmillpark.co.uk   website: www.newtonmillpark.co.uk

DAVID & JACKIE BISHOP, TOGHILL HOUSE FARM, FREEZING HILL, WICK, NEAR BATH BS30 5RT (01225 891261; Fax: 01225 892128). Luxury barn conversions on working farm 3 miles north of Bath. Each equipped to very high standard, bed linen provided. Also en suite B&B accommodation in 17th century farmhouse. [pw! Pets £5 per night, £20 per week]
website: www.toghillhousefarm.co.uk

MR JOHN NAPIER, EAGLE HOUSE BED AND BREAKFAST, CHURCH STREET, BATHFORD, BATH BA1 7RS (01225 859946). Stylish 250-year-old Georgian Stone Mansion in peaceful location only 3 miles from Bath, an ideal base for exploring the city and the surrounding area. Friendly hosts; six well equipped bedrooms, including large family rooms. [Pets £4.50 per night; £30 per week].
e-mail: jonap@eagleho.demon.co.uk   website: www.eaglehouse.co.uk

Blue Anchor

Hamlet two miles west of Watchet. Beautiful beaches, and rocks and cliffs of geological interest.

PRIMROSE HILL HOLIDAYS, WOOD LANE, BLUE ANCHOR TA24 6LA (01643 821200). Award-winning, spacious, comfortable accommodation in a terrace of four bungalows. Private gardens with panoramic views. A dog-friendly beach is a 10-minute walk away, with other lovely walks from your doorstep. Fully wheelchair accessible. VB ★★★★ [Pets £15 per week].
e-mail: info@primrosehillholidays.co.uk   website: www.primrosehillholidays.co.uk

Brean

Coastal village with extensive sands. To north is the promontory of Brean Down. Weston-Super-Mare 9 miles.

WESTWARD RISE HOLIDAY PARK, SOUTH ROAD, BREAN, NEAR BURNHAM ON-SEA TA8 2RD (01278 751310). Highly Recommended Luxury 2/6 berth Chalet bungalows. 2 double bedrooms, shower, toilet, TV, fridge, cooker, duvets and linen. Open all year. Call for free brochure. [Pets £15 per week.]
website: www.westwardrise.com

Bridgwater

An Area of Outstanding Natural Beauty at the foot of the Quantocks, a paradise for walkers.

THE HOOD ARMS, KILVE, BRIDGWATER TA5 1EA (01278 741210; Fax: 01278 741477). 17thC coaching inn on the A39 at the foot of the Quantock Hills. 12 en suite bedrooms, including four-posters. Beamed restaurant offering full à la carte menu; bar snacks and real ales available. Large garden. [🐾]
e-mail: info@thehoodarms.com   website: www.thehoodarms.com

Chard

At an altitude of 121 metres Chard is the highest town in Somerset. 15 miles south west of Yeovil.

LORDLEAZE HOTEL, HENDERSON DRIVE, FORTON ROAD, CHARD TA20 2HW (01460 61066). Once an 18th centry farmhouse, now a country hotel, close to the South Coast and minutes away from town centre. 25 en suite bedrooms, excellent restaurant and bar. AA ★★★ [Pets £5 per night]
e-mail: info@lordleazehotel.com   website: www.lordleazehotel.com

Cheddar

Picturesque little town in the Mendips, famous for its Gorge and unique caves. Cheese-making is a speciality. Good touring centre. Bath 24 miles, Burnham-on-sea 13, Weston-Super-Mare 11.

BROADWAY HOUSE HOLIDAY PARK, AXBRIDGE ROAD, CHEDDAR BS27 3DB (01934 724610; Fax: 01934 744950). A fun-filled family holiday park in picturesque Somerset. Convenience shop. Licensed bar and restaurant. Swimming pool & cafe. Adventure playground. Mains electricity and waste disposal point. Enjoy England ★★★★. [Pets £2.50 per night]
e-mail: enquiries@broadwayhousepark.co.uk   website: www.broadwayhousepark.co.uk

SUNGATE HOLIDAY APARTMENTS, CHURCH STREET, CHEDDAR BS27 3RA. Ideally situated for walking, cycling and touring the Mendips and the West Country. Competitively priced for short or longer holidays. For full details contact MRS M. FIELDHOUSE (01934 842273/742264) ETC ★★ [Quote for Pets].
e-mail: enquiries@sungateholidayapartments.co.uk   web: www.sungateholidayapartments.co.uk

Clevedon

Small town on Bristol Channel with restored Victorian pier.

MRS JENNY HOPKINS, ROSE COTTAGE, 36 THACKERAY AVE, CLEVEDON BS21 7JJ (01275 879491) You are assured of a warm welcome at this pleasant semi-detached B&B. Private parking. Non smoking. Bristol 15 miles. Well behaved dogs by arrangement. [Pets £1 per night]
e-mail: jenny22hopkins@virginmedia.com   website: www.rosecottage-bandb.co.uk

Dunster

Pretty village with interesting features, including Yarn Market, imposing 14th century Castle. Priory Church and old houses and cottages. Minehead 3 miles.

DUDDINGS COUNTRY COTTAGES, TIMBERSCOMBE DUNSTER TA24 7TB (01643 841123) Thatched longhouse and 12 cottages for 2-16 persons, beautifully converted from old stone barns and stables. Two miles from the village of Dunster in the Exmoor National Park. Pets and families welcome. Open all year. Visit Britain ★★★★ Self Catering. [pw!, Pets £20 per week].
e-mail: richard@duddings.co.uk   website: www.duddings.co.uk

THE YARN MARKET HOTEL, HIGH STREET, DUNSTER TA24 6SF (01643 821425; Fax: 01643 821475). An ideal location for walking and exploring Exmoor. Family-run hotel with a friendly, relaxed atmosphere, home cooking, en suite rooms with colour TV and tea making facilities. Non-smoking. Mid-week breaks a speciality – Pets Welcome. ETC ★★★ Hotel [pw! 🐕]
e-mail: hotel@yarnmarkethotel.co.uk   website: www.yarnmarkethotel.co.uk

BURNELLS GARDENS, KNOWLE LANE, DUNSTER TA24 6TX (01643 822045; 07796 833183). Quality Exmoor farmhouse bed and breakfast. Pets very welcome, multiple pets no problem; superb breakfasts, wonderful walking. From £32 pppn, discounts available for stays of 3 nights or more. [pw! 🐕]
e-mail: libbyportch@yahoo.co.uk   website: www.burnellsgardens.moonfruit.com

Exford

Fine touring centre for Exmoor and North Devon, on River Exe. Dulverton 10 miles.

CHAPEL COTTAGE, EXFORD TA24 7PY (01788 810275). Enjoy walking or riding on the moors, by the rivers or the beach. Return to our cosy cottage, log fire and beams. Two bedrooms (sleeps 4+2), two bathrooms. Excellent inns within 100 yards. Open all year. [🐕 Up to 2 dogs welcome, free of charge]
e-mail: stay@chapelcottage-exmoor.co.uk   website: www.chapelcottage-exmoor.co.uk

STILEMOOR, EXFORD, EXMOOR NATIONAL PARK TA24 7NA. Charming cosy centrally heated detached bungalow with enclosed garden, superb views, walking, fishing, riding. Sleeps 6. ETC ★★★★. JOAN ATKINS, 2 EDGCOTT COTTAGE, EXFORD, MINEHEAD TA24 7QG (01643 831564; mobile: 078914 37293) [Pets £2.50 per night, £16 per week]
e-mail: info@stilemoorexmoor.co.uk   website: www.stilemoorexmoor.co.uk

WESTERMILL, EXFORD, EXMOOR TA24 7NJ (01643 831238; Fax: 01643 831216). Idyllic Scandinavian cottages in grass paddocks by stream, with views across river valley. Heart of Exmoor. Woodburners. Four waymarked walks over 500 acre working farm. Disabled Category 2. Separate campsite by river. VisitBritain ★★★, David Bellamy Gold Award for Conservation. [Pets £2.50 per night, £15 per week.]
e-mail: pw@westermill.com   website: www.westermill.com

LEONE & BRIAN MARTIN, RISCOMBE FARM HOLIDAY COTTAGES, EXFORD, EXMOOR NATIONAL PARK TA24 7NH (01643 831480). Beside River Exe – centre of Exmoor National Park – close to coast. Four charming self-catering cottages. Dogs and horses welcome. Stabling available. VB ★★★★ [Pets £2.50 per night, £15 per week.]
website: www.riscombe.co.uk (with up-to-date vacancy info.)

Exmoor

265 square miles of unspoiled heather moorland with deep wooded valleys and rivers, ideal for a walking, pony trekking or fishing holiday.

WEST HOLLOWCOMBE SELF-CATERING COTTAGES, HAWKRIDGE, EXMOOR TA22 9QL (01398 341400). Four spacious, well appointed barn conversions. Open-plan living accommodation, fully equipped kitchens, wood-burning stoves. Sleep 4-6. Parking. Stables. Pets welcome. [Pets £3 per night.]
e-mail: cottages@westhollowcombe.co.uk   website: www.westhollowcombe.co.uk

WOODCOMBE LODGES, BRATTON, NEAR MINEHEAD TA24 8SQ (Tel & Fax: 01643 702789). Four self-catering lodges in a tranquil rural setting on the edge of Exmoor National Park, standing in a beautiful 2½ acre garden with wonderful views. VisitBritain ★★★★ [Pets £10 per week]
e-mail: nicola@woodcombelodge.co.uk   website: www.woodcombelodge.co.uk

JENNY COPE, NORTH DOWN FARM, PYNCOMBE LANE, WIVELISCOMBE, TAUNTON TA4 2BL (01984 623730). Traditional working farm. All rooms en suite, furnished to high standard. Log fires. Central heating. B&B £36pppn. BB&EM: 7 nights £299pp, 3-night B&B and evening meal £145pp. Dogs welcome. ETC ★★★★ Silver Award. [Pets £5 per night].
e-mail: jennycope@btinternet.com   website: www.north-down-farm.co.uk

JANE STYLES, WINTERSHEAD FARM, SIMONSBATH TA24 7LF (01643 831222). Five tastefully furnished and well-equipped cottages situated in the midst of beautiful Exmoor. Pets welcome, stabling and grazing, DIY livery. Colour brochure on request. ETC ★★★★ [Dogs £15 per week, Horses £20 per week.]
website: www.wintershead.co.uk

THE PACK HORSE, ALLERFORD, NEAR PORLOCK TA24 8HW (Tel & Fax: 01643 862475). Self-catering apartments and cottage within picturesque National Trust village. Immediate access to the beautiful surrounding countryside. Stabling available. Open all year. ETC ★★★★ [Pets £15 per week]
e-mail: holidays@thepackhorse-exmoor.co.uk   website: www.thepackhorse-exmoor.co.uk

WESTERCLOSE HOUSE, WITHYPOOL, EXMOOR NATIONAL PARK TA24 7QR (01643 831302). Stunning views, complete peace, and wonderful moorland location. Five cosy cottages, including two bungalows, all with log fires and individual gardens. Pub/shop 300 metres. Dogs and horses welcome. ETC ★★★★ [pw! Dogs £12 per week]
website: www.westerclose.co.uk

IAN & LORENA MABBUTT, WEST WITHY FARM, UPTON, NEAR DULVERTON, TAUNTON TA4 2JH (01398 371322). Two local stone barns converted to spacious, comfortable self-catering cottages on a 23-acre smallholding. Sleep 4/5. Enclosed gardens. ETC ★★★★ [Pets £12 per week]
e-mail: westwithyfarm@exmoor-cottages.com   website: www.exmoor-cottages.com

Minehead

Neat and stylish resort on Bristol Channel. Sandy bathing beach, attractive gardens, golf course and good facilities for tennis, bowls and horse riding. Within easy reach of the beauties of Exmoor.

MINEHEAD 16TH CENTURY THATCHED COTTAGES. Rose Ash - Sleeps 2, prettily furnished, all electric. Willow - Inglenook, oak panelling, electricity, gas, CH, Sleeps 6. Little Thatch - Sleeps 5, Inglenook, Cosy location, Electricity. Gas. CH. Private car park. Enclosed gardens. Pets welcome. SAE: MR T. STONE, TROYTES FARMSTEAD, TIVINGTON, MINEHEAD TA24 8SU (01643 704531). [🐕]

SUNFIELD, 83 SUMMERLAND AVENUE, MINEHEAD TA24 5BW (01643 703565). Delightful family-run guest house only a few minutes' level walking distance from sea front. Delicious home cooking. 8 en suite bedrooms. Children and well behaved pets welcome. Totally non-smoking. ETC ★★★★ [🐕] website: www.sunfieldminehead.co.uk

Porlock

Small resort near coast at foot of steep hill. Lynton 11 miles, Minehead 6.

THE SHIP INN, HIGH STREET, PORLOCK TA24 8QD (01643 862507). Thatched 13th century family-run inn within walking distance of sea and moor. Genuine old bar with stone floor and log fire. Home cooked food. Six real ales, three ciders. Five B&B bedrooms, all en suite. [Pets £5 per stay] e-mail: enquiries@shipinnporlock.co.uk   website: www.shipinnporlock.co.uk

Quantock Hills

Granite and limestone ridge running north-west and south-east from Quantoxhead and Kingston.

THE OLD CIDER HOUSE, 25 CASTLE STREET, NETHER STOWEY TA5 1LN (01278 732228). In picturesque, historic village at the foot of the Quantocks. All en suite; licensed dining. Own car parking, walled garden. B&B from £30pppn. Wonderful dog-walking country; only 4 miles from coast. EnjoyEngland ★★★★ Guest Accommodation. [Pets £3 per night]. e-mail: info@theoldciderhouse.co.uk   website: www.theoldciderhouse.co.uk

Stoke St Gregory

Rural settlement in te Somerset Levels. Taunton 10 miles.

HOLLY FARM HOLIDAY COTTAGES, STOKE ST GREGORY, NEAR TAUNTON TA3 6HS (01823 490828). Five self-catering cottages, all furnished and equipped to a high standard, sleep 4/5. Each with own enclosed garden. Heated indoor pool, hot tub, games room. ETC ★★★★ e-mail: robhembrow@btinternet.com   www.holly-farm.com

Taunton

County capital in Vale of Taunton Deane. Museum, Civic Centre, remains of Norman castle.

FARTHINGS HOTEL & RESTAURANT, HATCH BEAUCHAMP, TAUNTON TA3 6SG (01823 480664; Fax: 01823 481118). Nestled in the midst of the wild and fertile countryside of Somerset, just 3 miles from the M5 and Taunton. An elegant Georgian Hotel with beautiful grounds and gardens, orchards, roses, and our own poultry for your breakfast eggs. AA ★★★ Two Rosettes. [🐕] e-mail: farthingshotel@yahoo.co.uk   website: www.farthingshotel.co.uk

ASHE FARM, THORNFALCON, TAUNTON TA3 5NW (01823 443764) Quiet, informal family-run site in the Vale of Taunton. Two sheltered meadows with lovely views of the hills. Electric hook-ups. Disabled toilet facilities. Laundry. Information room. Play area. AA Three Pennants. EnjoyEngland ★★★ [🐕] e-mail: info@ashefarm.co.uk   website: www.ashefarm.co.uk

HOLLY BUSH PARK, CULMHEAD, TAUNTON TA3 7EA (01823 421515). Hidden in Somerset's Blackdown Hills, along a maze of narrow lanes. A genuine "away from it all" site. Tents, campervans, caravans, dogs, quiet families and couples welcome. AA 3 Pennants. website: www.hollybushpark.com

et

Small port and resort with rocks and sands. Good centre for Exmoor and the Quantocks. Bathing, boating, fishing, rambling. Tiverton 24 miles, Bridgwater 19, Taunton 17, Dunster 6.

SUNNYBANK HOLIDAY PARK, DONIFORD, WATCHET TA23 0UD (01984 632237). Relax at this five star holiday park nestled in the Quantock Hills, Somerset. Well-appointed static caravans for hire. Convenience shop. Outdoor swimming pool. Children's play area. Laundry facilities. Enjoy England ★★★★★ . [Pets £2.50 per night]
e-mail: enquiries@sunnybankpark.co.uk   website: www.sunnybankpark.co.uk

MRS K. MUSGRAVE, CROFT HOLIDAY COTTAGES, THE CROFT, ANCHOR STREET, WATCHET TA23 0BY (01984 631121) Courtyard of six cottages/bungalows situated in a quiet backwater of the small harbour town of Watchet. Parking, central heating. TV, DVD, washing machine, fridge/freezer, microwave. Use of heated indoor pool. Sleeps 2-6 persons. £215-£795 per property per week. EnjoyEngland ★★★★ [Pets £15 per week]
e-mail: croftcottages@talk21.com   website: www.cottagessomerset.com

Wells

England's smallest city. West front of Cathedral built around 1230 shows superb collection of statuary.

INFIELD HOUSE, 36 PORTWAY, WELLS BA5 2BN (01749 670989; Fax: 01749 679093). Richard and Heather invite you and your dog (if older than one year) to visit England's smallest city. Wonderful walks on Mendip Hills. No smoking. Bountiful breakfasts, dinners by arrangement. AA ★★★★ [🐾]
website: www.infieldhouse.co.uk

Weston-Super-Mare

Popular resort on the Bristol Channel with a wide range of entertainments and leisure facilities. An ideal base for touring the West Country.

SOMERSET COURT COTTAGES, WICK ST LAWRENCE, NEAR WESTON-SUPER-MARE BS22 7YR (01934 521383). Converted stone cottages in mediaeval village. 1, 2 or 3 beds. Some with four-posters, luxury whirlpool/spa baths. Superb centre for touring West Country. Short Breaks available. £220-£730 per week. [Pets £2 per night]
e-mail: peter@somersetcourtcottages.co.uk   website: www.somersetcottages.com

BRAESIDE HOTEL, 2 VICTORIA PARK, WESTON-SUPER-MARE BS23 2HZ (01934 626642). Delightful, family-run Hotel, close to shops, beach and park. Parking available. All rooms en suite, colour TV, tea/coffee making. Members of the Bed and Breakfast Association. [🐾]
e-mail: enquiries@braesidehotel.com   website: www.braesidehotel.com

LOWER FARM COTTAGES. Three luxury spacious cottages with enclosed gardens, sleep 3/6/7. Peaceful rural setting, lovely views. Three miles to sea. Families and dogs welcome. Off-peak Short Breaks. EnjoyEngland ★★★★. CHRISTINE AND ROY BALL, LOWER FARM HOUSE, SOUTH ROAD, LYMPSHAM, WESTON-SUPER-MARE BS24 0DY (01934 750206). [Pets £20 per week].
e-mail: holidays@lowerfarmcottages.co.uk   website: www.lowerfarmcottages.co.uk

Williton

Village 2 miles South of Watchet.

THE WHITE HOUSE, 11 LONG STREET, WILLITON TA4 4QW (01984 632306). B & B from only £39pppn including a beautifully cooked Full English breakfast. Friendly and relaxed atmosphere. Families and pets welcome. AA ★★★★ [🐾]
e-mail: whitehouselive@btconnect.com   website: www.whitehousewilliton.co.uk

Yeovil

Vibrant market town situated at the southern boundary of Somerset 40 miles from Bristol and 30 miles from Taunton.

THE HALFWAY HOUSE INN COUNTRY LODGE, CHILTHORNE DOMER, NEAR YEOVIL BA22 8RE (01935 840350; Fax: 01935 849006) The very best in country hospitality and an ideal base from which to tour Somerset and Dorset. 20 en suite rooms including a disabled-friendly lodge and four-poster Bridal Suite. Well behaved pets by arrangement. AA ★★★ INN.
e-mail:paul@halfwayhouseinn.com   website:www.halfwayhouseinn.net

Grittleton, Purton, Westbury

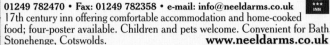

Grittleton

Village 6 miles north west of Chippenham.

THE NEELD ARMS INN, THE STREET, GRITTLETON SN14 6AP (01249 782470; Fax: 01249 782358). 17th century inn offering comfortable accommodation and home-cooked food; four-poster available. Children and pets welcome. Convenient for Bath, Stonehenge, Cotswolds. EnjoyEngland ★★★ Inn.
e-mail: info@neeldarms.co.uk   website: www.neeldarms.co.uk

Purton

Village 4 miles north west of Swindon. Situated between Cricklade and Wootton Bassett.

THE PEAR TREE AT PURTON, CHURCH END, SWINDON SN5 4ED (01793 772100; Fax: 01793 772369). Elegant stone Cotswold hotel set in 7 acres, just 5 miles from Swindon. 17 en suite bedrooms, many with spa baths, one with four-poster, furnished to a high standard. Well-behaved dogs welcome. [🐾]
website: www.peartreepurton.co.uk

Salisbury

13th century cathedral city, with England's highest spire at 404ft. Many fine buildings.

MR A. SHERING, SWAYNES FIRS FARM, GRIMSDYKE, COOMBE BISSETT, SALISBURY SP5 5RF (01725 519240). Small working farm with cattle, poultry, geese and duck ponds. Spacious rooms, all en suite with colour TV. Ideal for visiting the many historic sites in the area. ETC ★★★ [Pets £5 per night]
e-mail: swaynes.firs@virgin.net   website: www.swaynesfirs.co.uk

Westbury

Town at foot of Salisbury Plain, 4 miles south of Trowbridge.

SPINNEY FARMHOUSE, THOULSTONE, CHAPMANSLADE, WESTBURY BA13 4AQ (01373 832412). Enjoy farm fresh food in a warm, friendly, family atmosphere. Off A36, 16 miles from Bath. All rooms with washbasins, tea/coffee making. TV lounge. No smoking. Children and pets welcome. [🐾]
e-mail: isabelandbob@btinternet.com

The Christopher

110 High Street, Eton, Windsor SL4 6AN

A former Coaching Inn dating back to 1711, the hotel is situated in the heart of Eton, ideal for amenities and attractions. The rooms have a clean and simple design and are equipped with the latest technology and home comforts. Each room has internet access, laptop safe, and power shower and some have full air-conditioning. Many of our rooms are suitable for families and have either a sofa bed or space for extra beds. Christopher's Bar and Grill offers all day dining.

AA
★★★
HOTEL

Tel: 01753 852359 • Fax: 01753 830914
e-mail: reservations@thechristopher.co.uk • www.thechristopher.co.uk

Eton

Town located 20 miles west of London on the west bank of the River Thames. opposite Windsor Castle.

THE CHRISTOPHER, 110 HIGH STREET, ETON, WINDSOR SL4 6AN (01753 852359; Fax: 01753 830914). Modernised hotel, centrally situated for amenities and attractions. Rooms are equipped with internet access, laptop safe, power shower. Family rooms available. Bar and Grill offers all day dining. AA ★★★. [Pets £10 per night]
e-mail: reservations@thechristopher.co.uk   website: www.thechristopher.co.uk

Membury

Located close to Swindon, Newbury and Reading.

DAYS INN MEMBURY, WESTBOUND JUNCTION 14/15, M4 (01908 514047). Modern, comfortable accommodation in peaceful setting. All rooms en suite, FREE SKY TV, Broadband WIFI, trouser press, hot drinks tray and free parking. Ideally located for visiting Swindon, Chippenham, Bristol, Bath, The Cotswolds, Gloucester and Oxford. AA Approved & Pet Friendly. [🐾]
e-mail: membury.hotel@welcomebreak.co.uk   website: www.welcomebreak.co.uk

---

🐾 Pets are welcome free of charge.

£ A charge is made for pets: nightly or weekly.

pw! Special provision for pets; exercise facility, feeding or accommodation arrangement.

⌂ Separate pets accommodation.

Classified Symbols

Chesham

Town on south side of Chiltern Hills. Ideal walking area.

GEORGE ORME, 49 LOWNDES AVENUE, CHESHAM HP5 2HH (01494 792647). B&B in detached house, 10 minutes from the Underground. Private bathroom, tea/coffee, TV. Good walking country - Chiltern Hills three minutes. ETC ★★★ [🐾]

Milton Keynes

Purpose-built new city, home to the Open University. Midway between London, Birmingham, Leicester, Oxford and Cambridge.

DIFFERENT DRUMMER HOTEL, HIGH STREET, STONY STRATFORD, MILTON KEYNES MK11 1AH (01908 564733; Fax: 01908 260646) Ancient inn transformed into a superbly furnished hotel. En suite bedrooms, restaurant, wine bar. EnjoyEngland ★★★, AA ★★.
e-mail: info@hoteldifferentdrummer.co.uk   website: www.hoteldifferentdrummer.co.uk

SWAN REVIVED HOTEL, HIGH STREET, NEWPORT PAGNELL, MILTON KEYNES MK16 8AR (01908 610565; Fax: 01908 210995). Delightful 16thC former coaching inn, extensively modernised to provide 40 comfortable guest rooms, two bars, à la carte restaurant, meeting rooms and banqueting facilities. Pets very welcome. [🐾]
e-mail: info@swanrevived.co.uk   website: www.swanrevived.co.uk

Ashurst, Crawley, Fordingbridge

A useful index of towns/counties appears on pages 455-461

FHG Guides publish a large range of well-known accommodation guides. We will be happy to send you details or you can use the order form at the back of this book.

Lyndhurst, New Forest

SHAMBA HOLIDAYS, RINGWOOD ROAD, ST LEONARDS BH24 2SB (01202 873302). Ideally situated to explore Hampshire and Dorset. Shamba offers touring and camping facilities with heated pool and clubhouse. Close to New Forest and Bournemouth with its fine beaches. Seasonal pitches available. ETC ★★★★ [pw! Pets £2.50 per night, £17.50 per week].
website: www.shambaholidays.co.uk

Ashurst

Residential location 3 miles NE of Lyndhurst.

WOODLANDS LODGE HOTEL, BARTLEY ROAD, ASHURST, WOODLANDS SO40 7GN ((023) 80 292257; Fax: (023) 80 293090). Luxury Hotel offering peace and tranquillity. 16 bedrooms, all en suite with whirlpool bath, TV, hairdryer, telephone etc. Award winning Restaurant. Direct access to Forest. ETC ★★★ [Pets £5 per night].
e-mail: reception@woodlands-lodge.co.uk   website: www.woodlands-lodge.co.uk

Crawley

Small village 5 miles north-west of Winchester.

MRS ROSEMARY PICKUP, FOLLY FARM TOURING CARAVAN PARK. CRAWLEY, WINCHESTER SO21 2PH (01962 776486). Site on small working farm catering for all ages. Pitches for tents, caravans andmotorhomes. Showers, toilets and kitchen with microwave and washing machine. Shops and local facilities four miles. [🐾]

Fordingbridge

Town on River Avon 6 miles North of Ringwood.

THREE LIONS, STUCKTON, NEAR FORDINGBRIDGE SP6 2HF (01425 652489; Fax: 01425 656144) Relax in a beautiful setting and come and go as you please without the formality of a hotel. Hot tub and sauna. Three times Hampshire 'Restaurant of the Year', Good Food Guide. [pw! Pets £10 per week]
website: www.thethreelionsrestaurant.co.uk

Lymington

Residential town and yachting centre 15 miles east of Bournemouth.

HONEYSUCKLE HOUSE, 24 CLINTON ROAD, LYMINGTON SO41 9EA (01590 676635). Ground floor double room/single, en suite, non-smoking. Woodland walks, park, quay and marinas nearby. B&B from £30.00 pppn. [🐾]
e-mail: derekfarrell317@btinternet.com   website: http://explorethenewforest.co.uk/honeysuckle.htm

MRS P. J. ELLIS, EFFORD COTTAGE, EVERTON, LYMINGTON SO41 0JD (01590 642315). Outstanding B&B with old world charm in proprietor's own Georgian home. Excellent touring centre for New Forest and South Coast. All rooms en suite with luxury facilities. B&B from £25-£35pppn. No children. AA ★★★★, Michelin. [PW! Pets from £2 per night]
e-mail: effordcottage@aol.com   website: www.effordcottage.co.uk

Lyndhurst

Good base for enjoying the fascinating New Forest as well as the Hampshire coastal resorts. Bournemouth 20 miles, Southampton 9.

THE CROWN HOTEL, LYNDHURST, NEW FOREST S043 7NF (023 8028 2922; Fax: 023 8028 2751). A mellow, Listed building in the centre of the village, an ideal base for exploring the delights of the New Forest with your canine friend(s). Free parking, quiet garden, three star luxury and animal loving staff. AA ★★★ [Pets £7 per night].
e-mail: reception@crownhotel-lyndhurst.co.uk   website: www.crownhotel-lyndhurst.co.uk

ORMONDE HOUSE HOTEL, SOUTHAMPTON ROAD, LYNDHURST SO43 7BT (023 8028 2806, Fax: 023 8028 2004). Opposite open forest, easy drive to Exbury Gardens and Beaulieu. Elegant, family-run Two Star Hotel with pretty, en suite rooms with CTV, phone and beverage making. Superior rooms and ground floor suites, all with kingsize bed and some with whirlpool bath. Bar, lounge and delicious dinners available. AA ★★. [Pets £3.50 per night, max. 2 per room]
e-mail: enquiries@ormondehouse.co.uk   website: www.ormondehouse.co.uk

New Forest

Area of heath and woodland of nearly 150 square miles, formerly Royal hunting grounds.

MRS E.E. MATTHEWS, THE ACORNS, OGDENS, NEAR FORDINGBRIDGE SP6 2PY (01425 655552).
Luxury two bedroom residential-type caravan. Sleeps 4/6. Maintained to high standard, kitchen,
shower room, sitting/diningroom, outside laundry area, own garden. Lovely New Forest setting.
Non-smoking, ample parking. Children over five years. Well-behaved dogs welcome (max. 2).
Terms £205 - £385, Easter to mid-October. [pw! Pets £12 each per week].
e-mail: e_matthews@mypostoffice.co.uk   website: www.dogscome2.co.uk

MRS J. PEARCE, ST. URSULA, 30 HOBART ROAD, NEW MILTON BH25 6EG (01425 613515).
Excellent facilities and warm welcome for well behaved pets and owners! Ground floor suite
suitable for disabled guests, plus single and twin rooms. Bed & Breakfast from £27.50. [🐾]

LITTLE THATCH, 15 SOUTH STREET, PENNINGTON (01582 842831) Beautiful Grade II Listed thatched
cob cottage, sleeps 4 in 2 bedrooms. Superbly renovated to offer traditional cottage features,
tastefully combined with luxury modern comforts. Secluded secure garden.[🐾]
e-mail: suzannah@littlethatchcottage.com   website: www.littlethatchcottage.com

NEW FOREST - HIGHFIELDS COTTAGE. Charming, secluded cottage. Quiet country hamlet. Great
walks. Pets welcome. Sleeps 2+2. Tel: 01425 471372 . [Pets £25 per week]
e-mail: 07enquiries@highfields-cottage.co.uk   website: www.highfields-cottage.co.uk

GORSE COTTAGE, BALMER LAWN ROAD, BROCKENHURST. Cottage/bungalow on open forest road
close to village in New Forest. Sleeps 4 in 2 bedrooms. Conservatory, luxury bathroom, log fire,
TV/Freeview/DVD, secluded sunny garden. Pets welcome. Contact: MRS E. GILBERT (01727 850659).
ETC ★★★★ [Pets £15 per week]
e-mail: info@gorsecottage.co.uk   website: www.gorsecottage.co.uk

THE WATERSPLASH HOTEL, THE RISE, BROCKENHURST SO42 7ZP (01590 622344). Prestigious
New Forest family-run country house hotel set in large garden. Noted for fine personal service,
accommodation and traditional English cuisine at its best. All rooms en suite. Luxury four-poster
with double spa bath. Swimming pool. Short walk to open forest. AA ★★ Colour brochure available.
[Pets from £5 per night.]
e-mail: bookings@watersplash.co.uk   website: www.watersplash.co.uk

Ringwood

Busy market town, centre for trout fishing, trekking and rambling. Bournemouth 13 miles.

LITTLE FOREST LODGE, POULNER HILL, RINGWOOD BH24 3HS (01425 478848; Fax: 01425
473564). A warm welcome to you and your pets at this charming Edwardian house set in two acres
of woodland. Six en suite bedrooms. All well behaved dogs welcome. AA ★★★★ Guest House.
[Pets £5 per night].

DAVID SATCHELL, THE HIGH CORNER INN, LINWOOD, RINGWOOD, HANTS BH24 3QY (01425
473973, Fax: 01425 483052). Seven en suite bedrooms deep in the heart of The New Forest. Real
ales, home-cooked food, Sunday carvery and log fires. Pets welcome. [🐾]
website: www.highcornerinn.com

Southsea

Residential and holiday district of Portsmouth 2km South of the city centre.

Quality Hotel accommodation with a superb sea front location. Good walking! All rooms en suite,
etc. Passenger lift, licensed bar/restaurant, car park. Small charge for pets. Contact: MARK & JENNY
BRUNNING, THE SEACREST HOTEL, 12 SOUTH PARADE, SOUTHSEA, PORTSMOUTH PO5 2JB
(02392 733192; Fax: 02392 832523). AA ★★ 75%.
e-mail: office@seacresthotel.co.uk   website: www.seacresthotel.co.uk

---

Please mention PETS WELCOME!

when making enquiries about accommodation featured in this guide

www.holidayguides.com

Carisbrooke, Cowes, Freshwater, Totland Bay, Ventnor

Ventnor, Yarmouth

ISLAND VIEW HOLIDAYS, Great value holidays, the best facilities, and beautiful Isle of Wight locations. Island View Holidays offer something for dogs and dog-lovers alike. Booking: (01983 721606). [Pets £30 per week]
e-mail: info@islandviewholidays.co.uk   website: www.islandviewholidays.co.uk

ISLAND COTTAGE HOLIDAYS (01929 481555). Large range of pet and dog friendly cottages in beautiful rural and coastal locations.
website: www.islandcottageholidays.com

Bonchurch

One mile north-east of Ventnor.

THE LAKE, SHORE ROAD, LOWER BONCHURCH PO38 1RF (01983 852613). Lovely country house in a beautiful quiet two-acre garden. First class food and service, all in a relaxed and friendly atmosphere. All rooms en suite. Car ferry inclusive prices available. ETC ★★★★ [Pets £5 per night]
e-mail: fhg@lakehotel.co.uk   website: www.lakehotel.co.uk

MRS J. LINES, ASHCLIFF HOLIDAY APARTMENT, BONCHURCH PO38 1NT (01983 853919). Self-contained ground floor apartment (sleeps 2) adjoining Victorian house. Large south-facing gardens. Sea views from garden. Large private car park. Pets welcome to use garden. ETC ★★★ [🐾]
e-mail: linessidney@aol.com

MRS A. EVANS, "THE WATERFALL", SHORE ROAD, BONCHURCH, VENTNOR PO38 1RN (01983 852246). Spacious, self-contained Flat. Sleeps 3 adults. Colour TV. Sun verandah and garden. The beach, the sea and the downs. [🐾]
e-mail: benbrook.charioteer@virgin.net

Carisbrooke

Historic town with Carisbrooke Castle where Charles I was imprisoned prior to his trial.

CARISBROOKE. Two bedroom bungalow. Lovely enclosed garden. Pets welcome. Fully equipped. Sleeps 2/6. Private parking. Excellent touring position. Also two bedroom bungalow near Cowes. [Pets £10 per week]. Contact: (01983 524359/522173).

Cowes

Yachting centre with yearly regatta since 1814. Newport 4 miles.

SUNNYCOTT CARAVAN PARK, COWES PO31 8NN (01983 292859). Small, quiet, family-run park close to Cowes. All caravans have full cooker, microwave, fridge and colour TV. Shop and laundry room on site. We welcome pets. Short breaks arranged. ETC ★★★★ [Pets £20 per week]
e-mail: info@sunnycottcaravanpark.co.uk   website: www.sunnycottcaravanpark.co.uk).

Freshwater

Two kilometres south of Totland. South-west of Farringford, formerly the home of Tennyson.

MR AND MRS B. MOSCOFF, SEAHORSES, VICTORIA ROAD, FRESHWATER PO40 9PP (Tel & Fax: 01983 752574). Peaceful 19th century rectory set in two-and-a-half acres of lovely gardens. Good area for walking, golfing, sailing, paragliding and bird watching. Double, family and twin rooms, all en suite. TV lounge, log fires. B&B pppn: £33-£40 depending on season. Children half price. [🐾 pw!]
e-mail: seahorses-iow@tiscali.co.uk   website: www.seahorsesisleofwight.com

Totland Bay

Small resort 3 miles south-west of Yarmouth Bay.

SENTRY MEAD HOTEL, MADEIRA ROAD, TOTLAND BAY PO39 0BJ (01983 753212; Fax: 01983 754710). This beautiful Victorian villa is set in its own spacious gardens in the tranquil surroundings of West Wight. Just 150 yards from the beach, and with scenic downland walks on the doorstep, this is the perfect place to relax and unwind. All bedrooms en suite. ETC ★★★ Silver Award [Pets £3 per day, £15 per week]
e-mail: info@sentrymead.co.uk   website: www.sentrymead.co.uk

THE HERMITAGE BED & BREAKFAST, CLIFF ROAD, TOTLAND BAY PO39 0EW (01983 752518). Friendly, homely en suite accommodation in quiet setting. All rooms have TV and tea/coffee facilities. An ideal base from which to tour the island. Evening meals on request. Pets welcome.
e-mail: blake_david@btconnect.com   website: www.thehermitagebnb.co.uk

Ventnor

Well-known resort with good sands, downs, popular as a winter holiday resort. Nearby is St Boniface Down, the highest point on the island. Ryde 13 miles, Newport 12, Sandown 7, Shanklin 4.

VENTNOR HOLIDAY VILLAS, WHEELERS BAY ROAD, VENTNOR PO38 1HR (01983 852973). Apartments and Villas on south facing hillside leading down to a small rocky bay. Apartments open all year, villas April to October. Write or phone for a brochure. Pets welcome in villas. ETC ★★★ [Pets £20 per week]
e-mail: sales@ventnorholidayvillas.co.uk   website: www.ventnorholidayvillas.co.uk

MRS F. CORRY, LITTLE SPAN FARM, REW LANE, WROXALL, VENTNOR PO38 3AU (Tel & Fax: 01983 852419, Freephone 0800 2985819). Working farm in an Area of Outstanding Natural Beauty, close to footpaths and holiday attractions. Ideal for family holidays. B&B in farmhouse from £30 pppn or Self-Catering Cottages from £225-£725 per week. Dogs welcome. [pw! Pets £4 per night, £25 per week].
e-mail: info@spanfarm.co.uk   website: www.spanfarm.co.uk

Yarmouth

Coastal resort situated 9 miles west of Newport. Castle built by Henry VIII for coastal defence.

THE ORCHARDS HOLIDAY CARAVAN & CAMPING PARK, NEWBRIDGE, YARMOUTH PO41 0TS (Dial-a-brochure 01983 531331). Luxury holiday caravans, most with central heating and double glazing. Well maintained touring pitches. Excellent facilities including indoor pool with licensed coffeeshop. Dog exercise area. Ideal walking and cycling. Open late February to New Year. Located in an Area of Outstanding Natural Beauty. Spectacular views. [First dog free, 2nd dog £2 per night]
e-mail: info@orchards-holiday-park.co.uk   website:www.orchards-holiday-park.co.uk

Ashford, Boughton Monchelsea, Broadstairs, Canterbury

Deal, Margate, St Margaret's Bay, Sevenoaks, Thurnham

Hidden Gem
By the Sea, 59 Gladstone Road, Deal, Kent CT14 7ET
Sleeps 2 (Double Bed) • No Smoking
Pets Welcome FREE

A serene, luxuriously furnished and equipped, modern, stairless, one-bedroom bungalow. Situated in a delightful side street next to Deal Castle and the beach. Private off-street parking and secure private garden.
Ideally located for golf, fishing, cyclists and walkers. Dog lovers can walk either on the beach, the promenades, the cliffs or countryside.
Numerous local entertainments and places to visit ...... something for everyone.
Tel: Lucy 07590 756833 • e-mail via the website: www.selfcatering-deal.co.uk

Smiths Court Hotel
AA
21-27 Eastern Esplanade, Cliftonville, Margate CT9 2HL

Margate's highest starred hotel with 43 standard and executive rooms, many with sea view, all en suite with direct-dial telephone, tea and coffee making facilities and hospitality tray. 15 studio, one and two-bedroom suites with pantry kitchens and dining area, ideal for families, long-stay guests and self-catering breaks.
The beautiful Orangery Restaurant, with marble floors, soaring windows and sea view balcony, offers great seasonal, locally produced food. Disabled facilities, private car parking and free wifi available. Pets welcome. Perfect for short breaks.

Tel: 01843 222310 or e-mail info@smithscourt.co.uk
quoting reference PET11 • www.smithscourt.co.uk

Reach Court Farm Cottages
St Margaret's Bay

Situated in the heart of a family-run, working farm, surrounded by open countryside, these five luxury self-contained cottages are very special. They are set around the old farm yard in an attractive setting of lawns and shrubs with open views from the front or rear. The cottages sleep from two to six plus cot, and the accommodation is of the highest standard, giving them a relaxing country feel, with the kitchens equipped with ovens, fridges, microwaves, toasters, coffee makers, etc. There is also a washing machine and tumble dryer in an adjoining laundry room.
Reach Court Farm is the nearest farm to France and was known as the "Front Line Farm" during World War II. St Margaret's is a rural village with shops and public houses offering a range of eating facilities. Dover, Folkestone, Canterbury and Sandwich are all within easy reach.
Mrs J. Mitchell, Reach Court Farm, St Margaret's-at-Cliff, St Margaret's Bay, Dover CT15 6AQ
Tel & Fax: 01304 852159
e-mail: enquiries@reachcourtfarmcottages.co.uk • www.reachcourtfarmcottages.co.uk

GOLDING HOP FARM COTTAGE
Plaxtol, Near Sevenoaks TN15 0PS • Tel: 07771 520229
★★★ Cottage on 13-acre cobnut farm in Bourne Valley. Sleeps 5 plus cot. Children and pets welcome. Open all year. £240-£450 pw.
info@goldinghopfarm.com • www.goldinghopfarm.com

BLACK HORSE INN Pilgrims Way, Thurnham, Maidstone ME14 3LD
Tel: 01622 737185 • info@wellieboot.net • www.wellieboot.net
A homely and welcoming inn with its origins in the 18thC, The Black Horse is adorned with hops and beams, and has an open log fireplace to welcome you in winter. A separate annexe has 30 beautiful en suite bedrooms.

Wrotham Heath

GARDEN OF ENGLAND COTTAGES IN KENT & SUSSEX, CLAYFIELD HOUSE, 50 ST JOHNS ROAD, TUNBRIDGE WELLS, KENT TN4 9NY (01892 510117). Pets welcome in many of our holiday homes and go free. All properties VisitBritain quality assured. On-line booking and availability. [🐾]
e-mail: holidays@gardenofenglandcottages.co.uk   website: www.goec.co.uk

Ashford

Market town on Great Stour River, 13 miles south-west of Canterbury.

Luxury pine lodges, superior self-catering accommodation overlooking two lakes in beautiful Kent countryside. Rough shooting and coarse fishing on our farms. Weeks or short breaks. Contact: ASHBY FARMS LTD, PLACE FARM, KENARDINGTON, ASHFORD TN26 2LZ (01233 733332; Fax: 01233 733326). [Pets £10 per stay]
e-mail: info@ashbyfarms.com   website: www.ashbyfarms.com

Boughton Monchelsea

Village 3 miles south of Maidstone.

COCK INN, BOUGHTON MONCHELSEA, MAIDSTONE ME17 4JD (01622 743166) Glorious 16thC timbered black and white inn with inglenook fireplace and oak-beamed bar and restaurant. Patio and outside eating area. Real ales. Sensational food. [pw! 🐾]
e-mail: cockinnboughtonmonchelsea@hotmail.com   website: www.cockinnmaidstone.co.uk

Broadstairs

Quiet resort, once a favourite of Charles Dickens. Good sands and promenade.

THE HANSON, 41 BELVEDERE ROAD, BROADSTAIRS CT10 1PF (01843 868936). Small, friendly licensed Georgian Hotel. Home comforts; children and pets welcome. Attractive bar. SAE. [pw! Pets £1 per night, £5 per week]
website: www.hansonhotel.co.uk

Canterbury

Cathedral City on River Great Stour, 54 miles east of London.

DOREEN ADY, HAWTHORN FARM COTTAGES, WARE, NEAR SANDWICH (01304 813560). Four converted two-bedroom cottages, sleeping 4-5. Ideally situated for relaxing or exploring the Kent coastline. Children's play field. Ample parking. Pets welcome by arrangement. ETC ★★★/★★★★. [pw! Pets £20 per week]
e-mail: hawthornfarmcottages@dsl.pipex.com   website: www.hawthornfarmcottages.co.uk

Deal

Cinque Port and resort on East coast 8 miles N.E. of Dover.

HIDDEN GEM, 59 GLADSTONE ROAD, DEAL CT14 7ET. Luxuriously furnished one bedroom bungalow, with gas central heating, secure private garden and off-street parking. Near Deal Castle, the beach, the town, and endless beach and country walks. No smoking. For details please tel Lucy on: 07590 756833 or e-mail via the website. ETC ★★★★ [🐾]
website: www.selfcatering-deal.co.uk

Margate

Traditional seaside resort, with a vibrant cultural quarter and several historic buildings.

SMITHS COURT HOTEL, 21-27 EASTERN ESPLANADE, CLIFTONVILLE, MARGATE CT9 2HL (01843 222310). Elegant, Victorian family-run premier hotel. 43 individually decorated rooms and suites, many with superb sea views. Perfect for short breaks. Pets welcome. EnjoyEngland/AA ★★★. [Pets £10 per stay].
e-mail: info@smithscourt.co.uk   website: www.smithscourt.co.uk

St Margaret's Bay

4 miles north-east of Dover

DEREK AND JACQUI MITCHELL, REACH COURT FARM COTTAGES, REACH COURT FARM, ST MARGARET'S BAY, DOVER CT15 6AQ (Tel & Fax: 01304 852159). Situated in the heart of the Mitchell family farm, surrounded by open countryside, these five luxury self-contained cottages are very special. The cottages are set around the old farmyard, which has been attractively set to lawns and shrubs, with open views of the rural valley both front and back. [🐎]
e-mail: enquiries@reachcourtfarmcottages.co.uk   website: www.reachcourtfarmcottages.co.uk

Sevenoaks

Town on edge of North Downs 21 miles south east of London.

GOLDING HOP FARM COTTAGE, PLAXTOL, NEAR SEVENOAKS TN15 0PS (07771 520229). Three Star cottage on 13-acre cobnut farm in Bourne Valley. Sleeps 5 plus cot. Children and pets welcome. Open all year. £240-£450 pw. [Pets £12 per week each].
e-mail: info@goldinghopfarm.com   website: www.goldinghopfarm.com

Thurnham

Located in a beautiful and secluded area of Kent and just 3 miles north east of the County Town of Maidstone.

BLACK HORSE INN, PILGRIMS WAY, THURNHAM, MAIDSTONE ME14 3LD (01622 737185). Homely and welcoming inn with its origins in the 18thC, The Black Horse is adorned with hops and beams, and has an open log fireplace. A separate annexe has 30 beautiful en suite bedrooms. [Pets £6 per night].
e-mail: info@wellieboot.net   website: www.wellieboot.net

Wrotham Heath

Village situated at foot of North Downs.

PRETTY MAID HOUSE B&B, LONDON ROAD, (A20) WROTHAM HEATH, SEVENOAKS TN15 7RU (01732 886445; F: 01732 886439). Guest house offering bed and breakfast accommodation located in the heart of Kent between Sevenoaks, Maidstone & Brands Hatch Racing Circuit. AA ★★★★ Highly Commended. [🐎]
e-mail: stay@prettymaid.co.uk   website: www.prettymaidhouse.com

---

🐎   Pets are welcome free of charge.   **Classified Symbols**

£   A charge is made for pets: nightly or weekly.

pw!   Special provision for pets; exercise facility, feeding or accommodation arrangement.

⌂   Separate pets accommodation.

Abingdon, Bicester, Burford, Oxford, Standlake, Tackley/Kidlington

Little Acre, Tetsworth, Thame OX9 7AT

Traditional cottage-style accommodation, set in 20 acres. Well appointed en suite bedrooms, including one with direct access to garden. Pets welcome by arrangement. Ideal for exploring Chilterns.

01844 281423 • 07798 625252 • julia@little-acre.co.uk
www.little-acre.co.uk

Abingdon

Market town and civil parish 5 miles south of Oxford in the Thames Valley.

KINGFISHER BARN HOLIDAY COTTAGES, ABINGDON OX14 3NN (Tel & Fax: 01235 537538). Self-catering cottages, from one-bedroom loft apartments to four-bedroom lodges. Sleep 4/10. All fully equipped, with TV with Freeview. Wi-Fi. Indoor swimming pool. Pets welcome. ETC ★★★★
e-mail: info@kingfisherbarn.com   website: www.kingfisherbarn.com

Bicester

Town 11 miles NE of Oxford.

TODDY AND CLIVE HAMILTON-GOULD, TOWER FIELDS, TUSMORE ROAD, NEAR SOULDERN, BICESTER OX27 7HY (01869 346554). Ground floor en suite rooms, all with own entrance and ample parking. Breakfast using local produce. Easy reach of Oxford, Stratford-upon-Avon, many National Trust houses. Silverstone, Towcester. Dogs and horses welcome by arrangement. [🐾]
e-mail: toddyclive@towerfields.com   website: www.towerfields.com

Burford

Small Cotswold Town on River Windrush, 7 miles west of Witney.

THE INN FOR ALL SEASONS, THE BARRINGTONS, NEAR BURFORD OX18 4TN (01451 844324). Family-run and owned, an unspoilt former 16th century English Coaching Inn. Genuinely dog-friendly; ground floor room available with direct access to exercise area. AA ★★ and Rosette. [Pets £5.00 each per night]
email: info@innforallseasons.com   website: www.innforallseasons.com

Oxford

City 52 miles from London. University dating from 13th century. Many notable buildings.

MR B. CRONIN, NANFORD GUEST HOUSE, 137 IFFLEY ROAD, OXFORD OX4 1EJ (01865 244743; Fax: 01865 249596). Period guest house located five minutes on foot from the University of Oxford. Wide range and number of rooms, all with private shower and toilet. [🐾]
e-mail: b.cronin@btinternet.com   website: www.nanfordguesthouse.com

Standlake

Village approximately 5 miles south east of Witney and 7 miles west of Oxford.

LINCOLN FARM PARK, HIGH STREET, STANDLAKE OX29 7RH (01865 300 239). Small, quiet Family Park. Super and Hard standing pitches.Tenters' Kitchen. Games Room. Play-area. Indoor heated swimming pools, spas, saunas, children's pool & steam room, solarium, fitness suite. AA Best Campsite of the Year 2010. Best Regional Park 2007 Finalist 2008/2009. Practical Caravan. [Pets £1.25 per night]
website: www.lincolnfarmpark.co.uk

Tackley/Kidlington

Village 3 miles north-east of Woodstock; approximately 5 miles north of Oxford.

JUNE AND GEORGE COLLIER, 55 NETHERCOTE ROAD, TACKLEY, KIDLINGTON, OXFORD OX5 3AT (01869 331255; mobile: 07790 338225). Bed and Breakfast in Tackley. An ideal base for touring, walking, cycling and riding. Central for Oxford, The Cotswolds, Stratford-on-Avon, Blenheim Palace. Woodstock four miles. There is a regular train and bus service with local Hostelries serving excellent food. [⚲ 🏠]
e-mail: junecollier@btinternet.com   website: www.colliersbnb.co.uk

Thame

Town on River Thame 9 miles SW of Aylesbury.

MS. JULIA TANNER, LITTLE ACRE, TETSWORTH, NEAR THAME OX9 7AT (01844 281423; mobile: 07798 625252). Traditional cottage-style accommodation, set in 20 acres. Well appointed en suite bedrooms, including one with direct access to garden. Pets welcome by arrangement. Ideal for exploring Chilterns. [Pets £3 per night. Bring dog basket with you.]
e-mail: julia@little-acre.co.uk   website: www.little-acre.co.uk

Farnham

Bustling town at the western end of Surrey, bordering on Hampshire. Remains of Roman, Saxon and Stone Age dwellings have been found within the town boundaries.

TILFORD WOODS LODGES, TILFORD ROAD, FARNHAM GU10 2DD (01252 792199). A serene and relaxing retreat in the heart of beautiful rural Surrey. Well-appointed luxurious lodges for hire. Seven golf clubs nearby. Short stroll to local pub. Launderette. Saunas and outdoor hot tubs available. Enjoy England ★★★★. [Pets £2.50 per night]
e-mail: enquiries@tilfordwoods.co.uk   website: www.tilfordwoods.co.uk

Kingston Upon Thames

Market town, Royal borough and administrative centre of Surrey. Kingston is ideally placed for London and environs.

CHASE LODGE HOTEL, 10 PARK ROAD, HAMPTON WICK, KINGSTON UPON THAMES KT1 4AS (020 8943 1862; Fax: 020 8943 9363). Award-winning hotel offering quality en suite bedrooms. Easy access to town centre and major transport links. ★★★ [🐾]
e-mail: info@chaselodgehotel.com   website: www.chaselodgehotel.com

🐾 Pets are welcome free of charge.

£ A charge is made for pets: nightly or weekly.

pw! Special provision for pets; exercise facility, feeding or accommodation arrangement.

⌂ Separate pets accommodation.

Classified Symbols

Alfriston

Attractive village in heart of the South Downs, with old market square and village green.

THE GEORGE INN, HIGH STREET, ALFRISTON BN26 5SY (01323 870319; Fax: 01323 871384). Six relaxing and charming bedrooms. Delicious food, refreshing ales, oak beams, open log fires. Friendly atmosphere, quality service and a beautiful location.
e-mail: info@thegeorge-alfriston.com　　　　website: www.thegeorge-alfriston.com

THE STAR, HIGH STREET, ALFRISTON BN26 5TA (01323 870495). Historic country hotel with 37 spacious en suite bedrooms, all traditionally furnished. Wi-Fi. The award-winning Restaurant uses fresh, locally sourced ingredients; meals also served in bar and lounge. Pets welcome in all public areas except restaurant. Special Pet Package available. AA ★★★ and Rosette.
e-mail: bookings@thestaralfriston.co.uk　　　　website: www.thestaralfriston.co.uk

Chiddingly

Charming village, 4 miles north-west of Hailsham. Off the A22 London-Eastbourne road.

Adorable, small, well-equipped cottage in grounds of Tudor Manor. Two bedrooms, sleeps 4-6. Full central heating. Colour TV. Fridge/freezer, laundry facilities. Large safe garden. Use indoor heated swimming pool, sauna/jacuzzi and tennis. From £420 to £798 per week inclusive. ETC ★★★. Contact: EVA MORRIS, "PEKES", 124 ELM PARK MANSIONS, PARK WALK, LONDON SW10 0AR (020 7352 8088; Fax: 020 7352 8125). [pw! 2 dogs free, extra two £7 each].
e-mail: pekes.afa@virgin.net　　　　website: www.pekesmanor.com

Terms quoted in this publication may be subject to increase if rises in costs necessitate

Fairlight

Village 3 miles east of Hastings

JANET & RAY ADAMS, FAIRLIGHT COTTAGE, WARREN ROAD, FAIRLIGHT TN35 4AG (01424 812545). Country house in idyllic location with clifftop walks. Tasteful en suite rooms, comfortable guest lounge. Delicious breakfasts. No smoking. Dogs stay with owners. VB ★★★★ [🐾]
e-mail: fairlightcottage@supanet.com   website: www.fairlightcottage.co.uk

Polegate

Quiet position, 5 miles from the popular seaside resort of Eastbourne. London 58 miles, Lewes 12.

MRS P. FIELD, 20 ST JOHN'S ROAD, POLEGATE BN26 5BP (01323 482691). Homely private house. Quiet location; large enclosed garden. Parking space. Ideally situated for walking on South Downs and Forestry Commission land. All rooms, washbasins and tea/coffee making facilities. Bed and Breakfast. Pets very welcome. [pw! 🐾]

Rye

Picturesque hill town with steep cobbled streets. Many fine buildings of historic interest. Hastings 12 miles, Tunbridge Wells 28.

MRS JANE APPERLY, BRANDY'S COTTAGE, CADBOROUGH FARM, RYE TN31 6AA (01797 225426). Recently converted cottage provides luxurious and spacious accommodation for two people. Private courtyard. One small well-behaved dog and children over 12 welcome. No-smoking. Short breaks available. ETC ★★★★ [🐾]
e-mail: apperly@cadborough.co.uk   website: www.cadborough.co.uk

RYE LODGE HOTEL, HILDER'S CLIFF, RYE TN31 7LD (01797 223838; Fax: 01797 223585). Luxury, elegance and charm in a relaxed atmosphere. Luxurious rooms, full room service and an elegant Champagne Bar. Indoor swimming pool, spa and sauna. Ideal for exploring historic Rye. AA/VB ★★★ Gold Award. [Pets £8 per night, £50 per week]
website: www.ryelodge.co.uk

Seaford

On the coast midway between Newhaven and Beachy Head.

BEACH COTTAGE, CLAREMONT ROAD, SEAFORD BN25 2QQ. Well-equipped, three-bedroomed terraced cottage on seafront. CH, open fire and woodburner. South-facing patio overlooking sea. Downland walks (wonderful for dogs), fishing, golf, wind-surfing, etc. Details from JULIA LEWIS, 47 WANDLE BANK, LONDON SW19 1DW (020 8542 5073). [pw! 🐾]
e-mail: cottage@beachcottages.info   website: www.beachcottages.info

Arundel, Chichester, Eastergate, Henfield, Horsham

Pulborough, Selsey, Worthing

Arundel

Arundel lies between Chichester and Brighton, 5 miles from Littlehampton on the south coast. Magnificent Arundel Castle with its impressive grounds overlooks the River Arun, and the town is also home to the Wildfowl and Wetlands Trust where thousands of rare and migratory birds can be seen.

MRS VICKI RICHARDS, WOODACRE, ARUNDEL ROAD, FONTWELL, ARUNDEL BN18 0QP (01243 814301). Bed & Breakfast in traditional family home. Ideal for Chichester, Goodwood and seaside. Clean, spacious rooms, two on ground floor. ETC ★★★★
e-mail: wacrebb@aol.com website: www.woodacre.co.uk

Chichester

County town 9 miles east of Havant. Town has cathedral and 16th century market cross.

SPIRE COTTAGE, CHURCH LANE, HUNSTON, CHICHESTER PO20 1AJ (01243 778937). Stylish bed and breakfast accommodation in a friendly and relaxed atmosphere. Excellent facilities. Village pub and two golf courses. [Dogs £5 per night]
e-mail: jan@spirecottage.co.uk website: www.spirecottage.co.uk

Eastergate

Village between the sea and South Downs. Fontwell Park nearby. Bognor Regis 5 miles south.

WANDLEYS CARAVAN PARK, EASTERGATE PO20 3SE (01243 543235 or 01243 543384). You will find peace, tranquillity and relaxation in one of our comfortable holiday caravans. All have internal WC and shower. Dogs welcome. Many historic and interesting places nearby. Telephone for brochure. [🐕]
e-mail: amandagent@btinternet.com　　　　　　website: www.wandleyscaravanpark.com

Henfield

Large village in the Horsham District of West Sussex, 33 miles south of London, 12 miles north west of Brighton and 30 miles north east of Chichester.

GARDEN COTTAGE AND DAIRYMAID'S COTTAGE, NEW HALL, HENFIELD BN5 9YJ (01403 733982) Comfortable and well equipped cottages in owner's grounds offer a tranquil and pleasant retreat. Garden Cottage sleeps 2/4, Dairymaid's Cottage sleeps 5. Children and pets welcome. Open all year. ETC ★★★ [Pets £15 per week]
e-mail: norman.carreck@btinternet.com

Horsham

Town 8 miles south west of Crawley.

SUMNERS PONDS CAMPSITE & FISHERY, BARNS GREEN, HORSHAM RH13 0PR (01403 732539). Set in tranquil countryside amongst 1000 acres of woodland and lakes. Cottages, Log Cabins, Pods, Pitches, Fishing Lakes. Working farm. Ideal location for touring South Downs.
e-mail: sumnersponds@dsl.pipex.com　　　　　website: www.sumnersponds.co.uk

Pulborough

Town on River Arun 12 miles NW of Worthing.

BEACON LODGE, LONDON ROAD, WATERSFIELD, PULBOROUGH RH20 1NH (01798 831026; 07941 884891). Charming self-contained annexe in centre of South Downs National Park. B&B accommodation, en suite, TV, coffee/tea making facilities. Wonderful countryside views. B&B from £65 per night, family room. Excellent for country walks. No charge for your pets! [🐕]
e-mail: gbwingfield@yahoo.co.uk　　　　　　website: www.beaconlodge.co.uk

Selsey

Seaside resort 8 miles south of Chichester. Selsey Bill is headland extending into the English Channel.

ST ANDREWS LODGE, CHICHESTER ROAD, SELSEY PO20 0LX (01243 606899; Fax: 01243 607826). 10 bedrooms, all en suite, with direct dial telephones and modem point, some on ground floor. Dining room overlooking garden; licensed bar for residents only. Wheelchair accessible room. Dogs welcome in rooms overlooking large garden. Apply for brochure and prices. ETC★★★★ [Pets £3 per stay (donation to local project)]
e-mail: info@standrewslodge.co.uk　　　　　website: www.standrewslodge.co.uk

Worthing

Residential town and seaside resort with 5-mile seafront. Situated 10 miles west of Brighton..

CAVENDISH HOTEL, 115/116 MARINE PARADE, WORTHING BN11 3QG (01903 236767). Recently refurbished sea front hotel with views over English Channel. All rooms en suite, with TV, tea/coffee making and telephone. A la carte and snack menus available. Ideal base for touring.
e-mail: reservations@cavendishworthing.co.uk　　website: www.cavendishworthing.co.uk

Burwell, Ely

Burwell

One of the largest villages in Cambridgeshire, with over 60 listed buildings of interest, and the 15th century Church of St Mary's. Ideal area for walkers, fishing enthusiasts and nature lovers.

THE MEADOW HOUSE, 2A HIGH STREET, BURWELL, CAMBRIDGE CB25 0HB (01638 741926; Fax: 01638 741861). Modern house in two acres of wooded grounds offering superior Bed and Breakfast. Variety of en suite accommodation. All rooms have TV, central heating and tea/coffee facilities. No smoking. Family rate on request. ETC ★★★★ [🐾]
e-mail: hilary@themeadowhouse.co.uk   website: www.themeadowhouse.co.uk
                                                              www.hilaryscottage.co.uk

Ely

Magnificent Norman Cathedral dating from 1083. Ideal base for touring the fen country of East Anglia.

THE OLD SCHOOL B&B, THE OLD SCHOOL, SCHOOL LANE, COVENEY, ELY CB6 2DB (01353 777087; Mob: 07802 174541; Fax : 01353 777091). Former village school set in an acre of gardens and horse paddocks, with splendid views across the Fens. Three ground floor bedrooms. Dogs very welcome. Twin kennels available if required. EnjoyEngland ★★★★. [pw! £3 per dog per night]
e-mail: info@TheOldSchoolBandB.co.uk   website: TheOldSchoolBandB.co.uk

MRS C. H. BENNETT, STOCKYARD FARM, WISBECH ROAD, WELNEY PE14 9RQ (01354 610433; Fax: 01354 610422). Comfortable converted farmhouse, rurally situated between Ely and Wisbech. Conservatory breakfast room, guests' lounge. Free-range produce. Miles of riverside walks. Vegetarians welcome. B&B from £25. [🐾 pw!]

Clacton-on-Sea , Colchester, Mersea Island

Clacton-on-Sea

Sandy beaches, safe sea bathing, water sports and Victorian pier. 4 miles east of Colchester.

Colchester

Britain's oldest recorded town. Many great visitor attractions, including the children's favourite, Colchester Zoo.

Mersea Island

Winding lanes cross open countryside, joined to mainland by Strood Causeway.

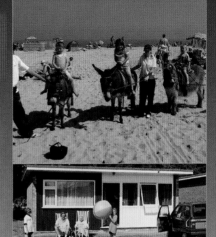

Norfolk Coastal Properties

Welcome to our 'Holiday Cottages' in North Norfolk

The Old Boathouse, Sheringham

If you are looking to escape, whether it be for a long weekend or a couple of weeks, and want to be guaranteed that you are renting a property that is clean, comfortable and something a little bit different, then Olly and I have just the places. Pets most welcome!

We take care of everything, from the initial enquiry to the cleaning, so you are guaranteed a personal service.

All properties are owned by us, looked after by us and include all the bed linen – so all you have to worry about is packing the car and getting there.

Take a look at **The Old Boathouse** in Sheringham, originally used to build crab boats for the local fishermen. Lots of character and spectacular sea views. Private parking – sleeps 6.

The Fisherman's Shed is a beautiful 'bolt hole', tastefully converted to sleep 4, and has wonderful sea views.

The Old Stables in Weybourne consists of 5 pretty cottages in a courtyard, sleeping from 1-5 people and all with private parking. Each cottage has fenced garden/patio areas. Located just 5 minutes from the sea.

"So come and dip into an area of outstanding beauty and I'll be happy to share some of my walks along the fabulous coastline with you and your owners!" OLLY

The Fisherman's Shed, Sheringham

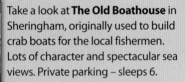

Olly

The Old Stables: Lavender Cottage

The Old Stables: Stable & Stable Lads Cottages

The Old Stables: Coach House & Grooms Cottages

Check out our website, there is a detailed calendar showing up-to-date bookings for each property.

Tel: 01263 588926 / 01777 872618

Mobile: 07989 567289

e-mail: info@norfolkcoastalproperties.co.uk

www.norfolkcoastalproperties.co.uk

Diss, Fakenham, Foxley, Great Yarmouth

Happisburgh, Holt, Hunstanton, King's Lynn

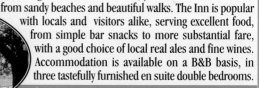

Go BLUE RIBAND for quality inexpensive self-catering holidays where your dog is welcome – choice of locations all in the borough of Great Yarmouth. Detached 3 bedroom bungalows, seafront bungalows, detached Sea-Dell chalets and modern sea front caravans. Free colour brochure: DON WITHERIDGE, BLUE RIBAND HOUSE, PARKLANDS, HEMSBY, GREAT YARMOUTH NR29 4HA (01493 730445). [Pets £10 per week; one pet free on some dates; one pet free on all holidays when booking for the first time through Pets Welcome!].
website: www.BlueRibandHolidays.co.uk

NORFOLK COASTAL PROPERTIES. Quality self-catering holiday cottages in North Norfolk. Clean, comfortable and something a little bit different. Properties sleep up to 6. Late availability discounted prices. [Pets £15 per week]. Contact EMMA COOLING (01263 588926/01777 872618: Mob: 07989 567289).
e-mail: info@norfolkcoastalproperties.co.uk   website: www.norfolkcoastalproperties.co.uk

NORFOLK COUNTRY COTTAGES (01603 871872). We have more than 360 self-catering cottages to choose from, many accepting pets. Sweeping beaches, pretty countryside and many rural footpaths make Norfolk the perfect destination for you and your discerning pets.
e-mail: info@norfolk.cottages.co.uk   website: www.norfolkcottages.co.uk

Bacton-on-Sea

Village on coast. 5 miles from North Walsham.

CASTAWAYS HOLIDAY PARK, PASTON ROAD, BACTON-ON-SEA NR12 0JB (01692 650436 and 650418). In peaceful village with direct access to sandy beach. Modern caravans, Pine Lodges and Flats, with all amenities. Licensed club, entertainment, children's play area. Ideal for discovering Norfolk. ETC ★★★. [Pets £20 per week]
website: www.castawaysholidaypark.net

Burnham Market

Village 5 miles West of Wells.

THE HOSTE ARMS, THE GREEN, BURNHAM MARKET PE31 8HD (01328 738777; Fax: 01328 730103). Stylish hotel with relaxing friendly atmosphere and attentive service. Individually designed bedrooms. Cosy bar with log fire, terraced dining area, conservatory. Locally sourced food. Midweek breaks. AA 2 Rosettes for food. [🐾].
e-mail: reception@hostearms.co.uk   website: www.hostearms.co.uk

Caister-on-Sea

Historic site with Roman ruins and 15th century Caister Castle with 100 foot tower.

Superior brick-built, tiled roof cottages with double glazing throughout. Adjacent golf course. Lovely walks on dunes and coast. 2-4 night breaks early/late season. Terms from £69 to £355. SAND DUNE COTTAGES, TAN LANE, CAISTER-ON-SEA, GREAT YARMOUTH NR30 5DT (01493 720352; mobile: 07785 561363). ETC ★★★ [Pets £15 per week]
e-mail: sand.dune.cottages@amserve.net
website: www.eastcoastlive.co.uk/sites/sanddunecottages.php

Cromer

Attractive resort built round old fishing village. Norwich 21 miles.

KNOLL GUEST HOUSE, ALFRED ROAD, CROMER NR27 9AN (01263 512753). A Victorian terraced house with five en suite bedrooms, one on the ground floor. All rooms with TV, tea/coffee making facilities and Wi-Fi. Only minutes stroll to the beach, pier and town centre. [🐾]
e-mail: knollguesthouse@btconnect.com   website: www.knollguesthouse.com

KINGS CHALET PARK, CROMER. Comfortable well-equipped chalets on quiet site; ideally placed for woodland and beach walks. 10 minutes' walk to town, shops nearby. Details from MRS I. SCOLTOCK, SHANGRI-LA, LITTLE CAMBRIDGE, DUTON HILL, DUNMOW, ESSEX (01371 870482; 07710 904048).
[one pet free]

KINGS CHALET PARK, CROMER (01263 511308). Well-equipped chalets sleeping 2 to 6; shower/bathroom, microwave and TV. One twin, one double bedroom, bed sofa in lounge, well-equipped kitchenette. Quiet site adjacent to woods, golf club and beaches. Local shops nearby. Pleasant 10 minutes' walk to town. Families welcome. [🐾]

All-electric two and three bedroom Holiday Cottages sleeping 4/6 in beautiful surroundings, also detached bungalow. Sandy beaches, sports facilities, Cinema and Pier (live shows). Parking. Children and pets welcome. ETC ★★-★★★ Brochure: BROADGATES COTTAGES, NORTHREPPS, FOREST PARK CARAVAN SITE LTD, NORTHREPPS ROAD, CROMER, NORFOLK NR27 0JR (01263 513290; Fax: 01263 511992) [Pets £10 weekly].
e-mail: info@broadgates.co.uk   website: www.broadgates.co.uk

KINGS CHALET PARK, CROMER. Self-catering holiday chalets set in an attractive landscaped park. Sleep 4-6 in two bedrooms and sofa bed. TV, cutlery, crockery, cooker and fridge provided. Dogs welcome. Contact: JACKIE ANDERSON, AMBLESIDE, PRIORY ROAD, BACTON NR12 0HQ (01692 650591; mobile: 07876 385609 OR 07747 517732).

CLIFTONVILLE HOTEL, SEAFRONT, CROMER NR27 9AS (01263 512543; Fax: 01263 515700). Ideally situated on the Norfolk coast. Beautifully restored Edwardian Hotel. 30 en suite bedrooms all with sea view. Executive suites. Seafood Bistro, à la carte Restaurant. AA ★★★ [pw! pets £4 per night]
e-mail: reservations@cliftonvillehotel.co.uk   website: www.cliftonvillehotel.co.uk

🐾	Pets are welcome free of charge.
£	A charge is made for pets: nightly or weekly.
pw!	Special provision for pets; exercise facility, feeding or accommodation arrangement.
⌂	Separate pets accommodation.

Classified Symbols

Dereham

Situated 16 miles west of Norwich. St Nicholas Church has 16th century bell tower.

BARTLES LODGE, CHURCH STREET, ELSING, DEREHAM NR20 3EA (01362 637177). B&B in en suite rooms in converted dairy. Central heating, tea/coffee, freeview TV. Village inn 100 yards for evening meal [pw! Pets £2 per night, £10 per week]
e-mail: bartleslodge@yahoo.co.uk   website: www.bartleslodge.co.uk

SCARNING DALE, SCARNING, EAST DEREHAM NR19 2QN (01362 687269). Self-catering cottages (not commercialised) in grounds of owner's house. On-site indoor heated swimming pool and full-size snooker table. Pets welcome by arrangement. Grazing and Stables available.
website: www.scarningdale.co.uk

Diss

Small market town on the River Waveney 19 miles SW of Norwich.

PAUL AND YOLANDA DAVEY, STRENNETH, AIRFIELD ROAD, FERSFIELD, DISS IP22 2BP (01379 688182; Fax 01379 688260). Family-run, fully renovated period property with two cottages. All rooms en suite, colour TVs, hospitality trays. Ground floor rooms. Non-smoking. Extensive breakfast menu. Licensed. Bed and Breakfast from £25. ETC ★★★★ Silver Award. [🐾]
e-mail: pdavey@strenneth.co.uk   website: www.strenneth.co.uk

WAVENEY VALLEY HOLIDAY PARK, AIRSTATION LANE, RUSHALL, DISS IP21 4QF (01379 741228/741690; Fax: 01379 741228). Touring Caravan and Camping Site. Licensed bar, electric hook-ups, restaurant, shop, laundry. Self-catering mobile homes. Outdoor swimming pool, horse riding on site; good fishing nearby.
e-mail: waveneyvalleyhp@aol.com   website: www.caravanparksnorfolk.co.uk

Fakenham

Historic market town halfway between Norwich and King's Lynn.

ABBOTT FARM BED & BREAKFAST, WALSINGHAM ROAD, BINHAM, FAKENHAM NR21 0AW (01328 830519). Liz and Alan welcome you to their home which has three comfortable en suite bedrooms. Breakfast is served in the conversatory which overlooks the beautiful countryside. Near to the North Norfolk coastline.
e-mail: enquiries@abbottfarm.co.uk   website: www.abbottfarm.co.uk

Foxley

Village 6 miles east of East Dereham.

Self-catering Cottages (2/3/4 bedrooms) on working farm. All fully equipped, with central heating. 20 miles from coast, 15 from Broads. Mature woodland nearby. Fishing in owners' lakes. Indoor heated swimming pool. ETC ★★★/★★★★. MOOR FARM STABLE COTTAGES, FOXLEY NR20 4QP (Tel & Fax: 01362 688523). [Pets £10 per week]
e-mail: mail@moorfarmstablecottages.co.uk   website: www.moorfarmstablecottages.co.uk

Great Yarmouth

Traditional lively seaside resort with a wide range of amusements, including the Marina Centre and Sealife Centre.

CAREFREE HOLIDAYS, CHAPEL BRIERS, YARMOUTH ROAD, HEMSBY, GREAT YARMOUTH NR29 4NJ (01493 732176). A wide selection of superior chalets for live-as-you-please holidays near Great Yarmouth and Norfolk Broads. All amenities on site. Parking. Children and pets welcome. [Pets £25 per week.]
website: www.carefree-holidays.co.uk

MRS MICHELLE BROWNE, SUNWRIGHT HOLIDAYS,50 MARINERS COMPASS, GORLESTON, GREAT YARMOUTH NR31 6TS (01493 304282) Sundowner Holiday Park, near Great Yarmouth. Fully furnished and equipped self catering chalets, sleep up to 6. Close to beach, Norfolk Broads and many attractions. [Pets £15 per week].
e-mail: sunwrightholiday@aol.com   website: www.sunwrightholidays.co.uk

Happisburgh

Coastal resort 6 miles East of North Walsham.

OLLANDS FARM BARN, SHORT LANE, HAPPISBURGH NR12 0RR (01692 652280).18thC barn with beamed cathedral ceiling, wood-burning stove, quaint paddle stairs, central heating, comfortable king-size bed in galleried bedroom, sofa-bed downstairs, fully fitted kitchen, shower room. Well behaved dogs welcome.[Pets £10 per week].
e-mail: mastuart@talk21.com   website: www.ollandsfarmbarn.co.uk

Holt

Small town 10 miles west of Cromer.

WEYBOURNE FOREST LODGES, SANDY HILL LANE, WEYBOURNE, HOLT NR25 7HW (01263 588440). Comfortable, well equipped lodges set in a tranquil forest glade with wonderful walks on the doorstep. Adjoining National Trust. 1½ miles from beach and cliffs, three miles from Holt and Sheringham. [Pets £20 per week]
e-mail: weybourneforestlodges@hotmail.com   website: www.weybourneforestlodges.co.uk

THE PHEASANT HOTEL, COAST ROAD, KELLING, HOLT NR25 7EG (01263 588382). Set in 2 acres of landscaped gardens. All rooms are en suite, with most on ground floor. Well behaved dogs with responsible owners welcome. ETC ★★ [Pets £6 per night]
e-mail: enquiries@pheasanthotelnorfolk.co.uk   website: www.pheasanthotelnorfolk.co.uk

Hunstanton

Coastal resort on the Wash 14 miles NE of King's Lynn.

ST CRISPINS, OLD HUNSTANTON (01485 534036). Near sandy beach, golf course; shop, pubs. A few miles Royal Sandringham, Norfolk Lavender, RSPB reserves. Bargain breaks early/late from £130. Pets welcome. [One dog £15 per week]
e-mail: st.crispins@btinternet.com

THE HAVEN, HUNSTANTON. Three-bedroom bungalow with large enclosed secluded garden. Sleeps 5. Minutes from town centre, cliff tops, the old lighthouse and beach. Convenient for Sandringham, Holkham, Peddars Way, RSPB Titchwell Reserve etc. Non-smoking. CONTACT: MRS SANDRA HOHOL, BIRDS NORFOLK HOLIDAY HOMES (01485 534267). (Please quote ref: SHF:HU61).
e-mail: shohol@birdsnorfolkholidayhomes.co.uk   www.norfolkholidayhomes-birds.co.uk

King's Lynn

Ancient market town and port on the Wash with many beautiful medieval and Georgian buildings.

MRS G. DAVIDSON, HOLMDENE FARM, BEESTON, KING'S LYNN PE32 2NJ (01328 701284). 17th century farmhouse situated in central Norfolk within easy reach of the coast and Broads. Sporting activities available locally, village pub nearby. One double room, one twin and one single. Pets welcome. Bed and Breakfast from £22.50pp; Evening Meal from £15. Weekly terms available and child reductions. Two self-catering cottages. Sleeping 4/8. Terms on request. ETC ★★★ [🐾]
e-mail: holmdenefarm@farmersweekly.net   website: www.holmdenefarm.co.uk

MRS J. E. FORD, 129 LEZIATE DROVE, POTT ROW, KING'S LYNN PE32 1DE (01553 630356). Detached bungalow sleeps 4. In quiet village close to Sandringham and beaches. Facilities include colour TV, video, microwave, fridge/freezer, washing machine, off road parking, dog run. [🐾]
website: www.southsideholidayhome.co.uk

Lowestoft

Resort town on the North Sea coast, 38 miles north east of Ipswich.

BROADLAND HOLIDAY VILLAGE, OULTON BROAD, LOWESTOFT NR33 9JY (01502 573033). Discover the delights of the forgotten Norfolk Broad with your faithful friend. Stay in cosy brick bungalows, some with outdoor hot tubs, or pine lodges. Indoor heated pool. The perfect holiday for the whole family! [Pets £30 per week].
website: www.broadlandvillage.co.uk

Mundesley-on-Sea

Small resort backed by low cliffs. Good sands and bathing. Norwich 20 miles, Cromer 7.

KILN CLIFFS CARAVAN PARK, CROMER ROAD, MUNDESLEY NR11 8DF (01263 720449). Peaceful family-run site situated around an historic brick kiln. Six-berth caravans for hire, standing on ten acres of grassy cliff top. All caravans fully equipped (except linen) and price includes all gas and electricity. [🐾].

47 SEAWARD CREST, MUNDESLEY. West-facing brick built chalet on private site with lawns, flowers and parking. Large lounge/dining room, kitchenette, two bedrooms, bathroom. Beach and shops nearby. Pets most welcome. SAE please: MRS DOAR, 4 DENBURY ROAD, RAVENSHEAD, NOTTS. NG15 9FQ (01623 798032). [🐾]

North Walsham

Market town 14 miles north of Norwich, traditional centre of the Norfolk reed thatchiing industry.

MRS. G. FAULKNER, DOLPHIN LODGE, 3 KNAPTON ROAD,TRUNCH, NORTH WALSHAM NR28 0QE (01263 720961; Mobile: 07901 691084). Friendly B&B in village within easy reach of all Norfolk attractions including Norfolk Broads. All rooms en suite, tea/coffee facilities, TVs, hairdryers etc. Enquiries by telephone only. [🐾]
website: www.dolphinlodge.net

Norwich

Historic city with Cathedral, Castle, shops, restaurants and lots to see and do. Many medieval streets and lanes, with attractive timbered houses.

WHITE LODGE FARM COTTAGES, HINGHAM NR9 4LY (01953 850435 or 07768 156680). Set in the heart of the Norfolk countryside, but within walking distance of the beautiful village of Hingham, the three cottages offer comfort and modern convenience all year round for weekend, midweek or longer stays. Dogs very welcome. EnjoyEngland ★★★★★ Gold Award.
e-mail: fhgp@whitelodgefarmcottages.co.uk   www.whitelodgefarmcottages.co.uk

Sheringham

Small, traditional resort with sandy beaches, which has grown around a flint-built fishing village.

SHERINGHAM COTTAGES. Six traditional self-catering properties within walking distance of the beach. Comfortable and fully equipped. Sleep 4/8. Dogs welcome by arrangement. For details contact: TREVOR CLAYDON, CAMELOT HOUSE, HOLT ROAD, GRESHAM, NORWICH NR11 8AD (01263 577560).
e-mail: trevor.claydon@which.net   website: www.sheringhamcottages.com

Stiffkey

Village on the north coast of Norfolk. 25 miles north west of the city of Norwich.

STIFFKEY RED LION, 44 WELLS ROAD, STIFFKEY NR23 1AJ (01328 830552) Five ground floor en suite bedrooms, five on first floor; all with their own external door. Pets warmly welcomed. [Pets £5 per week]
e-mail: redlion@stiffkey.com   website: www.stiffkey.com

MOUNT TABOR, WELLS ROAD, STIFFKEY. A quaint cottage hideaway with lounge, compact galley kitchen with dining area, bathroom and twin bedroom. Coastal walks nearby. Contact: MRS NORRIS, 30 COTSWOLD DRIVE, ROYTON OL2 5HD (0161 633 6834). [Pets £10 per week]
e-mail: stiffkeycottage@ntlworld.com   website: www.stiffkeycottage.com

Terms quoted in this publication may be subject to increase if rises in costs necessitate

Thornham

Village 4 miles east of Hunstanton. Site of Roman signal station.

THE LIFEBOAT INN, SHIP LANE, THORNHAM PE36 6LT (01485 512236; Fax: 01485 512323). A welcome sight for the weary traveller for centuries. Dogs welcome. Restaurant (one AA rosette). Bird watching and walking along miles of open beaches. Please ring for brochure and tariff. [Pets £8 per week.]
e-mail: lifeboatinn@maypolehotels.com   website: www.maypolehotels.com

Thorpe Market

Village 4 miles south of Cromer.

POPPYLAND TOURING PARK & HOLIDAY COTTAGE, THE GREEN, THORPE MARKET NR11 8AJ (01263 833219). Ideal for guests who want to relax or explore local area. Puddleduck Cottage (sleeps 2) has private enclosed garden. Touring park (adults only) in landscaped gardens surrounded by trees. Excellent food nearby. [Pets £12 per week.]
e-mail: enquiries@poppyland.com   website: www.poppyland.com

Thurne

Idyllic Broadland village. Great Yarmouth 10 miles.

HEDERA HOUSE AND PLANTATION BUNGALOWS, THURNE NR29 3BU (01692 670242 or 01493 844568). Adjacent river, seven bedroomed farmhouse, 10 competitively priced bungalows in peaceful gardens. Outdoor heated pool. Enjoy boating, fishing, walking, touring, nearby golf, sandy beaches and popular resorts. [Pets £20 per week]
website: www.hederahouse.co.uk

Weybourne

Located in an Area of Outstanding Natural Beauty and part of the Heritage Coastline. Sheringham and Holt 4 miles.

BOLDING WAY HOLIDAYS, THE BARN, BOLDING WAY, WEYBOURNE, HOLT NR25 7SW (01263 588666). The Stables (SC) sleeps 8, Biddles Cottage (SC) sleeps 2; Tack Room (room only) sleeps 2. In an Area of Outstanding Natural Beauty and on the Heritage Coast. Well behaved pets welcome. Fenced gardens. Shared use of hot tub and sauna. ETC ★★★★ Gold Award. [🐾]
e-mail: holidays@boldingway.co.uk   website: www.boldingway.co.uk

Winterton-on-Sea

Good sands and bathing. Great Yarmouth 8 miles.

WINTERTON HOLIDAYS, WINTERTON-ON-SEA. Privately owned one and two-bedroom chalets, furnished and equipped to a high standard, on picturesque park few minutes' walk from sea. Dogs allowed on beach all year. Ideal for quiet, relaxing break and for exploring Broads, coast, Norwich. Village has pub, restaurant and shops. MRS JUNE HUDSON, 15 LARK WAY, BRADWELL, GREAT YARMOUTH NR31 8SB (01493 444700). [Pets £5 per night, £20 per week]
website: www.wintertonholidays.com

FISHERMANS RETURN, THE LANE, WINTERTON-ON-SEA NR29 4BN (01493 393305). 300-year-old brick and flint pub, just a few minutes' stroll from sandy beaches and beautiful walks. Excellent food, simple bar snacks and good choice of real ales and fine wines. B&B available in 3 tastefully furnished en suite double bedrooms.
e-mail: fishermansreturn@yahoo.co.uk   website: www.fishermans-return.com

WINTERTON CHALET HOLIDAYS. Peaceful well appointed self-catering chalets (sleep 2/5) with sea views, on Winterton Valley estate. Children and pets very welcome. Short walk to village with shops and dog-friendly pub. Phone or e-mail for details (07799 386834). [Pets £20 per week]
e-mail: mail@wintertonchaletholidays.co.uk   website:www.wintertonchaletholidays.co.uk

WINTERTON VALLEY HOLIDAYS. A selection of modern superior fully appointed holiday chalets in a choice of locations near Great Yarmouth. Enjoy panoramic views from WINTERTON, a quiet and picturesque 35-acre estate, while CALIFORNIA has all the usual amenities, with free entry to the pool and clubhouse. Pets are very welcome at both sites. For colour brochure: 15 KINGSTON AVENUE, CAISTER-ON-SEA NR30 5ET (01493 377175).
website: www.wintertonvalleyholidays.co.uk

Barnoldby-le-Beck

Village 4 miles SW of Grimsby.

GRANGE FARM COTTAGES & RIDING SCHOOL, WALTHAM ROAD, BARNOLDBY-LE-BECK DN37 0AP (01472 822216; Fax: 01472 233550; mobile: 07947 627663). Three well appointed cottages and riding school situated in the heart of the Lincolnshire Wolds. Sleep 4/6. ETC ★★★★. Equestrian Centre offers tuition, all-weather riding, stabling. [Pets £10 per week]
website: www.grangefarmcottages.com

Ipswich, Kessingland, Laxfield, Long Melford

Nayland, Orford, Saxmundham

Tattingstone

Badgers' Bend

Detached 18th century cottage with plenty of character, situated close to Alton Water in the pleasant village of Tattingstone. Ideal base for touring Essex/Suffolk, seaside towns such as Felixstowe, Walton-on-Naze or Clacton-on-Sea, or for visiting Ipswich (6 miles) and Woodbridge. *Three bedrooms (one double and two twin); lounge, sitting room, dining room; downstairs bathroom.* Children and dogs welcome. Non-smoking. All prices include heating, electricity, linen and towels. Please call Margaret & Howard for more information.

Tel: 01473 311309
e-mail: howardnuttallm@supanet.com

Aldeburgh

Coastal town 6 miles south-east of Saxmundham. Annual music festival at Snape Maltings.

WENTWORTH HOTEL, ALDEBURGH IP15 5BD (01728 452312). Country House Hotel overlooking the sea. Immediate access to the beach and walks. Two comfortable lounges with log fires and antique furniture. Refurbished bedrooms with all facilities and many with sea views. Restaurant specialises in fresh produce and sea food. ETC Silver Award. AA ★★★ Two Rosettes. [Pets £2 per day]
e-mail: stay@wentworth-aldeburgh.co.uk   website: www.wentworth-aldeburgh.com

Bungay

Attractive town in the Waveney Valley, with a wealth of historic sites. Town centre has a Roman well, a Saxon church, and the remains of a Norman castle and Benedictine priory. 14 miles south east of Norwich.

EARSHAM PARK FARM, OLD RAILWAY ROAD, EARSHAM, BUNGAY NR35 2AQ (01986 892180). Superb Victorian property overlooking open countryside. Bedrooms attractively furnished; excellent breakfasts. All rooms en suite. ETC/AA ★★★★ Gold Award. [Pets £5 per night]
website: www.earsham-parkfarm.co.uk

ANNIE'S COTTAGE, SUFFOLK. Peaceful, rural location in open countryside. 2 bedrooms, sleeps 4. Large lounge/dining room, woodburning stove. Linen and towels provided. Electricity included. Enclosed private garden. Contact: LYNNE MORTON, HILL FARM HOLIDAYS, ILKETSHALL ST JOHN, BECCLES NR34 8JE (01986 781240). [🐾]
website: www.hillfarmholidays.com

Bury St Edmunds

This prosperous market town on the River Lark lies 28 miles east of Cambridge.

RAVENWOOD HALL COUNTRY HOUSE HOTEL AND RESTAURANT, ROUGHAM, BURY ST EDMUNDS IP30 9JA (01359 270345; Fax: 01359 270788). 16th century beamed Tudor Hall set in seven acres of perfect dog walks. Individually furnished en suite bedrooms; renowned restaurant; relaxing inglenook fires. AA ★★★, AA 2 Rosettes. [🐾 pw!]
e-mail: enquiries@ravenwoodhall.co.uk   website: www.ravenwoodhall.co.uk

REDE HALL FARM PARK, REDE, BURY ST EDMUNDS IP29 4UG (01284 850695; Fax: 01284 850345). Two well equipped cottages, ideal for touring East Anglia and the coast. Totally non-smoking. Hot Tub Spa available for exclusive use (inclusive). Well behaved dogs welcome. ETC ★★★★ [🐾 ⬜]
e-mail: chris@redehallfarmpark.co.uk   website: www.redehallfarmpark.co.uk

CULFORD FARM COTTAGES, BURY ST EDMUNDS IP28 6DS (Tel/Fax: 01284 728334). Three cottages set in 250 acres of peaceful farmland. Comfortable converted accommodation with all amenities. Sleep 4. Each with own hot tub and shared heated outdoor pool in summer. [Pets £25 per week]
e-mail: enquiries@homefarmculford.co.uk   website: www.culfordfarmcottages.co.uk

Hadleigh

Historic town on River Brett with several buildings of interest including unusual 14th century church. Bury St Edmunds 20 miles, Colchester 14, Sudbury 11, Ipswich 10.

EDGE HALL, 2 HIGH STREET, HADLEIGH IP7 5AP (01473 822458). Truffles invites you to stay in her master's comfortable lodge house. Well behaved owners will enjoy the perfect walks and super breakfasts. Twin/double £85 per night, single £57.50. Self-catering also available. ETC/AA ★★★★★, ETC Silver Award. [Pets £5 per stay]
e-mail: r.rolfe@edgehall.co.uk　　　　　　　website: www.edgehall.co.uk

Ipswich

County town and port 66 miles NE of London.

WAYNE & SUE LEGGETT, DAMERONS FARM HOLIDAYS, HENLEY, IPSWICH IP6 0RU (01473 832454 or 07881 824083). Five cottages, each sleeping 1-6. The Old Dairy has a high level of accessibility for disabled visitors; three others have ground floor bedrooms and bathrooms. Games room with table tennis, pool and table football. Short Breaks out of season.
website: www.dameronsfarmholidays.co.uk

Kessingland

Little seaside place with expansive beach, safe bathing, wildlife park, lake fishing. To the south is Benacre Broad, a beauty spot. Norwich 26 miles, Adleburgh 23, Lowestoft 5.

Quality seaside bungalows in lawned surrounds overlooking the sea. Open all year, fully eqipped. Sleep 1/6. Direct access to award-winning beach. Parking Pets very welcome. APPLY– KNIGHTS HOLIDAY HOMES, 22 HARROP DALE, CARLTON COLVILLE, LOWESTOFT, SUFFOLK NR33 8UY (FREEPHONE 0800 269067). [🐾]
e-mail: info@knightsholidays.co.uk　　　　　website: www.knightsholidays.co.uk

Laxfield

Village 6 miles North of Framlingham.

LODGE COTTAGE, LAXFIELD. Pretty 16C thatched cottage retaining some fine period features. Sleeps 4. Pets welcome. Fenced garden. One mile from village. 30 minutes to Southwold and coast. Rural, quiet and relaxing. ETC ★★★★. For brochure phone: MRS JANE BREWER, LODGE COTTAGE, LAXFIELD ROAD, CRATFIELD, HALESWORTH IP19 0QG (01986 798830 or 07788 853884). [🐾].
e-mail: janebrewer@live.co.uk

Long Melford

Village in the beautiful countryside of Suffolk, in the River Stour valley, just north of Sudbury, beside the A314 road to Bury St Edmunds.

THE BLACK LION HOTEL & RESTAURANT, THE GREEN, LONG MELFORD CO10 9DN (01787 312356). The Georgian Black Lion Hotel overlooks the famous green, and the cosy bar and restaurant offer a range of innovative dishes. 10 en suite bedrooms refurbished to luxury status. Idyllic dog walks. [🐾]
e-mail: enquiries@blacklionhotel.net　　　　　website: www.blacklionhotel.net

Pet-Friendly
Pubs, Inns & Hotels
on pages 448-453

These establishments may not feature in the main section of the book

Nayland

Small town on River Stour, 6 miles north of Colchester.

GLADWINS FARM, HARPER'S HILL, NAYLAND CO6 4NU (01206 262261). Self-catering cottages (sleep 2-8) set in 22 acres of Suffolk countryside. Indoor heated pool, sauna, hot tub, tennis court and playground. Loads of dog walking. [Pets £20 per week] ETC ★★★★/★★★★★.
e-mail: contact@gladwinsfarm.co.uk   website: www.gladwinsfarm.co.uk

Orford

Village on River Ore, 9 miles east of Woodbridge.

THE CROWN AND CASTLE, ORFORD, WOODBRIDGE IP12 2LJ (01394 450205). Comfortable and very dog-friendly hotel situated close to 12th century castle in historic and unspoilt village of Orford. Honest good food served in award-winning Trinity Restaurant. [Pets £5 per night]
e-mail: info@crownandcastle.co.uk   website: www.crownandcastle.co.uk

Saxmundham

Small town 18 miles NE of Ipswich.

SWEFFLING HALL FARM, SWEFFLING, SAXMUNDHAM IP17 2BT (Tel & Fax: 01728 663644). In a quiet location. One double and one family room with en suite/private bathrooms. Ideal for walking/cycling and Heritage Coast. Open all year. Always a warm welcome. [pw! 🐕 🏠]
e-mail: stephen.mann@unicombox.com   website: www.swefflinghallfarm.co.uk

Tattingstone

Small village 6 miles south of Ipswich.

BADGERS' BEND. Detached 18th century cottage ideally situated for touring Essex/Suffolk, visiting the seaside, or shopping in Ipswich and Woodbridge. Three bedrooms (one double, two twin). Children and dogs welcome. Please call Margaret and Howard for more information (01473 311309). [🐕]
e-mail: howardnuttallm@supanet.com

PEAK COTTAGES (0844 770 8924). Quality self-catering accommodation in the Derbyshire Dales and Peaks. Whether you are a walker, climber, potholer, antiquarian, historian, naturalist, gardener or sportsman – Derbyshire has it all. Pets welcome in many. Telephone for colour brochure. [Pets £12 per week.]
website: www.peakcottages.com

Derbyshire
Ashbourne

Bentley Brook Inn is a busy country inn in the beautiful Peak Park, providing quality accommodation, an award-winning restaurant and an all-day bar offering informal meals and snacks. The Inn has a large child and pet-friendly garden. Favourite centre for walking and for visiting Dovedale, the Manifold Valley, Chatsworth and Alton Towers. Eleven refurbished en suite rooms of great character. Free wireless broadband in the bar. Pets welcome by prior arrangement.

Bentley Brook Inn

Fenny Bentley, Ashbourne, Derbyshire DE6 1LF
Tel: 01335 350278 • Fax: 01335 350422
e-mail: all@bentleybrookinn.co.uk • www.bentleybrookinn.co.uk

Paddock House Farm Holiday Cottages
★★★★ *Luxury Holiday Cottage Accommodation*

Surrounded by 5 acres of delightful grounds and reached along its own long drive, Paddock House nestles peacefully in a secluded spot between the famous villages of Alstonefield and Hartington. Arranged around a courtyard, these charming cottages enjoy uninterrupted views. The area is a walker's paradise, and there are excellent cycle trails along Dovedale, Tissington and the Manifold Valley. Ideal base for families, many attractions closeby. Nearby Ashbourne offers shops, restaurants and other town amenities. Alton Towers 20 minutes.

Peak District National Park, Alstonefield, Ashbourne, Derbyshire DE6 2FT
Tel: 01335 310282 • Mobile: 07977 569618
e-mail: info@paddockhousefarm.co.uk • www.paddockhousefarm.co.uk

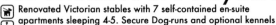

Dronfield, Hope Valley, Matlock, Peak District National Park

Please mention PETS WELCOME!
when making enquiries about accommodation featured in this guide

Ashbourne

Market town on River Henmore, close to its junction with River Dove. Several interesting old buildings. Birmingham 42 miles, Nottingham 29, Derby 13.

MR & MRS LENNARD, WINDLEHILL FARM, SUTTON ON THE HILL, ASHBOURNE DE6 5JH (Tel & Fax: 01283 732377). Converted beamed barns on small organic farm - the Chop House sleeps 6 and has a fenced garden, the Hayloft sleeps 2 and is a first floor apartment. Well behaved pets welcome. ETC ★★★★ [pw! Pets £10 per week minimum]
e-mail: windlehill@btinternet.com   website: www.windlehill.btinternet.co.uk

MRS M.A. RICHARDSON, THROWLEY HALL FARM, ILAM, ASHBOURNE DE6 2BB (01538 308202/ 308243). Self-catering accommodation in farmhouse for up to 12 and cottages for five and seven people. Also Bed and Breakfast in farmhouse. Central heating, en suite rooms, TV, tea/coffee facilities in rooms. No smoking. Children and pets welcome. Near Alton Towers and stately homes. ETC ★★★★. [Pets £5 per week.]
e-mail: throwleyhall@btinternet.com   website: www.throwleyhallfarm.co,uk

BENTLEY BROOK INN, FENNY BENTLEY, ASHBOURNE DE6 1LF(01335 350278; Fax: 01335 350422) Busy country inn in the beautiful Peak Park. Quality accommodation, award-winning restaurant and all day bar. Pet-friendly garden. Eleven refurbished en suite rooms of great character. Pets welcome by prior arrangement. Enjoy England ★★★ Inn. [Pets £10]
e-mail: all@bentleybrookinn.co.uk   website: www.bentleybrookinn.co.uk

PADDOCK HOUSE FARM HOLIDAY COTTAGES, PEAK DISTRICT NATIONAL PARK, ALSTONEFIELD, ASHBOURNE DE6 2FT (01335 310282; Mobile: 07977 569618). Surrounded by 5 acres of delightful grounds and arranged around a courtyard, these charming cottages enjoy uninterrupted views. Ideal base for families, many attractions close by; Alton Towers 20 minutes. ETC ★★★★ [Pets £20 per week].
e-mail: info@paddockhousefarm.co.uk   website: www.paddockhousefarm.co.uk

MRS M.M. STELFOX, DOG AND PARTRIDGE COUNTRY INN, SWINSCOE, ASHBOURNE DE6 2HS (01335 343183). 17th century Inn offering ideal holiday accommodation. Many leisure activities available. All bedrooms with washbasins, colour TV, telephone and private facilities. ETC/AA ★★ [🐾, pw!]
e-mail: info@dogandpartridge.co.uk   website: www.dogandpartridge.co.uk

Belper

Town 7 miles North of Derby.

FLEET COTTAGE, 66 THE FLEET BELPER DE56 1NW (Tel: 01773 823240; Mobile: 0786 626 5446). Renovated 18th century Grade II listed 2 bedroomed cottage, beamed throughout. Ideal base for many attractions and lovely walks. ETC ★★★★ [🐾].
e-mail: info@thefleetcottage.co.uk   website: www.thefleetcottage.co.uk

Burnaston

Village 5 miles SW of Derby.

STABLES LODGE, GRASSY LANE, BURNASTON DE65 6LN (01332 510000). Renovated stables with seven self-contained en suite self-catering apartments, sleeping 4-5. Dog runs and optional kennels. Overnight accommodation and weekend breaks also available. [🐾 🏠]
website: www.stableslodge.co.uk

Buxton

Well-known spa and centre for the Peak District. Beautiful scenery and good sporting amenities. Leeds 50 miles, Matlock 20, Macclesfield 12.

PRIORY LEA HOLIDAY FLATS. Close to Poole's Cavern Country Park. Fully equipped. Full central heating. Sleep 2/6. Cleanliness assured. Terms from £125-£295. Open all year. Short Breaks available. ETC ★★/★★★. MRS GILL TAYLOR, 50 WHITE KNOWLE ROAD, BUXTON SK17 9NH (01298 23737). [pw! Pets £2 per night.]
e-mail: priorylea@hotmail.co.uk   website: www.priorylea.co.uk

ALISON PARK HOTEL, 3 TEMPLE ROAD, BUXTON SK17 9BA (01298 22473; Fax: 01298 72709). Situated close to the Pavilion Gardens and Opera House. 17 bedrooms, all en suite or private bathroom. Lunches, bar meals and dinner available daily. Wheelchair ramp access; ground floor bedrooms. Licensed. ETC ★★ [🐾]
e-mail: reservations@alison-park-hotel.co.uk   website: www.alison-park-hotel.co.uk

Dronfield

Situated between Sheffield and Chesterfield on the River Drone in north east Derbyshire.

MILL FARM HOLIDAY COTTAGES, CROWHOLE, BARLOW, DRONFIELD S18 7TJ (0114 2890543: Fax: 0114 2891473) Five cottages fully equipped to a very high standard. Cots, folding beds and high chairs are available on request. Four-poster bed in Wood View. Launderette on site. Dogs always welcome. [Pets £10 per week]
e-mail: cottages@barlowlakes.co.uk   website: www.millfarmcottages.com

Hope Valley

Large valley in Peak District, 4 miles from Hathersage.

THE LITTLE JOHN HOTEL, STATION ROAD, HATHERSAGE, HOPE VALLEY S32 1DD (01433 650225). Ideal for a relaxing drink or meal after walking the high moors. Popular local pub with award-winning ales and good selection of refreshments. Home cooked food. Six en suite rooms and three charming cottages [🐾].
e-mail: littlejohnhotel@btconnect.com   website: www.littlejohnhotel.co.uk

Matlock

County town of Derbyshire, situated on a bend of the River Derwent.

ALISON HOUSE, INTAKE LANE, CROMFORD, MATLOCK DE4 3RH (01629 822211; Fax: 01629 822316). Georgian-style house set in the Derwent Valley World Heritage site. Beautiful gardens in a peaceful setting. 16 en suite rooms. Bar, lounge and restaurant. AA ★★★★ [pw! 🐾].
e-mail: info@alison-house-hotel.co.uk   website: www.alison-house-hotel.co.uk

Peak District National Park

A green and unspoilt area at the southern end of the Pennines, covering 555 square miles.

WHEELDON TREES FARM, EARL STERNDALE, BUXTON SK17 0AA (01298 83219). Relax and unwind with your dog(s) in our unique award-winning dairy barn conversion. Nine cosy, superbly equipped holiday cottages sleeping 1-5 (total 30). ETC ★★★★ [pw! 🐾]
e-mail: stay@wheeldontreesfarm.co.uk   website: www.wheeldontreesfarm.co.uk

BIGGIN HALL, PEAK PARK (01298 84451). Close Dove Dale. 17th century hall sympathetically restored. Bathrooms en suite, log fires, C/H comfort, warmth and quiet. Fresh home cooking. Beautiful uncrowded footpaths and cycle trails. ETC ★★[🐾]
website: www.bigginhall.co.uk

Tideswell

Village in the Peak District situated 1000ft above sea level, 6 miles east of Buxton.

WELYARDE. A delightful single cottage with three bedrooms, with a beautiful landscaped garden. Sleeps 6, occasionally 8. We truly welcome dogs. And THE OLD PIGGERY – an equally dog friendly establishment with fabulous views. For details contact: PAUL HARRISON AND CARRIE WARR, DEVONSHIRE HOUSE, HIGH STREET, TIDESWELL SK17 8LB (01298 872285).
e-mail: info@oldpiggery.co.uk   website: www.welyarde.co.uk

Wirksworth

An ancient Saxon town, once the principal lead mining centre of the Peak District, 4 miles south of Matlock.

THE WILD CHERRY BED & BREAKFAST, 78 GREENHILL, WIRKSWORTH DE4 4EN (01629 824712). A family run bed and breakfast in a quiet location with panoramic views over the Ecclesbourne Valley. Two double bedrooms with tea/coffee facilities. Wi-Fi. Parking. Pets welcome.
e-mail: thewildcherry78@hotmail.co.uk   website: www.peakdistrictinformation.com

Bromyard, Hereford, Ledbury, Much Cowarne

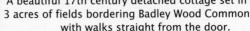
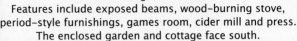

FHG Guides publish a large range of well-known accommodation guides. We will be happy to send you details or you can use the order form at the back of this book.

Bromyard

Medieval market town 12 miles west of Worcester; the streets are lined with half-timbered buildings.

ELCOCKS COTTAGE, NEAR BROMYARD. A beautiful 17th century detached cottage set in 3 acres bordering Badley Wood Common. Features include exposed beams, wood-burning stove, period-style furnishings. Enclosed garden and cottage face south. Pets welcome. ETC ★★★ Contact: MIKE HOGG (0121 427 1395).
e-mail: Mike@elcocks.net   website: www.elcocks.net

Hereford

Cathedral town on River Wye 45 miles SW of Birmingham.

SINK GREEN FARM, ROTHERWAS, HEREFORD HR2 6LE (01432 870223). 16th century farmhouse overlooking picturesque Wye Valley. En suite rooms, one four-poster. Extensive garden with summer house and hot tub. Fishing. Prices from £35pp. Children welcome. Pets by arrangement. [★]
e-mail: enquiries@sinkgreenfarm.co.uk   website: www.sinkgreenfarm.co.uk

Ledbury

Town 12 miles east of Hereford with many timbered houses.

CHURCH FARM, CODDINGTON, LEDBURY HR8 IJJ (01531 640271). Black and white 16th-century Farmhouse on a working farm close to the Malvern Hills — ideal for touring and walking. Two double and one twin bedrooms. Excellent home cooking. Warm welcome assured. Open all year. From £37. Single supplement. AA ★★★★ [Small charge for pets]
website: www.dexta.co.uk

Leominster

Known as "The Town in the Marches", this historic market town is located in the heart of the beautiful border countryside and possesses some fine examples of architecture throughout the ages, such as The Priory Church and Grange Court. Ludlow 9 ½ miles, Hereford 12 miles.

**CLIVE & CYNTHIA PRIOR, MOCKTREE BARNS, LEINTWARDINE, LUDLOW SY7 0LY (01547 540441). Gold Award winning cottages around a sunny courtyard. Sleep 2-6. Comfortable, well-equipped. Friendly owners. Dogs and children welcome. Non-Smoking. Lovely country walks. Ludlow, seven miles. Brochure. NAS Level 1 Accessibility. VB ★★★ [★] See also colour advertisement page 242
e-mail: mocktreebarns@care4free.net   website: www.mocktreeholidays.co.uk**

DOCKLOW MANOR, DOCKLOW, LEOMINSTER HR6 0RX (01568 760668) Two delightful stone cottages quietly secluded in five acres of garden and woodland. Superb westerly views. Table tennis, croquet and trampolining available. Excellent fishing, golf and walking nearby.
website: www.docklow-manor.co.uk

Much Cowarne

Village 5 miles SW of Bromyard.

RICHARD & MARGARET BRADBURY, COWARNE HALL COTTAGES, MUCH COWARNE HR7 4JQ (01432 820317) Historic, comfortable cottages 'twixt the Malvern Hills and Wye Valley. Large garden. Private enclosed patios. Convenient for nearby towns and attractions. Free brochure and 'planner pack'.
e-mail: rm@cowarnehall.co.uk   website: www.cowarnehall.co.uk

---

★	Pets are welcome free of charge.
£	A charge is made for pets: nightly or weekly.
pw!	Special provision for pets; exercise facility, feeding or accommodation arrangement.
⌂	Separate pets accommodation.

Classified Symbols

Ross-on-Wye

An attractive town standing on a hill rising from the left bank on the Wye. Cardiff 47 miles, Gloucester 17.

THE HOSTELRIE AT GOODRICH, GOODRICH, ROSS-ON-WYE HR9 6HX (01600 890241). Enjoy comfort and good food at this fully centrally heated 17th Century Inn. We have a reputation for quality food at a reasonable price. Dogs welcome in bedrooms, main bar and garden. ETC/AA ★★ [🐾]
e-mail: info@thehostelrieatgoodrich.com   website: www.thehostelrieatgoodrich.com

LEA HOUSE BED & BREAKFAST, LEA, ROSS-ON-WYE HR9 7JZ (01989 750652). Spacious bedrooms with kingsize or twin beds and en suite bathrooms; all individually styled, with TV and beverage tray. Secluded garden. Dogs very welcome. AA ★★★★ [Dogs £7.50 per stay]. See Display Advert.
e-mail: enquiries@leahouse.co.uk   website: www.leahouse.co.uk

GAME LARDERS & OLD BAKEHOUSE, WYTHALL ESTATE, ROSS-ON-WYE HR9 3SD (01989 562688). Enjoy peace and quiet in the secluded setting of Wythall Estate. The self contained cottages sleep 2/4, each with sitting room, dining area, fully fitted kitchen, bedroom(s) and family bathroom.
e-mail: bookings@wythallestate.co.uk   website: www.wythallestate.co.uk

Symonds Yat

Well known beauty spot on River Wye, 4 miles from Monmouth.

THE ROCK B&B, HILLERSLAND, NEAR SYMONDS YAT GL16 7NY (01594 837893). Located on the ridge between the Wye and Ruardean Valleys. Quiet well behaved dogs welcome. All three dog-friendly bedrooms have direct access from the outside, meaning you and your dog can come and go as you please.[Pets £10 per stay]
website: www.stayattherock.com

Walterstone

Set at the base of the Black Mountains on the edge of the Brecon Beacons National Park.

ALLT YR YNYS COUNTRY HOUSE, WALTERSTONE, NEAR ABERGAVENNY HR2 0DU (01873 890307). Beautifully preserved 16thC manor house set in the foothills of the Black Mountains on the fringes of the Brecon Beacons National Park. 22 luxury en suite bedrooms. Award-winning restaurant and Cider Mill bar. Indoor heated swimming pool, sauna and spa pool. WTB ★★★
website: www.allthotel.co.uk

Market Harborough, Melton Mowbray

Market Harborough

Town on River Welland 14 miles south-east of Leicester.

BROOK MEADOW HOLIDAYS. Three self-catering chalets, Carp fishing, camping and caravan site
with electric hookups. Phone for brochure. ETC ★★★. MRS MARY HART, WELFORD ROAD,
SIBBERTOFT, MARKET HARBOROUGH LE16 9UJ (01858 880886). [🐕 camping, £12 Self-catering]
e-mail: brookmeadow@farmline.com   website: www.brookmeadow.co.uk

Melton Mowbray

Old market town, centre of hunting country. Large cattle market. Church and Ann of Cleves' House are of interest. Kettering 29 miles, Market Harborough 22, Nottingham 18, Leicester 15.

SYSONBY KNOLL HOTEL, ASFORDBY ROAD, MELTON MOWBRAY LE13 OHP (01664 563563; Fax:
01664 410364.). Family-run hotel on edge of market town. Grounds of five acres with river frontage.
Superb food, individually styled rooms, and a genuine welcome for pets. Please see website for
special offers and further details. ETC/AA ★★★ [🐕]
website: www.sysonby.com

🐕   Pets are welcome free of charge.   **Classified Symbols**

£   A charge is made for pets: nightly or weekly.

pw! Special provision for pets; exercise facility, feeding or accommodation arrangement.

⌂   Separate pets accommodation.

Boston, Gainsborough, Grantham, Horncastle

Langton-by-Wragby, Louth, Mablethorpe

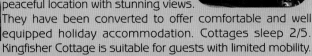

Boston

South east coast of Lincolnshire, 32 miles from Lincoln.

ELMS FARM COTTAGES, BOSTON PE20 3QP (01205 290840; mobile: 07887 652021). Fully equipped and furnished to a high standard with level access throughout. Walk to the village pub for good food. 2 miles from Boston, ideally located for Fens, Wolds and coast. ETC 4/5 Stars Gold Award.
e-mail carol@elmsfarmcottages.co.uk   website: www.elmsfarmcottages.co.uk

Gainsborough

Market town and River Port 15 miles NW of Lincoln.

THE BLACK SWAN GUEST HOUSE, 21 HIGH STREET, MARTON, GAINSBOROUGH DN21 5AH (01427 718878). Former 18th Century Coaching Inn, providing very comfortable accommodation. All rooms en suite, with digital TV and tea/coffee making facilities. Lincoln 12 miles away, many other attractions nearby. Non-smoking. AA ★★★★ [🐾]
e-mail: info@blackswanguesthouse.co.uk   website:www.blackswanguesthouse.co.uk

Grantham

Market town 24 miles south of Lincoln.

WOODLAND WATERS, WILLOUGHBY ROAD, ANCASTER, GRANTHAM NG32 3RT (Tel & Fax: 01400 230888). Set in 72 acres of beautiful woodland walks. Luxury holiday lodges, overlooking the lakes and excellently equipped. Dogs welcome in some lodges. Bar/restaurant on site. Fishing. Golf nearby. Short Breaks available. Open all year. [Pets £1 per night camping, £20 per week lodges.]
e-mail: info@woodlandwaters.co.uk   website: www.woodlandwaters.co.uk

Horncastle

Market town on banks of Rivers Waring and Bain noted for its many antique shops.

POACHERS HIDEAWAY HOLIDAY COTTAGES, FLINTWOOD FARM, BELCHFORD, HORNCASTLE LN9 5QN (01507 533555). Sleep 2-24. Gold award-winning self catering cottages set in 150 acres of wildflower meadows, fishing lakes and woodland. Jacuzzi and Therapies available. Linen and towels provided. Kennels available. ETC 4-5 Stars [Pets £10 per week]
e-mail: info@poachershideaway.com   website: www.poachershideaway.com

LITTLE LONDON COTTAGES, TETFORD, HORNCASTLE. Very well-equipped property standing in own garden, on our small estate. Lovely walks. Special offers. ETC ★★★★. Contact: MRS S.D. SUTCLIFFE, THE GARTH, LITTLE LONDON, TETFORD, HORNCASTLE LN9 6QL (01507 533697; mobile: 07767 321213). [🐾]
e-mail: debbie@sutcliffe11.freeserve.co.uk   website: www.littlelondoncottages.co.uk

Langton-by-Wragby

Village located south-east of Wragby.

MISS JESSIE SKELLERN, LEA HOLME, LANGTON-BY-WRAGBY, LINCOLN LN8 5PZ (01673 858339). Ground floor accommodation in chalet-type house. Central for Wolds, coast, fens, historic Lincoln. Market towns, Louth, Horncastle, Boston, Spilsby, Alford, Woodhall Spa. Two double bedrooms. Washbasin, TV; bathroom, toilet adjoining; lounge with colour TV, separate dining room. Drinks provided. Children welcome reduced rates. Car almost essential, parking. Numerous eating places nearby. B&B from £30 per person (double/single let). Open all year. Pets welcome free. Tourist Board Listed [🐾]

Louth

Quaint market town with old fashioned architecture. Knwn as the 'Capital of the Lincolnshire Wolds'. 26 miles from Lincoln.

GRASSWELLS FARM HOLIDAY COTTAGES, SOUTH COCKERINGTON, LOUTH. Two single barn conversions - spacious, comfortable and well equipped. Set in three acres of grounds with private fishing lake. Pets welcome. Sleep 2-5. ETC ★★★★ Contact: MS J. FOSTER, GRASSWELLS HOLIDAY COTTAGES (SADDLEBACK LEISURE LTD), SADDLEBACK ROAD, HOWDALES, SOUTH COCKERINGTON, LOUTH LN11 7DJ (01507 338508). [🐾]
website: www.grasswells.co.uk

BRACKENBOROUGH HALL COACH HOUSE HOLIDAYS. Winner: Best Self-Catering Holiday in England 2009, Silver Award. Three self-catering apartments in a listed 18thC Coach House in the beautiful county of Lincolnshire. Accommodates 1-24. Short Breaks available. PAUL & FLORA BENNETT, BRACKENBOROUGH HALL, LOUTH LN11 0NS (Tel/Fax: 01507 603193). ★★★★/ ★★★★★ [Pets £10 per dog]
e-mail: PaulandFlora@BrackenboroughHall.com　　　website: www.BrackenboroughHall.com

WESTFIELD FARM SELF-CATERING HOLIDAY COTTAGES, STEWTON, LOUTH LN11 8SD(01507 354892 or 07885 280787). One, two and three bedroom converted cottages, sleeping 2, 4 or 6 people. Set in open countryside, just 2 miles from Louth. Open all year, short breaks available. ETC★★★/★★★★.
website: www.westfieldfarmcottages.co.uk

CANAL FARM COTTAGES, AUSTEN FEN, GRAINTHORPE, LOUTH LN11 0NX (01472 388825). Three self-catering cottages which have been converted to offer comfortable and well equipped holiday accommodation. Sleep 2/5. One cottage suitable for guests with limited mobility. [Pets £15 per week] ETC ★★★★
e-mail: r-ma@canalfarmcottages.co.uk　　　　website: www.canalfarmcottages.co.uk

Mablethorpe

Coastal resort 11 miles from Louth.

MRS GRAVES, GRANGE FARM, MALTBY-LE-MARSH, ALFORD LN13 0JP (01507 450267). Farmhouse B&B and self-catering country cottages set in15 idyllic acres of Lincolnshire countryside. 2 miles from beach. Peaceful base for leisure, walking and sightseeing. Two private fishing lakes. Many farm animals. Brochure available. [Pets £5 per night B&B, £30 per week in cottages, ⌂]
website: www.grange-farmhouse.co.uk

North Somercotes

Large coastal village in the Marshes area.

THREE LUXURY 4-STAR COTTAGES, LINCOLNSHIRE COAST. On a quiet lane leading to the sea, an ideal holiday home for people who want the best modern comforts, the calm of the Lincolnshire coast,and plenty to see and do nearby. Each has 2 double bedrooms, sleeps 4/5. (01507 358256/07724 76434) . EnjoyEngland ★★★★.
e-mail: nurserycottage@hotmail.co.uk   website: www.mealsfarm.com

Skegness

Coastal resort 19 miles north east of Boston.

THE CHESTNUTS, WAINFLEET ROAD, BURGH LE MARSH PE24 5AH (Tel & Fax: 01754 810904) Farm and Country Cottages with private fishing on a real farm, only 5 miles from Skegness. Cottages have private fishing waters. Children's play area, farm animals. Brochure available.
e-mail: macka@freenetname.co.uk   website: thechestnutsfarm.co.uk

Northamptonshire
Long Buckby

Long Buckby

Village 5 miles north east of Daventry.

MURCOTT MILL FARMHOUSE, MURCOTT, LONG BUCKBY NN6 7QR (01327 842236). Beautiful Georgian mill house, all rooms well appointed. Friendly, animal-loving hosts. Delicious farmhouse breakfast. Off road, quiet, plenty of walks. ETC ★★★★ [🐾]
e-mail: carrie.murcottmill@virgin.net   website: www.murcottmill.com

A useful index of towns/counties appears on pages 455-461

Please mention PETS WELCOME!
when making enquiries about accommodation featured in this guide

Nottinghamshire

Burton Joyce

Residential area 4 miles north-east of Nottingham.

MRS V. BAKER, WILLOW HOUSE, BURTON JOYCE, NOTTINGHAMSHIRE NG14 5FD (0115 931 2070 or 07816 347706). Victorian house, authentically furnished, in quiet village near beautiful stretch of River Trent. Four miles city. Close to station/bus stop. Bright, clean rooms. TV. En suite. Parking. From £26pppn. Good local eating. Please phone first for directions. [🐾] website: www.willowhousebedandbreakfast.co.uk

Shropshire
Bridgnorth, Burford, Church Stretton

Bridgnorth

Town on cliff above River Severn.

THE GRANARY, THE OLD VICARAGE, DITTON PRIORS, BRIDGNORTH WV16 6SP (01746 712272; Fax: 01746 712288) Early 19th century Granary in hill country. Sleeps two/four with view over farmland. Antique furniture complements surroundings. Excellent walking, cycling. Pets welcome. Contact MRS S. ALLEN. VisitBritain ★★★. [🐾]
  e-mail: allens@oldvicditton.freeserve.co.uk   website: www.stmem.com/thegranary

Burford

Small village to the north of the River Teme. Many NT properties in the area.

MARGARET ANDERSON, HARPFIELDS HOP-KILN, BURFORD, TENBURY WELLS WR15 8HP (01584 810099 or 01584 811298). Unusual converted Victorian building in unspoilt countryside. Perfect for a rural self-catering holiday in a traditional farmyard setting. Sleeps 4. EnjoyEngland ★★★★.[🐾]
  e-mail: janderson117@btinternet.com   website: www.harpfields-hopkiln.co.uk

Church Stretton

Delightful little town in lee of Shropshire Hills. Walking and riding country. Facilities for tennis, bowls, gliding and golf. Knighton 22 miles, Bridgnorth 19, Ludlow 15, Shrewsbury 12.

THE LONGMYND HOTEL, CHURCH STRETTON SY6 6AG (01694 722244). In 10 acre grounds, with sweeping views over Welsh border country. Outdoor pool, pitch-and-putt, sauna. Excellent and varied cuisine. Self-catering lodges in grounds. AA ★★★ [Pets £6 per night].
  e-mail: info@longmynd.co.uk   website: www.longmynd.co.uk

MRS C.F. BRANDON-LODGE, NORTH HILL FARM, CARDINGTON, CHURCH STRETTON SY6 7LL (01694 771532). Rooms with a view! B&B in beautiful Shropshire hills. TV in rooms, tea etc. Ideal walking country. From £28 per person; en suite available. AA ★★★★ [pw! Pets £2 per night, 🏠]
  e-mail: cbrandon@btinternet.com   website: www.virtual-shropshire.co.uk/northhill/

Craven Arms

Surrounded by hills, Craven Arms is home to the Shropshire Hills Discovery Centre where you can experience virtual balloon rides and meet the "hairy mammoth". Beautiful Stokesey Castle lies just outside the town. Ludlow 6½ miles, Shrewsbury 19 miles.

Two modern static caravans, each sleeps 6. Pets and children welcome; horses also accommodated. Open Easter to October. Also campsite for all types of unit. THE ANCHORAGE, ANCHOR, NEWCASTLE ON CLUN, CRAVEN ARMS SY7 8PR (01686 670737). [🐾].
  e-mail: nancynewcwm@btinternet.com   website: www.adamsanchor.co.uk

Ludlow

Lovely and historic town on Rivers Teme and Corve with numerous old half-timbered houses and inns. Worcester 29 miles, Shrewsbury 27, Hereford 24, Bridgnorth 19, Church Stretton 16.

CLIVE & CYNTHIA PRIOR, MOCKTREE BARNS, LEINTWARDINE, LUDLOW SY7 0LY (01547 540441). Gold Award winning self-catering cottages around a sunny courtyard. Sleep 2-6. Comfortable, well-equipped. Friendly owners. Dogs and children welcome. Non-smoking. Lovely country walks. Ludlow, seven miles. Brochure. NAS Level 1 Accessibility. VB ★★★ [🐾] See also colour advertisement page 242.
e-mail: mocktreebarns@care4free.net　　　　website: www.mocktreeholidays.co.uk

SIR HENRY SIDNEY APARTMENT, LUDLOW CASTLE. Superbly renovated apartment, full of charm and character. Sitting/dining room, two twin bedrooms with en suite bathrooms. Parking space in the heart of Ludlow. A unique opportunity to reside within the walls of Ludlow Castle. Open all year. 01584 87446 for full colour brochure. EnjoyEngland★★★★★ *SELF CATERING.* [Pets £4 per night].
e-mail: info@ludlowcastle.com　　　　website: www.castle-accommodation.com

SALLY AND TIM LOFT, GOOSEFOOT BARN, PINSTONES, DIDDLEBURY, CRAVEN ARMS, SHROPSHIRE SY7 9LB (01584 861326). Four delightful cottages thoughtfully converted and equipped to the highest standard. All with en suite facilities and garden or seating area. One cottage with disabled access. Situated in a secluded valley and ideally located to explore the beautiful South Shropshire countryside. Sleep 2-6. ETC ★★★★ [🐾]
e-mail: info@goosefootbarn.co.uk　　　　website: www.goosefootbarn.co.uk

THE MOOR HALL, NEAR LUDLOW SY8 3EG (01584 823209). Built in 1789, a splendid example of the Georgian Palladian style. Breathtaking views, 5-acre garden. B&B from £30 pppn. AA ★★★★ [🐾]
e-mail: info@moorhall.co.uk　　　　website: www.moorhall.co.uk

Oswestry

Borderland market town. Many old castles and fortifications. Shrewsbury 16, Vyrnwy 18.

PEN-Y-DYFFRYN COUNTRY HOTEL, NEAR RHYDYCROESAU, OSWESTRY SY10 7JD (01691 653700). Picturesque Georgian Rectory quietly set in Shropshire/ Welsh Hills. 12 en suite bedrooms, four with private patios. 5-acre grounds. No passing traffic. Johansens recommended. Dinner, Bed and Breakfast from £92 per person per day. AA ★★★. [🐾 pw!]
e-mail: stay@peny.co.uk　　　　website: www.peny.co.uk

Shrewsbury

Fine Tudor town with many beautiful black and white timber buildings, Abbey and Castle. Riverside walks, Quarry Park and Dingle flower gardens. 39 miles north-west of Birmingham.

ELIZABETH DAWSON, BRIMFORD HOUSE, CRIGGION, SHREWSBURY SY5 9AU (01938 570235) An elegant Georgian farm house set in the beautiful tranquil Welsh/Shropshire countryside between Shrewsbury and Welshpool. Country pub 3 minutes walk. Three en suite bedrooms AA ★★★★ Highly Commended. [🐾]
e-mail: info@brimford.co.uk　　　　website: www.brimford.co.uk

🐾　Pets are welcome free of charge.

£　A charge is made for pets: nightly or weekly.

pw!　Special provision for pets; exercise facility, feeding or accommodation arrangement.

⌂　Separate pets accommodation.

Classified Symbols

Leek

Busy market town in Staffordshire Moorlands on edge of Peak District.

THE HOLLYBUSH INN, DENFORD ROAD, DENFORD, LEEK ST13 7JT (01538 371819). A 17th century former corn mill, a favourite with people cruising the Caldon Canal. A good selection of beers, wines and ales. Food available seven days a week, prepared using fresh, locally sourced produce whenever possible. Pets welcome.

EDITH & ALWYN MYCOCK, ROSEWOOD COTTAGE, LOWER BERKHAMSYTCH FARM, BOTTOM HOUSE, NEAR LEEK ST13 7QP (Tel & Fax: 01538 308213). Cosy three bedroomed cottage with four-poster, sleeps six. Fully equipped and carpeted. Electricity and linen inclusive, laundry room. Ideal base for Alton Towers, Potteries and Peak District. Terms £230 to £375. [Pets £7.50 per week] website: www.rosewoodcottage.co.uk

THE BOTHY, RUDYARD LAKE. Sleeps 5. Fully equipped, two-bedroom cottage set in its own gardens with waterfront terrace, private pontoon and fishing and boating rights. Find out more by calling 07957 856629 or 01565 633636. EnjoyEngland ★★★★. website: www.thebothy-rudyard.co.uk

Stafford

Town on River Sow, 14 miles south of Stoke-on-Trent.

MRS N. ROBINSON, WYNDALE GUEST HOUSE, 199 CORPORATION STREET, STAFFORD ST16 3LQ (01785 223069). Comfortable Victorian Guest House situated quarter mile from Stafford town centre and 3 miles from County Showground. Small nature reserve across the road ideal for dog walking. ETC ★★★ [🐾]
e-mail: wyndale@aol.com   website: www.wyndaleguesthouse.co.uk

Tutbury

Village 4 miles north west of Burton-Upon-Trent. Ruins of 14c castle.

LITTLE PARK HOLIDAY HOMES, PARK LANE, TUTBURY, NEAR BURTON-ON-TRENT DE13 9JQ (Tel & Fax: 01283 812654; Mobile: 07884 343460). Barn Conversion Units. Full self-catering. Facilities situated near to medieval castle and tourist village. Spectacular views. Near Alton Towers and other theme parks. Ample parking. Please phone for brochure. [🐾]

CLIFTON CRUISERS, CLIFTON WHARF, CLIFTON, RUGBY, WARWICKSHIRE CV23 0EY (01788 543570; Fax: 01788 579799). Varied choice of boat layouts and accommodation to satisfy the requirements of most family and holiday groups (sleeping 2-8). Starting base centrally situated on the waterway network. [🐕]
e-mail: info@cliftoncruisers.com　　　　　　website: www.cliftoncruisers.com

Leamington Spa

Spa town on River Leam, 8 miles South of Coventry.

MRS HARRISON, BUBBENHALL HOUSE, PAGET'S LANE, BUBBENHALL CV8 3BJ. (Tel/Fax: 02476 302409). A charming country house offering superior bed and breakfast accommodation, located in the heart of Warwickshire, between Royal Leamington Spa and Coventry. Pet friendly. AA ★★★★ [🐕]
e-mail: wharrison@bubbenhallhouse.freeserve.co.uk　　website: www.bubbenhallhouse.com

Stratford-Upon-Avon

Historic town famous as Shakespeare's birthplace and home. Birmingham 24, Warwick 8 miles.

RIVERSIDE CARAVAN PARK, TIDDINGTON ROAD, STRATFORD-UPON-AVON CV37 7BE (01789 292312). Luxury Caravans, sleep 6. Fully equipped kitchens, bathroom/ shower/WC. Also two riverside Cottages, all modern facilities to first-class standards. Private fishing. On banks of River Avon. [Pets £15 weekly.]
e-mail: riverside@stratfordcaravans.co.uk　　website: www.stratfordcaravans.co.uk

Warwick

Town on the River Avon, 9 miles south-west of Coventry, with medieval castle and many fine old buildings.

DAVID & PATRICIA CLAPP, CROFT GUESTHOUSE, HASELEY KNOB, WARWICK CV35 7NL (Tel & Fax: 01926 484 447). All bedrooms en suite or with private bathroom, some ground floor. Non-smoking. Picturesque rural setting. Central for NEC, Warwick, Stratford, Stoneleigh and Coventry. B&B single £40, double/twin £60. ETC/AA ★★★★ [Dogs £3 per night]
e-mail: david@croftguesthouse.co.uk　　　　website: www.croftguesthouse.co.uk

🐕　Pets are welcome free of charge.　**Classified Symbols**

£　A charge is made for pets: nightly or weekly.

pw!　Special provision for pets; exercise facility, feeding or accommodation arrangement.

⌂　Separate pets accommodation.

Bishop's Frome, Droitwich, Great Malvern

Great Malvern, Malvern, Tenbury Wells

Please mention PETS WELCOME!
when making enquiries about accommodation featured in this guide

Bishop's Frome

Village 4 miles south of Bromyard.

FIVE BRIDGES COTTAGES, NEAR BISHOP'S FROME, WORCESTER WR6 5BX (01531 640340). Nestled in the heart of the Herefordshire cider apple and hop growing regions, the cottages are set within the owner's 4-acre garden and smallholding. [pw!]
e-mail: info@fivebridgescottages.co.uk   website: www.fivebridgescottages.co.uk

Droitwich

Town 6 miles north east of Worcester. Former spa status due to saline springs.

MRS SALLI HARRISON, MIDDLETON GRANGE, SALWARPE, DROITWICH SPA WR9 0AH (01905 451678). Traditional 18th century country house surrounded by picturesque gardens. Children welcome. Well behaved pets welcome; dog sitting available. All rooms en suite. M5 motorway six minutes. Worcester 10 minutes. [🐾].
e-mail: salli@middletongrange.com   website: www.middletongrange.com

Great Malvern

The historical centre of the town of Malvern, famous for its large priory, dating from the 11thC.

WHITEWELLS FARM COTTAGES, RIDGEWAY CROSS, NEAR MALVERN WR13 5JR (01886 880607; Fax: 01886 880607). Charming converted Cottages, sleep 2–6. Fully equipped with colour TV, microwave, barbecue, fridge, iron, etc. Linen, towels also supplied. One cottage suitable for the disabled with full wheelchair access. Short breaks, long lets, large groups. ETC ★★★★ [pw! Pets £10 per week.] Also see Display Advert. Contact: DENIS KAVANAGH.
e-mail: info@whitewellsfarm.co.uk   website: www.whitewellsfarm.co.uk

HARMONY HOUSE, 184 WEST MALVERN ROAD, MALVERN WR14 4AZ (01684 891650). On the western side of the Malvern Hills. Wonderful views, breakfast tailored to your specific desires, and three spacious en suite bedrooms. Non-smoking. Well behaved dogs welcome. [🐾]
e-mail: Catherine@HarmonyHouseMalvern.com   website: www.HarmonyHouseMalvern.com

Malvern

Victorian spa town, now a busy shopping centre and home to an annual music festival.

MALVERN HILLS HOTEL, WYNDS POINT, MALVERN WR13 6DW (01684 540690). Enchanting family-owned and run hotel nestling high in the hills. Direct access to superb walking with magnificent views. Oak-panelled lounge, log fire, real ales, fine food and friendly staff. Great animal lovers. AA ★★★ [Pets £5 per night].
website: www.malvernhillshotel.co.uk

Pirton

Midway between Worcester and Pershore.

PIRTON HOUSE FARM, PIRTON, WORCESTER WR8 9EJ (01905 820728). Set in tranquil countryside, this 19th century farmhouse offers an away from it all break. Two double rooms. Children, dogs and horses welcome. Lots of footpaths. Close to Malvern Showground. [🐎]
e-mail: info@pirtonhousefarm.com   website: www.pirtonhousefarm.com

Tenbury Wells

Market town on the south bank of the River Teme which forms the border between Shropshire and Worcestershire.

LONG COVER COTTAGE & THE COACH HOUSE. Two properties with a home-from-home feel. Long Cover Cottage has three double rooms and sleeps 6. Coach House is open plan and sleeps 2. Acres of outdoor space. ETC ★★★★. For details contact: FISHPOOL COTTAGE, KYRE, TENBURY WELLS WR15 8RL (01885 410208).
e-mail: ellie_vanstraaten@yahoo.co.uk   website: www.a-country-break.co.uk

Worcester

Cathedral city on River Severn, 24 miles south-west of Birmingham.

MOSELEY FARM BED & BREAKFAST, MOSELEY ROAD, HALLOW, WORCESTER WR2 6NL (01905 641343).17th Century former farmhouse with large enclosed garden. Rural location, 4 miles from Worcester. Full English Breakfast or Room only. Three family (two en suite) and one twin room, all with Freeview TV, radio alarm clock, tea/coffee making facilities and free Wi-Fi access. Off-road parking. 20 minutes drive from M5, J5 or J7. From £25pppn. [pw! 🐎]
e-mail: moseleyfarmbandb@aol.com   website: www.moseleyfarmbandb.co.uk

Hornsea, Howden, Kilnwick Percy

Beverley

Popular medieval market and county town in the East Riding of Yorkshire, 8 miles from Kingston upon Hull, 10 miles from Market Weighton and 12 from Hornsea.

ROBEANNE HOUSE, DRIFFIELD LANE, SHIPTONTHORPE, YORK YO43 3PW (01430 873312). Family B&B, country location, 18 miles from historic York. Ideal for coast, Moors, racing, Beverley, Cycle Route 66 and Wolds Way. Beautiful country house and gardens. All rooms en suite. Contact: JEANNE WILSON. AA ★★★ [pw! Pets £5 per night]
e-mail: enquiries@robeannehouse.co.uk   website: www.robeannehouse.co.uk

HOLME WOLD COTTAGE, HOLME ON THE WOLDS, NEAR BEVERLEY HU17 7PX (01430 810535). A three bedroom holiday cottage on working arable farm. Views over the Yorkshire Wolds. Large garden with patio area. Within easy reach of the coast, towns and cities; close to the Wolds Way for walking or cycling holidays. ETC ★★★★ [Pets £3 per night]
e-mail: info@yorkshirewoldscottage.co.uk   website: www.yorkshirewoldscottage.co.uk

Bridlington

Traditional family resort with picturesque harbour and a wide range of entertainments and leisure facilities. Ideal for exploring the Heritage coastline and the Wolds.

THE TENNYSON, 19 TENNYSON AVENUE, BRIDLINGTON YO15 2EU (01262 604382). Friendly, good quality guest house offering spacious en suite rooms. Ground floor room available. Non-smoking. Evening meals by arrangement. An easy walk to town centre, North Beach and cliff walks. B&B from £25pppn. AA ★★★ [Pets £5 per stay].
website: www.thetennyson-brid.co.uk

Driffield

Town 11 miles south west of Bridlington.

OLD COBBLER'S COTTAGE, NORTH DALTON. Pretty cottage with garden looking over village mere with ducks and fish. Good walking area and easy access to York and coast. Open fire. Local pub serving real ale and good food within 20 yards. Short breaks available. For details contact (01377 219901/217523 or 07801 124264). ETC ★★★ [🐾]
e-mail: chris.wade@adastra-music.co.uk   website: www.waterfrontcottages.co.uk

Flamborough

Village 4 miles NE of Bridlington.

THORNWICK & SEA FARM HOLIDAY CENTRE, FLAMBOROUGH YO15 1AU (01262 850369). Set on the spectacular Heritage Coast with unrivalled coastal scenery. Six-berth caravans and chalets for hire. Tents and tourers welcome. Bars, entertainment, shop, pool and gym on site. ETC ★★★★, David Bellamy Silver Award. [Pets £10 per week.]
e-mail: enquiries@thornwickbay.co.uk   website: www.thornwickbay.co.uk

Grindale

Rural hamlet 4 miles from Bridlington. Ideal for touring Wolds, moors and coast.

SMITHY COTTAGE, GRINDALE YO16 4XU (01904 448933). Unique and charming four-star rated detached single storey 200-year-old former Blacksmiths. Ideal for exploring Heritage Coast. Four-poster bed, log fire, restored to high standard. Parking. Sleeps 4.
e-mail karen.coman@virgin.net   website: www.thesmithy.info

Hornsea

Coastal resort 14 miles NE of Hull.

CHERRY TREE, HORNSEA. Cosy well appointed holiday bungalow in quiet cul-de-sac off town centre. Fully equipped. Large conservatory. Open all year. Contact: MRS RITA LEONARD, COWDEN PARVA FARM, MAIN ROAD, COWDEN, ALDBROUGH HU11 4UG (01964 527245; Fax: 01964 527521). Visit Britain ★★★. [Pets £10 per week]
e-mail: leonardritaruth@yahoo.co.uk   website: www.cherrytreeyorkshire.co.uk

Howden

Small town 3 miles North of Goole.

VIVIENNE & JOHN SWEETING, APPLE TREE COTTAGES, THE DAIRY FARM, SALTMARSHE, HOWDEN DN14 7RX. (01430 430 677; Mobile: 07960 300 337). Two self-catering Cottages or Farmhouse B&B on a Yorkshire family farm. A wonderful stay in friendly, well appointed comfortable surroundings. [Pets £5 per night]
e-mail: vivienne.sweeting@btinternet.com   website: www.appletree-cottages.co.uk

Kilnwick Percy

Located 2 miles east of Pocklington

PAWS-A-WHILE, KILNWICK PERCY, POCKLINGTON YO42 1UF (01759 301168; Mobile: 07711 866869). Small family B & B set in forty acres of parkland twixt York and Beverley. Golf, walking, riding. Pets and horses most welcome. Brochure available. ETC ★★★★ [pw! 🐾]
e-mail: paws.a.while@lineone.net   website: www.pawsawhile.net
                                        www.dickyphotos.com

Terms quoted in this publication may be subject to increase if rises in costs necessitate

Bentham, Carperby, Clapham, Coverdale

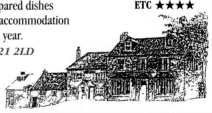

FHG Guides publish a large range of well-known
accommodation guides. We will be happy to send you details or
you can use the order form at the back of this book.

Valley View Farm Cottages

Old Byland, Helmsley YO62 5LG
Tel: 01439 798221
Fax: 01439 798477

enjoyEngland.com
★★★★
SELF CATERING

HOLIDAY COTTAGES

Our six cottages, sleeping 2-10 are
situated on a working farm within the
scenic countryside of the
North Yorkshire Moors National Park,
close to Rievaulx Abbey and five miles
from the delightful market town of
Helmsley. Enjoy rural peace and
tranquillity in an ideal location for
exploring Yorkshire.
- Private parking.
- Good walking area.
- Choice of cottages for 2.
- Short breaks are offered, subject
  to availability.
- Dogs welcome by arrangement.
- Optional on-line booking.

e-mail: sally@valleyviewfarm.com
www.valleyviewfarm.com

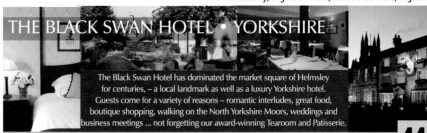

Kirkbymoorside, Knaresborough, Leyburn, Malham, Northallerton, Nunthorpe

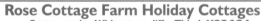

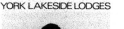

York

Bentham

Quiet village amidst the fells. Good centre for rambling and fishing. Ingleton 5 miles north-east.

MRS L. J. STORY, HOLMES FARM, LOW BENTHAM, LANCASTER LA2 7DE (015242 61198). Cottage conversion in easy reach of Dales, Lake District and coast. Central heating, fridge, TV, washer, games room. ETC ★★★★. [🐾]
e-mail: lucy@holmesfarmcottage.co.uk   website: www.holmesfarmcottage.co.uk

Carperby

Village one mile North of Aysgarth.

THE WHEATSHEAF, CARPERBY, NEAR LEYBURN DL8 4DF (01969 663216; Fax: 01969 663019) Excellent en suite accommodation in 12 bedrooms (including four posters), at this comfortable family-owned hotel offering the best of local cuisine and comfort. [Pets £5 per week].
e-mail: info@wheatsheafinwensleydale.co.uk   website: www.wheatsheafinwensleydale.co.uk

Clapham

Village 6 miles NW of Settle.

NEW INN, CLAPHAM, NEAR INGLETON LA2 8HH (015242 51203; Fax: 015242 51824). 'As relaxed as you like'. A comfortable hotel in the Yorkshire Dales National Park. The ideal holiday destination for your pet, be assured of a warm and friendly reception, sit back, close your eyes and soak up the history and atmosphere. ETC ★★ [Pets £5 per night]
e-mail: info@newinn-clapham.co.uk   website: www.newinn-clapham.co.uk

Coverdale

Located in the Yorkshire Dales National Park, famous for Middleham Castle, Richard III and the Forbidden Corner..

MRS JULIE CLARKE, MIDDLE FARM, WOODALE, COVERDALE, LEYBURN DL8 4TY (01969 640271). Peacefully situated farmhouse away from the madding crowd. B&B with optional Evening Meal. Home cooking. Pets sleep where you prefer. Ideally positioned for exploring the beautiful Yorkshire Dales. [🐾 pw!]
e-mail: j-a-clarke@hotmail.co.uk

Danby

Village on River Esk 12 miles west of Whitby.

THE FOX & HOUNDS INN, AINTHORPE, DANBY YO21 2LD (01287 660218). Residential country pub and restaurant. All rooms en suite. Enjoy our real ales or quality selected wines. Freshly prepared food served every day. Open all year. ETC ★★★★ Inn [Pets £2.75 per night.]
e-mail: info@foxandhounds-ainthorpe.com   website: www.foxandhounds-ainthorpe.com

Goathland

Small village high on the North York Moors, famous as the village of Aidensfield in the TV series "Heartbeat".

EMMA BRICE, ROSE COTTAGE B&B, GOATHLAND YO22 5AN (01947 896253; Mobile: 07920 474321). One of the most beautiful cottages in the North Yorkshire Moors. Good location for walks and local amenities. Pets allowed. Non smoking. Private parking. Beauty Treatments available. [🐾]
e-mail: emmabrice@rosecottage-heartbeat.com   website: www.rosecottage-heartbeat.com

Grassington

Wharfedale village in attractive moorland setting. Ripon 22 miles, Skipton 9.

FORESTERS ARMS, MAIN STREET, GRASSINGTON, SKIPTON BD23 5AA (01756 752349). The Foresters Arms is situated in the heart of the Yorkshire Dales and provides an ideal centre for walking or touring. Within easy reach of York and Harrogate. ETC ★★★ [🐾]
e-mail: theforesters@totalise.co.uk   website: www.forestersarmsgrassington.co.uk

Harrogate

Charming and elegant spa town set amid some of Britain's most scenic countryside. Ideal for exploring Herriot Country and the moors and dales. York 22 miles, Bradford 19, Leeds 16.

ALEXA HOUSE, 26 RIPON ROAD, HARROGATE HG1 2JJ (01423 501988). Harrogate's only 4 Star Highly Commended guest accommodation. Private parking, licensed bar, Wi-Fi. Short stroll to town. AA ★★★★ Highly Commended. [🐾]
e-mail: enquires@alexa-house.co.uk   website: www.alexa-house.co.uk

ROSEMARY HELME, HELME PASTURE LODGES & COTTAGES, OLD SPRING WOOD, HARTWITH BANK, SUMMERBRIDGE, HARROGATE HG3 4DR (01423 780279). Country accommodation for owners and dogs and numerous walks in unspoilt Nidderdale. Central for Harrogate, York, Herriot and Bronte country. National Trust area. ETC ★★★★, ETC Category 1 for Disabled Access. [pw! Pets £5 per night, £25 per week; some free.]
e-mail: info@helmepasture.co.uk   website: www.helmepasture.co.uk

SOUTHFIELD FARM HOLIDAY COTTAGES, DARLEY, HARROGATE HG3 2PR (01423 780258). Two well equipped holiday cottages between Harrogate and Pateley Bridge. Ideal for touring the Dales, with York within easy driving distance. Ample parking. Well behaved pets welcome. [🐾]
e-mail: info@southfieldcottages.co.uk   website: www.southfieldcottages.co.uk

THE COURTYARD AT DUKE'S PLACE, BISHOP THORNTON, NEAR HARROGATE HG3 3JY (01765 620229 or 07979 521960). In glorious Nidderdale, group of well maintained and equipped holiday cottages. Sleep 2/6; linen, fully equipped kitchens. Riding stables on site. B&B now available. Pets, horses and children most welcome. ETC ★★★/★★★★ [🐾]
e-mail: enquiries@dukesplace-courtyard.co.uk   website: www.dukesplace-courtyard.co.uk

RUDDING HOLIDAY PARK, FOLLIFOOT, HARROGATE HG3 1JH (01423 870439; Fax: 01423 870859). ★★★ cottages and lodges sleeping two to seven people. All equipped to a high standard. Pool, licensed bar, golf and children's playground in the Parkland. Illustrated brochure available. [£2.75 per dog]
e-mail: stay@ruddingpark.com   website: www.ruddingholidaypark.co.uk

Hawes

Small town in Wensleydale, 14 miles south east of Kirkby Stephen.

COUNTRY COTTAGE HOLIDAYS, DRYDEN HOUSE, MARKET PLACE, HAWES DL8 3RA (01969 667654). 80 cottages in the lovely Yorkshire Dales. Colour TV, central heating, open fires. Gardens, private parking. Many allow pets. Rents from £200 per week. Sleep 1-10. [Pets from £8 per week]
website: www.countrycottageholidays.co.uk

COCKLAKE HOUSE, MALLERSTANG CA17 4JT (017683 72080). Charming, High Pennine Country House B&B in unique position above Pendragon Castle in Upper Mallerstang Dale offering good food and exceptional comfort to a small number of guests. Two double rooms with large private bathrooms. Three acres riverside grounds. Dogs welcome. [🐾]

SIMONSTONE HALL, HAWES, WENSLEYDALE DL8 3LY (01969 667255; Fax: 01969 667741). Facing south across picturesque Wensleydale. All rooms en suite with colour TV. Fine cuisine. Extensive wine list. Friendly personal attention. A relaxing break away from it all. AA ★★ [Pets £10 per stay]
e-mail: enquiries@simonstonehall.com   website: www.simonstonehall.com

STONE HOUSE HOTEL, SEDBUSK, HAWES DL8 3PT (01969 667571). This fine Edwardian country house has spectacular views and serves delicious Yorkshire cooking with fine wines. Comfortable en suite bedrooms, some ground floor. Phone for details. [🐾]
website: www.stonehousehotel.co.uk

Helmsley

A delightful stone-built town on River Rye with a large cobbled square. Thirsk 12 miles.

JOHN & SALLY ROBINSON'S VALLEY VIEW FARM, OLD BYLAND, HELMSLEY, YORK YO62 5LG (01439 798221). Fully equipped self-catering cottages on working farm in North York Moors. Ideal for touring Yorkshire, or just walking the hills and lanes around. Rural peace and tranquillity. Dogs free. Kennel and run available. ETC ★★★★ [🐾]
e-mail: sally@valleyviewfarm.com   website: www.valleyviewfarm.com

THE BLACK SWAN HOTEL, MARKET PLACE, HELMSLEY YO62 5BJ (01439 770466). Luxury Yorkshire hotel in Helmsley market square. Romantic interludes, great food, boutique shopping, walking on the North Yorkshire Moors, weddings and business meetings. AA ★★★. [Pets £10 per stay]
e-mail: enquiries@blackswan-helmsley.co.uk   website: www.blackswan-helmsley.co.uk

SUE SMITH, LASKILL GRANGE, HAWNBY, NEAR HELMSLEY YO62 5NB (01439 798268). Delightful country house set in one-acre gardens; all rooms en suite. Generous cuisine of a high standard using fresh local produce, vegetarians catered for. Newly installed hot tubs. Open all year. Also 7 luxury self-catering cottages. ETC ★★★★ Silver Award, AA ★★★★.[🐾]
e-mail: laskillgrange@tiscali.co.uk   website: www.laskillgrange.co.uk

High Bentham

Small market town situated between the Yorkshire Dales and the Lake District.

MRS I. CARR, LOWTHER HILL CARAVAN PARK, HIGH BENTHAM LA2 7AN, (01524 261657). Small licensed site set in the Yorkshire Dales with uninterrupted panoramic views. Easy access to the Dales, coast and Lakes. Rally field and barn for use in wet weather. [🐾]
website: www.caravancampingsites.co.uk/northyorkshire/lowtherhill.htm

Hutton-Le-Hole

Small village about 7 miles north west of Pickering.

MOORLAND COTTAGES, HAMMER AND HAND HOUSE, HUTTON-LE-HOLE, YORK YO62 6UA (01751 417743). In a picturesque village location, three separate self catering cottages, fully equipped with all that you would require for your stay. Sleep 3-5. An ideal base for touring. [Pets £10 per week]
e-mail: moorlandcottages@btinternet.com   website: www.moorlandcottages.com

Ingleton

Small village in the heart of Three Peaks Country in the Yorkshire Dales.

JILL HOWARTH, GALE GREEN COTTAGE, INGLETON LA6 3NJ (015242 41245) A warm welcome, great food and superb scenery at our friendly B&B ideally located for all types of hill and mountain walking in one of England's natural beauty spots. Two double and one twin rooms, all en suite. Guest lounge. AA ★★★★. [🐾]
e-mail: jill@galegreen.com   website: www.galegreen.com

Kirkbymoorside

Small market town which lies approximately 25 miles north of York midway between Pickering and Helmsley.

MRS F. WILES, SINNINGTON COMMON FARM, KIRKBYMOORSIDE, YORK YO62 6NX (01751 431719). One and two bedroomed cottages (all en suite) situated in beautiful countryside. Many farmyard and rescue animals, horses and abundant wildlife. Pets welcome. [🐾]
e-mail: felicity@scfarm.demon.co.uk   website: www.sinningtoncommonfarm.co.uk

Knaresborough

Town on escarpment above the River Nidd, 3 miles NE of Harrogate..

NEWTON HOUSE, KNARESBOROUGH. Winner of the AA Pet Friendly Award – pets genuinely welcomed and lots of great walks nearby. Spacious and comfortable, newly refurbished ensuite accommodation and great breakfasts. AA ★★★★ Highly Commended, AA Breakfast Award. Contact MARK & LISA WILSON, NEWTON HOUSE, 5-7 YORK PLACE, KNARESBOROUGH HG5 OAD (Tel: 01423 863539). [🐾]
e-mail: newtonhouse@btinternet.com   website: www.newtonhouseyorkshire.com

Leyburn

Small market town, 8 miles south-west of Richmond, standing above the River Ure in Wensleydale.

BARBARA & BARRIE MARTIN, THE OLD STAR, WEST WITTON, LEYBURN DL8 4LU (01969 622949). Former 17th century Coaching Inn now run as a guest house. Oak beams, log fire, home cooking. En suite B&B from £28 pppn. ETC ★★★ [🐾]
e-mail: enquiries@theoldstar.com   website: www.theoldstar.com

Malham

Village in upper Airedale, 5 miles east of Settle, across the moors.

MR C. SHARP, MIRESFIELD FARM, MALHAM, SKIPTON BD23 4DA (01729 830414). In beautiful gardens bordering village green and stream. Excellent food. 11 bedrooms, all with private facilities. Full central heating. Two well-furnished lounges and conservatory. B&B from £24pppn. ETC ★★★ [🐾 pw!]

Northallerton

Town 14 miles South of Darlington.

JULIE & JIM GRIFFITH, HILL HOUSE FARM, LITTLE LANGTON, NORTHALLERTON DL7 0PZ (01609 770643). Sleep 2/4. Four well-equipped cottages, cosily heated for year round appeal. Centrally located between Dales and Moors. Weekly rates from £195 incl. Short breaks available. Golf 2 miles, shops 3 miles, pub food 1.5 miles. Pets welcome. VisitBritain ★★★★ [pw! 🐾]
e-mail: info@hillhousefarmcottages.com   website: www.hillhousefarmcottages.com

Nunthorpe

Between Middlesbrough and Stokesley, on edge of North York Moors National Park

BLACKTHORN GATE, EASTFIELDS FARM, NUNTHORPE TS7 0PB (01642 324496). Four luxury lodges, each with living room/dining room, fully equipped kitchen and two bedrooms; each also has own sauna. Sleep 4-6. On edge of North Yorks Moors National Park. Pets welcome in two lodges. ETC ★★★★
e-mail: info@blackthorngate.co.uk   website: www.blackthorngate.co.uk

A useful index of towns/counties appears on pages 455-461

Pickering

Pleasant market town on southern fringe of North York Moors National Park with moated Norman Castle. Bridlington 31 miles, Whitby 20, Scarborough 16, Helmsley 13, Malton 3.

THE WHITE SWAN INN AT PICKERING (01751 472288). 16th century inn with a buzz. Dog friendly with excellent: service, rooms, food and wine. "...consistently brilliant.." Please phone or visit our website for a brochure. ETC ★★★, AA Rosette [Pets £12.50 per stay].
e-mail: welcome@white-swan.co.uk   website: www.white-swan.co.uk

Port Mulgrave

Located 1km north of Hinderwell.

NORTH YORK MOORS NATIONAL PARK. Stone Cottage (sleeps) 4 in North York Moors National Park. Sea view, near Cleveland coastal footpath. Log fire, non-smoking. Whitby 9 miles. Brochure available (01642 613888). [🐾]

Scalby Nabs (Scarborough)

Small town and suburb 2 miles north west of Scarborough.

EAST FARM COUNTRY COTTAGES, SCALBY NABS, SCALBY, SCARBOROUGH (01723 353635). Three single-storey two-bedroom stone cottages (no steps/stairs) in national Park; only 5 minutes from Scarborough. All completely non-smoking. Ideal base for walking or touring. VisitBritain ★★★ [Pets from £10 per week.]
e-mail: joeastfarmcottages@hotmail.co.uk   website: www.eastfarmcountrycottages.co.uk

Scarborough

Very popular family resort with good sands. York 41 miles, Whitby 20, Bridlington 17, Filey 7.

SUE AND TONY HEWITT, HARMONY COUNTRY LODGE, LIMESTONE ROAD, BURNISTON, SCARBOROUGH YO13 0DG (0800 2985840). A peaceful retreat set in two acres of private grounds with 360° panoramic views of the National Park and sea. An ideal centre for walking or touring. En suite centrally heated rooms with superb views. Non-smoking, licensed, private parking facilities. B&B from £29.50 to £38. ETC ★★★★ [Pets £4 per night, £15 per week]
e-mail: mail@harmonylodge.net   website: www.harmonycountrylodge.co.uk

CAYTON VILLAGE CARAVAN PARK LTD, MILL LANE, CAYTON BAY, SCARBOROUGH YO11 3NN (01723 583171). Luxurious facilities, adventure playground, site shop, 4-acre floodlit dog walk. Seasonal pitches, supersites, hardstanding and storage. Open 1st March - 31st October. Half-a-mile to beach adjoining village. ETC ★★★★★, David Bellamy Gold Award. [Pets £1 per night].
e-mail: info@caytontouring.co.uk   website: www.caytontouring.co.uk

Skipton

Airedale market town, centre for picturesque Craven district. Fine Castle (14th cent). York 43 miles, Manchester 42, Leeds 26, Harrogate 22, Settle 16.

DEVONSHIRE ARMS COUNTRY HOUSE HOTEL & SPA, BOLTON ABBEY BD23 6AJ (01756 710441; Fax: 01756 710564). Luxury country house with a relaxed feel. Each bedroom individually decorated and designed. Overlooking Yorkshire Dales; surrounding area offers fishing, mountain biking, horse riding and walking. Dog Friendly Service. AA/Enjoy England ★★★★.
e-mail: reception@thedevonshirearms.co.uk   website: www.thedevonshirearms.co.uk

BECK HALL, MALHAM BD23 4DJ (01729 830332). 18th century B&B on the Pennine Way, log fires and huge breakfasts. Midweek and 4-night specials. Ideal for exploring the Yorkshire Dales. AA ★★★, WELCOME HOST [🐾]
e-mail: simon@beckhallmalham.com   website: www.beckhallmalham.com

CRAVEN HOUSE, 56 KEIGHLEY ROAD, SKIPTON BD23 2NB (01756 794657/07960 864916). Large terraced house with 7 bedrooms, sleeps up to 14. Suitable for large groups, extended families or just for the luxury of plenty of space! Dogs welcome by arrangement. Well equipped kitchen, dining room, lounge and cosy basement TV room. ETC ★★★★ [🐾]
e-mail: info@craven-house.co.uk   website: www.craven-house.co.uk

Over 250 super self-catering Cottages in the Yorkshire Dales, York, Coast, Moors, Lancashire, Peak and Lake District. For our fully illustrated brochure apply: HOLIDAY COTTAGES YORKSHIRE LTD (INCORPORATING RED ROSE COTTAGES), WATER STREET, SKIPTON BD23 1PB (01756 700872). [🐾]
website: www.holidaycotts.co.uk

THE CONISTON HOTEL, CONISTON COLD, SKIPTON BD23 4EA (01756 748080). Set in a stunning 1400-acre estate, an ideal base for guests wishing to explore the Yorkshire Dales. 50 en suite bedrooms with full facilities. Special rates for leisure breaks and family rooms. ETC ★★★ Silver Award, AA ★★★. [pw! Pets £10 per stay]
e-mail: info@theconistonhotel.com   website: www.theconistonhotel.com

Stainforth

Picturesque village in the Yorkshire Dales, 2½ miles from Settle.

2 HOLLIES COTTAGES. Traditional Dales 2-bedroom cottage situated in the Yorkshire Dales National Park. Sleeps 4. Open coal fire. Linen provided. Pets welcome. Contact: BRIDGE COTTAGE, STAINFORTH, NEAR SETTLE BD24 9PG (01729 822649). [🐾]
e-mail: vivmills30@hotmail.com   website: www.stainforth-holiday-cottage-settle.co.uk

Staithes

Fishing village on North Sea coast 9 miles NW of Whitby.

WAYCOT HOLIDAY COTTAGE (01947 841396). Character cottage sleeping 4 adjacent to our B&B. One double and one twin bedroom. Multi-fuel stove. No smoking. Children and pets welcome. Contact: MS M.J. HEALD, BROOKLYN B&B, BROWN'S TERRACE, STAITHES TS13 5BG [🐾]
e-mail: margaret@heald.org.uk   website: www.brooklynuk.co.uk

MS M.J. HEALD, BROOKLYN B&B, BROWN'S TERRACE, STAITHES TS13 5BG (01947 841396). Situated in the old part of picturesque and historic Staithes. Two double and one twin bedrooms available, generous breakfasts, vegetarians catered for. Pets and children most welcome. ETC ★★★ [🐾]
e-mail: margaret@heald.org.uk   website: www.brooklynuk.co.uk

PENNYSTEEL COTTAGE. Beamed and wood-panelled old fisherman's cottage located in the beautiful fishing village of Staithes. Breathtaking views from every room and from its sun terrace. One double, twin and single bedroom. CONTACT: CHRIS WADE, 2 STAR ROW, NORTH DALTON, DRIFFIELD YO25 9UX (01377 219901 day; 01377 217523 eve; 07801 124264). EnjoyEngland ★★★ [🐾]
e-mail:chris.wade@adastra-music.co.uk   website: www.waterfrontcottages.co.uk

Thirsk

Market town with attractive square. Excellent touring area. Northallerton 3 miles.

ROSE COTTAGE FARM HOLIDAY COTTAGES, SUTTON-UNDER-WHITESTONECLIFFE, THIRSK YO7 2QA (01845 597309). Self-catering holiday cottages with superb scenery and wonderful walking. Each sleeps two. All linen, towels, welcome pack and heating included. Shared patio area. Well behaved pets accepted by arrangement.
website: www.rose-cottage-farm.co.uk

FOXHILLS HIDEAWAYS, FELIXKIRK, THIRSK YO7 2DS (01845 537575). 4 Scandinavian log cabins, heated throughout, linen provided. A supremely relaxed atmosphere on the edge of the North York Moors National Park. Open all year. Village pub round the corner. [🐾]

POPLARS HOLIDAY COTTAGES AND BED & BREAKFAST, THIRSK. The Poplars stands in two acres of lovely gardens with a field for dog walking. We have brick cottages as well as log cabins, with bed and breakfast in the main house. Contact AMANDA RICHARDS, THE POPLARS, CARLTON MINIOTT, THIRSK YO7 4LX (01845 522712). ETC ★★★★, Silver Award. [Pets £5 per night B&B, £10 per week SC]
website: www.thepoplarsthirsk.com

Whitby

Charming resort with harbour and sands. Of note is the 13th century ruined Abbey. Stockton-on-Tees 34 miles, Scarborough 20, Saltburn-by-the-Sea 19.

THE SEACLIFFE HOTEL, 12 NORTH PROMENADE, WHITBY YO21 3JX (Freephone 0808 1682118). Magnificent seafront position overlooking beach and harbour entrance. Lovely scenic walks. Restaurant, bar, lounge, patio garden. Evening meals from £12.95: Lamb Shank to Fillet Steak, Whitby Scampi to Lobster. Private car park (8). Dogs by arrangement. See website for menus and special offers. VB ★★★★ Guest Accommodation [🐾]
e-mail: stay@seacliffehotel.com   website: www.seacliffehotel.com

WHITE ROSE HOLIDAY COTTAGES, NEAR WHITBY. Quality cottages and bungalows offering a warm and friendly welcome. Sleep 1-9. Private parking. Ideal for coast and country. APPLY: MRS J. ROBERTS (PW), 5 BROOK PARK, SLEIGHTS, NEAR WHITBY YO21 1RT (01947 810763) ETC ★★★-★★★★. [Pets £5 per week, pw!]
website: www.whiterosecottages.co.uk

BOLTHOLE COTTAGE, WALKERS YARD, CLIFF STREET, WHITBY. Secluded cottage offering lounge, modern kitchen, double bedroom. Gas and electricity incl. Central location for restaurants, museum, art gallery etc. An ideal location for touring the Whitby area. Pets welcome. Contact: MRS K.E. NOBLE, STORMVILLE, ROBIN HOOD'S BAY, WHITBY YO22 4RA (01947 880063; mobile: 07881 523141).
e-mail: enquiries@boltholecottage.co.uk   website: www.boltholecottage.co.uk

MR NEIL HARLAND, CLITHERBECKS FARM, DANBY YO21 2NT (01287 660321). Self catering accommodation for up to seven people in this traditional hill farmhouse. Near Danby and the National Parks Moors Centre. Own entrance. Open all year. VisitBritain ★★★.[🐾]
e-mail: enquiries@clitherbecks.co.uk   website: www.clitherbecks.co.uk

SWALLOW HOLIDAY COTTAGES. Discover historic Whitby, pretty fishing villages, way-marked walks. Four cottages, one or two bedrooms. Private parking. Children and dogs welcome. Weekly rates from £195 to £500. Please phone or write for a brochure. KARL HEYES, 15 BEECHFIELD, HIGH HAWSKER, WHITBY YO22 4LQ (07545 641943). [Pets: first free, second pet £20 per week].
e-mail: karl@swallowcottages.co.uk   website: www.swallowcottages.co.uk

RAVEN HALL COUNTRY HOUSE HOTEL, LODGES & GOLF COURSE, RAVENSCAR, SCARBOROUGH YO13 0ET (01723 870353; Fax: 01723 870072). This imposing hotel offers comfortable accommodation, superb cuisine and an impressive range of leisure facilities including a 9-hole golf course. A family holiday paradise. AA ★★★. Finnish Log Lodges also available. [pw! Pets £5 per night.]
e-mail: enquiries@ravenhall.co.uk   website: www.ravenhall.co.uk

York

Historic cathedral city and former Roman Station on River Ouse. Magnificent Minster and 3 miles of ancient walls. Facilities for a wide range of sports and entertainments. Horse-racing on Knavesmire. Bridlington 41 miles, Filey 41, Leeds 24, Harrogate 22.

HIGH BELTHORPE, BISHOP WILTON, YORK YO42 1SB (01759 368238; Mobile: 07786 923330). Set on an ancient moated site at the foot of the Yorkshire Wolds, this comfortable Victorian farmhouse offers huge breakfasts, private fishing and fabulous walks. Dogs and owners will love it! Open all year except Christmas. Prices from £25. ETC ★★★ [pw! 🐾]
e-mail: meg@highbelthorpe.co.uk

THE NEW INN MOTEL, MAIN STEEET, HUBY, YORK YO61 1HQ (01347 810219) Modern, motel-style accommodation in quiet location 9 miles north of York. Comfortable en suite bedrooms. Breakfast from locally sourced produce served in dining room. Pets by arrangement. [Pets £5 per night]
e-mail: enquiries@newinnmotel.freeserve.co.uk   website: www.newinnmotel.co.uk

ASCOT HOUSE, 80 EAST PARADE, YORK YO31 7YH (01904 426826; Fax: 01904 431077). Attractive Victorian villa with easy access to city centre. Family and double rooms en suite. Comfortable residents' lounge, dining room. Single room £60-£70, double room £68-£80. Free private enclosed car park. ETC/AA ★★★★, ETC Silver Award. [🐾]
e-mail: admin@ascothouseyork.com   website: www.ascothouseyork.com

YORK LAKESIDE LODGES, MOOR LANE, YORK YO24 2QU (01904 702346). Self-catering pine lodges. Mature parkland setting. Large fishing lake. Nearby superstore with coach to centre every 10 mins. ETC ★★★★/★★★★★ [pw! Pets £25 per week]
e-mail: neil@yorklakesidelodges.co.uk   website: www.lakesidelodges.co.uk

ST GEORGE'S, 6 ST GEORGE'S PLACE, YORK YO24 1DR (01904 625056). Family-run guest house in quiet cul-de-sac near racecourse. All rooms en suite with colour TV, tea/coffee making facilities. Private parking. Pets welcome by arrangement. £65 double or twin room. ETC/AA ★★★ [🐾]
e-mail: sixstgeorg@aol.com   website: www.stgeorgesyork.com

Bingley, Haworth, Ossett

Bingley

Town on River Aire 5 miles north-west of Bradford.

THE FIVE RISE LOCKS HOTEL & RESTAURANT, BECK LANE, BINGLEY BD16 4DD (01274 565296).
Large Victorian house in tranquil area, but close main roads, tourist sites. Good views, individual
decor, informal style. Historic canal locks and excellent walking (dogs and humans) close by. AA/
VisitBritain ★★★★ [Pets £5 per night]
e-mail: info@five-rise-locks.co.uk   website: www.five-rise-locks.co.uk

Haworth

Rural village located in the Pennines, 3 miles south west of Keighley and 10 miles west of Bradford in the heart of Bronte Country..

WESTFIELD LODGE (BRONTELAND) LIMITED, NEW WESTFIELD FARM, UPPER MARSH, OXEN-
HOPE, KEIGHLEY, BD22 9RH (07780 602524) Twenty high quality self-catering apartments that face
out onto the moors above Haworth. All come fully furnished with bedding, linen, towels, power,
water services, free satellite TV and Wi-Fi included in the price. Enjoy England ★★★ [pw! 🐕]
email: enquiry@westfield-lodge.co.uk   website:www.westfield-lodge.co.uk

Ossett

Market town situated halfway between Dewsbury and Wakefield.

HEATH HOUSE, CHANCERY ROAD, OSSETT WF5 9RZ (01924 260654). An elegant Victorian house
set in 4 acres; all rooms comfortably furnished with TV, tea/coffee tray. Breakfast freshly cooked to
order. Open all year. Easy drive to Leeds, Bradford and Dewsbury. AA ★★★★
e-mail: bookings@heath-house.co.uk   website: www.heath-house.co.uk

Barnard Castle

Named after the castle it was built around, 34 miles south of Newcastle upon Tyne. The Bowes Museum is a popular attraction.

LAVEROCK MULTI-DOG COTTAGES, BARNARD CASTLE (01833 650695). Two cottages each sleeping up to 5 people. Fantastic views on sheep farm, enclosed gardens, doggy shower room, 5-acre stock free field. 120 foot indoor Agility Building and sheepdog lessons on site. [pw! 1st 4 dogs free!! Small charge for 5+].
e-mail: comebyanaway@hotmail.com　　　　　website: www.multidogcottages.co.uk

Bishop Auckland

Town on right bank of River Wear, 9 miles south-west of Durham. Castle, of varying dates, residence of the Bishop of Durham.

ALISON & KEITH TALLENTIRE, LOW LANDS FARM, LOW LANDS, COCKFIELD, BISHOP AUCKLAND DL13 5AW (01388 718251; mobile: 07745 067754). Two self-catering cottages on a working livestock farm. Each sleeps up to 4, plus cot. Prices from £160-£360. Call for a brochure. Pets and children most welcome. ETC ★★★★ ETC CATEGORY 3 DISABLED ACCESSIBILITY (one cottage). [Pets £10 per week]
e-mail: info@farmholidaysuk.com　　　　　website: www.farmholidaysuk.com

Castleside

A suburb 2 miles south-west of Consett.

DAVID BLACKBURN AND IRENE MORDEY, BEE COTTAGE FARMHOUSE, CASTLESIDE, CONSETT DH8 9HW (01207 508224). Charming farmhouse with stunning views. You will be most welcome. Ideal for Newcastle, Durham, Beamish etc. Bed and Breakfast; dinner available, licensed. Great for pets. VisitBritain ★★★★ [pw! ᵀ▯]
e-mail: beecottage68@aol.com　　　　　website: www.beecottage.co.uk

---

ᵀ▯　Pets are welcome free of charge.

£　A charge is made for pets: nightly or weekly.

pw!　Special provision for pets; exercise facility, feeding or accommodation arrangement.

▯　Separate pets accommodation.

Classified Symbols

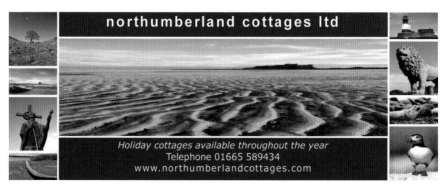
Alnmouth, Alnwick, Alwinton, Bamburgh

www.holidayguides.com

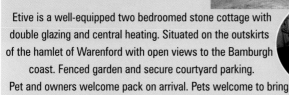

Berwick-Upon-Tweed, Chathill, Corbridge, Eals, Guyzance

2, THE COURTYARD, BERWICK-UPON-TWEED

Secluded Self Catering Townhouse in heart of old Berwick. Planted courtyard garden and sunny verandah. Historic ramparts 400 yards. Choice of walks. Ideal for exercising pets.

Contact: J Morton, 1, The Courtyard, Church Street, Berwick-Upon-Tweed, TD15 1EE (01289 308737)
e-mail: patmosphere@yahoo.co.uk • www.berwickselfcatering.co.uk

Doxford Farm Cottages • Northumberland

Comfortable self-catering family accommodation on working farm situated amidst unspoilt wooded countryside, five miles from the coast. 8 stone built terrace cottages.

Contact: Sarah Shell, Doxford Farm, Chathill, Alnwick, Northumberland NE67 5DY
Tel: 01665 579348 • mobile: 07734 247277 • e-mail: sarah@doxfordfarmcottages.com
www.doxfordfarmcottages.com   VisitBritain ★★★/★★★★

Fellcroft Bed & Breakfast

Delightful family-run B&B in a large Edwardian house close to the centre of Corbridge. Special facilities for walkers, cyclists and tourists. Families, children and dogs welcome.
Mrs T. Brown, Fellcroft, Station Road, Corbridge, Northumberland NE45 5AY
Tel: 01434 632384 Fax: 01434 633918 • E-mail: tove.brown@ukonline.co.uk
www.fellcroftbandb.com

The Hayes • Corbridge www.hayes-corbridge.co.uk

Formerly stables, now converted into two cottages, each sleeps up to 5. Each has one double and one twin bedroom, and shower room upstairs; downstairs cloakroom; lounge and dining areas. Electric cooker, fridge, microwave, washing machine and dishwasher; TV, CD/DVD; central heating throughout. Wifi available. Pets welcome.
Newcastle Road, Corbridge, Northumberland NE45 5LP
Tel: 01434 632010 • e-mail: camon@onebillinternet.co.uk   *Stable* and *Bothy*

Stay in stunning Northumberland • • Stonecrop

Nestling in the South Tyne Valley in the small hamlet of Eals is this white-washed cottage with its own orchard. Recently renovated, with modern comforts - a new kitchen and bathroom, a cosy log stove and 3 bedrooms. Well behaved pets welcome.
Contact: Richard Parker, Eastgate, Milburn, Penrith, Cumbria CA10 1TN
Tel: 01768 361509 • www.stonecrop.co.uk

Guyzance, Northumberland

BANK HOUSE
HOLIDAY COTTAGES

One, two, three and four-bedroom luxuriously converted stone buildings and farmhouse, set in natural woodland close to the beautiful Northumberland coastline.

Contact: Linda Taylor, Bank House Holiday Cottages, Guyzance, Northumberland NE65 9AP • 07957 100615
e-mail: info@bankhouseholidaycottages.co.uk • www.bankhouseholidaycottages.co.uk

Visit www.holidayguides.com
for pet-friendly accommodation in Britain

Please mention PETS WELCOME!

when making enquiries about accommodation featured in this guide

NORTHUMBERLAND COTTAGES LTD. A local booking agency with a Green Tourism Bronze Award, offering a range of traditional and contemporary cottages, both inland and along the stunning North Northumberland coastline. Several of our cottages welcome more than 1 dog. Telephone 01665 589434 or check availability online. [Pets £20 per week]
e-mail: enquiries@northumberlandcottages.com   website: www.northumberlandcottages.com

Alnmouth

Seaside village situated at the mouth of the River Aln.

SADDLE B&B, 24/25 NORTHUMBERLAND STREET, ALNMOUTH NE66 2RA (01665 830476). Friendly, family-run B&B on the Northumberland coast. Car park. All bedrooms en suite. Children and pets most welcome. [🐾]
e-mail: thesaddlebedandbreakfast@hotmail.com   website: www.thesaddlebedandbreakfast.co.uk

🐾   Pets are welcome free of charge.

£   A charge is made for pets: nightly or weekly.

pw!   Special provision for pets; exercise facility, feeding or accommodation arrangement.

⌂   Separate pets accommodation.

Classified Symbols

Alnwick

Town situated 32 miles south of Berwick-Upon-Tweed and the Scottish Border.

ALNWICK LODGE   WEST CAWLEDGE PARK, ALNWICK NE66 2HJ (01665 604363/603377). In a picturesque setting close to the A1, with 15 well equipped en suite bedrooms, decorated and furnished to the highest standards. Locally sourced produce features in the splendid breakfast; evening meals available if ordered in advance. Children and dogs welcome. ETC ★★★ [Pets £6 per night]
e-mail: bookings@alnwicklodge.com   website: www.alnwicklodge.com

Alwinton

Village in Upper Coquetdale, 9 miles from Rothbury.

FELLSIDE COTTAGE, ALWINTON. Cosy cottage nestling in beautiful Upper Coquet Valley. Fully furnished to a high standard. Open fire. Lovely garden and patio. Sleeps 3. A walker's paradise. Walkers and Cyclists Welcome. VisitBritain ★★★★. Contact: MRS D. STRAUGHAN, BEDLINGTON LANE FARM, BEDLINGTON NE22 6AA (01670 823042). [🐾]
e-mail: stay@fellsidecottcheviots.co.uk   website: www.fellsidecottcheviots.co.uk

Bamburgh

Village on North Sea coast with magnificent castle. Grace Darling buried in churchyard.

WAREN HOUSE HOTEL, WAREN MILL, BAMBURGH NE70 7EE (01668 214581). Luxurious Country House Hotel. Excellent accommodation, superb food, moderately priced wine list. Rural setting. No children under 14 please. ETC ★★★ Silver Award, AA ★★★ One Rosette.[🐾]
e-mail: enquiries@warenhousehotel.co.uk   website: www.warenhousehotel.co.uk

THE MIZEN HEAD HOTEL, BAMBURGH NE69 7BS (01668 214254; Fax: 01668 214104). A warm welcome awaits owners and pets alike at the Mizen Head. Close to the beautiful Northumbrian coastline and just a short drive from many lovely walks in the Ingram Valley. The hotel boasts log fires, live music, good food and real ales.
e-mail: info@mizenheadhotel.co.uk   website: www.mizenheadhotel.co.uk

Belford

Village 14 miles SE of Berwick-Upon-Tweed.

ETIVE COTTAGE, WARENFORD, NEAR BELFORD NE70 7HZ. Well-equipped two-bedroomed cottage with double glazing, central heating. Open views to coast. Fenced garden; secure parking. Pet and owners welcome pack. Pets welcome to bring along well behaved owners. Regional Winner, Winalot 'Best Place to Stay'. VisitBritain ★★★★★ Self-catering. Brochure: JAN THOMPSON (01668 213233). [🐾]
e-mail: janet.thompson1@homecall.co.uk   website: www.etivecottage.co.uk

Berwick-upon-Tweed

Border town at mouth of River Tweed 58 miles north west of Newcastle and 47 miles south east of Edinburgh. Medieval town walls, remains of a Norman Castle.

FRIENDLY HOUND COTTAGE, FORD COMMON, BERWICK-UPON-TWEED TD15 2QD (01289 388554) Set in a quiet rural location, convienient for Holy Island, Berwick, Bamburgh and the Heritage coastline. Come and enjoy our top quality accommodation, excellent breakfasts, and warm welcome. Arrive as our guests and leave as our friends. EnjoyEngland ★★★★ [🐾]
website: www.friendlyhoundcottage.co.uk

2, THE COURTYARD, BERWICK-UPON-TWEED. Secluded Self catering Townhouse in heart of old Berwick. Planted courtyard garden and sunny verandah. Historic ramparts 400 yards. Choice of walks. Ideal for exercising pets. Contact: J. MORTON, 1, THE COURTYARD, CHURCH STREET, BERWICK -UPON-TWEED, TD15 1EE (01289 308737). [pw! 🐾]
e-mail: patmosphere@yahoo.co.uk   website: www.berwickselfcatering.co.uk

Chathill

Hamlet 4 miles SW of Seahouses.

SARAH SHELL, DOXFORD FARM COTTAGES, CHATHILL, ALNWICK NE67 5DY (01665 579348; mobile: 07734 247277). Comfortable self-catering family accommodation on working farm situated amidst unspoilt wooded countryside, five miles from the coast. 8 stone built terrace cottages. VisitBritain ★★★/★★★★ [Pets £20 per week].
e-mail: sarah@doxfordfarmcottages.com   website: www.doxfordfarmcottages.com

Corbridge

Small town on the north bank of the River Tyne, 3 miles west of Hexham. Nearby are remains of Roman military town of Corstopitum.

MRS T. BROWN, FELLCROFT BED & BREAKFAST, STATION ROAD, CORBRIDGE NE45 5AY (01434 632384; Fax: 01434 633918). Delightful family-run B&B in a large Edwardian house close to the centre of Corbridge. Special facilities for walkers, cyclists and tourists. Families, children and dogs welcome. EnjoyEngland ★★★★.
e-mail: tove.brown@ukonline.co.uk   website: www.fellcroftbandb.com

MR & MRS MATTHEWS, THE HAYES GUEST HOUSE, NEWCASTLE ROAD, CORBRIDGE NE45 5LP (01434 632010). Stone-built stables in grounds of large country house converted into two self-catering cottages, each accommodating 4/5. WiFi available. ETC ★★★ [Pets £15 per week]
e-mail: camon@onebillinternet.co.uk   website: www.hayes-corbridge.co.uk

Eals

Village 7 miles from Haltwhistle, 8 miles from Alston.

STONECROP. A delightful white-washed cottage with its own orchard and large garden in a beautiful valley; recently renovated, with modern comforts - 3 bedrooms. Well behaved pets welcome. Close to Hadrian's Wall. Contact: RICHARD PARKER, EASTGATE, MILBURN, PENRITH, CUMBRIA CA10 1TN (01768 361509) [🐾]
website: www.stonecrop.co.uk

Guyzance

Hamlet located south east of Alnwick on the River Coquet.

LINDA TAYLOR, BANK HOUSE HOLIDAY COTTAGES, GUYZANCE NE65 9AP (07957 100615). One, two, three and four-bedroom luxuriously converted stone buildings and farmhouse, set in natural woodland close to the beautiful Northumberland coastline. VisitBritain ★★★★ Self Catering. [🐾]
e-mail: info@bankhouseholidaycottages.co.uk   website: www.bankhouseholidaycottages.co.uk

Haltwhistle

Small market town about one mile South of Hadrian's Wall.

KATH AND BRAD DOWLE, SAUGHY RIGG FARM, TWICE BREWED, HALTWHISTLE NE49 9PT (01434 344120). Close to the best parts of Hadrian's Wall. A warm welcome and good food. All rooms en suite. Parking. TV. Central heating. Children and pets welcome. Open all year. Prices from £35 pppn. ETC ★★★★ [Pets £5 per night]
e-mail: info@saughyrigg.co.uk   website: www.saughyrigg.co.uk

Hexham

Market town on south bank of the River Tyne, 20 miles west of Newcastle-upon-Tyne.

MRS RUBY KEENLEYSIDE, STRUTHERS FARM, CATTON, ALLENDALE, HEXHAM NE47 9LP (01434 683580). Panoramic views, splendid walks. Double/twin rooms, en suite bathrooms, central heating. Good farmhouse cooking. Ample safe parking. Children welcome. Pets by prior arrangement. Open all year. ETC ★★★★.
website: www.struthersfarmbandb.com

BATTLESTEADS HOTEL & RESTAURANT, WARK, HEXHAM NE48 3LS (01434 230209). Friendly family-run hotel with 17 en suite bedrooms including ground floor with disabled access. Excellent bar meals and à la carte menus; good choice wines and beers. Pets by arrangement only. Enjoy England ★★. [Pets £5 per night].
e-mail: info@battlesteads.com   website: www.battlesteads.com

High Buston

Hamlet near Shilbottle, ideal base for exploring Northumbrian coastline.

APPLE ORCHARD HOUSE, THE OLD STABLES, HIGH BUSTON HALL, HIGH BUSTON, ALNMOUTH NE66 3QH (01913 863888). 3-bedroom cottage with sea views on all sides. Lounge, fully equipped kitchen/diner. Two downstairs bedrooms, plus en suite master bedroom. Enclosed gardens.
e-mail: kathlewis1@hotmail.com   website: www.hemmelcottage.co.uk

Longhorsley

Village 6 miles NW of Morpeth.

★★★★ SELF-CATERING HOLIDAY COTTAGE (Mobile: 0781 624 5678). Sleeps 8. Bring your horses and dogs on holiday and explore our fabulous countryside, beaches and many local equestrian facilities. For further information and contact details visit our website. [🐴].
e-mail: carolyn@westmoorfarm.co.uk   website: www.westmoorfarm.co.uk

Otterburn

Site of the Battle of Otterburn in 1388, part of the continuing skirmishes between the Scottish and English.

THE BORDER FOREST CARAVAN PARK, COTTONSHOPEBURNFOOT, NEAR OTTERBURN NE19 1TF (01830 520259). Small secluded family run park, ideal for touring, and with many outdoor pursuits and historic sites within easy reach. A paradise for dogs and nature lovers. [🐴]
e-mail: borderforest@btinternet.com   website: www.borderforest.com

Wooler

Small town on Harthope Burn 15 miles NW of Alnwick.

LYNNEY HOLDEN, CROOKHOUSE, KIRKNEWTON, WOOLER NE71 6TN (01668 216113). Superior self catering accommodation in a traditional Northumbrian steading, Secluded and tranquil. Sleeps 2-12. Horses and dogs welcome. VisitBritain ★★★★. [🐴 pw!]
e-mail: stay@crookhousecottages.co.uk   website: www.crookhousecottages.co.uk

Balterley, Chester, Macclesfield, Rostherne

FHG Guides publish a large range of well-known accommodation guides. We will be happy to send you details or you can use the order form at the back of this book.

Tattenhall

Balterley

Small village two miles west of Audley.

MR & MRS HOLLINS, BALTERLEY GREEN FARM, DEANS LANE, BALTERLEY, NEAR CREWE CW2 5QJ (01270 820214). 145-acre farm in quiet and peaceful surroundings. Within easy reach of Junction 16 on the M6. Bed and Breakfast from £25pp. Also cottage for self-catering. Caravans and tents welcome. [pw! Pets £2 per night]

Chester

Former Roman city on the River Dee, with well-preserved walls and beautiful 14th century Cathedral. Liverpool 25 miles

THE EATON HOTEL, CITY ROAD, CHESTER CH1 3AE (01244 320840; Fax: 0870 6221691). Ideally located for you and your dog, in the heart of Chester, with parking, and bordering the Shropshire Union Canal towpath. [🐾]
website: www.eatonhotelchester.co.uk

MRS ANNE ARDEN, NEWTON HALL, TATTENHALL, CHESTER CH3 9NE (01829 770153; Mobile: 07974 745676). Part 16thC country house on a family-run farm, surrounded by beautiful scenery, with views of Beeston and Peckforton Castles. Ideal for a quiet, relaxing holiday. Chester 15 minutes' drive. ETC ★★★★ Silver Award [🐾]
e-mail: saarden@btinternet.com   website: www.newtonhallfarm.co.uk

Macclesfield

Town 10 miles south of Stockport.

MRS STUBBS, ASTLE FARM EAST, CHELFORD, MACCLESFIELD SK10 4TA (Tel & Fax: 01625 861270). A warm and friendly welcome awaits on this picturesque arable farm surrounded by a large garden. We offer you a quiet stay in an idyllic setting. All bedrooms en suite, open all year. ETC ★★. [⌂ 🐾]
e-mail: stubg@aol.com   website: www.astlefarmeast.co.uk

Rostherne

Village in east Cheshire, one mile from Tatton Park.

ROSTHERNE COUNTRY HOUSE, ROSTHERNE LANE, ROSTHERNE, NEAR KNUTSFORD WA16 6RY (01565 832628). Beautiful Grade 2 listed Victorian House retaining many original features, ideal for exploring Cheshire. A real, 'home from home' which offers every conceivable comfort. AA★★★★.
e-mail: info@rostherehouse.co.uk   website: www.rostherehouse.co.uk

Tattenhall

Village 8 miles south east of Chester.

THE PHEASANT INN, HIGHER BURWARDSLEY, TATTENHALL CH3 9PF (01829 770434; Fax: 01829 771097). With panoramic views of Cheshire plains. Twelve en suite bedrooms. Freshly cooked food using local produce. Listed in the Michelin Good Pub Guide and Egon Ronay Guide. AA ★★★★★ [🐾]
e-mail: info@thepheasantinn.co.uk   website: www.thepheasantinn.co.uk

Alston

Please mention PETS WELCOME!
when making enquiries about accommodation featured in this guide

Appleby-in-Westmorland, Bowness-on-Windermere, Brampton

Brampton, Broughton-in-Furness, Carlisle, Cartmel, Cockermouth

Elterwater, Eskdale, Gosforth, Grange-over-Sands

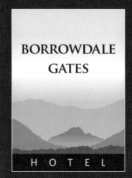

Grasmere, Hawkshead, Ireby, Kendal

Keswick

Kirkby Lonsdale, Kirkby Stephen

Lake District, Lamplugh (near Loweswater)

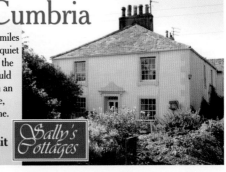

Lamplugh (near Loweswater), Langdale, Little Langdale, Loweswater, Millom, Newby Bridge

Taking your pet on holiday?
for quality properties where pets will be warmly welcomed visit:
www.pets-welcome.co.uk

Penrith

Penrith, Ravenstonedale, St Bees, Silloth-on-Solway, Skelwith Bridge

Ullswater, Wasdale

Please mention PETS WELCOME!

when making enquiries about accommodation featured in this guide

Pet-Friendly
Pubs, Inns & Hotels
on pages 448-453
These establishments may not feature in the main section of the book

The Wild Boar
Inn, Grill & Smokehouse

Nestling in a peaceful setting in the Gilpin Valley, The Wild Boar benefits from beautiful surrounding countryside, including its own private 72 acres of woodland, and many other Lake District attractions close by.

A special venue for many an occasion, whether that be a romantic or adventurous break, family get-together, intimate business meeting or as one of our very valued frequent diners.

After undergoing a refurbishment The Wild Boar now offers individually designed bedrooms, Grill and Smokehouse with an open kitchen and chef's table.

THE WILD BOAR
INN, GRILL & SMOKEHOUSE
CROOK, NEAR WINDERMERE
CUMBRIA LA23 3NF
RESERVATIONS: 08458 504604
www.wildboarinn.co.uk

English Lakes Hotels Resorts & Venues

STAY LAKELAND. A range of high quality self-catering holiday accommodation in the Lake District and Cumbria, including traditional cottages, houses, timber lodges and holiday static caravans. All ★★★ minimum and inspected annually by Quality in Tourism (0845 468 0936) [🐾]
website: www.staylakeland.co.uk

CUMBRIAN COTTAGES. Choose from 300 pet-friendly cottages. Superb locations throughout the Lake District and Cumbria. All VisitBritain graded. Contact us for a brochure or visit our website. Tel: 01228 599950 (lines open 7 days 9am-9pm (5.30pm Sat). [Pets £15 per week.]
website: www.cumbrian-cottages.co.uk

Alston

Small market town 16 miles NE of Penrith.

CUMBERLAND INN, TOWNFOOT, ALSTON CA9 3HX (01434 381875). A comfy retreat in the secluded North Pennines. Home-made hearty fare available all day. All 5 bedrooms are en suite. Muddy dogs and boots welcome. Pets welcome in bedrooms and bar. No charge for pets.
e-mail: stay@cumberlandinnalston.com   website: www.cumberlandinnalston.com.

PAUL & CAROL HUISH, ROCK HOUSE ESTATE, VALLEY VIEW, NENTHEAD, ALSTON CA9 3NA (01434 382 684). Five luxury cottages sleeping 2, 4, 7, 7, or 14. Undiscovered Cumbria, accessible to the Lakes, Dales and Borders. 100 acre estate is surrounded by spectacular views. Short breaks available. Open all year. VisitBritain ★★★/★★★★. [Pets £20 each].
e-mail: Info@RockHouseEstate.co.uk   website: www.RockHouseEstate.co.uk

Ambleside

Popular centre for exploring Lake District at northern end of Lake Windermere. Picturesque Stock Ghyll waterfall nearby, lovely walks. Associations with Wordsworth. Penrith 30 miles, Keswick 17, Windermere 5.

BRATHAY LODGE, ROTHAY ROAD, AMBLESIDE LA22 0EE (015394 32000) Spacious en suite bedrooms, spa baths with shower over. Ground floor rooms with own entrance. Double, twin and family rooms, rates from £30 pppn. Pets welcome. Private off-road parking. EnjoyEngland ★★★★. [Pets £5 per pet per night]
e-mail: info@brathay-lodge.co.uk   website: www.brathay-lodge.co.uk

SMALLWOOD HOUSE, COMPSTON ROAD, AMBLESIDE LA22 9DJ (015394 32330). Where quality and the customer come first. En suite rooms, car parking, leisure club membership. ETC ★★★★ [Pets £3 per night]
website: www.smallwoodhotel.co.uk

**THE OLD VICARAGE, VICARAGE ROAD, AMBLESIDE LA22 9DH (015394 33364). 'Rest a while in style'. Quality B&B set in tranquil wooded grounds in the heart of the village. Car park. All rooms en suite. Kettle, clock/radio, TV. Heated indoor pool, sauna, hot tub, sun lounge and rooftop terrace. Special breaks. Friendly service where your pets are welcome. Telephone Ian or Helen Burt. [🐾]
website: www.oldvicarageambleside.co.uk**

2 LOWFIELD, OLD LAKE ROAD, AMBLESIDE. Ground floor garden flat half a mile from town centre; sleeps 4. Lounge/diningroom, kitchen, bathroom/WC, two bedrooms, one with en suite shower. Linen supplied. Children and pets welcome. Parking. Terms from £160 to £300 per week. Contact: MR P. F. QUARMBY, 3 LOWFIELD, OLD LAKE ROAD, AMBLESIDE LA22 0DH (015394 32326) [🐾]
e-mail: paul.quarmby@zen.co.uk

GREENHOWE CARAVAN PARK, GREAT LANGDALE, AMBLESIDE LA22 9JU (015394 37231; Fax: 015394 37464). Permanent Caravan Park with Self Contained Holiday Accommodation. An ideal centre for Climbing, Fell Walking, Riding, Swimming, or just a lazy holiday. [Pets £6 per night, £30 per week]
website: www.greenhowe.com

A useful index of towns/counties appears on pages 455-461

KIRKSTONE FOOT, KIRKSTONE PASS ROAD, AMBLESIDE LA22 9EH (015394 32232; Fax: 015394 32805). Superior cottage and apartment complex, set in peaceful gardens, adjoining the Lakeland fells and village centre. Open all year. ETC ★★★★ and ETC ★★★★ GOLD AWARD [pw! Pets £5.00 per night.]
e-mail: enquiries@kirkstonefoot.co.uk   website: www.kirkstonefoot.co.uk

LYNDALE GUEST HOUSE LAKE ROAD, AMBLESIDE LA22 0DN (015394 34244) Nestled midway between Lake Windermere and Ambleside village, with superb views of Loughrigg Fell and the Langdales beyond. Excellent base for walking, touring, or just relaxing. [🐕]
e-mail: alison@lyndale-guesthouse.co.uk   website: www.lyndale-guesthouse.co.uk

BETTY FOLD, HAWKSHEAD HILL, AMBLESIDE LA22 0PS (015394 36611). Ground floor apartment sleeping four. Private entrance. Set in peaceful and spacious grounds, ideal for walkers and families with pets. Open all year. [pw! Pets £2 per night.]
e-mail: claire@bettyfold.co.uk   website: www.bettyfold.co.uk

Appleby-in-Westmorland

Located in the Eden Valley, ideal for walking, riding, fishing and cycling. Annual events include The Gypsy Horse Fair and the Jazz Festival.

MILBURN GRANGE HOLIDAY COTTAGES, KNOCK, APPLEBY CA16 6DR (017683 61867) 1,2 & 3 bedroom cottages and a snug apartment in a stunning rural location. Two National Parks on the doorstep. Dogs very welcome and open all year. VisitBritain ★★★ Self Catering. [Pets £20 per week]
e-mail: petswelcome@milburngrange.co.uk   website: www.milburngrange.co.uk

KEITH AND DIANE BUDDING, SCALEBECK HOLIDAY COTTAGES, SCALEBECK, GREAT ASBY, APPLEBY CA16 6TF (01768 351006). Comfortable and well-equipped self-catering accommodation in the tranquil and picturesque Eden Valley. Sleep 2/5. No smoking. ETC ★★★★ [pw! £20 per week]
e-mail: mail@scalebeckholidaycottages.co.uk   website: www.scalebeckholidaycottages.co.uk

RAY & FREI WALKER, HALL CROFT, DUFTON, APPLEBY-IN-WESTMORLAND CA16 6DB (017683 52902). Large, detached, beautifully restored Victorian house in peaceful village, offering high quality facilities in an idyllic setting. Three large guest rooms. Ideal for peaceful break, or centre for activity holiday. B&B from £31 pppn. AA ★★★★. [🐕]
e-mail: hallcroft@phonecoop.coop

Bassenthwaite

Village on Bassenthwaite Lake with traces of Norse and Roman settlements.

SKIDDAW VIEW HOLIDAY HOME PARK, BOTHEL, NEAR BASSENTHWAITE CA7 2JN (016973 20919). Award winning 20 acre holiday home park situated in a secluded and delightful setting in the Northern Lake District. Range of self catering properties including static caravans, timber lodges as well as holiday cottages in the surrounding towns and villages. David Bellamy Gold Award. ETC ★★★★ Holiday Park.
website: www.skiddawview.co.uk

Bowness-on-Windermere

Location on East shore of Lake Windermere adjoining Windermere town.

OAKFOLD HOUSE, BERESFORD ROAD, BOWNESS-ON-WINDERMERE LA23 2JG (015394 43239) Award-winning Victorian Guesthouse. Free WiFi. Close to Lake, steamers, shops, restaurants and Beatrix Potter attraction. Car park. Gardens. VisitBritain ★★★★ Gold Award. [🐕]
e-mail: oakfoldhouse@fsmail.net   website: www.oakfoldhouse.co.uk

WINDERMERE LAKE HOLIDAYS. Holiday houseboats on the lake shore with stunning views. Sleep 4. Open all year round. Pets welcome. For brochure: 015394 43415. [Pets £10 per week]
e-mail: email@lakewindermere.net   website: www.lakewindermere.net

Brampton

Market town with cobbled streets. Octagonal Moat Hall with exterior staircases and iron stocks.

FARLAM HALL HOTEL, BRAMPTON CA8 2NG (016977 46234; Fax: 016977 46683). Standing in four acres of gardens, with its own lake, Farlam Hall offers fine quality cuisine and individually decorated guest rooms. Ideal touring centre for the Lakes, Borders and Hadrian's Wall. AA Three Stars Inspectors' Choice and Two Rosettes, Relais & Chateaux. [🐴]
e-mail: farlam@relaischateaux.com   website: www.farlamhall.co.uk

LONG BYRES AT TALKIN HEAD (016977 3435). Walk your dog straight from the cottages up the hill and on to the fells. 7 cottages on North Pennines farm, sleeping 2-8; excellent base for Hadrian's Wall, Scottish Borders and the Lake District. Local food cooked by Harriet and delivered to your cottage. [🐴]
e-mail: stay@longbyres.co.uk   website: www.longbyres.co.uk

Broughton-in-Furness

Village 8 miles NW of Ulverston.

J. JACKSON, THORNTHWAITE FARM, WOODLAND HALL, WOODLAND, BROUGHTON-IN-FURNESS LA20 6DF (Tel & Fax: 01229 716340). Two well-equipped cottages and two caravans in excellent walking area. Wildlife/birdwatchers paradise. Private fishing lake. Ancient woodlands, quiet, relaxing, warm welcome. Established 1968. ETC ★★★★ GOLD AWARD [Pets £15 per week]
e-mail: info@lakedistrictcottages.co.uk   website: www.lakedistrictcottages.co.uk

PAUL SANDFORD, WOODEND COTTAGES, WOODEND, ULPHA, BROUGHTON-IN-FURNESS LA20 6DY (019467 23277). Woodend is remote and surrounded by hills and moorland, with views towards Scafell Pike. The cottages and house offer cosy accommodation for two to six people. Short breaks available out of season.
website: www.woodendcottage.com

Carlisle

Important Border city and former Roman station on River Eden. Castle is of historic interest, also Tullie House Museum and Art Gallery. Good sports facilities inc. football and racecourse. Kendal 45 miles, Dumfries 33, Penrith 18.

GRAHAM ARMS HOTEL, ENGLISH STREET, LONGTOWN, CARLISLE CA6 5SE (01228 791213; Fax: 01228 794110). 16 bedrooms en suite, including four-poster and family rooms, all with tea/coffee facilities, TV and radio. Secure courtyard locked overnight. Pets welcome with well-behaved owners. ETC ★★ [🐴]
e-mail: office@grahamarms.com   website: www.grahamarms.com

Cartmel

Village 4 miles south of Newby Bridge.

RATHER SPECIAL COTTAGES. Seven cottages sleeping 2-6. Set behind a large Georgian house set in parkland on the side of Hamps Fell. Beautiful garden, great walks. Pets and children welcome. Open all year. Please telephone for details. ETC ★★★★. Contact: MR M. AINSCOUGH, LONGLANDS AT CARTMEL, GRANGE-OVER-SANDS LA11 6HG (015395 36475; Fax: 015395 36172). [🐴]
e-mail: longlands@cartmel.com   website: www.cartmel.com

🐴	Pets are welcome free of charge.
£	A charge is made for pets: nightly or weekly.
pw!	Special provision for pets; exercise facility, feeding or accommodation arrangement.
⌂	Separate pets accommodation.

Classified Symbols

Cockermouth

Market town and popular touring centre for Lake District and quiet Cumbrian coast. On Rivers Derwent and Cocker. Penrith 30 miles, Carlisle 26, Whitehaven 14, Keswick 12.

THE PHEASANT, BASSENTHWAITE LAKE, NEAR COCKERMOUTH CA13 9YE (017687 76234; Fax: 017687 76002). Traditional Cumbrian hostelry with tastefully renovated accommodation, fine dining and outstanding hospitality. ETC ★★★ Silver Award, AA ★★★ and Rosette
e-mail: info@the-pheasant.co.uk　　　　　website: www.the-pheasant.co.uk

ROSE COTTAGE GUEST HOUSE, LORTON ROAD, COCKERMOUTH CA13 9DX (Tel & Fax: 01900 822189). Family-run guest house on the outskirts of Cockermouth. Warm, friendly atmosphere. Parking. All rooms en suite with colour TV, tea/coffee, central heating. Pets welcome. ETC/AA ★★★★ [🐾]
website: www.rosecottageguest.co.uk

THE MANOR HOUSE, OUGHTERSIDE, ASPATRIA CA7 2PT (016973 22420). 18th century manor farmhouse retaining many original features and several acres of land. Spacious en suite rooms, tea/coffee making facilities, TV and lots of little extras. All pets welcome. Inspection Commended. [🐾]
e-mail: richardandjudy@themanorhouse.net　　　website: www.themanorhouse.net

Coniston

Village 8 miles south-west of Ambleside, dominated by Old Man of Coniston (2635ft).

THE COPPERMINES AND CONISTON LAKES COTTAGES (015394 41765). Unique Lakeland cottages for 2 – 30 of quality and character in stunning mountain scenery. Log fires, exposed beams. Pets welcome! ★★★ - ★★★★ Book online. [Pets £25 per stay]
website: www.coppermines.co.uk

THE SUN, CONISTON LA21 8HQ (015394 41248; Fax 015394 41219). Unique mix of great bar, diner and Four Star inn in extremely comfortable and informal atmosphere. Locally sourced food. Eight refurbished bedrooms with superb views. ETC ★★★★ [Pets £10 per night]
e-mail: info@thesunconiston.com　　　website: www.thesunconiston.com

THE YEWDALE HOTEL, YEWDALE ROAD, CONISTON LA21 8DU (015394 41280). Central for activities such as fishing, boating, canoeing, walking and pony trekking. 8 en suite bedrooms with TV and tea-making. Bar and dining room offer varied menus featuring fresh local produce. Excellent Cumbrian breakfasts. ETC ★★★ [Pets £6 per night]
e-mail: info@yewdalehotel.com　　　　　website: www.yewdalehotel.com

WATERHEAD HOTEL, CONISTON LA21 8AJ (015394 41244; Fax: 015394 41193). Situated alongside Coniston Water, The Waterhead Hotel makes a perfect retreat. 24 en suite bedrooms, two junior suites. Mountain View Restaurant, lounge bar with views across the Lake. Non-smoking. Ideal base for outdoor activities, also lake cruises and historic houses. ETC ★★★ [Pets £10 per night].
website: www.waterhead-hotel.co.uk

BLUEBIRD LODGE, WATERHEAD, CONISTON LA21 8AJ (Tel/Fax: 01539 441442) In a quiet corner of the English Lakes, with comfortable rooms, a warm welcome and some of the best views in the area. An ideal location for fell walkers, dog owners and cyclists. All bedrooms are of a high standard.[🐾]
website: www.bluebirdlodge.co.uk

Crosby-on-Eden

Combined name for two small villages situated by the River Eden, north east of Carlisle.

THE WALLFOOT, PARK BROOM, CROSBY-ON-EDEN, CARLISLE CA6 4QH. (01228 573696; Fax: 01228 573240). Popular hotel just 3 miles east of Carlisle. Surrounded by fabulous scenery and lovely walks. Fantastic base for visiting the Lake District and South West Scotland.
e-mail: info@wallfoot.co.uk　　　　　website: www.wallfoot.co.uk

Crosthwaite

Hamlet 5 miles west of Kendal.

DAMSON DENE HOTEL, CROSTHWAITE LA8 8JE (015395 68676). Tranquil location only 10 minutes from Lake Windermere. Best Lakes Breaks from £118 per person for 2 nights. [Pets £5 per stay].
e-mail: info@damsondene.co.uk   website: www.bestlakesbreaks.co.uk

ROBIN AND MARNIE DAWSON, CROSTHWAITE HOUSE, CROSTHWAITE, NEAR KENDAL LA8 8BP (015395 68264). Comfortable, relaxing B&B in area of real natural beauty, with pleasant fell and woodland walks. Relax, unwind and enjoy the easy-going atmosphere. AA ★★★★.[🐾]
e-mail: bookings@crosthwaitehouse.co.uk   website: www.crosthwaitehouse.co.uk

Duddon Valley

Majestic valley running between Cockley Beck and Duddon Bridge.

COCKLEY BECK FARM COTTAGE, SEATHWAITE, BROUGHTON-IN-FURNESS LA20 6EQ (01229 716480). In the heart of the Lake District National Park, just 4 miles from the summit of Scafell Pike. Self-contained holiday cottage (sleeps 4). Large open-plan kitchen. Well behaved dogs free of charge. Available all year. Private enclosed garden with patio and parking. [🐾 pw!]
e-mail: Sandra@cockleybeck.co.uk   website: www.cockleybeck.co.uk

Elterwater

Village lying half a mile north west of Lake Elter Water.

THE BRITANNIA INN, ELTERWATER, AMBLESIDE LA22 9HP (015394 37210; Fax: 015396 78075). 500-year-old traditional Lakeland inn. Extensive, home-cooked menu, real ales, cosy bars, log fires. Comfortable, high quality en suite accommodation. Well-behaved pets welcome. ETC ★★★.[🐾] Use Promo code 'Pets' on our online booking system.
e-mail: info@britinn.co.uk   website: www.britinn.co.uk

Eskdale

Lakeless valley, noted for waterfalls and ascended by a light-gauge railway. Tremendous views. Roman fort. Keswick 35 miles, Broughton-in-Furness 10 miles.

FISHERGROUND FARM, ESKDALE. Traditional hill farm, with a stone cottage and three pine lodges, ideal for walkers, nature lovers, dogs and children. Games room, raft pool and a station on the miniature railway! Good pubs nearby. PETER & KATHRYN KETCHEN, BETWEEN GUARDS, GOSFORTH CA20 1EN (01946 720810) [🐾]
e-mail: holidays@fisherground.co.uk   website: www.fisherground.co.uk

THE BOOT INN (FORMERLY THE BURNMOOR INN), BOOT, ESKDALE CA19 1TG (019467 23224). Nine en suite bedrooms. Dogs and their owners made very welcome. Special breaks available all year on our web site. [🐾]
e-mail: enquiries@bootinn.co.uk   website: www.bootinn.co.uk

Gosforth

Village in the Western Lake District, St Mary's Church is home to the tallest and oldest Viking Cross in England. Seascale 2 miles.

BLENG BARN COTTAGE, MILL HOUSE FARM, WELLINGTON, SEASCALE CA20 1BH (07801 862237 & 07775 512918; Fax: 01946 725671. Self-catering 3-bedroom holiday cottage on a large working farm. Sleeps 6+4. Many traditional features and modern facilities. ETC ★★★★ Self Catering.[🐾]
e-mail: info@blengfarms.co.uk   website: www.blengfarms.co.uk

Grange-in-Borrowdale

Hamlet in Borrowdale at the end of Derwent Water.

THE BORROWDALE GATES HOTEL, GRANGE-IN-BORROWDALE, KESWICK CA12 5UQ (017687 77204; Fax: 017687 77195). Superbly situated amidst breathtaking scenery. Comfortable lounges, log fires and antiques will welcome you. 26 comfortable bedrooms and award-winning food. VisitBritain/AA ★★★, VisitBritain SILVER AWARD.
e-mail: hotel@borrowdale-gates.com   website: www.borrowdale-gates.com

Grange-over-Sands

Edwardian seaside resort on the edge of the Lake District National Park.

HAMPSFELL HOUSE HOTEL, HAMPSFELL ROAD, GRANGE-OVER-SANDS LA11 6BG (015395 32567). In two acres of private grounds, just a few minutes' walk from the town centre. The eight en suite bedrooms are well appointed. Enjoy the best of fresh Cumbrian produce in the elegant dining room. Ideal base for exploring the Lake District. AA ★★ [Pets from £5 per night].
e-mail: enquiries@hampsfellhouse.co.uk   website: www.hampsfellhouse.co.uk

Grasmere

Village famous for Wordsworth associations; the poet lived in Dove Cottage (preserved as it was), and is buried in the churchyard. Museum has manuscripts and relics.

GRASMERE HOTEL, BROADGATE, GRASMERE LA22 9TA (015394 35277). Charming 13 bedroom Country House Hotel, with ample parking and a licensed lounge. All rooms recently refurbished with en suite facilities. Award-winning restaurant overlooking gardens, river and surrounding hills. Special breaks throughout the year. AA ★★ 81%; ETC ★★ Silver Award.[Pets £10 per stay].
e-mail: enquiries@grasmerehotel.co.uk   website: www.grasmerehotel.co.uk

LAKE VIEW COUNTRY HOUSE & SELF-CATERING APARTMENTS, GRASMERE LA22 9TD (015394 35384/35167). 4 rooms B&B or 3 Self-Catering apartments in unrivalled, secluded location in the village with wonderful views and lakeshore access. All B&B rooms en suite, some with whirlpool baths. Ground floor accommodation available. No smoking. Featured in Michelin Guide.
website: www.lakeview-grasmere.com

Hawkshead

Quaint village in Lake District between Coniston Water and Windermere. The 16th century Church and Grammar School, which Wordsworth attended, are of interest. Ambleside 5 miles.

LAKELAND HIDEAWAYS, THE SQUARE, HAWKSHEAD LA22 0NZ (015394 42435). Cottages in and around Hawkshead. Great walks and lakes for swimming, dog friendly pubs, open fires to lie in front of... owners will enjoy it too. [Pets £20 per week].
e-mail: bookings@lakeland-hideaways.co.uk   website: www.lakeland-hideaways.co.uk

THE KINGS ARMS HOTEL, HAWKSHEAD, AMBLESIDE LA22 0NZ (015394 36372). Join us for a relaxing stay amidst the green hills and dales of Lakeland, and we will be delighted to offer you good food, homely comfort and warm hospitality in historic surroundings. We hope to see you soon! Self-catering cottages also available.[🐾, pets £20 per week s/c]
website: www.kingsarmshawkshead.co.uk

Ireby

A peaceful and uncrowded village just outside the Lake District National Park. Carlisle 18 miles.

2 MOOT HALL, IREBY CA7 1DU (01423 360759). Lovely cottage, part of 16th century Moot Hall in unspoilt village; delightful walks in Uldale Fells and northern Lake District. Sleeps 4. Linen/fuel/electricity incl. Open all year. Reductions for PAT, Assistance and Rescue Dogs. [🐾]
e-mail: ruthboyes@virgin.net   website: www.irebymoothall.co.uk

Kendal

Market town and popular centre for touring the Lake District. Of historic interest is the Norman castle, birthplace of Catherine Parr. Penrith 25 miles, Lancaster 22, Ambleside 13.

ANNE TAYLOR, RUSSELL FARM, BURTON-IN-KENDAL, CARNFORTH, LANCS. LA6 1NN (01524 781334). Bed and Breakfast. Ideal centre for touring Lakes and Yorkshire Dales. Good food, friendly atmosphere on working dairy farm. Modernised farmhouse. Guests' own lounge. [🐕]
e-mail: miktaylor@farming.co.uk

RIVERSIDE HOTEL, BEEZON ROAD, KENDAL LA9 6EL (015397 34861). Lovely riverside location. Best Lakes Breaks from £118 per person for 2 nights. [Pets £5 per stay].
e-mail: info@riversidekendal.co.uk   website: www.bestlakesbreaks.co.uk

STONECROSS MANOR HOTEL, MILNTHORPE ROAD, KENDAL LA9 5HP (01539 733559; Fax: 01539 736386). Stonecross Manor offers easy access to town, ample parking, local cuisine, conference and banquet facilities, indoor swimming pool, and four-poster bedrooms. [Pets £10 per stay]
e-mail: info@stonecrossmanor.co.uk   website: www.stonecrossmanor.co.uk

MRS HELEN JONES, PRIMROSE COTTAGE, ORTON ROAD, TEBAY CA10 3TL (015396 24791). Adjacent M6 J38 (10 miles north of Kendal). Excellent rural location for North Lakes and Yorkshire Dales. Superb facilities, jacuzzi bath, king and four-poster beds. One acre garden. Self-contained ground floor flat and 3 purpose-built self-catering bungalows for disabled guests, with electric bed, jacuzzi and large, wheel-in bathroom. Pets welcome, very friendly. VisitBritain ★★★★ Guest Accommodation. [Pets £3 per night]
e-mail: primrosecottebay@aol.com   website: www.primrosecottagecumbria.co.uk

MR WARREN PROBYN, THE GLEN GUESTHOUSE, OXENHOLME, KENDAL LA9 7RF (01539 726386). Family-run Kendal Bed and Breakfast, with an excellent reputation for warm and friendly service, excellent comfortable accommodation and large freshly cooked breakfasts. Set in a quiet location in its own grounds under the "The Helm". EnjoyEngland ★★★★. [Pets £3 per night]
e-mail: greenintheglen@btinternet.com   website: www.glen-kendal.co.uk

MRS L. HODGSON, PATTON HALL FARM, KENDAL LA8 9DT (01539 721590). 2 Modern caravans, fully double glazed, gas central heating. Double and twin bedrooms, kitchen, spacious lounge/dining area, toilet and shower. Traditional working farm set in 140 acres of beautiful countryside. [Pets £10/£15 per week].
e-mail: stay@pattonhallfarm.co.uk   website: www.pattonhallfarm.co.uk

Keswick

Famous Lake District resort at north end of Derwentwater with Pencil Museum and Cars of the Stars Motor Museum. Carlisle 30 miles,

MRS A. TRUE, LOW NEST FARM B&B, CASTLERIGG, KESWICK CA12 4TF (017687 72378) Small, family run farm offering B&B in the heart of the Lake District, just two miles south of Keswick. All bedrooms en suite. Pets most welcome; many extra facilities. AA ★★★★.
e-mail: info@dogfriendlylakedistrict.co.uk   website: www.dogfriendlylakedistrict.co.uk

ROYAL OAK HOTEL, BORROWDALE, KESWICK CA12 5XB (017687 77214). Traditional Lakeland hotel with friendly atmosphere. Home cooking, cosy bar, comfortable lounge and some riverside rooms. Winter and Summer discount rates. Brochure and tariff available. [🐕]
e-mail: info@royaloakhotel.co.uk   website: www.royaloakhotel.co.uk

KESWICK COTTAGES, LAKELAND VIEW, 3 HOW LANE, PORTINSCALE, KESWICK CA12 5RS (017687 80088). Cottages and apartments in and around Keswick. Properties are well maintained and clean. From traditional Lakeland cottages to luxurious apartments. Children and pets welcome. ETC ★★★★-★★★★★ [Pets £15 per week]
e-mail: info@keswickcottages.co.uk   website: www.keswickcottages.co.uk

OVERWATER HALL, OVERWATER, NEAR IREBY, KESWICK CA7 1HH (017687 76566). Elegant Country House Hotel in spacious grounds. Dogs very welcome in your room. 4 night mid-week breaks from £400 per person, inclusive of Dinner and Breakfast. Mini breaks also available all year. Award-winning restaurant. Northwest of England Tourism Award - Small Hotel of the Year 2010. AA ★★★ and Two Rosettes. See also advertisement on page 302 [pw! 🐕]
e-mail: welcome@overwaterhall.co.uk   website: www.overwaterhall.co.uk

MARY MOUNT HOTEL, BORROWDALE, NEAR KESWICK CA12 5UU (017687 77223). Set in 4½ acres of gardens and woodlands on the shores of Derwentwater. 2½ miles from Keswick in picturesque Borrowdale. Superb walking and touring. All rooms en suite with colour TV and tea/coffee making facilities. Licensed. Brochure on request. ETC ★★ [pw! Pets £10 per week.]
e-mail: info@marymounthotel.co.uk   website: www.marymounthotel.co.uk

HORSE AND FARRIER INN, THRELKELD, KESWICK CA12 4SQ (017687 79688; Fax: 017687 79823). Ideal location for walking or touring the Lake District. All 15 bedrooms en suite, with TV, tea/coffee making and hairdryer. Award-winning food and restaurant. Open all year. Pets welcome. ETC ★★★★ [Pets £7.50 per week].
e-mail: info@horseandfarrier.com   website: www.horseandfarrier.com

ANDY & CHARLOTTE PETERS, ROOMS 36, 36 LAKE ROAD, KESWICK CA12 5DQ (01768 772764; Freephone: 0800 0566401; mobile: 07721 957899). Set in quiet cul-de-sac, 3 minutes' walk from town centre, Theatre by the Lake, and Derwentwater (Queen of the Lakes). 7 well appointed rooms, all en suite. Special diets catered for, as well as normal English breakfast. Open all year including Christmas. [Pets £9 per night]
e-mail: andy@rooms36.co.uk   website: www.rooms36.co.uk

MARK & HELEN SMITH, GREYSTOKE HOUSE, 9 LEONARD STREET, KESWICK CA12 4EL (017687 72603) Warm and comfortable accommodation in a quiet location within walking distance of Keswick town centre. Safe cycle storage; drying room. Non-smoking, dog-friendly. [Pets £10 per stay]
e-mail: info@greystokeguesthouse.co.uk   website:www.greystokeguesthouse.co.uk

WOODSIDE, PENRITH ROAD, KESWICK CA12 4LJ (017687 73522). Friendly family-run establishment. All our rooms are en suite. We have ample private parking and large gardens. Non-smoking. Dogs welcome. [🐾]
website: www.woodsideguesthouse.co.uk

LOW BRIERY HOLIDAYS (017687 72044). A peaceful and scenic riverside location just outside Keswick. A choice of cottages, timber lodges and holiday caravans to suit all budgets. ETC ★★★★ [Pets £20 per week]
website: www.keswick.uk.com

Warm, comfortable houses and cottages in Keswick and beautiful Borrowdale, welcoming your dog. Inspected and quality graded. LAKELAND COTTAGE HOLIDAYS, KESWICK CA12 4QX (017687 76065; Fax: 017687 76869). [Pets £2 per day, £14 per week]
e-mail: info@lakelandcottages.co.uk   website: www.lakelandcottages.co.uk

DERWENT WATER MARINA, PORTINSCALE, KESWICK CA12 5RF (017687 72912). Lakeside self-catering apartments. Three apartments sleep 2, one apartment sleeps 6. Superb views over the lake and fells. Includes TV/DVD, heating and bed linen. Free Wi-Fi. Non-smoking. Watersports and boat hire available on site. [🐾]
e-mail: info@derwentwatermarina.co.uk   website: www.derwentwatermarina.co.uk

COLEDALE INN, BRAITHWAITE, NEAR KESWICK CA12 5TN (017687 78272). Friendly, family-run Victorian Inn in peaceful situation. Warm and spacious en suite bedrooms with TV. Children and pets welcome. Open all year. ETC ★★★ [🐾]
website: www.coledale-inn.co.uk

Kirkby-in-Furness

Small coastal village (A595). 10 minutes to Ulverston. Lakes within easy reach. Ideal base for walking and touring.

SUNSET COTTAGE. Self-catering 17th century two/three bedroom character cottage with garden. Original features. Panoramic views over sea/mountains; Coniston/Windermere 30 minutes. Non-smoking. Open all year. VisitBritain ★★★★ Contact: JANET AND PETER, 1 FRIARS GROUND, KIRKBY-IN-FURNESS LA17 7YB (01229 889601). [Pets £20 per pet per week]
e-mail: enquiries@southlakes-cottages.com   website: www.southlakes-cottages.com

A useful index of towns/counties appears on pages 455-461

Kirkby Lonsdale

Georgian buildings and quaint cottages. Riverside walks from medieval Devil's Bridge.

BARBON INN, BARBON, NEAR KIRKBY LONSDALE LA6 2LJ (015242 76233). Friendly 17th century Coaching Inn with 10 bedrooms. Country pursuits within the immediate area. Nestling in Lune Valley between Lake District and Yorkshire Dales. [pw! Pets £10 per stay]
e-mail: info@barbon-inn.co.uk   website: www.barbon-inn.co.uk

THE SNOOTY FOX, KIRKBY LONSDALE LA6 2AH (01524 271308). Charming Jacobean Inn, offering 9 en suite rooms, award-winning restaurant and lounge bar, the perfect base from which to explore both the Lake District and Yorkshire Dales. AA ★★★★ [🐾]
e-mail: snootyfoxhotel@talktalk.net   website: www.thesnootyfoxhotel.co.uk

MRS PAULINE BAINBRIDGE, ULLATHORNS FARM, MIDDLETON, KIRKBY LONSDALE LA6 2LZ (015242 76214; Mobile: 07800 990689). 17th Century farmhouse on a working farm situated in the Lune Valley. B&B from £27. Children and well-behaved pets welcome. Non-smoking. VisitBritain ★★★★ [🐾]
e-mail: pauline@ullathorns.co.uk   website: www.ullathorns.co.uk

Kirkby Stephen

Small town on River Eden, 9 miles South of Appleby.

COCKLAKE HOUSE, MALLERSTANG CA17 4JT (017683 72080). Charming, High Pennine Country House B&B in unique position above Pendragon Castle in Upper Mallerstang Dale offering good food and exceptional comfort to a small number of guests. Two double rooms with large private bathrooms. Three acres riverside grounds. Dogs welcome. [🐾]

Kirkoswald

Village in the Cumbrian hills, lying north west of the Lake District. Ideal for touring. Penrith 7 miles.

SECLUDED COTTAGES WITH PRIVATE FISHING, KIRKOSWALD CA10 1EU (24 hour brochure line 01768 898711, manned most Saturdays). Quality cottages, clean, well equipped and maintained. Centrally located for Lakes, Pennines, Hadrian's Wall, Borderland. Enjoy the Good Life in comfort. Pets' paradise. Guests' coarse fishing. Bookings/enquiries 01768 898711. ETC ★★★ [pw! £2 per pet per night, £14 per week].
e-mail: info@crossfieldcottages.co.uk   website: www.crossfieldcottages.co.uk

Lake District

North west corner of England between A6/M6 and the Cumbrian Coast. Fells, valleys and 16 lakes, the largest being Lake Windermere.

LAKE DISTRICT. Two luxury houses available to rent in the Lake District. Routen House, sleeps 12 plus cot. Fully modernised, outstanding position in 4 acres. Little Parrock, sleeps 10 plus cot, short walk from centre of Grasmere with real log fire and private garden. Both houses non-smoking. MRS J. GREEN (01604 505115).
e-mail: joanne@routenhouse.co.uk   www.routenhouse.co.uk/www.littleparrock.co.uk

GRIZEDALE LODGE, HAWKSHEAD, AMBLESIDE LA22 0QL (015394 36532; Fax: 015394 36572). In the heart of Grizedale Forest National Park, within easy reach of Windermere, Coniston, Beatrix Potter country and other attractions. All rooms en suite, some with four-posters. Open all year.
e-mail: enquiries@grizedale-lodge.com   website: www.grizedale-lodge.com

Lamplugh (near Loweswater)

Hamlet 7 miles south of Cockermouth.

ROSE COTTAGE. Three miles from Loweswater and four miles from Ennerdale, lovely throughout. Open plan kitchen and sitting room, cosy coal fire, two bedrooms and enclosed garden. Pets welcome. Contact SALLY FIELDING (01768 779445). [Pets £15 per week]
website: www.millgillhead.co.uk

FELLDYKE COTTAGE HOLIDAYS, LAMPLUGH. Visiting the Western Lakes? Then why not stay in this lovely 19th century cottage. Sleeps 4, short breaks can be arranged. Pets are welcome. Open all year. Contact MRS A. WILSON (01946 861151). VB ★★★★ [pw!🐾] .
e-mail: dockraynook@talk21.com   website: www.felldykecottageholidays.co.uk

Langdale

Dramatic valley area to the west of Ambleside, in the very heart of the National Park.

WHEELWRIGHTS HOLIDAY COTTAGES, ELTERWATER, NEAR AMBLESIDE LA22 9HS (015394 38305; Fax: 015394 37618). Some of the loveliest cottages in the Lake District with stunning scenery on their doorsteps are ready to welcome you and your pets. Prices vary. Please visit our website. ETC ★★★ - ★★★★★ [🐾]
e-mail: enquiries@wheelwrights.com   website: www.wheelwrights.com

Little Langdale

Hamlet 2 miles west of Skelwith Bridge. To west is Little Langdale Tarn, a small lake.

HIGHFOLD COTTAGE, LITTLE LANGDALE. Very comfortable Lakeland cottage, ideally situated for walking and touring. Superb mountain views. Sleeps 5. Personally maintained. Pets welcome. Weekly £260–£550. VB ★★★. MRS C.E. BLAIR, 8 THE GLEBE, CHAPEL STILE, AMBLESIDE LA22 9JT (015394 37686). [🐾]
website: www.highfoldcottage.co.uk

Loweswater

A small hamlet situated between the lakes Loweswater and Crummock Water in the Lake District National Park. Cockermouth 6 miles.

SCALE HILL, LOWESWATER, COCKERMOUTH CA13 9UX (01900 85232). With walking distance of Loweswater, Crummock Water, Buttermere. Four posters, bed linen. Good food and real ales served at local country inns. Open February to December. See also advert on p308. [Pets £30 per week].
e-mail: thompson@sc.alehillloweswater.co.uk   website: www.scalehillloweswater.co.uk

Millom

Small coastal town in the South Western Lake District.

HOLIDAY COTTAGE - LAKE DISTRICT (01229 717174). 300-year- old two-bedroom cottage on the west coast of Cumbria within the National Park. Traditional cottage, oak beams etc. Secure garden and an attached 3-acre deer-fenced playground for dogs. Close to miles of dog-friendly beaches. [pw! 🐾]

Newby Bridge

Village 8 miles NE of Ulverston

NEWBY BRIDGE HOTEL, NEWBY BRIDGE LA12 8NA (015395 31222). Overlooking the southern shores of Lake Windermere. Best Lakes Breaks from £118 per person for 2 nights. [Pets £5 per stay].
e-mail: info@newbybridgehotel.co.uk   website: www.bestlakesbreaks.co.uk

MR A.S.G. SCOTT, OAK HEAD CARAVAN PARK, AYSIDE, GRANGE-OVER-SANDS LA11 6JA (015395 31475). A well tended, uncrowded and wooded site set amidst picturesque fells. Flush toilets, hot showers, laundry facilities, hair dryers, deep freeze, gas on sale. Tourers (30 pitches), Tents (30 pitches), Auto Homes. Open March 1st to October 31st. [🐾]
website: www.oakheadcaravanpark.co.uk

Penrith

Market town and centre for touring Lake District. Of interest are 14th century castle, Gloucester Arms (1477) and Tudor House. Excellent sporting facilities. Windermere 27 miles, Keswick 18.

NORTH BANK, EAMONT BRIDGE, PENRITH (01768 862153; 07939 240214). Detached bungalow with private gardens. Two lounges, kitchen, utility room; two bathrooms, one with jacuzzi, the other a walk-in shower. Four bedrooms, sleeps 8/9. Parking. [Pets £20 per week]
website: www.northbankholidaycottage.com

THE GEORGE HOTEL, DEVONSHIRE STREET, PENRITH CA11 7SU (Freephone 0800 840 1242). Situated in the attractive town of Penrith the George Hotel provides the ideal base from which to explore the Lake District and Eden Valley. 35 comfortable en suite rooms. Bar or restaurant meals available. Discounted golf available. [Pets £10 per night].
e-mail: georgehotel@lakedistricthotels.net   website: www.lakedistricthotels.net

CARROCK COTTAGES. Four renovated, award-winning, stone-built cottages set on the fringe of the Lakeland Fells. Games room. Home cooked meals service. Ideal for fell walking. Excellent restaurants nearby. A warm welcome guaranteed. ETC ★★★★★ GOLD AWARD. Contact MALCOLM OR GILLIAN (01768 484111; Fax: 01768 488850). [Pets £25 per week each].
e-mail: info@carrockcottages.co.uk   website: www.carrockcottages.co.uk

LYVENNET COTTAGES. Five different cottages in and around the small farming village of Kings Meaburn in beautiful unspoilt 'Lyvennet Valley'. Ideal touring centre for the Lakes and Dales. JANET ADDISON, KELD FARM, KINGS MEABURN, PENRITH CA10 3BS (01931 714661/714226; Fax: 01931 714598). ETC ★★★★/★★★★★
website: www.lyvennetcottages.co.uk

Ravenstonedale

Conservation village in the Eden Valley, 5 miles from Kirkby Stephen.

MRS D. METCALFE, HIGH GREENSIDE, RAVENSTONEDALE, KIRKBY STEPHEN CA17 4LU (015396 23671). Superb B&B accommodation in 18th century farmhouse on 120-acre working hill farm. Double and single room with private shower; twin and double en suite. All have colour TV and tea/coffee making. Superb views across Eden Valley. [🐾]
website: www.farmhousebandbcumbria.com

St Bees

Village 4 miles south of Whitehaven.

SEACOTE PARK, THE BEACH, ST BEES CA27 0ET(01946 822777; Fax: 01946 824442). Adjoining lovely sandy beach on fringe of Lake District, modern luxury holiday caravans for hire. Full serviced touring pitches and tent area. St Bees is convenient for touring. We also have two other Caravan Parks close by, Tarnside and Seven Acres. ETC ★★★★. Rose Award Park. [Pets £3 per night, £20 per week in hire caravans; free of charge in tourers and tents]
e-mail: reception@seacote.com   website: www.seacote.com

Silloth-on-Solway

Solway Firth resort with harbour and fine sandy beach. Mountain views. Golf, fishing. Penrith 33 miles, Carlisle 23, Cockermouth 17.

MR AND MRS M.C. BOWMAN, TANGLEWOOD CARAVAN PARK, CAUSEWAY HEAD, SILLOTH CA7 4PE (016973 31253). Friendly country site, excellent toilet and laundry facilities. Tourers welcome or hire a luxury caravan. Open 1st March to January 31st. Telephone or e-mail for a brochure. AA THREE PENNANTS. [🐾]
e-mail: tanglewoodcaravanpark@hotmail.com   website: www.tanglewoodcaravanpark.co.uk

Skelwith Bridge

Small village in the southern area of the Lake District. 3 miles south of Grasmere.

MIDDLE BRIG HOW (015394 37635). Tucked away up a private drive surrounded by a well kept garden. Good sized living room with open fire and French doors. Large kitchen/dining area. Bathroom and separate wc; double bedroom with king size bed. Sleeps 2. [🐾]
e-mail: enquiries@wheelwrights.com   website: www.wheelwrights.com

Ullswater

Lake stretching for 7 miles with attractive Lakeside walks.

LAND ENDS CABINS, WATERMILLOCK, NEAR ULLSWATER CA11 0NB (017684 86438). Only 1.5 miles from Ullswater, our four detached log cabins have a peaceful fellside location in 25-acre grounds with two pretty lakes. Doggy heaven! Sleep 2-5. ETC ★★★ [🐾]
e-mail: infolandends@btinternet.com   website: www.landends.co.uk

FARRIERS LOFT, FELL VIEW, GLENRIDDING, PENRITH CA11 0PJ (017684 82795). Sleep 2-5. Lovely, comfortable, well equipped accommodation in an idyllic location between Glenridding and Patterdale. Magnificent views of the surrounding fells. Short Breaks available out of season.
e-mail: enquiries@farriersloft.com   website: www.farriersloft.com

COVE CARAVAN & CAMPING PARK, WATERMILLOCK, PENRITH CA11 0LS (017684 86549). Well-maintained and peaceful park overlooking Lake Ullswater surrounded by Fells. Ideally situated for walking, watersports and all Lake District attractions. Electric hook-ups with hardstandings, sheltered grass for campers. AA 3 PENNANTS. [Pets £1 per night]
website: www.cove-park.co.uk

Wasdale

Hamlet 1 mile north east of Wast Water

THE BRIDGE INN, SANTON BRIDGE, HOLMROOK CA19 1UX (019467 26221; Fax: 019467 26026). Award-winning country inn providing good food and accommodation. 16 en suite bedrooms. Ideal for exploring the Western Lakes and fells. Well behaved dogs welcome. [Pets £6 per stay].
e-mail: info@santonbridgeinn.com   website: www.santonbridgeinn.com

Wigton

Market town 11 miles SW of Carlisle.

FOXGLOVES COTTAGE, WIGTON. Sleeps 2-8. Spacious, well-equipped comfortable cottage on working farm. Children and pets very welcome. Easy reach Lake District, Scottish Borders and Roman Wall. Available all year. Short breaks by arrangement. MR & MRS E. & J. KERR, GREENRIGG FARM, WESTWARD, WIGTON CA7 8AH (016973 42676). [pw! First pet free, second or more £10 per week]
e-mail: kerr_greenrigg@hotmail.com

Windermere

Famous resort on lake of same name, the largest in England. Magnificent scenery. Car ferry from Bowness, one mile distant. Kendal 9 miles.

WATERMILL INN & BREWERY, INGS, NEAR WINDERMERE LA8 9PY (01539 821309; Fax: 01539 822309). Ruby and friends (Dogs) welcome you to the award-winning Inn. 16 real ales. Cosy fires, en suite rooms, excellent bar meals. Doggie water and biscuits served in the bar. Good doorstep dog walking. ETC ★★★★ [Pets £4 per night (includes donation to Dogs' Trust].
e-mail: info@Lakelandpub.co.uk   website: www.Lakelandpub.co.uk

Hundreds of self-catering holiday homes in a variety of wonderful locations, all well equipped and managed by our caring staff. Pets welcome. For brochure, contact: LAKELOVERS, BELMONT HOUSE, LAKE ROAD, BOWNESS-ON-WINDERMERE LA23 3BJ. (015394 88855; Fax: 015394 88857). ETC ★★★ - ★★★★★ [Pets £20 per week.]
e-mail: bookings@lakelovers.co.uk   website: www.lakelovers.co.uk

LANGDALE CHASE HOTEL, WINDERMERE LA23 1LW (015394 32201). Magnificent country house hotel with grounds sloping to the edge of Lake Windermere. Panoramic views, log fires, excellent food and friendly professional staff all ensure a memorable stay. ETC ★★★ [Pets £10 per night]
e-mail: sales@langdalechase.co.uk   website: www.langdalechase.co.uk

THE WILD BOAR INN, GRILL & SMOKEHOUSE, CROOK, NEAR WINDERMERE LA23 3NF (08458 504 604). Nestled in the beautiful Gilpin Valley, former coaching Inn set within its own private 72 acres of woodland. Excellent restaurant with local produce and real ales. Windermere Golf Club and Leisure Club nearby. [Pets £25, up to 2 dogs per stay - max. 4 nights.]
website: www.wildboarinn.co.uk

Blackburn, Blackpool, Carnforth, Cockerham, Preston, Thornley

Blackburn

Former mill town with a rich industrial heritage, set in the heart of Lancashire's Hill Country.

THE BROWN LEAVES COUNTRY HOTEL, LONGSIGHT ROAD, COPSTER GREEN, NEAR BLACKBURN BB1 9EU (01254 249523; Fax: 0845 557 0608). Situated on the A59 halfway between Preston and Clitheroe, five miles from Junction 31 on M6 in beautiful Ribble Valley. All rooms ground floor, en suite facilities, satellite TV, tea-making and hairdryer. Guests' lounge and bar lounge. Car parking. Pets by arrangement. All credit cards welcome. [🐾]
website: www.brownleavescountryhotel.co.uk

Blackpool

Famous resort with fine sands and many attractions and vast variety of entertainments. Blackpool Tower (500ft). Three piers. Manchester 47 miles, Lancaster 26, Preston 17, Fleetwood 8.

THE BRAYTON, 7-8 FINCHLEY ROAD, GYNN SQUARE, BLACKPOOL FY1 2LP (01253 351645). Quiet licensed hotel overlooking Gynn Gardens and the promenade. Full 'restaurant style' menu served daily. Dogs most welcome. Open all year. [🐾]
e-mail: info2@the-brayton-hotel.com   website: www.the-brayton-hotel.com

Carnforth

Town 6 miles North of Lancaster.

LOCKA OLD HALL COTTAGE, ARKHOLME, NEAR KIRKBY LONSDALE LA6 1BD (015242 21561). Small cottage with open fire in easy reach of Lake District, Yorkshire Dales and Lancashire coast. Lawned garden with views over fells and Ingleborough. Quiet location. Sleeps 2 (+2 on sofa bed). [🐾]
e-mail: cottage@locka.co.uk   website: www.locka.co.uk

Cockerham

Village 6 miles south of Lancaster.

COCKERHAM SANDS COUNTRY PARK, COCKERHAM, LANCASTER LA2 0BB (01524 751387). Family park with access to Lancashire Coastal Walk. Heated outdoor swimming pool, shop, launderette, Cockerham Country Club. Modern 4 and 6-berth fully equipped caravans for hire. [Pets £20 per week]

Preston

Large town on River Ribble, 27 miles from Manchester.

SIX ARCHES CARAVAN PARK, SCORTON, GARSTANG, NEAR PRESTON PR3 1AL (01524 791683). Modern 4 and 6-berth caravans, touring pitches; large two-bedroom flats to sleep 6. Blackpool 14 miles, Lake District 30 miles. Licensed club with entertainment. Controlled dogs welcome. [Pets £20 per week]

Thornley

Town 7 miles West of Clitheroe, 4 miles from Longridge.

LOUDVIEW BARN. Self-catering stone barn conversion in peaceful location in Forest of Bowland. Exceptional views across unspoilt countryside. Unit 1: one double, one twin and bunk beds; Unit 2: one double and one twin. ETC ★★★★ Contact: MR & MRS STARKEY, LOUDVIEW BARN, RAMS CLOUGH FARM, THORNLEY, PRESTON PR3 2TN (01995 61476). [🐾]
e-mail: loudview@ic24.net   website: www.loudview.co.uk

www.holidayguides.com

Accommodation Standards: Star Grading Scheme

The AA, VisitBritain, VisitScotland, and the VisitWales now use a single method of assessing and rating serviced accommodation. Irrespective of which organisation inspects an establishment the rating awarded will be the same, using a common set of standards, giving a clear guide of what to expect. They have full details of the grading system on their websites.

 www.enjoyEngland.com

Scottish TOURIST BOARD www.visitScotland.com

 Cymru Wales www.visitWales.com

www.theaa.com

Using a scale of 1-5 stars the objective quality ratings give a clear indication of accommodation standard, cleanliness, ambience, hospitality, service and food.

This shows the full range of standards suitable for every budget and preference, and allows visitors to distinguish between the quality of accommodation and facilities on offer in different establishments. All types of board and self-catering accommodation are covered, including hotels, B&Bs, holiday parks, campus accommodation, hostels, caravans and camping, and boats.

Gold and Silver awards are given to Hotels and Guest Accommodation that provide exceptional quality, especially in service and hospitality.

The more stars, the higher level of quality

★
acceptable quality; simple, practical, no frills

★★
good quality, well presented and well run

★★★
very good level of quality and comfort

★★★★
excellent standard throughout

★★★★★
exceptional quality, with a degree of luxury

National Accessible Scheme Logos for mobility impaired and older people

If you have particular mobility impairment. look out for the National Accessible Scheme. You can be confident of finding accommodation or attractions that meet your needs by looking for the following symbols.

 Older and less mobile guests
If you have sufficient mobility to climb a flight of steps but would benefit from fixtures and fittings to aid balance.

 Part-time wheelchair users
You have restricted walking ability or may need to use a wheelchair some of the time and can negotiate a maximum 3 steps.

 Independent wheelchair users
You are a wheelchair user and travel independently. Similar to the international logo for independent wheelchair us

 Assisted wheelchair users
You're a wheelchair user and travel with a friend or family member who helps you with everyday tasks.

Kintail Lodge Hotel, Glen Shiel, Ross-shire (p368)

Visit **www.holidayguides.com**
for pet-friendly accommodation in Britain

Rattray Head, Stonehaven, Turriff

Ballater

Village and resort 14 miles east of Braemar.

GLEN LUI HOTEL, 14 INVERCAULD ROAD, BALLATER AB35 5PP (013397 55402). Friendly, family-run hotel set in 2 acres of woodlands. Pets are welcome in our comfortable Pine Terrace twin rooms. Come to the Glen Lui for a great Scottish experience. Fantastic food and wines. Short breaks.
e-mail: infos@glen-lui-hotel.co.uk   website: www.glen-lui-hotel.co.uk

CAMBUS O'MAY HOTEL, BALLATER AB35 5SE (Tel & Fax: 013397 55428). Family-run country house hotel 4 miles east of Ballater. Excellent food; 12 en suite bedrooms. Ideal area for hill walking, golf, fishing and visiting Balmoral Castle etc. [🐾]
e-mail: mckechnie@cambusomay.freeserve.co.uk   website: www.cambusomayhotel.co.uk

🐾 Pets are welcome free of charge.   **Classified Symbols**

£   A charge is made for pets: nightly or weekly.

pw! Special provision for pets; exercise facility, feeding or accommodation arrangement.

⌂   Separate pets accommodation.

Braemar

Village 16 miles south west of Ballater. Popular tourist centre with famous Highland Games.

BRAEMAR HOLIDAY LODGES, GLENSHEE ROAD, BRAEMAR AB35 5YO. SELF CATERING LOG CABINS (Tel/Fax: 013397 41627). One and three bedroom cabins set in hotel grounds. Spacious open-plan layout with French doors leading to verandah. Open all year round. STB ★★★
e-mail: mail@braemarlodge.co.uk   website: www.braemarlodge.co.uk

Glenlivet

Located 8 miles north of Tomintoul. Distilleries and State forest.

BEECHGROVE COTTAGES, GLENLIVET. Traditional stone cottages set amidst beautiful surroundings near rivers Avon and Livet. All modernised and very comfortable. Fishing available. Ideal for exploring Highlands, Castle and Whisky Trails, walking, skiing, golf. Contact: THE POST OFFICE, TOMNAVOULIN, BALLINDALLOCH AB37 9JA (01807 590220) [🐕]
website: www.beechgrovecottages.co.uk

Rattray Head

Fishing port on the north east coast 27 miles north of Aberdeen. The most easterly town on the Scottish mainland.

SAND DUNES & SECLUDED 11-MILE BEACH. Eco-hostel and holiday flat in doggy heaven. Homely, relaxing retreat on generally sunny, dry, midge-free coast. Suit nature lovers, cyclists, walkers, even giant dogs. Washroom for clothes, kit and pets. ROB & VAL, LIGHTHOUSE COTTAGES, RATTRAY HEAD, PETERHEAD AB42 3HA (01346 532236) STB ★★★ Hostel.[pw! 🐕]
e-mail: hostel@rattrayhead.net   website: www.rattrayhead.net/hostel

Stonehaven

Fishing port on East Coast, 13 miles south of Aberdeen.

MRS AILEEN PATON, 'WOODSIDE OF GLASSLAW', STONEHAVEN AB39 3XQ (01569 763799). Modern bungalow with six centrally heated en suite bedrooms with colour TV and hospitality trays. Stonehaven two miles. Accessible for disabled guests. STB/AA ★★★★ [🐕]
e-mail: aileen@woodsideofglasslaw.co.uk   website: www.woodsideofglasslaw.co.uk

Turriff

Small town in agricultural area, 9 miles south of Banff.

SIMON PEARSE, COUNTRY COTTAGES, FORGLEN ESTATE, TURRIFF AB53 4JP (01888 562918). Estate on the beautiful Deveron River. Sandy beaches only nine miles away, Turriff two miles. 5 cottages sleeping 4–9. From £209 weekly. Open all year. Ideal for top golf courses, free brown trout fishing. Well-behaved dogs welcome. [🐕]
e-mail: reservations@forglen.co.uk   website: www.forglen.co.uk

ARDTUR COTTAGES

Two adjacent cottages in secluded surroundings. Ideal for hill walking, climbing, pony trekking, boating and fly fishing. Shop one mile; sea 200 yards; car essential; pets allowed.

MRS J PERY, ARDTUR, APPIN PA38 4DD (01631 730223 or 01626 834172)
e-mail: pery@btinternet.com • www.ardturcottages.com

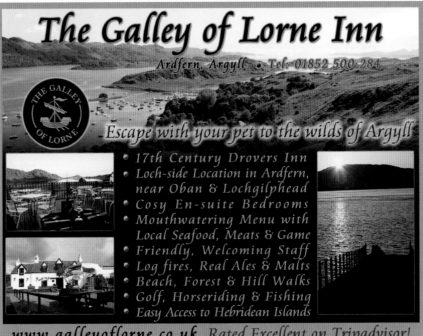

The Galley of Lorne Inn
Ardfern, Argyll • Tel: 01852 500 284

Escape with your pet to the wilds of Argyll

- 17th Century Drovers Inn
- Loch-side Location in Ardfern, near Oban & Lochgilphead
- Cosy En-suite Bedrooms
- Mouthwatering Menu with Local Seafood, Meats & Game
- Friendly, Welcoming Staff
- Log fires, Real Ales & Malts
- Beach, Forest & Hill Walks
- Golf, Horseriding & Fishing
- Easy Access to Hebridean Islands

www.galleyoflorne.co.uk Rated Excellent on Tripadvisor!

ARDNAMURCHAN & MULL

Self Catering Cottages in an unspoilt wilderness

01972 510 262
WWW.STEADING.CO.UK

Miles & miles of forestry, coastal & hill walks amidst spectacular scenery. Pets welcome in our cosy cottages, many of which have sea views & log fires.
Book your escape today!

Please mention PETS WELCOME!

when making enquiries about accommodation featured in this guide

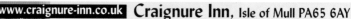
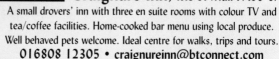

FHG Guides publish a large range of well-known accommodation guides. We will be happy to send you details or you can use the order form at the back of this book.

Appin

Mountainous area bounded by Loch Linnhe, Glen Creran and Glencoe.

MRS J PERY, ARDTUR, APPIN PA38 4DD (01631 730223 or 01626 834172). Two adjacent cottages in secluded surroundings. Ideal for hill walking, climbing, pony trekking, boating and fly fishing. Shop one mile; sea 200 yards; car essential; pets allowed.[🐾]
e-mail: pery@btinternet.com   website: www.ardturcottages.com

Ardfern

On west side of Loch Craignish, 4 miles west of Kilmartin.

THE GALLEY OF LORNE INN, ARDFERN PA31 8QN (01852 500284). 17thC drovers' inn in lochside location near Oban and Lochgilphead. Cosy en suite bedrooms, mouthwatering menu, friendly staff. Log fires, real ales and malts. Pets welcome, with miles of beach, forest and hill walks. [Pets £7.50 per night]
website: www.galleyoflorne.co.uk

Ardnamurchan

Peninsula on West Coast running from Salen to Ardnamurchan Point.

STEADING HOLIDAYS, ARDNAMURCHAN & MULL (01972 510262). Miles and miles of forestry, coastal and hill walks amidst spectacular scenery. Pets welcome in our cosy self-catering cottages, many of which have sea views and log fires.
website: www.steading.co.uk

Cairndow

Village at mouth of Kinglas Water on Loch Fyne in Argyll, near head of Loch.

Comfortable holiday cottage at the head of the longest sea loch in Scotland, in lovely walking country. Sleeps up to eight people. Linen and electricity included. STB ★★★ Self Catering. MRS DELAP, ACHADUNAN, CAIRNDOW, ARGYLL PA26 8BJ (Tel & Fax: 01499 600238).
website: www.argyllholidaycottages.com

CAIRNDOW STAGECOACH INN, CAIRNDOW PA26 8BN (01499 600286; Fax: 01499 600220). Well-appointed en suite bedrooms. Excellent cuisine in Stables Restaurant and lounge meals all day. Amenities include lochside beer garden, sauna and solarium. AA ★★★ Inn.
website: www.cairndowinn.com

Craignure (Isle of Mull)

Village and main ferry port on Isle of Mull located around the bay.

CRAIGNURE INN, ISLE OF MULL PA65 6AY (016808 12305). A small drovers' inn with three en suite rooms with colour TV and tea/coffee facilities. Home-cooked bar menu using local produce. Well behaved pets welcome. Ideal centre for walks, trips and tours.
e-mail: craignureinn@btconnect.com   website: www.craignure-inn.co.uk

Dalmally

Small town in Glen Orchy to the south-west of Loch Awe, with romantic Kilchurn Castle (14th century). Edinburgh 98 miles, Glasgow 69, Ardrishaig 42, Oban 25, Inveraray 16.

ROCKHILL WATERSIDE COUNTRY HOUSE, ARDBRECKNISH, BY DALMALLY PA33 1BH (01866 833218). 17th century guest house on waterside with spectacular views over Loch Awe. Three delightful rooms with all modern facilities. First-class home cooking.
website: www.rockhillfarmguesthouse.co.uk

Dunoon

Town and resort in Argyll, 4 miles west of Gourock across Firth of Clyde.

ABBOTS BRAE HOTEL, WEST BAY, DUNOON PA23 7QJ (01369 705021; Fax: 01369 701191). Small welcoming hotel at the gateway to the Western Highlands with breathtaking views. Comfortable, spacious, en suite bedrooms, quality home cooking and select wines. STB ★★★★ [🐾]
e-mail: info@abbotsbrae.co.uk   website: www.abbotsbrae.co.uk

Inveraray

18thC Royal burgh on the shores of Loch Fyne, 35 miles south of Oban.

HALFTOWN COTTAGES, ST CATHERINE'S (01369 860750). Heart of the West Highlands. 55 miles from Glasgow and across Loch Fyne from Inveraray. Two radically modernised 18thC farm cottages. Wholly secluded woodland site just above the loch. A real 'chill out' place for humans and animals. [Pets £10 per week.]
website: www.argyllcottages.com

Isle of Gigha

A tranquil island, one of the Inner Hebrides just of the west coast of Scotland. A haven for birds and wildlife.

GIGHA HOTEL, ISLE OF GIGHA PA41 7AA (01583 505254; Fax: 01583 505244). Beautiful, tranquil island. Explore the white sandy bays and lochs; famous Achamore Gardens. Easy walking, bike hire, birds, wildlife and wild flowers. Dog-friendly. Holiday cottages also available. [🐾]
website: www.gigha.org.uk

Kilchattan Bay

Quiet seaside village with wide bay on the East coast of Bute.

ST BLANE'S HOTEL, KILCHATTAN BAY, ISLE OF BUTE PA20 9NW (01700 831224). Traditional, family-run, pet-friendly, licensed Hotel offering superior en suite accommodation. Perfect base for walking, golf, windsurfing and other water sports. Open to non-residents. [🐾]
e-mail: info@stblaneshotel.com   website: www.stblaneshotel.com

Loch Crinan

The village of Crinan is at the entrance to the canal at the eastern end of the Loch.

DUNTRUNE CASTLE HOLIDAY COTTAGES. Sleep 2-5. Five traditional self-catering cottages in spacious grounds of castle. Estate comprises 5000 acres and 5 miles of coastline. For further details please contact: ROBIN MALCOLM, DUNTRUNE CASTLE, KILMARTN, ARGYLL PA31 8QQ (01546 510283). STB ★★★ Self Catering. [🐾]
website: www.duntrune.com

Loch Goil

Six mile long loch stretching from Lochgoilhead to Loch Long.

DARROCH MHOR, CARRICK CASTLE, LOCH GOIL PA24 8AF (01301 703249; Fax: 01301 703348). Five self-catering Chalets on the shores of Loch Goil in the heart of Argyll Forest Park. Fully equipped except linen. Colour TV, fitted kitchen, carpeted. Pets very welcome. Open all year. [🐾]
e-mail: mail@argyllchalets.com   website: www.argyllchalets.com

Oban

Popular Highland resort and port, yachting centre, ferry services to Inner and Outer Hebrides. Sandy bathing beach at Ganavan Bay. McCaig's Tower above town is Colosseum replica built in 1890s.

THE LANCASTER, ESPLANADE, OBAN PA34 5AD (01631 562587). A family-run, sea front hotel with 27 bedrooms. All public rooms enjoy sea views. Indoor swimming pool, steam room, sauna and spa. An ideal location from which to explore the Highlands and Islands.
e-mail: lancasteroban@btconnect.com   website: www.lancasteroban.co.uk

BARCALDINE HOUSE, NEAR OBAN PA37 1SG (01631 720219). An ideal location from which to explore Argyll and the Highlands. Spacious en suite bedrooms are equipped with TV, DVD, CD player and tea/coffee facilties. Full Scottish Breakfast. Dogs welcome. Self catering cottages also available. AA ★★★★ and 2 Rosettes.
e-mail: enquiries@barcaldinehouse.co.uk   website: www.barcaldinehouse.co.uk

MRS LINDA BATTISON, COLOGIN COUNTRY CHALETS, LERAGS GLEN, BY OBAN PA34 4SE (01631 564501; Fax: 01631 566925). Cosy chalets, lodges, cottages and houses, all conveniences. Situated on farm, wildlife abundant. Launderette, licensed bar serving home-cooked food. Free fishing. Playpark. STB ★★★/★★★★ Self-Catering [pw! Pets £20 per week.]
e-mail: info@cologin.co.uk   website: www.cologin.co.uk

COLIN & JO MOSSMAN, LAGNAKEIL HIGHLAND LODGES, LERAGS, OBAN PA34 4SE (01631 562746). Our Timber Lodges and four cottages are set in a tranquil, scenic wooded glen overlooking Loch Feochan, only 3 miles from the picturesque harbour town of Oban: "Gateway to the Isles". Lodges equipped to a high standard, including linen and towels, country pub a short walk. OAP discount. Free loch fishing. Special Breaks from £65 per lodge per night, weekly from £290-£1450. Sleep 1-12 comfortably. VisitScotland ★★★/★★★★ Self-Catering. [Pets £3 per night].
e-mail: info@lagnakeil.co.uk   website: www.lagnakeil.co.uk

TRALEE BAY HOLIDAYS, BENDERLOCH, BY OBAN PA37 1QR (01631 720255/217). Overlooking Ardmucknish Bay. The wooded surroundings and sandy beaches make Tralee the ideal destination for a self-catering lodge or caravan holiday anytime of the year. STB ★★★★★ [Pets £15 per week]
e-mail: tralee@easynet.co.uk   website: www.tralee.com

LOCH MELFORT HOTEL & RESTAURANT, ARDUAINE, BY OBAN PA34 4XG (01852 200233; Fax: 01852 200214). Stunning views down the Sound of Jura to the Islands. Located between Inveraray and Oban, beside the famous Arduaine Gardens. Excellent award-winning cuisine, comfortable accommodation, and friendly and attentive service. [Pets £8.50 per night]
e-mail: reception@lochmelfort.co.uk   website: www.lochmelfort.co.uk

MRS STEWART, GLENVIEW, SOROBA ROAD, OBAN PA34 4JF (01631 562267). Small family-run guest house, 10 minutes' walk from train, boat and bus terminal. A warm welcome awaits you all year round. [🐾]

MELFORT PIER AND HARBOUR, KILMELFORD, BY OBAN PA34 4XD (01852 200333; Fax: 01852 200329). Superb Lochside houses each with Sauna, Spa bath, Digital TV, Telephone, Wifi, on the shores of Loch Melfort. Excellent base for touring Argyll and the Isles. From £90 to £240 per night. Sleeps 2-6. 2 pets very welcome. Service with a smile. [Pets £15 each per stay]
website: www.mellowmelfort.com

Rothesay

Principal town on the Isle of Bute. Reached by ferry from Wemyss Bay.

DAVID & ELAINE DANIELS, ARDENCRAIG HOUSE APARTMENTS, ARDENCRAIG ROAD, ROTHESAY PA20 9EP (Tel & Fax: 01700 505077; Mobile: 07881 825653 or 07990 838350). Five spacious and comfortable apartments in a beautifully converted Georgian mansion. Overlooking the Firth of Clyde. Pets are welcome by prior arrangement. STB ★★★★.[🐾]
e-mail: EBDan10@aol.com   website: www.ardencraig.org.uk

Strontian

Village lying on the north shore of Loch Sunart, close to the head of the Loch.

KILCAMB LODGE HOTEL & RESTAURANT, STRONTIAN PH36 4HY (01967 402257). If good food, fine wine and fine dining and a touch of luxury are on your list of priorities when looking for a small, pet-friendly hotel, look no further than this Country House on the edge of Loch Sunart. STB ★★★ Gold, AA ★★★ and 2 Rosettes.
e-mail: enquiries@kilcamblodge.co.uk   website: www.kilcamblodge.co.uk

Tarbert

Fishing port on isthmus connecting Kintyre to the mainland.

Peaceful, unspoilt West Highland estate. Traditional cottages, with open fires. Sleep 4–10. Pets welcome. Walks, pony trekking, golf nearby. APPLY SOPHIE JAMES, SKIPNESS CASTLE, BY TARBERT PA29 6XU (01880 760207; Fax: 01880 760208). STB ★★/★★★ [🐾]
e-mail: sophie@skipness.freeserve.co.uk

DUNMORE COURT, KILBERRY ROAD, NEAR TARBERT PA29 6XZ (01880 820654). Four cottages sleeping 2-7. Wonderful walks and scenery, peace and quiet. Winter breaks available. Easy access to island ferries. Terms from £250-£600. Open all year. ASSC member. STB ★★ SELF CATERING. [🐾]
e-mail: bookings@dunmorecourt.com   website: www.dunmorecourt.com

Taynuilt

Village in Argyll 1km south west of Bonawe.

INVERAWE COTTAGES, TAYNUILT PA35 1HU (01866 822777). Three self-catering cottages offer a wonderful haven to relax. Comfortable, cosy and welcoming. Sleep 2, 4 and 6. Inverawe is a paradise for dogs, children and adults alike.
e-mail: cottages@inverawe.co.uk   website: www.inverawe-cottages.co.uk

www.holidayguides.com

Esplanade, Ayr KA7 1DT

Ayr's only seafront hotel, just five minutes'
walk from town centre.
Lunches, dinners and bar suppers served.

HORIZON HOTEL

A welcome guest. In all my years of experience of this business, I have never received a complaint about a dog slamming bedroom doors late at night, talking loudly in the corridors or driving away noisily from the car park when other guests are trying to sleep. Never has a dog made cigarette burns on the carpets, furniture or in the bath. No dog has ever stolen my towels, sheets or ashtrays. No cheque written by a dog has ever bounced and no dog has ever tried to pay with a stolen credit card. Never has a dog insulted my waitress or complained about food or wine. Neither have we ever had a dog who was drunk. In short you are welcome whenever you wish to come to this hotel and if you can vouch for your master, you are welcome to bring him along too!!

Phone now for free colour brochure. Under the personal supervision of Mr & Mrs A.H. Meikle.

Tel: 01292 264384 • Fax: 01292 264011
e-mail: reception@horizonhotel.com
www.horizonhotel.com

The Isle of Arran

AA "Inspectors' Choice" Hotel
VisitScotland "Gold Award" Hotel
& 5-Star Self-catering Cottages
www.kilmichael.com • 01770 302219

Kilmichael

Dyemill Lodges · Isle of Arran

Six Scandinavian designed pinewood lodges and two holiday homes offer comfortable accommodation in surroundings full of natural beauty and interest, yet close to all the amenities of Lamlash village .

**Contact: Dyemill House, Monamhor Glen, Lamlash, Isle of Arran KA27 8NT
Tel: 01770 600419 • e-mail: enquiries@dyemill.co.uk • www.dyemill.co.uk**

Strathconon Cottage · Self Catering Accommodation · Isle of Arran

Luxury self catering holiday accommodation in a beautiful secluded location. 300 yards from the seafront and within easy reach of shops and restaurants. Ideal base for up to 10 people. Category 3 Disabled Access. Well behaved pets are welcome by prior arrangement.

Jim and Moira Finlayson,
"Suilven", Southend, Argyll PA28 6RF
Phone: 01586 830323
Email: enquiries@arranselfcatering.com
www.arranselfcatering.com

ASSC

FHG Guides publish a large range of well-known accommodation guides. We will be happy to send you details or you can use the order form at the back of this book.

Ayr

Popular family holiday resort with sandy beaches. Excellent shopping, theatre, racecourse.

HORIZON HOTEL, ESPLANADE, AYR KA7 1DT (01292 264384; Fax: 01292 264011). Highly recommended for golf breaks; special midweek rates. Coach parties welcome. Lunches, dinners and bar suppers served. Phone now for free colour brochure. [🐶]
e-mail: reception@horizonhotel.com　　　　　website: www.horizonhotel.com

Brodick

Resort on east coast of Isle of Arran, Ferry connection to mainland.

KILMICHAEL HOTEL (01770 302219). AA "Inspectors' Choice" Hotel. VisitScotland "Gold Award" Hotel and 5-Star Self-catering Cottages
website: www.kilmichael.com

Lamlash

Village on east coast of Isle of Arran, 3 miles south of Brodick.

DYEMILL LODGES, ISLE OF ARRAN. Six Scandinavian designed pinewood lodges and two holiday homes offer comfortable accommodation in surroundings full of natural beauty and interest, yet close to all the amenities of Lamlash village. Contact: PAUL & SUE ARCHER, DYEMILL HOUSE, MONAMHOR GLEN, LAMLASH, ISLE OF ARRAN KA27 8NT (01770 600419). STB ★★★.
e-mail: enquiries@dyemill.co.uk　　　　　website: www.dyemill.co.uk

Whiting Bay

Village on east coast of Isle of Arran.

STRATHCONON COTTAGE, ISLE OF ARRAN. Luxury self catering holiday accommodation in a beautiful secluded location, 300 yards from the seafront. For up to 10 people. Category 3 Disabled Access. Well behaved pets welcome by prior arrangement. Contact: JIM AND MOIRA FINLAYSON, "SUILVEN", SOUTHEND, ARGYLL PA28 6RF (01586 830323). STB ★★★★.
e-mail: enquiries@arranselfcatering.com　　　　　website: www.arranselfcatering.com

Bonchester Bridge, Cockburnspath, Coldstream

A useful index of towns/counties appears on pages 455-461

Eyemouth, Galashiels, Jedburgh, Kelso

Selkirk, West Linton

Bonchester Bridge

Village on Rule Water, 6 miles east of Hawick. To east is Bonchester Hill surmounted by ancient earthworks.

Cockburnspath

Village situated at the eastern extremity of the Southern Upland Way.

MARION LAUDER, CLOVERKNOWE COTTAGES, PATHHEAD FARM,COCKBURNSPATH TD13 5XB (01368 830318). Two detached sandstone cottages on the border of Berwickshire and East Lothian. Modernised and equipped to high standards. Large enclosed gardens . Ample parking. En suite and ground floor bedrooms available. [🐕]
e-mail: mlauder@supanet.com

Coldstream

Town lying on the north bank of the River Tweed in Berwickshire. Home of the Coldstream Guards British Army Regiment.

LITTLE SWINTON HOLIDAY COTTAGES, coldstream (01890 882173). Three farm cottages, Cotoneaster, Ivy and Honeysuckle, in a row of single storey cottages built of traditional stone. Clean, comfortable, spacious and well equipped. Ample car parking. Children and pets welcome; large grass play area. [🐕]
e-mail: suebrewis@littleswinton.co.uk website: www.littleswinton.co.uk

Eyemouth

Small town on coast, 8 miles north-west of Berwick-upon-Tweed.

THE HERRING QUEEN. Water-front listed Georgian apartment sleeping 4+4 with glorious views of Eyemouth harbour from every room. Carefully upgraded, with modern day essentials. Also, ANTONINE WALL COTTAGES (STB ★★★★), two very well equipped self-catering cottages in Bonnybridge, Stirlingshire. Contact: FIONA BRIGGS, BONNYSIDE ROAD, BONNYBRIDGE FK4 2AA (01324 811875).
websites: www.theherringqueen.co.uk website: www.antoninewallcottages.co.uk

Galashiels

Picturesque town on the A7 Carlisle to Edinburgh. with a good choice of shops and leisure activities.

KINGSKNOWES HOTEL, SELKIRK ROAD, GALASHIELS TD1 3HY (01896 758375; Fax: 01896 750377). A Baronial mansion set in attractive gardens and close to the River Tweed. Elegant public areas, spacious bedrooms. Ideal base for touring. AA ★★★
e-mail: enq@kingsknowes.co.uk website: www.kingsknowes.co.uk

Jedburgh

Small town on Jed water, 10 miles north-east of Hawick. Ruins of abbey founded in 1138.

CHRISTINE SWANSTON, FERNIEHIRST MILL LODGE, JEDBURGH TD8 6PQ (01835 863279). A chalet style guest house set in grounds of 25 acres. All rooms en suite with tea/coffee making facilities. Well behaved pets (including horses) welcome by arrangement. AA ★★ [🐕]
e-mail: ferniehirstmill@aol.com website: www.ferniehirstmill.co.uk

CRAILING OLD SCHOOL, CRAILING, BY JEDBURGH TD8 6TL (01835 850382). Peacefully situated B&B close to the River Teviot. Ideal area for walking, fishing, golf and horse riding. Self contained lodge with wheelchair/disabled friendly access. Self catering possible. Evening meals by arrangement. AA ★★★★ [pw! Pets £2 per night, £10 per week]
e-mail: info@crailingoldschool.co.uk website: www.crailingoldschool.co.uk

Classified Symbols

- 🐕 Pets are welcome free of charge.
- £ A charge is made for pets: nightly or weekly.
- pw! Special provision for pets; exercise facility, feeding or accommodation arrangement.
- ⌂ Separate pets accommodation.

Kelso

Market town 18 miles north-west of Hawick and 20 miles south-west of Berwick-upon-Tweed.

WESTWOOD HOUSE, OVERLOOKING SCOTLAND'S FAMOUS RIVER TWEED. Enclosed and secluded riverside cottage with walled gardens and own private island. Sleeps 2-8 persons plus child, from £385 per week. 2 person discounts. For brochure contact: DEBBIE CRAWFORD, PIPPIN HEATH FARM, HOLT, NORFOLK NR25 6SS (07788 134832). [🐾]

MRS KIRSTY B. SHAW, SMAILHOLM MAINS FARM COTTAGES, BY KELSO TD5 7RT (01573 460318). Two cosy farm cottages, each sleeping 5, in a peaceful setting 6 miles from Kelso. Both with open fires, central heating, Sky TV. Close to golf, fishing, walking or a day at the races. Short breaks available. STB ★★★★[🐾]
e-mail: info@smailholm-mains.co.uk   website: www.kelsoaccommodation.co.uk

GLEBE HOUSE SELF-CATERING (07971 522 040). By Kelso and Jedburgh. Sleeps 10+2+cots. Large handsomely furnished rooms. Easy driving distance pubs, shops etc. Dogs welcome. STB ★★★★ *SELF-CATERING.* [🐾]
e-mail: enquiries@holidayhomescotland.co.uk   website: www.holidayhomescotland.co.uk

Newcastleton

Small village nestling in the valley of Liddesdale, ideal base for touring.

BAILEY MILL COURTYARD, BAILEY MILL, NEWCASTLETON TD9 0TR (016977 48617). Self-catering apartments nestling on the Roxburghshire / Cumbrian border. Also riding holidays with B&B or Full Board. Licensed bar. Colour brochure available. ETC★★/★★★ [🐾]
e-mail: baileymillaccom@aol.com   website: www.baileycottages-riding-racing.com

Peebles

Royal Burgh 23 miles south of Edinburgh with a good choice of shops and outdoor activities.

TONTINE HOTEL, HIGH STREET, PEEBLES EH45 8AJ (01721 720892). Dog-friendly hotel in the heart of Peebles. 36 en suite bedrooms, some with views of the river and Tweed Green. Parking. Wonderful walks on the door step. STB ★★★ [🐾]
e-mail: stay@tontinehotel.com   website: www.tontinehotel.com

CRINGLETIE HOUSE HOTEL, PEEBLES EH45 8PL (01721 725750). Our idyllic rural setting allows our guests to escape the stress and noise of everyday life. We welcome well-behaved children and dogs, and we have two rooms where dogs can be accommodated. Open all year. AA/STB ★★★★ [Pets £10 per night]
e-mail: enquiries@cringletie.com   website: www.cringletie.com

Selkirk

Town on hill above Ettrick Water, 9 miles north of Hawick

THE GARDEN HOUSE, WHITMUIR, SELKIRK TD7 4PZ (01750 721728; Mobile: 07768 707700). Comfortable, warm modern farm house B&B. Spacious bedrooms, private bathrooms. Good home cooking. Fishing, walking, cycling and horse riding nearby. Grazing available. Open all year. [🐾]
e-mail: whitmuir@btconnect.com   website: www.whitmuirfarm.co.uk.

West Linton

Village on east side of Pentland hills, 7 miles south-west of Penicuik. Edinburgh 18 miles.

MRS C. M. KILPATRICK, SLIPPERFIELD HOUSE, WEST LINTON EH46 7AA (01968 660401). Two lovely cottages on hideaway country estate near Edinburgh. Sleep 4/6. Available all year. Perfect dog-friendly location. STB ★★★/★★★★★ [🐾]
e-mail: cottages@slipperfield.com   website: www.slipperfield.com

Crossmichael, Dalbeattie, Dumfries, Drummore, Gatehouse of Fleet

Visit **www.holidayguides.com**
for pet-friendly accommodation in Britain

HILLCREST HOUSE

Maidland Place, Wigtown DG8 9EU
Tel: 01988 402018

Beautiful Victorian character villa set on
edge of national book town.
Fabulous views over nature reserve.
Six bedrooms, residents' lounge.
Evening meals using fresh local produce.

e-mail: info@hillcrest-wigtown.co.uk • www.hillcrest-wigtown.co.uk

Auchencairn

Village 7 miles south of Dalbeattie.

BALCARY BAY COUNTRY HOUSE HOTEL, AUCHENCAIRN, NEAR CASTLE DOUGLAS DG7 1QZ (01556 640217: Fax: 01556 640272). Ideal location for exploring South West Scotland. Well appointed bedrooms, all en suite. Imaginative cuisine based on local produce. STB ★★★, AA ★★★, 2 Rosettes. [🐾]
e-mail: reservations@balcary-bay-hotel.co.uk   website: www.balcary-bay-hotel.co.ukv

Auldgirth

Small village on A76.

FRIARS CARSE COUNTRY HOUSE HOTEL, AULDGIRTH DG2 0SA (01387 740388; Fax: 01387 740550). 21 en suite bedrooms. Restaurant serving excellent local cuisine. Private fishing. Snooker room. Putting Green. Golf & Cycling nearby. STB★★★.
website: www.friarscarse.co.uk

Castle Douglas

Old market town at the northern end of Carlingwalk Loch, good touring centre for Galloway

LOCHHILL QUALITY COTTAGES, LOCHHILL FARM, RINGFORD, CASTLE DOUGLAS DG7 2AR (01557 820225). Peaceful, quiet, relaxing, tranquil. Horses, riding school and trekking centre. Fantastic views, working farm, cycling. STB ★★★.
e-mail: lochhill@tiscali.co.uk   website: www.lochhill.net

MRS CELIA PICKUP, "CRAIGADAM", CASTLE DOUGLAS DG7 3HU (Tel & Fax: 01556 650233). Family-run 18th century famhouse. All bedrooms en suite. Billiard room/honesty bar. Lovely oak-panelled dining room offering Cordon Bleu cooking using local produce such as venison, pheasant and salmon. Trout fishing, walking and golfing available. STB ★★★★; AA ★★★★ and Breakfast & Dinner Awards. [🐾]
e-mail: inquiry@craigadam.com   website: www.craigadam.com

ROSE COTTAGE, GELSTON, CASTLE DOUGLAS DG7 1SH (01556 502513). Holiday cottage near secluded sandy beaches, water sports, birdwatching, walking, golf and fishing. Two double and two twin bedrooms; two bathrooms. Fully equipped kitchen. Sun room. Utility room. Enclosed courtyard. Ample parking. No smoking.

CATHY AND RICHARD AGNEW, GLENLEE HOLIDAY HOUSES, NEW GALLOWAY, CASTLE DOUGLAS DG7 3SF (01644 430212). Five charming holiday cottages in quiet secluded woodland set around a central courtyard. Each cottage is well equipped and comfortably furnished. An excellent base for exploring Galloway. STB ★★★. [🐾]
e-mail: agnew@glenlee-holidays.co.uk   website: www.glenlee-holidays.co.uk

Crossmichael

Small village on east side of Loch Ken, 4 miles north of Castle Douglas.

DEESIDE BED & BREAKFAST 42 MAIN STREET, CROSSMICHAEL, CASTLE DOUGLAS DG7 3AU (01556 670239) Small, family-run accommodation, surrounded by the unspoiled beauty of the Galloway countryside. One double en suite, twin/double with private facilities. STB ★★★. [Pets £3 per night].
e-mail: info@deesidebandb.co.uk   website: www.deesidebandb.co.uk

Dalbeattie

Small town in wooded valley on Urr Water, 12 miles form Dumfries.

BAREND HOLIDAY VILLAGE, SANDYHILLS, DALBEATTIE DG5 4NU (01387 780663). On the beautiful South West Colvend coast. Our log cabins are well equipped and centrally heated for all year comfort. On-site boules courts, bar, restaurant, sauna and indoor pool. Wi-Fi internet access available. [Pets £3 per night].
website: www.barendholidayvillage.co.uk

Dumfries

County town of Dumfries-shire and a former seaport. Dumfries contains many interesting buildings including an 18th century windmill containing a camera obscura. Robert Burns lived in the town before his death in 1796.

DAVID & GILL STEWART, AE FARM COTTAGES, GUBHILL FARM, DUMFRIES DG1 1RL (01387 860648). Modern accommodation in old stone buildings on a traditional farm, overlooking a peaceful valley. Beautiful views, plentiful wildlife and endless paths on the doorstep. Between Dumfries, Moffat and Thornhill. STB ★★★ SELF CATERING, CATEGORY ONE DISABILITY. [🐾]
e-mail: gill@gubhill.co.uk   website: www.aefarmcottages.co.uk

Drummore

Coastal location, 4 miles north of Mull of Galloway.

MULL OF GALLOWAY, DRUMMORE. A few short steps from the beach. STB 3/4-Star cottages; non-smoking cottages available. Tranquil and unspoiled village. Logan Botanical Gardens, golf, fishing, birdwatching nearby. Unrestricted beaches. ASSC. Contact SALLY COLMAN (01776 840631). [Pets £15 per pet per week]
website: www.harbourrow.co.uk

Gatehouse of Fleet

Small town near mouth of Water of Fleet, 6 miles north-west of Kirkcudbright

RUSKO HOLIDAYS, GATEHOUSE OF FLEET, CASTLE DOUGLAS DG7 2BS (01557 814215). Spacious farmhouse and three charming, cosy cottages near beaches, hills, gardens, castles and golf course. Walking, fishing, tennis. Pets, including horses, welcome. Sleep 2-12. STB ★★ to ★★★★ Self-Catering. Disabled Awards. [Pets £20 per week.]
e-mail: info@ruskoholidays.co.uk   website: www.ruskoholidays.co.uk

CARRICK HOLIDAY COTTAGES. Range of self-catering cottages and chalets in beautiful Carrick Bay and Brighouse Bay. Safe sandy beaches, sailing, cycling, walking, birdwatching, golf. Pets welcome. Contact CATHIE TENNANT, OWL COTE BYRE, CARRICK SHORE, GATEHOUSE OF FLEET DG7 2DT (01556 505485; Mobile: 07719 263098). [🐾]
e-mail: cathie.tennant@googlemail.com   website: www.carrickcottagesscotland.com

BANK OF FLEET HOTEL, 47 HIGH STREET, GATEHOUSE OF FLEET DG7 2HR (01557 81430) Situated in the picturesque and historic town of Gatehouse of Fleet. En suite single, double and family rooms from £32.50 pppn. Lounge Bar and Restaurant. Short Breaks £240 DB&B. STB ★★★.
e-mail: bankoffleet@btconnect.com   website: www.bankoffleet.co.uk

Kirkcudbright

Town in a sheltered position on north Solway shore, 25 miles from Dumfries.

BAYTREE HOUSE, 110 HIGH STREET, KIRKCUDBRIGHT DG6 4JQ (01557 330824). Award-winning Georgian townhouse in a conservation area of the historic harbour town of Kirkcudbright. Four en suite bedrooms. Dogs welcome by arrangement. STB ★★★★.
e-mail: info@baytreekirkcudbright.co.uk   website: www.baytreekirkcudbright.co.uk

GORDON HOUSE HOTEL,116 HIGH STREET, KIRKCUDBRIGHT DG6 4JQ (01557 330670; Fax: 01557 331040). Family-run hotel with an informal and relaxed atmosphere. Finest Scottish food, excellent accommodation and real value for money. Well behaved pets welcome by arrangement. [🐾]
e-mail: mail@gordon-house-hotel.co.uk   website: www.gordon-house-hotel.co.uk

Moffat

At head of lovely Annandale, grand mountain scenery. Good centre for rambling, climbing, angling and golf. The 'Devil's Beef Tub' is 5 miles, Edinburgh 52, Peebles 33, Dumfries 21.

HEATHERYHAUGH LODGES, MOFFAT DG10 9LD (01683 220107). For people who want extra comfort. Four fully equipped detached lodges, each with 3 large bedrooms, one en suite, plus main bathroom, laundry room, comfortable lounge. Set in secluded parkland. [Pets £10 per week]
e-mail: heatheryhaugh@aol.com   website: www.heatheryhaugh.co.uk

BARNHILL SPRINGS COUNTRY GUEST HOUSE, MOFFAT DG10 9QS (01683 220580). Early Victorian country house overlooking some of the finest views of Upper Annandale. Comfortable accommodation, residents' lounge with open fire. Situated on the Southern Upland Way half-a-mile from A74/M74 Moffat Junction. Pets free of charge. Bed & Breakfast from £33; Evening Meal by arrangement. AA ★★ [pw!]
e-mail: barnhillsprings@yahoo.co.uk

Newton Stewart

Small town on River Cree 7 miles north of Wigtown.

KINGS GREEN CARAVAN PARK, PORT WILLIAM DG8 9SG (01988 700489). A local community-run site with 30 pitches (22 have electricity) set on the edge of the fishing village of Port William. Toilet/shower/laundry block with disabled facility. [🐾]
website: www.portwilliam.com

BARGALY ESTATE COTTAGES, PALNURE, NEWTON STEWART DG8 7BH (01671 401048). Three cottages. The Gatehouse Cottage to the historic Bargaly Estate stands proudly looking over the countryside beyond. Gardener's Cottage was once the home fo the head gardener and lies adjacent to the walled garden. Nestling in a woodland setting lies Squirrel Cottage. Salmon and trout fishing. [🐾].
e-mail: bargalyestate@callnetuk.com   website: www.bargaly.com

Portpatrick

Village on the extreme south-westerly tip of mainland Scotland cut into a cleft in steep cliffs.

1D OLD STATION COURT, PORTPATRICK. A modern fully equipped two-bedroom flat with satellite TV and DVD player. Sleeps 4. Off-street parking. Pets by prior arrangement. STB ★★★ CONTACT: MR J REID, 46 RODGER AVENUE, NEWTON MEARNS, GLASGOW G77 6JS (0141-616 2808; 07515 952500 / 07752 120527).

Stranraer

Scotland's gateway to Ireland, only 90 minutes away by fast ferry. Ideal base for outdoor activities.

CROSS HAVEN GUEST HOUSE, LEWIS STREET, STRANRAER DG9 7AL (01776 700598). Family-run Guest House close to ferry, offering quality service and value for money. En suite bedrooms. Ideal for couples, ferry passengers and visitors to Ireland. Pets welcome. STB ★★★. [Pets £7 per night]
e-mail: crosshavengh@yahoo.co.uk   website: www.crosshaven.co.uk

Thornhill

Small town on River Nith 13 miles north-west of Dumfries. Site of Roman signal station lies to the south.

TEMPLAND COTTAGES, TEMPLAND MAINS, THORNHILL DG3 5AB (01848 330775). Set in the heart of the Nith Valley near Thornhill, with shops, hotels and restaurants. Tastefully converted cottages sleep from 2-6. Own patio with BBQ, heated indoor pool and sauna. [🐕]
e-mail: jacqui@templandcottages.co.uk   website: www.templandcottages.co.uk

TRIGONY HOUSE HOTEL, THORNHILL DG3 5EZ (01848 331211). Standing in over 4 acres of woodland and gardens, Trigony is a luxury Country House Hotel with a combination of relaxed style and excellent rustic cuisine. Should you have a dog they will be more than welcome at our pet-friendly hotel. [pw!]
e-mail: info@trigonyhotel.co.uk   website: www.countryhousehotelscotland.com

HILLCREST BARN. One mile from Drumlanrig Castle estate, offering fishing, mountain biking, walking, and 4x4 tours. One double room, shower room, enclosed garden. Digitial TV, DVD; fully fitted kitchen. Short Breaks available all year; includes heating, towels and linen. For details contact: 01848 331557. STB ★★★ [🐕]
website: www.thornhillselfcatering.co.uk

HOPE COTTAGE, THORNHILL DG3 5BJ (01848 331510; Fax: 01848 331810). Pretty stone cottage in the peaceful conservation village of Durisdeer. Well-equipped self-catering cottage with large secluded garden. Sleeps 5/6. Towels, linen, heating and electricity included. Phone MRS S. STANNETT for brochure. STB ★★★★ [🐕]
e-mail: a.stann@btinternet.com   website: www.pet-dog-friendly-selfcatering-hopecottage.co.uk

Whithorn

Small town 9 miles south of Wigtown.

MIKE AND HELEN ALEXANDER, CRAIGLEMINE COTTAGE B&B, GLASSERTON, NEAR WHITHORN DG8 8NE (01988 500594). Our rural location makes this a wonderful place to unwind. Ideal for touring, your dog will love the nearby beaches. Evening meal available. STB ★★ [🐕]
e-mail: cottage@fireflyuk.net   website: www.startravel.fireflyinternet.co.uk

KATH & TIM ANNISON, CHAPEL OUTON FARMHOUSE B&B, WHITHORN DG8 8DH (01988 500136) Old-fashioned hospitality in comfortable and informal surroundings.Non-smoking, spacious yet cosy accommodation and wholesome home cooked food. Let us spoil you and your family and pamper your pet. [pw! 🐕]
e-mail: kath@chapelouton.co.uk   website: www.chapelouton.co.uk

Wigtown

Small town on hill above River Cree, known as "Scotland's Book Town".

HILLCREST HOUSE, MAIDLAND PLACE, WIGTOWN DG8 9EU (01988 402018). Beautiful character Victorian villa set on edge of national book town. Fabulous views over nature reserve. Six bedrooms, residents' lounge. Evening meals using fresh local produce. [Pets free in kennels, £1 per night indoors]
e-mail: info@hillcrest-wigtown.co.uk   website: www.hillcrest-wigtown.co.uk

🐕   Pets are welcome free of charge.

£   A charge is made for pets: nightly or week

Classified Symbols

pw! Special provision for pets; exercise facility, feeding or accommodation arrangement.

⌂   Separate pets accommodation.

Bonhill (near Loch Lomond)

Bonhill (near Loch Lomond)

Small town on the eastern bank of the River Leven, ideal for touring Loch Lomond and beyond.

SUNNYSIDE B&B, MAIN STREET NORTH, BONHILL, NEAR LOCH LOMOND G83 9JX (01389 750282).
Family-run B&B in deceptively large cottage, set in its own grounds. Six en suite bedrooms. Close
to Loch Lomond, Glasgow, Stirling, Edinburgh and the Trossachs. [Pets £5 per week]
e-mail: enquiries@sunnysidebb.co.uk   website: www.sunnysidebb.co.uk

Edinburgh & Lothians

North Berwick, Rosewell, West Calder

North Berwick

Town and resort 19 miles east of Edinburgh.

WEST FENTON COURT, WEST FENTON, NORTH BERWICK EH39 5AL(01620 842154). Luxury self-catering holiday cottages near North Berwick, perfect for families, golf, walking, beaches and relaxation. Just 35 minutes from Edinburgh. Superbly equipped. STB ★★★★ [Pets £10 per week].
e-mail: info@westfenton.co.uk   website: www.westfenton.co.uk

Rosewell

Village 4 miles south west of Dalkeith.

HUNTER HOLIDAY COTTAGES, THORNTON FARM, ROSEWELL, EDINBURGH EH24 9EF (0131 448 0888; Fax: 0131 440 2082). 2 x two-bedroom cottages and 1 x 3-bedroom cottage on working farm 20 minutes' drive Edinburgh. Great walks on tracks and through woods. Contact MARGOT CRICHTON. [Pets £10 per night/week].
e-mail: info@edinburghcottages.com   website: www.edinburghcottages.com

West Calder

Village in West Lothian 4 miles west of Livingston.

CROSSWOODHILL FARM HOLIDAY COTTAGES, NEAR EDINBURGH. Well equipped and spacious properties, family, pet and disabled friendly. Ideal base for exploring this scenic area and for visiting Edinburgh. STB 3/5 Stars. Contact: GERALDINE HAMILTON, CROSSWOODHILL, WEST CALDER, WEST LOTHIAN EH55 8LP (01501 785205).[Pets £20 per week]
e-mail: cottages@crosswoodhill.co.uk   website: www.crosswoodhill.co.uk
www.fivestarholidaycottage.co.uk

Lower Largo, St Andrews

The Crusoe Hotel

Main Street, Lower Largo, Fife KY8 6BT
Tel: 01333 320759 • Fax: 01333 320865
email: relax@crusoehotel.co.uk
www.crusoehotel.co.uk

Old-world ambience with fine harbour views. En suite accommodation, outstanding cuisine, free house. Excellent centre for sailing, golf, birdwatching, wind surfing, coastal walks.

ST ANDREWS COUNTRY COTTAGES

Idyllic Country Cottages and Farmhouses in St Andrews and on a beautiful Country Estate. Perfect for golf, exploring or relaxing. Enclosed gardens, log fires, private walking. Sleep 4 to 14.

ASSC Brochure:- Mountquhanie Estate, FREEPOST, Cupar, Fife KY15 4BR
Tel: 01382 330318 • Fax: 01382 330480
e-mail: enquiries@standrews-cottages.com • www.standrews-cottages.com

Lower Largo

Village on the bay, 2 miles NE of Leven. Birth place of Alexander Selkirk of Robinson Crusoe fame.

THE CRUSOE HOTEL, MAIN STREET, LOWER LARGO, NEAR ST ANDREWS KY8 6BT. (01333 320759; Fax: 01333 320865). Old-world ambience with fine harbour views. En suite accommodation, outstanding cuisine, free house. Excellent centre for sailing, golf, birdwatching, wind surfing, coastal walks. STB ★★★ Hotel. [🐾]
email: relax@crusoehotel.co.uk   website: www.crusoehotel.co.uk

St Andrews

Home of golf - British Golf Museum has memorabilia dating back to the origins of the game. Remains of castle and cathedral. Sealife Centre and beach Leisure Centre. Excellent sands. Ideal base for exploring the picturesque East Neuk.

MR & MRS PATRICK WEDDERBURN, ST ANDREWS COUNTRY COTTAGES, MOUNTQUHANIE ESTATE, FREEPOST, CUPAR KY15 4BR (01382 330318; Fax: 01382 330480). Quality self-catering houses and cottages in St Andrews and on a tranquil Country Estate. Central heating, TV. Enclosed gardens. STB ★★★ to ★★★★★ Self Catering. [pw! Dogs £15 per week, Cats F.O.C.].
e-mail: enquiries@standrews-cottages.com   website: www.standrews-cottages.com

Pet-Friendly
Pubs, Inns & Hotels
on pages 448-453
These establishments may not feature in the main section of the book

Fort William

Gairloch, Glencoe, Glen Shiel, Invermoriston, Inverness, Killin

Balbeag • Kincraig   STB ★★★

01963 220250 • camacg@talk21.com • www.balbeag.co.uk

A comfortable S/C family holiday cottage built of pine logs and set in the Cairngorm National Park. Living/dining room, open-plan kitchen, bathroom and 4 bedrooms. Sleeps 1-8. Satellite TV, DVD, wood-burning stove. Available March to December. Nearby activities include watersports, horse riding, gliding, golf and walks.

"Fraser" & "Telford" Cottages

Close to Loch Insh and Glenfeshie, an ideal holiday base from which to explore the Cairngorms National Park. In the Highland village of Kincraig, equidistant from Aviemore and Kingussie. Well behaved dogs and children welcome!

STB ★★★
Silver GTBS Award

Contact: Nick & Patsy Thompson, Glebe House, Kincraig PH21 1NU (01540 651377)
e-mail: glebecottages@gmail.com • www.glebecottages.co.uk

Allt Gynack Guest House

Tel:
01540 661081

Gynack Villa, 1 High Street, Kingussie, Near Aviemore PH21 1HS
Family owned Victorian guest house in a beautiful part of the Highlands. In its own grounds with private car park. Open all year. Huge range of activities. Excellent restaurants nearby.
e-mail: alltgynack@tiscali.co.uk • www.alltgynack.com

COLUMBA HOUSE
HOTEL & GARDEN RESTAURANT

In an area of oustanding natural beauty. An oasis amidst the magnificent scenery, stunning landscapes and tranquillity, in the foothills of snow-capped peaks of the Cairngorm and Monadhliath mountains, in the Cairngorms National Park. Quiet Highland retreat, nestling in a secluded, landscaped, walled garden with patio for summer time dining. Offering the highest standards of welcoming hospitality, accommodation and customer care, friendly atmosphere. Rooms with their own front doors, perfect for doggie holidays. Candlelit Garden Restaurant, renowned for excellent cuisine and attentive service. Homely, enchanting lounge and cosy bar, offering modern facilities while retaining their original charm. Wi-Fi. Nearby Leisure Club free. Wheelchair friendly; wet room. Suberb Penthouse Suite. **B&B from £40.**
Manse Road, Kingussie PH21 1JF • Tel: 01540 661402
e-mail: myra@columbahousehotel.com • www.columbahousehotel.com

---

LOCH NESS
Wildside, Whitebridge, Inverness IV2 6UN

Exceptional riverside lodges close to the spectacular Loch Ness. Mountains, lochs, waterfalls and wildlife abound.

Charming riverside lodges with private lawns, log fires and mountain views. Lodges range from 1, 2 & 3 bedrooms, sleeping from 2 to 8 people. All lodges are non-smoking and enjoy magnificent views. Quiet location with excellent walks from your lodge. Pets welcome. Free fishing.

Tel: 01456 486 373 • Fax: 01456 486 371
e-mail: info@wildsidelodges.com
www.wildsidelodges.co.uk

ASSC — Scottish Tourist Board ★★★★ Self Catering

Tigh an Eilean Hotel
& Shieldaig Bar and Coastal Kitchen

Tigh an Eilean (*"House of the Island"*) is in the picturesque 200-year-old fishing village of Shieldaig in Wester Ross, one of Scotland's last great wildernesses. Here the magnificent Torridon Mountains meet the Western Seas: spectacular walking, deserted beaches, home for seals, otters and sea eagles. Our award-winning hotel restaurant and the Coastal Kitchen next door both look across the sea to the sunset, and serve seafood delivered from the jetty to the kitchen door each day, together with other local specialities.

Good Hotel Guide ★ AA Britain's Best Hotels ★ Good Food Guide.

Shieldaig on Loch Torridon, Ross-shire, IV54 8XN • Tel: 01520 755251 • Fax: 01520 755321
e-mail: tighaneilean@keme.co.uk • www.tighaneilean.co.uk

Ord House Hotel, Muir of Ord, Ross-shire IV6 7UH

AA ★★ SMALL HOTEL

17th Century country house. Extensive gardens and woodlands for dogs to run around in. Large, airy bedrooms. Log fires. Restaurant with AA Rosette.
Telephone: 01463 870492
e-mail: admin@ord-house.co.uk • www.ord-house.co.uk

01309 672505

Speyside Cottages
Nethy Bridge, Inverness-shire | in Cairngorms National Park

Relax in 2 comfortable cottages (sleep 2-6) with fenced gardens, on riverbank with wonderful forest walks. Pets welcome. £170-£435 per week, includes full linen and towels.
Brian and Moira Patrick, 1 Chapelton Place, Forres, Moray IV36 2NL
brian@speysidecottages.co.uk • www.speysidecottages.co.uk

ASSC
VisitScotland ★★★★

Nethy Bridge, Highlands • Balnagowan Mill and Woodlark

Comfortable, modern 3 bedroom cottages in secluded locations in the Cairngorms National Park with extensive network of woodland and riverside walks on the doorstep, which is ideal for pets. Furnished to a high standard with full central heating.
£260 - £590 per week inclusive of electricity, bed linen and towels.
Contact Paula Fraser, 33 Argyle Grove, Dunblane, Perthshire FK15 9DT
Tel: 01786 824957   email: paulajfraser@aol.com

Please mention PETS WELCOME!

when making enquiries about accommodation featured in this guide

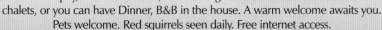

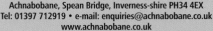

ISLANDS & HIGHLANDS COTTAGES, BRIDGE ROAD, PORTREE, ISLE OF SKYE IV51 9ER (01478 612123). Self catering accommodation in the beautiful, unspoilt Outer Hebrides, Isle of Skye and West Coast mainland. Come and relax in one of our holiday homes and experience the holiday of a lifetime. Quote Ref: PWFHG.
website: www.islands-and-highlands.co.uk

HIGHLAND HOTEL COLLECTION. A warm welcome awaits you in the Highlands of Scotland. BALLACHULISH HOTEL (0844 855 9133). ISLES OF GLENCOE HOTEL, BALLACHULISH (0844 855 9134). OBAN CALEDONIAN HOTEL, OBAN (0844 855 9135). STB ★★★
e-mail: reservations@akkeronhotels.com   website: www.akkeronhotels.com

Aviemore (Inverness-shire)

Scotland's leading ski resort in Spey valley with superb sport and entertainment facilities. All-weather holiday centre.

PINE BANK CHALETS, AVIEMORE (01479 810000). Self-catering log cabins, chalets and apartments by the River Spey. STB ★★★/★★★★ accommodation with easy access to the mountains and the stunning scenery of the Cairngorm National Park, yet also within walking distance of the village. Pine Bank Chalets is your ideal base for a stay in Aviemore. Pets welcome.
e-mail: info@pinebankchalets.co.uk   website: www.pinebankchalets.co.uk

FIONA GRANT, AVIELOCHAN FARM HOLIDAY COTTAGES, AVIELOCHAN FARM, AVIEMORE PH22 1QD (01479 810846). Situated beside a small loch within the Cirngorms National Park, Avielochan Holiday cottages enjoy spectacular views of the mountains. Sleep 5/7; caravan also available. Pets welcome. STB ★★★, Green Tourism Silver Award. [🐾]
e-mail: info@avielochancottages.co.uk   website:www.avielochancottages.co.uk

CAIRNGORM HIGHLAND BUNGALOWS, GLEN EINICH, 29 GRAMPIAN VIEW, AVIEMORE PH22 1TF (01479 810653, Fax: 01479 810262). Well equipped bungalows ranging from one to four bedrooms. Open all year. Leisure facilities nearby. Children and pets welcome. Phone for brochure. STB ★★★-★★★★ [🐾]
e-mail: linda.murray@virgin.net   website: www.cairngorm-bungalows.co.uk

Beauly (Inverness-shire)

Town at head of Beauly Firth, 11 miles west of inverness.

FRANK & JULIET SPENCER-NAIRN, CULLIGRAN COTTAGES, GLEN STRATHFARRAR, STRUY, NEAR BEAULY IV4 7JX (Tel & Fax: 01463 761285). Pure magic! Come for a spell in a chalet or cottage and this glen will cast one over you! Nature Reserve with native woodlands and wildlife. Open March - November. Brochure. Terms from £199-£529. [🐾]
e-mail: info@culligrancottages.co.uk   website: www.culligrancottages.co.uk

KERROW HOUSE, GLEN AFFRIC, CANNICH, BY BEAULY IV4 7NA (01456 415243; Mobile: 07944 726489). A selection of self-catering accommodation situated in 12 acres of wooded grounds, from Scandinavian-style chalets to a traditional riverside lodge. Sleep 2-7. Free fishing; rod hire available.   B&B also available (no pets). [Pets £20 per week - SC only].
email: info@kerrow-house.co.uk   website: www.kerrow-house.co.uk

www.holidayguides.com

Carrbridge (Inverness-shire)

Village on River Dulnain, 7 miles north of Aviemore. Landmark Visitor Centre has exhibition explaining history of local environment.

THE PINES COUNTRY GUESTHOUSE, DUTHIL, CARRBRIDGE PH23 3ND (01479 841220). Relax and enjoy our Highland hospitality, woodland setting; all rooms en suite. Traditional or vegetarian home cooking. B&B from £30 daily; DB&B from £268 weekly. Children and pets welcome. AA ★★★ [🐎]
website: www.thepines-duthil.co.uk

Contin (Ross-shire)

Village 2 miles south west of Strathpeffer.

COUL HOUSE HOTEL, CONTIN, BY STRATHPEFFER IV14 9ES (01997 421487; Fax: 01997 421945). Privately owned and operated 20-bedroom Country House Hotel with miles of forest walks, many log fires, and great food. Both you and your dog are made to feel most welcome.
e-mail: stay@coulhousehotel.com　　　　　website: www.coulhousehotel.com

Drumnadrochit (Inverness-shire)

Village on the shores of Loch Ness with "Monster" visitor centre. Sonar scanning cruises.

TORRAN HOUSE, UPPER DRUMBUIE, DRUMNADROCHIT IV63 6UX (01456 459 3530). Dog-friendly accommodation in the heart of the beautiful Scottish Highlands! B&B in guest wing, sleeps 5. Dogs and owners can roam for miles. [🐎]
e-mail: enquiries@torranbandb.net　　　　　website: www.torranbandb.net

GLENURQUHART LODGES, BY DRUMNADROCHIT IV63 6TJ (01456 476234; Fax: 01456 476286). Situated between Loch Ness and Glen Affric in a spectacular setting ideal for walking, touring or just relaxing in this tranquil location. Four spacious chalets all fully equipped for six people, set in wooded grounds. Owner's hotel adjacent where guests are most welcome in the restaurant and bar. [Pets £10 per week.]
e-mail: carol@glenurquhartlodges.co.uk　　　　　website: www.glenurquhart-lodges.co.uk

Fort William (Inverness-shire)

Small town at foot of Ben Nevis, ideal base for climbers and hillwalkers.

THE MOORINGS HOTEL, BANAVIE, FORT WILLIAM PH33 7LY (Tel: 01397 772797; Fax: 01397 772441). Situated alongside the Caledonian Canal, offering friendly personal service, comfort and style. Modern bedrooms feature hospitality trays, free Wi-Fi and satellite TV. Restaurant and Bar serve locally sourced produce. STB/AA ★★★ and Rosette. [pw! Pets £7 per stay]
e-mail: reservations@moorings-fortwilliam.co.uk　　website: www.moorings-fortwilliam.co.uk

THE CLAN MACDUFF HOTEL, FORT WILLIAM PH33 6RW (01397 702341; Fax: 01397 706174). This family-run hotel overlooks Loch Linnhe, two miles south of Fort William, excellent for touring the West Highlands. All rooms have TV, hairdryer, hospitality tray and private facilities. B&B from £27.50pppn. Three nights DB&B from £129pp (Spring/Autumn). STB ★★★ Hotel. Phone or write for colour brochure and tariff. [🐎]
e-mail: reception@clanmacduff.co.uk　　　　　website: www.clanmacduff.co.uk

LINNHE LOCHSIDE HOLIDAYS, CORPACH, FORT WILLIAM PH33 7NL (01397 772376; Fax: 01397 772007). Linnhe is unique and one of the most beautiful lochside parks in Britain. Close to Ben Nevis and Fort William. Excellent facilities. Pets welcome. Open mid December-end October. Colour brochure. (Pets £5 per night, £25 per week).
e-mail: relax@linnhe-lochside-holidays.co.uk　　website: www.linnhe-lochside-holidays.co.uk

🐎　Pets are welcome free of charge.

£　A charge is made for pets: nightly or weekly.

pw!　Special provision for pets; exercise facility, feeding or accommodation arrangement.

⌂　Separate pets accommodation.

Classified Symbols

GREAT GLEN HOLIDAYS, TORLUNDY, FORT WILLIAM PH33 6SW (Tel/Fax: 01397 703015). Sleep 4-6. Eight spacious, two-bedroom timber chalets on working Highland farm. Riding, fishing and walking on farm. Ideal for family holidays, excellent touring base. [Pets £15 per week]
e-mail: chris.carver@btconnect.com   website: www.fortwilliam-chalets.co.uk

LOCH LEVEN HOTEL, OLD FERRY ROAD, NORTH BALLACHULISH, NEAR FORT WILLIAM PH33 6SA (01855 821236). Twelve en suite rooms, many with loch views. Meals using freshly prepared Scottish produce. Secluded garden down to shore. Safe, private parking. Extensive grounds. Great walks. [pw! 🐕]
e-mail: reception@lochlevenhotel.co.uk   website: www.lochlevenhotel.co.uk

Gairloch (Ross-shire)

Small village on shore of Loch Gairloch.

THE OLD INN, FLOWERDALE GLEN, GAIRLOCH IV21 2BD (01445 712006: Fax: 01445 712933). A Traditional Highland Coaching Inn overlooking Gairloch harbour on the west coast of Scotland. Well known for its friendly welcome and relaxed atmosphere. Excellent accommodation, outstanding seafood, "Pub of the Year" awards. STB ★★★.
e-mail: enquiries@theoldinn.net   website: www.theoldinn.net

Glencoe (Inverness-shire)

Valley of River Coe, running west to Loch Leven, 3 miles east of Ballachulish. Site of notorious massacre in 1692.

INCHREE CHALETS & ROOMS, ONICH, NEAR FORT WILLIAM PH33 6SE (Tel & Fax: 01855 821287). Between Ben Nevis and Glencoe. 8 self-catering chalets, 4 or 6 berth. Pub and Restaurant on site. Discount for couples. Short-stay breaks available all year. [Pets £3 per night, £15 per week]
e-mail: stay@inchreecentre.co.uk   website: www.inchree.co.uk

Glen Shiel (Inverness-shire)

Valley on River Shiel in Skye & Lochalsh District.

KINTAIL LODGE HOTEL, SHIEL BRIDGE, GLENSHIEL IV40 8HL (01599 511275). Beautifully situated on the shores of Loch Duich 6 miles south of Eilean Donan Castle. We guarantee your comfort and we promise you the best of Highland food and hospitality. Dogs welcome.
e-mail: kintaillodgehotel@btinternet.com   website: www.kintaillodgehotel.co.uk

Invermoriston (Inverness-shire)

Small village 7 miles north of Fort Augustus, site of the Thomas Telford Bridge.

INVERMORISTON HOLIDAY CHALETS, GLENMORISTON, BY LOCH NESS IV63 7YF (01320 351254; Fax: 01320 351343) Centrally located in spectacular scenery, holiday accommodation which sleeps 2-4. All have free satellite TV, private patio area with barbecue. Dogs welcome in some chalets. Excellent base to explore, hill walk, fish and much more. [Pets £20 per week]
e-mail: info@invermoriston-holidays.co.uk   website: www.invermoriston-holidays.co.uk

Inverness (Inverness-shire)

Known as "The Capital of the Highlands". Airport, excellent shopping. Ideal touring base.

LOCH NESS HIDEAWAYS. Charming timber cottage and chalet (quarter-mile apart). Fully equipped. Lovely views. Ideal for dog lovers. Contact: MRS JANET SUTHERLAND, LOCH NESS HIDEAWAYS, AULTNAGOIRE, ERROGIE, BY INVERNESS IV2 6UH (01456 486711). [First 2 dogs free, £10 per week for additional dogs]
e-mail: janet@lochnesshideaways.co.uk   website: www.lochnesshideaways.co.uk

---

Terms quoted in this publication may be subject to increase if rises in costs necessitate

Killin (Perthshire)

Picturesque village at Western head of Loch Tay.

LYNNE AND ALISTAIR FERGUSON, 'BROCHANACH' 43 FINGAL ROAD, KILLIN FK21 8XA (01567 820028). Bed and varied Scottish Breakfast in small, tranquil village in the heart of Highland Perthshire. Ideal touring base. "Good walkies area" – dogs are especially welcome and stay free. [🐾 pw!]
e-mail: alifer@msn.com

Kincraig (Inverness-shire)

Attractive Highland village close to Loch Insh and Glenfeshie, midway between Aviemore and Kingussie.

BALBEAG, KINCRAIG. A Scandinavian-style pine log cottage. Self catering accommodation of living room/dining room, open-plan kitchen and 4 bedrooms. Sleeps 1-8. Satellite TV, DVD, wood burning stove. Nearby are watersports, horse riding, gliding and golf. Pets welcome by arrangement. Contact: MRS C. MACGREGOR (01963 220250).
e-mail: camacg@talk21.com   website: www.balbeag.co.uk

"FRASER" and "TELFORD" cottages, close to Loch Insh and Glenfeshie, are an ideal holiday base to explore the Cairngorms National Park. In the Highland village of Kincraig, equidistant from Aviemore and Kingussie. Well behaved dogs and children welcome. STB ★★★ Silver GTBS Award. Contact: NICK & PATSY THOMPSON, GLEBE HOUSE, KINCRAIG PH21 1NU (01540 651377). [🐾]
e-mail: glebecottages@gmail.com   website: www.glebecottages.co.uk

Kingussie (Inverness-shire)

Small town on River Spey 28 miles south of Inverness.

ALLT GYNACK GUEST HOUSE, GYNACK VILLA, 1 HIGH STREET, KINGUSSIE, NEAR AVIEMORE PH21 1HS. Family-owned Victorian guest house in a beautiful part of the Highlands. In its own grounds with private car park. Open all year. Huge range of activities. Excellent restaurants nearby. STB ★★★. [🐾]
e-mail: alltgynack@tiscali.co.uk   website: www.alltgynack.com

COLUMBA HOUSE HOTEL AND GARDEN RESTAURANT, MANSE ROAD, KINGUSSIE PH21 1JF (01540 661402). Quiet Highland retreat offering highest standards of hospitality, care and accommodation. Candlelit Garden Restaurant. Ground-floor rooms with own front doors, perfect for doggie holidays. STB ★★★ [pw! Pets £5 per night, £15 per week]
e-mail: myra@columbahousehotel.com   website: www.columbahousehotel.com

Kinlochbervie (Sutherland)

Village on north side of Loch Inchard.

THE KINLOCHBERVIE HOTEL, KINLOCHBERVIE, SUTHERLAND IV27 4RP (01971 521 275; Fax: 01971 521 438). Pet-friendly, family-run hotel in stunning location. Superb sea and hill views, beautiful beaches and an abundance of wildlife. Very comfortable en suite rooms, restaurant, bars, coffee shop. STB ★★★. [🐾]
e-mail: klbhotel@btconnect.com   website: www.kinlochberviehotel.com

Loch Ness (Inverness-shire)

Home of 'Nessie', extending for 23 miles from Fort Augustus to south of Inverness.

WILDERNESS COTTAGES. Quality self-catering properties throughout Scotland, including small cottages, large houses and luxury apartments on banks of Loch Ness. Pets welcome. Please see website for details or for a brochure contact: WILDERNESS COTTAGES, ROEBUCK COTTAGE, ERROGIE IV2 6UH (01456 486358). STB★★★/★★★★/★★★★★ SELF CATERING
e-mail: server@wildernesscottages.co.uk   website: www.wildernesscottages.co.uk

JUSTINE HUDSON, WILDSIDE HIGHLAND LODGES, WILDSIDE, WHITEBRIDGE, INVERNESS IV2 6UN. (01456 486373; Fax: 01456 486371). Charming riverside lodges. Log fires and mountain views. Sleep 2 to 8 people. Pets welcome. Free fishing. STB ★★★★ Self-catering. [Pets £15 per booking].
e-mail: info@wildsidelodges.com   website: www.wildsidelodges.com

Loch Torridon (Wester Ross)

Sea loch in an area of dramatic mountain scenery.

TIGH AN EILEAN HOTEL & SHIELDAIG BAR AND COASTAL KITCHEN, SHIELDAIG ON LOCH TORRIDON IV54 8XN (01520 755251; Fax: 01520 755321). In the picturesque 200-year-old fishing village of Shieldaig. Spectacular walking, deserted beaches. Award-winning restaurant. Fresh seafood delivered daily. Good Hotel Guide, AA Britain's Best Hotels, Good Food Guide. [pw! 🐕]
e-mail: tighaneilean@keme.co.uk   website: www.tighaneilean.co.uk

Muir of Ord (Inverness-shire)

Village 20km west of Inverness.

ORD HOUSE HOTEL, MUIR OF ORD IV6 7UH (01463 870492). 17th Century country house. Extensive gardens and woodlands for dogs to run around in. Large, airy bedrooms. Log fires. Restaurant. AA ★★ and Rosette. [pw! 🐕]
e-mail: admin@ord-house.co.uk   website: www.ord-house.co.uk

Nethy Bridge (Inverness-shire)

Popular resort on River Nethy with extensive Abernethy Forest to the south. Impressive mountain scenery. Grantown-on-Spey 5 miles.

SPEYSIDE COTTAGES, NETHY BRIDGE. Relax in 2 comfortable cottages (sleep 2-6) with fenced gardens, on riverbank with wonderful forest walks. Pets welcome. £170-£435 per week, includes full linen and towels. Contact BRIAN AND MOIRA PATRICK, 1 CHAPELTON PLACE, FORRES, MORAY IV36 2NL (01309 672505). [First dog FREE, extra dogs £25 per week]
e-mail: brian@speysidecottages.co.uk   website: www.speysidecottages.co.uk

BALNAGOWAN MILL AND WOODLARK, NETHY BRIDGE. Comfortable, modern 3 bedroom cottages in secluded locations in the Cairngorms National Park. Woodland and riverside walks on the doorstep. Ideal for pets. Furnished to a high standard with full central heating. £260-£590 per week incl. of electricity, bed linen and towels. VisitScotland ★★★★. ASSC MEMBER. Contact PAULA FRASER, 33 ARGYLE GROVE, DUNBLANE FK15 9DT (01786 824957) [🐕]
e-mail: paulajfraser@aol.com

MONDHUIE CHALETS & B&B, NETHY BRIDGE PH25 3DF (01479 821062). Situated in the country between Aviemore and Grantown-on-Spey, two comfortable, self-catering chalets, or you can have Dinner, B&B in the house. A warm welcome awaits you. Pets welcome. Red squirrels seen daily. Free internet access. [🐕]
e-mail: david@mondhuie.com   website: www.mondhuie.com

Newtonmore (Inverness-shire)

Small village at the heart of the Scottish Highlands. Officially the geographic centre of Scotland.

CRUBENBEG HOUSE, FALLS OF TRUIM, BY NEWTONMORE PH20 1BE (01540 673300) Relaxing country haven, in stunning surroundings, perfect for dog-walking. Delightful, spacious bedrooms, a splendid lounge, crackling fire, home-cooked evening meals, great wines, beer, malts and a warm welcome all ensure you'll enjoy your stay to the full. Dogs welcome! VisitScotland ★★★★ GOLD AWARD, AA ★★★★ Highly Commended.
e-mail: enquiries@crubenbeghouse.com   website: www.crubenbeghouse.com

Poolewe (Ross-shire)

Village lying between Lochs Ewe and Maree with the River Ewe flowing through.

MR A. URQUHART, CROFTERS COTTAGES, 15 CROFT, POOLEWE IV22 2JY (01445 781 268). Two traditional cottages situated in a scenic and tranquil area, ideal for a "get away from it all" holiday. Comfortably furnished with all mod cons. [🐕]
e-mail: croftcottages@btopenworld.com   website: www.crofterscottages.co.uk

Rhiconich (Sutherland)

Locality at the head of Loch Inchard on west coast of Sutherland District.

RHICONICH HOTEL, SUTHERLAND, N. W. HIGHLANDS IV27 4RN (01971 521224; Fax: 01971 521732). She's your best friend so why leave her at home, bring her to Rhiconich Hotel, she'll be made equally as welcome as you will. A place where we put service, hospitality and really fresh food as a priority, but why don't you come and see for yourself? STB ★★★ [🐾]
e-mail: info@rhiconichhotel.co.uk   website: www.rhiconichhotel.co.uk

Spean Bridge (Inverness-shire)

Village on River Spean at foot of Loch Lochy. Site of WWII Commando Memorial.

NEIL & ELIZABETH OCKENDEN, ACHNABOBANE FARMHOUSE, ACHNABOBANE, SPEAN BRIDGE PH34 4EX (01397 712919). Excellent accommodation and comfort. An ideal central base for exploring the Highlands. Local area has wide variety of outdoor pursuits, wildlife and attractions. STB ★★★. [£5 per dog per stay]
e-mail: enquiries@achnabobane.co.uk   website: www.achnabobane.co.uk

RIVERSIDE LODGES, INVERGLOY, SPEAN BRIDGE PH34 4DY (01397 712684). The ultimate Highland location. Three lodges, each sleep 6, in 12 acres of woodland garden on Loch Lochy. Free fishing. Open all year. Pets welcome. Brochure on request. STB ★★★★ [🐾]
e-mail: enquiries@riversidelodge.org.uk   website: www.riversidelodge.org.uk

Tongue (Sutherland)

Village near north coast of Caithness District on east side of Kyle of Tongue.

BORGIE LODGE HOTEL, SKERRAY, TONGUE KW14 7TH (Tel & Fax: 01641 521332). Set in a secluded Highland glen lies Borgie Lodge. Try pony trekking, fishing and forest walks. Open fires and fine dining. AA ★★ and Rosette, STB ★★★★ [🐾]
e-mail: info@borgielodgehotel.co.uk   website: www.borgielodgehotel.co.uk

Whitebridge (Inverness-shire)

Hamlet in the heart of the Scottish Highlands, 4 miles from Loch Ness and 9 miles from Fort Augustus.

WHITEBRIDGE HOTEL, WHITEBRIDGE, SOUTH LOCH NESS IV2 6UN (01456 486226; Fax: 01456 486413). Peaceful location with magnificent mountain views and excellent walks. Friendly locals' bar with home-cooked food. 12 en suite rooms. B&B from £35pppn. AA ★★[🐾]
e-mail: info@whitebridgehotel.co.uk   website: www.whitebridgehotel.co.uk

Biggar

Small town set round broad main street. Gasworks museum, puppet theatre seating 100, street museum displaying old shop fronts and interiors. Peebles 13 miles.

CARMICHAEL COUNTRY COTTAGES, CARMICHAEL ESTATE, BY BIGGAR ML12 6PG (01899 308336; Fax: 01899 308481). Our stone cottages nestle in the woods and fields of our historic family-run estate. Ideal homes for families, pets and dogs. 15 cottages, 32 bedrooms. STB ★★/★★★★ Self catering. Open all year. £225 to £595 per week. [pw! 🐾]
e-mail: information@carmichael.co.uk   website: www.carmichael.co.uk

WALSTON MANSION FARMHOUSE, WALSTON, CARNWATH, BY BIGGAR ML11 8NF (01899 810338; Fax: 01899 810334). Well known for its real home-from-home atmosphere, hearty breakfast menu and delicious evening meals. Pets by arrangement. Ideal touring base. STB ★★★
e-mail: margaret.kirby@walstonmansion.co.uk   website: www.walstonmansion.co.uk

Harthill

Village 5 miles south-west of Bathgate.

MRS STEPHENS, BLAIRMAINS FARM, HARTHILL ML7 5TJ (01501 751278; Fax: 01501 753383). Attractive farmhouse on small farm. Ideal for touring. Children welcome. Bed and Breakfast from £20; weekly rates available. Reduced rates for children. Open all year. [🐾]
e-mail: heather@blairmains.freeserve.co.uk   website: www.blairmains.co.uk

🐾   Pets are welcome free of charge.   **Classified Symbols**

£   A charge is made for pets: nightly or weekly.

pw! Special provision for pets; exercise facility, feeding or accommodation arrangement.

⌂   Separate pets accommodation.

Killin, Kinloch Rannoch, Lochearnhead, Perth, Pitlochry

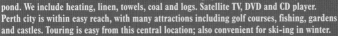

Strathyre

Aberfeldy

Small town standing on both sides of Uriar Burn near its confluence with the River Tay. Pitlochry 8 miles.

LOCH TAY LODGES, REMONY, ACHARN, ABERFELDY PH15 2HR (01887 830209). Enjoy hill walking, golf, sailing or touring. Salmon and trout fishing available. Log fires. Pets welcome. Walks along loch shore from house. STB ★★★ SELF CATERING in village close to Loch. For brochure, contact MRS P. W. DUNCAN MILLAR at above address. [🐾]
e-mail: remony@btinternet.com   website: www.lochtaylodges.co.uk

SHEILA AND PETER CAMPBELL, DULL FARM HOLIDAY LODGES, ABERFELDY PH15 2JQ (01887 820270). Luxury accommodation in 2 pine lodges on small farm. Fully equipped, well maintained; completely fenced. Panoramic views. Touring, walking, fishing, golf. Short Breaks available. [Pets £10 per week].
e-mail: info@dullfarm.freeserve.co.uk   website: www.self-cateringperthshire.com

DRUMCROY LODGES, MAINS OF MURTHLY, ABERFELDY PH15 2EA (01887 820978) Self-catering holiday accommodation in a stunning rural setting. Deluxe en suite chalets, sleeping 4-6. Ideal base to explore Central Scotland. Nature walks, fishing, mountain bike trails. £225-£450 per week. STB ★★★★
e-mail: info@highland-lodges.com   website: www.highland-lodges.com

FORTINGALL HOTEL, ABERFELDY PH15 2NQ (Tel/Fax: 01887 830367). A traditional country house hotel with a modern twist, offering a warm and friendly welcome to dog owners. Imaginative and award-winning cuisine served in a delightful atmosphere. STB/AA ★★★★, AA Two Rosettes. [Pets £15 per night].
e-mail:enquiries@fortingall.com   website: www.fortingall.com

Blairgowrie

Town in picturesque location near Ericht Gorge. Fine touring centre. Several castles in the vicinity. Pitlochry 23 miles, Dundee 20, Forfar 20, Perth 15.

ALTAMOUNT CHALETS, COUPAR ANGUS ROAD, BLAIRGOWRIE PH10 6JN (01250 872464). Sleep 2/4/6. Log cabins and chalets set in mature grounds with plenty of privacy and amenities, only five minutes' walk from Blairgowrie town centre. Ideal touring centre for Perthshire and the Highlands in all seasons.
e-mail: altamount@crownparks.com   website: www.crownparks.com

FHG Guides publish a large range of well-known accommodation guides. We will be happy to send you details or you can use the order form at the back of this book.

Crieff

Town and resort 16 miles west of Perth.

STRONACHLACHAR COTTAGE, MILNAB TERRACE, CRIEFF PH7 4ED (01764 655595; 07887 984240). Situated in the 'Gateway to the Highlands', the cottage is set within landscaped gardens. Lounge/dining room, kitchen, bathroom and two bedrooms. Sleeps 4. Pets welcome.
website: www.cottageguide.co.uk/stronachlachar

ABERTURRET COTTAGE, CRIEFF. Beautiful traditional cottage with enormous private garden by the river. Three bedrooms (sleeps 4 or 5). Excellent base for walking, cycling and exploring Perthshire. Heating, bedlinen and towels incl. in price. Contact JUDY WATT (01764 650064). [Pets £15 per week]
e-mail: judywatt@aberturret.com   website: www.aberturret.com

Glenshee

Very popular winter sports area, good base for touring.

FINEGAND FARM HOLIDAY COTTAGES, GLENSHEE PH10 7QB (01250 885234). Four well equipped traditional cottages individually sited on upland farm with river. Sleeping 4/7. Linen and towels provided. Electric heating. Cot, high chair. Fishing available. Prices from £250-£500.
e-mail: farm@finegandestate.com   website: www.finegandholidaycottages.com

Killiecrankie

Village on River Garry 3 miles south east of Blair Atholl.

ATHOLL COTTAGE, KILLIECRANKIE, PERTHSHIRE. Delightful stone cottage offers high quality accommodation for 5 people. Log fire. Private grounds. Ideal for exploring historic countryside. For further details contact: JOAN TROUP, DALNASGADH, KILLIECRANKIE, PITLOCHRY PH16 5LN (01796 470017; Fax: 01796 472183). [🐾]
e-mail: info@athollcottage.co.uk   website: www.athollcottage.co.uk

Killin

Village at confluence of Rivers Dochart and Lochay at head of Loch Tay.

GILL & DAVE HUNT, THE STEADING, WESTER LIX, KILLIN FK21 8RD (01567 820990 & 07747 862641). Two fully equipped self contained properties with Sky TV, wood-burning stove/open fire. One with sauna and private decking. Well behaved pet, or pets by arrangement. [Pets £15 per week for first pet, then £5 per pet]
e-mail: gill@westerlix.co.uk   website: www.westerlix.com

LYNNE AND ALISTAIR FERGUSON, 'BROCHANACH' 43 FINGAL ROAD, KILLIN FK21 8XA (01567 820028). Bed and varied Scottish Breakfast in small, tranquil village in the heart of Highland Perthshire. Ideal touring base. "Good walkies area" – dogs are especially welcome and stay free. [🐾 pw!]
e-mail: alifer@msn.com

Kinloch Rannoch

Village at foot of Loch Rannoch.

KILVRECHT CARAVAN & CAMP SITE, KINLOCH RANNOCH PH16 5QA (01350 727284; Fax: 01350 727811). Secluded campsite on a level open area in quiet, secluded woodland setting. Fishing available for brown trout on Loch Rannoch. Several trails begin from campsite. Please write, fax or telephone for further information. [🐾]
e-mail: tay.fd@forestry.gsi.gov.uk

Lochearnhead

Village at head of Loch Earn 6 miles South of Killin.

CLACHAN COTTAGE HOTEL, LOCHEARNHEAD FK19 8PU (01567 830247; Fax: 01567 830300). Well placed in central Scotland for touring. Excellent walking, mountain biking and fishing. Water-sports available from the hotel. Award-winning "Taste of Scotland" restaurant. [🐾]
website: www.clachancottagehotel.com

Perth

Town and Royal Burgh in central Scotland on the banks of the River Tay.

ORCHARD COTTAGE. Modern two-bedroom cottage in peaceful location, ideal for Perth city and for touring. Secluded private garden with pond. Linen, towels, coal and logs included. STB ★★★★ Contact: MRS G. MACKINTOSH, ORCHARD COTTAGE, HUNTINGTOWERFIELD, PERTH PH1 3JL (Tel & Fax: 01738 620783 / 07926 519574). [🐾]
e-mail: sales@perthcottage.co.uk   website: www.perthcottage.co.uk

Pitlochry

Popular resort on River Tummel in beautiful Perthshire Highlands. Excellent golf, loch and river fishing. Famous for summer Festival Theatre; distillery, Highland Games.

THE WHITE HOUSE, MOULIN, PITLOCHRY PH16 5EL. A mid 17th Century cottage on quiet village side street. Sleeps 6. Fully equipped. Many historical attractions and golf courses nearby. STB ★★. Contact: GUY JAMES, THE YELLOW HOUSE, SPRINGHILL, EASTINGTON, STONEHOUSE, GLOUCESTERSHIRE GL10 3AT (01453 823992/755552; Mob:07767 330986). [Pets £15 per week]
e-mail: whitehouse@jamesth9.co.uk   website: www.thewhitehousemoulin.co.uk

ROSEMOUNT HOTEL, PITLOCHRY PH16 5HT (01796 472302). We're just mad about dogs, and we have been known to welcome the occasional human companion, subject to behavioural considerations, naturally! Friendly, attentive service. Great food. Beautiful views. Fabulous walks. [🐾]
e-mail: rosemounthotel@tiscali.co.uk   website: www.scottishhotels.co.uk

St Fillans

Village at foot of Loch Earn, 5 miles west of Comrie.

THE FOUR SEASONS HOTEL, ST FILLANS PH6 2NF (01764 685333). Ideal holiday venue for pets and their owners. Spectacular Highland scenery, walking, fishing, watersports. Wonderful food. Full details on request. STB ★★★ Hotel, AA ★★★ and 2 Red Rosettes, Signpost, Best Loved Hotels. [pw! 🐾]
e-mail: sham@thefourseasonshotel.co.uk   website: www.thefourseasonshotel.co.uk

FORTRENN, ST FILLANS (01887 822819). Walkers and their dogs have forestry and open hillside at the door, with the Trossachs just across the loch. Sailors, waterskiers and fishermen need look no further than Loch Earn. Log fires, four poster master suite. Secure area for dogs. Sleeps 7. STB ★★★★ [Pets £25 per week]
e-mail: enquiries@heartofperthshire.co.uk   website: www.heartofperthshire.co.uk

Stanley

Pretty village on River Tay 8 miles south east of Dunkeld and 6 miles north of Perth.

TAYSIDE HOTEL, MILL STREET, STANLEY PH1 4NL (01738 828249). 12 en suite rooms with colour TV with freeview, DVD and media connections. The restaurant and bar offer a selection of home cooked food. An ideal base from which to tour the surrounding area. Pets welcome. [🐾]
e-mail: reception@taysidehotel.co.uk   website: www.taysidehotel.co.uk

Strathyre

Village set in the centre of Strathyre State Forest.

THE MUNRO INN, STRATHYRE FK18 8NA (01877 384333). Chilled out Robbie warmly welcomes doggy friends to the Munro Inn in beautiful Highland Perthshire. Perfect base for walking, cycling, climbing, water sports, fishing or relaxing! Great home cooking, lively bar, luxurious en suite bedrooms, drying room, broadband internet.
website: www.munro-inn.com

Aberfoyle

Small town at heart of Loch Lomond and Trossachs National Park.

TROSSACHS HOLIDAY PARK, BY ABERFOYLE FK8 3SA (01877 382 614; Fax: 01877 382 732; Freephone: 0800 1971192). 40 acre landscaped park with 45 exclusive touring pitches - mostly fully serviced. The perfect base to explore the Trossachs National Park. Enclosed dog walk. STB ★★★★★. David Bellamy Gold Award.
e-mail: info@trossachsholidays.co.uk   website: www.trossachsholidays.co.uk

Isle of Harris

Leverburgh

SCARISTA HOUSE, SGARASTA BHEAG, ISLE OF HARRIS HS3 3HX (01859 550238: Fax: 01859 550277). In one of the most beautiful and remote places to stay in Britain, traditional comfort in well-furnished guest rooms; skilled cooking and good wines, stunning views. STB ★★★★. Self catering cottage also available. [🐕]
e-mail: timandpatricia@scaristahouse.com   website: www.scaristahouse.com

Leverburgh

Village on S.W. Coast of Harris 4 miles N.W. of Rennish Point.

HOWARD AND SALLIE LOMAS, CARMINISH HOUSE, 1A STROND, LEVERBURGH HS5 3UD (01859 520400) Secluded, spacious, traditionally built B&B, with three twin/double en suite rooms. Panoramic views. Payphone, satellite TV, Wi-Fi. Garden and parking. Non-smoking. Children and pets welcome. STB ★★★★.[🐕]
e-mail: info@carminish.com   website: www.carminish.com

Isle of Lewis
Stornoway

Stornoway

Chief town of Lewis, with large natural harbour.

JANNEL BED & BREAKFAST, 5 STEWART DRIVE, STORNOWAY, ISLE OF LEWIS HS1 2TU (0800 634 3270). Excellent Stornoway-based Bed & Breakfast in light, modern and spacious 7-bedroomed family home. Enclosed garden. Off-street parking. Children and pets welcome. STB ★★★★.[🐕]
e-mail: stay@jannel-stornoway.co.uk   website: www.jannel-stornoway.co.uk

"Torlochan" • Isle of Mull

Torlochan is a small croft situated in the centre of the Isle of Mull, with views over Loch na Keal. It is an ideal base from which to explore all of Mull. We have two comfortable spacious log cabins, which have been completely refurbished in 2009 with new kitchens, bathrooms, lighting and wooden flooring. They can sleep 4 people and cost from £350 per week; short winter breaks from £60 per night, minimum 3 nights.

The Farmhouse has a lounge, kitchen/dining room, two sitting rooms with open fire and log stove. It sleeps 6 people from £595 per week and can sleep 8 when using a separate log cabin with twin bedroom for an additional £200 per week.

More information from:
Hylda Marsh,
Baliscate House,
Tobermory, Isle of Mull PA75 6QA
Tel: 01688 302048 • Fax: 01688 302251
e-mail: info@islandholidaycottages.com
www.torlochan.com
www.islandholidaycottages.com

Torlochan

Situated in the centre of Mull, 20 minutes from Tobermory and 25 minutes from Craignure.

TORLOCHAN, GRULINE, ISLE OF MULL. Situated in centre of Mull with views over Loch na Keal, two log cabins and a farmhouse for self-catering. [£10 per dog per week; other pets free]
e-mail: info@islandholidaycottages.com   www.torlochan.com/www.islandholidaycottages.com

Hannabreck · Dounby, Orkney

enquiries@lochlandchalets.co.uk • www.hannabreck.co.uk

Charming old-style cottage, two bedrooms. Bathroom with bath and level access shower, living room with open fire, kitchen. TV/internet access. Pets welcome. 15 miles Kirkwall, 10 miles ferry.

Contact: Mrs P. Norquoy, Bigging, Dounby KW17 2HR • 01856 771340

POINT OF NESS CAMPSITE • STROMNESS, ORKNEY

The 3-star camp site is situated in a quiet shoreline location one mile west of the pier head and ferry. There are numerous leisure activities near to the site. The site itself provides stunning views of Hoy and skies and is located in a quiet position near to a shoreline walk which is ideal for walking the dog!

IRRESISTIBLE ORKNEY

BIRSAY CARAVAN & CAMPING SITE • BIRSAY, ORKNEY

The camp site is in the stunning location of West Mainland Orkney, near spectacular cliffs, sandy beaches, quiet lochs and Orkney's Neolithic heartland. The camp site is suitable for touring caravans, motor homes and tents and has plenty of ground for walking the dog.

ORKNEY
ISLANDS COUNCIL

For bookings and further details please contact Orkney Islands Council

Tel: 01856 873535 ext 2430 • e-mail: leisure.culture@orkney.gov.uk • www.orkney.gov.uk or www.hostelsorkney.co.uk

LITTLE BU · ORPHIR · ORKNEY

Little Bu is a self-catering chalet-bungalow maintained to a very high standard and sleeping six. Open-plan livingroom/dining area and newly fitted kitchen, verandah, patio/decking area, large garden and garden furniture. Close to the sea.

Contact: Mrs Shephard, Windbreck, Butchers Lane, Boughton, Northampton NN2 8SL
Tel: 01604 843275 • jshephard@northamptonshire.gov.uk • www.littlebu.co.uk

Banks of Orkney Self-catering and B&B

Two cottages (STB ★★★) and converted barn (STB ★★★★). Located close to ferries, with stunning views over the Pentland Firth. Each cottage sleeps up to 2, and the barn sleeps 5/7. Licensed restaurant on site. For details contact:

Carole Fletcher, Banks of Orkney, South Ronaldsay KW17 2RW
Tel: 01856 831605 • www.banksoforkney.co.uk

Outbrecks in Orkney offer exceptional and unique self-catering cottages. Open all year – dogs welcome

Within an outstanding National Scenic Area, unwind and relax in comfort, explore the spectacular surrounding countryside and view incredible skies and sunsets. All our non-smoking accommodation is situated within its own private acres of dog-walking fields, in fabulous sea and loch locations by the archaeological World Heritage Site in Stenness.

Each cottage is within 200 metres of the shore, except for Harefields (which nestles in its own land). Please check our website for availability.

Harefields (sleeping up to 8) **Raingoose** (sleeping up to 5) and **Pine Trees** (sleeping 2) are all superbly finished, individually designed and spacious. Each, with its own garden, commands fabulous views and has plenty of space to exercise your dog.
£220 - £600 per week inclusive of electricity and linen.

Contact: Adrian and Lesley Francis, Outbrecks, Stenness, Orkney KW16 3EY
Tel: 01856 851 223 • e-mail: accommodation@outbreckscottages-orkney.co.uk
www.outbreckscottages-orkney.co.uk

Please mention PETS WELCOME!

when making enquiries about accommodation featured in this guide

Dounby

North of the Loch or Harray, 14 miles north west of Kirkwall. Nearby at Sandwick is the Neolithic village of Skara Brae.

HANNABRECK, DOUNBY. Charming old-style cottage, two bedrooms. Bathroom with bath and level access shower, living room with open fire, kitchen. TV/internet access. Pets welcome. 15 miles Kirkwall, 10 miles ferry. Contact: MRS P. NORQUOY, BIGGING, DOUNBY KW17 2HR (01856 771340). [🐾]
e-mail: enquiries@lochlandchalets.co.uk   website: www.hannabreck.co.uk

Kirkwall

Largest town in Orkney, ideal base for exploring the many historic attractions in the islands.

ORKNEY ISLANDS COUNCIL (01856 873535 ext 2430). Point of Ness Campsite, Stromness: 3-star campsite in quiet shoreline location. Birsay Caravan & Camping Site, Birsay: stunning location near Orkney's Neolithic heartland, suitable for touring caravans, motorhomes and tents.
e-mail: leisure.culture@orkney.gov.uk   www.orkney.gov.uk or www.hostelsorkney.co.uk

Orphir

Located midway between Stromness and Kirkwall.

LITTLE BU, ORPHIR, ORKNEY. Little Bu is a self-catering chalet-bungalow maintained to a very high standard and sleeping six. Open-plan livingroom/dining area and newly fitted kitchen, verandah, patio/decking area, large garden and garden furniture. Close to the sea. STB ★★★ Self Catering. Contact: MRS SHEPHARD, WINDBRECK, BUTCHERS LANE, BOUGHTON, NORTHAMPTON NN2 8SL (01604 843275) [🐾]
e-mail: jshephard@northamptonshire.gov.uk   website: www.littlebu.co.uk

South Ronaldsay

Most southerly of the main islands of Orkney   .

BANKS OF ORKNEY SELF-CATERING AND B&B. Two cottages (STB ★★★) and converted barn (STB ★★★★). Located close to ferries, with stunning views over the Pentland Firth. Each cottage sleeps up to 2, and the barn sleeps 5/7. Licensed restaurant on site. For details contact: CAROLE FLETCHER, BANKS OF ORKNEY, SOUTH RONALDSAY KW17 2RW (01856 831605). [Pets £15 per week]
website: www.banksoforkney.co.uk

Stenness

Situated at the south east end of Loch of Stenness, south west of Finstown on mainland Orkney.

ADRIAN AND LESLEY FRANCIS, OUTBRECKS, STENNESS KW16 3EY (01856 851 223) Exceptional self-catering cottages in fabulous sea and loch locations in outstanding National Scenic Area. Sleep 2-8. Open all year. Non-smoking. Dogs welcome. STB ★★★★.
e-mail: accommodation@outbreckscottages-orkney.co.uk
website: www.outbreckscottages-orkney.co.uk

Staffin

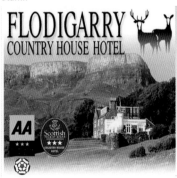

Substantially upgraded over the years Flodigarry Country House Hotel's traditional Highland character has been retained so guests can enjoy real Scottish hospitality in a stunning setting.
With numerous awards for accommodation and food over the years Flodigarry has achieved special status
Eighteen en suite bedrooms, all with great views.

Flodigarry Country House Hotel
Flodigarry, Isle of Skye IV51 9HZ
Tel: 01470 552203 • info@flodigarry.co.uk
www.flodigarry.co.uk

Staffin

Crofting and fishing village on rocky coast around Staffin Bay. 12 miles north of Portree.

FLODIGARRY COUNTRY HOUSE HOTEL, FLODIGARRY, ISLE OF SKYE IV51 9HZ (01470 552203). Flodigarry Country House Hotel has achieved special status with numerous awards for accommodation and food. Eighteen en suite bedrooms, all with great views. STB/AA ★★★. [🐾]
e-mail: info@flodigarry.co.uk   website: www.flodigarry.co.uk

North Uist
Locheport

Tigh Alasdair • North Uist Set on the family croft at Sidinish, Locheport, this beautiful self catering cottage is surrounded by moorland, sheep and water all at once. It enjoys unhindered views of Locheport, the hills of Bureaval, Eaval and Lees, not to mention spectacular sunsets. It offers all modern comforts in a traditional island setting, situated between the south shore of Loch Euphort (sea water) and Loch an Ghoil (fresh water). Sleeps 4. *For details contact:*
Janet MacDonald, Two Island Cottages, 285 Hillpark Drive, Glasgow G43 2SD
Tel: 0141 585 3155 / 0778 0937 278 • www.tighalasdair.co.uk

Locheport

Location on shore of sea loch, 5 miles south west of Lochmaddy.

TIGH ALASDAIR, NORTH UIST. Set on the family croft at Sidinish, Locheport, this beautiful self catering cottage enjoys unhindered views of Locheport, the hills of Bureaval, Eaval and Lees, not to mention spectacular sunsets. It offers all modern comforts in a traditional island setting. Sleeps 4. For details contact: JANET MACDONALD, TWO ISLAND COTTAGES, 285 HILLPARK DRIVE, GLASGOW G43 2SD (0141 585 3155 / 0778 0937 278). [pw! 🐾]
website: www.tighalasdair.co.uk

🐾   Pets are welcome free of charge.   **Classified Symbols**

£   A charge is made for pets: nightly or weekly.

pw! Special provision for pets; exercise facility, feeding or accommodation arrangement.

⌂   Separate pets accommodation.

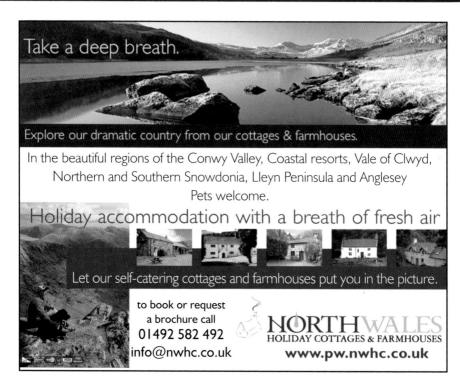

Bala, Bangor, Barmouth, Beaumaris

Caernarfon, Criccieth

TYDDYN HEILYN

CHWILOG, CRICCIETH LL53 6SW

Comfortably renovated Welsh stone cottage with character. Cosy, double-glazed, centrally heated and enjoying mild Gulf Stream climate with holiday letting anytime.

Two bedrooms with sea views. Ample grounds and doggy walks.

Positioned on Llyn Peninsula, 2 miles Criccieth, on edge Snowdonia, with 2 mile tree-lined walk to beach. Very central for touring.

Tel: 01766 810441 • e-mail: tyddyn.heilyn@tiscali.co.uk

Min Y Gaer, Porthmadog Road, Criccieth LL52 0HP · *01766 522151*

Family-run guest house overlooking the Esplanade, convenient for all amenities. 10 en suite bedrooms. Warm friendly atmosphere. Good food and comfortable accommodation at a reasonable price. Walkers and Cyclists Welcome.

e-mail: enquiry@minygaer.co.uk · www.minygaer.co.uk

Llwyn-Yr-Helm Farm

Quiet, small working farm site, four miles from Dolgellau in beautiful countryside, ideal for walking and mountain biking. Many places of interest in the area and nine miles from beaches. • Caravans, Dormobiles and tents; electric hook-ups. • Pets welcome. • Facilities for the disabled. • Toilet block • Laundry • Self-catering camping lodge also available.

Mrs Helen Rowlands • Llwyn-Yr-Helm Farm, Brithdir, Dolgellau LL40 2SA
Tel: 01341 450254 • e-mail: info@llwynyrhelmcaravanpark.co.uk
www.llwynyrhelmcaravanpark.co.uk

Award winning Country House standing in 20 acres of woodland, gardens and fields. High standard of accommodation in family, twin and double rooms, all en suite. Pets welcome. Stabling/grazing available.

MRS G. McCREADIE, DERI ISAF, DULAS BAY, ANGLESEY LL70 9DX
Tel: 01248 410536 • Mobile: 07721 374471
e-mail: mccreadie@deriisaf.freeserve.co.uk • www.angleseyfarms.com/deri.htm

Dyffryn Ardudwy, Llanbedr, Pentraeth, Pwllheli, Trearddur Bay

Pentre Mawr Farm
Relax in the peace and quiet of this working farm situated between Barmouth and Harlech. Inglenook fireplaces, spacious en suite bedrooms, and a homely atmosphere. Village shops, pubs. Cambrian Coast station and beach all within walking distance. Ample parking. Pets welcome. No children under 12. Phone Sue Owen for details. *Self catering also available.*

Dyffryn Ardudwy, Gwynedd LL44 2ES
Tel: 01341 247 413 • www.pentre-mawr.co.uk

Tan-y-Rhiw Holiday Cottage • Llanbedr
A detached secluded stone cottage set in its own grounds, offering a comfortable holiday whilst retaining its 18th century character. Sleeps up to eight people comfortably plus cot. Harlech 3 miles.

Carol & Paul Richardson, 15 Cheswardine Lane, Norton, Near Shifnal, Shropshire TF11 9EQ
Tel/Fax 01952 730212 • e-mail: tan.y.rhiw@btinternet.com • www.tan-y-rhiw.co.uk

---

WTB ★★★

Pen-y-Garnedd Farm Cottage
Near Pentraeth, Isle of Anglesey. Telephone bookings: 01248 450580
Fully refurbished detached cottage on a working smallholding. Electric heating and logburner in lounge. TV/DVD, stereo. One double bedroom; second bedroom with bunk beds and single bed. Fully equipped kitchen. Bathroom with power shower. Enclosed garden. Close to beaches and coastal walks.
Low Season Short Breaks. Caravan Club Approved Site (CCL5)
Well behaved children and pets welcome. Open all Year.

Tel: 01758 730375 • e-mail: post@crugeran.com
www.crugeran.com

CRUGERAN
Gwyliau fferm ~ Farm holidays

Self-catering holiday accommodation in farmhouse in beautiful North Wales.

Self-catering holiday accommodation in comfortable large farmhouse (sleeps 12). It has been lovingly furnished and decorated throughout, with some original furniture auction finds, quality reproduction pieces and welcoming colours on a neutral background. Abersoch, Aberdaron, Nefyn and all the beautiful sandy beaches of the peninsula are all close at hand. Walking, golf, sea fishing trips and plenty of water sport facilities are available. The market town of Pwllheli, the resorts of Criccieth and Porthmadog as well as numerous historic and scenic attractions such as the Snowdonia National Park, Ffestiniog Railway, castles and the Italianate village of Portmeirion are all easily reached.

Mrs R. Parry, Crugeran, Sarn Mellteyrn, Pwllheli, Gwynedd LL53 8DT

CEFN COED
Cefn Coed Holiday Cottages are situated on the south coast of the Lleyn Peninsula with sweeping panoramic views of Snowdonia, Cardigan Bay and the Meirionnydd Mountains. Three holiday cottages to let, all of which are of a very high standard and have enclosed gardens. Sleep 4/6.

Cefn Coed, Chwilog, Pwllheli, Gwynedd LL53 6NX
Telephone: 01766 810259
E-mail: enquiries@cefncoedholidays.co.uk • www.cefncoedholidays.co.uk

---

Blackthorn Farm is a family-run Bed and Breakfast, Self-Catering, Camping and Touring site. Situated in an idyllic spot on Holy Island in North Wales. Set in 18 acres of outstanding unspoilt beauty with panoramic views.
Blackthorn Farm, Penrhos Feilw, Trearddur Bay, Anglesey, North Wales LL65 2LT
01407 765262 • enquiries@blackthornfarm.co.uk • www.blackthornleisure.co.uk
WINNER: Best Caravan/Camping Site of the Year 2009 + 2011 • RUNNER-UP: Best Country House 2010

Comfortable self-catering holiday bungalows sleeping 2-7 near Trearddur's lovely beaches. Indoor heated swiming pool, licensed club, tennis court. Local, beautiful headland walks, fishing, golf and horse riding. Ideal location to explore Anglesey and the North Wales coast; near Holyhead.

TREARDDUR HOLIDAY BUNGALOWS
LON ISALLT TREARDDUR BAY ANGLESEY LL65 2UP
Tel: 01407 860494 • e-mail: trearholiday@btconnect.com • www.holiday-bungalows.co.uk

Bala

Natural touring centre for Snowdonia. Narrow gauge railway runs along side of Bala lake, the largest natural lake in Wales. Golf, sailing, fishing, canoeing.

TY GWYN - two-bedroomed luxury caravan in private grounds. Situated just two miles from Bala in beautiful country area, ideal for walking, sailing, fishing and canoeing. Only 30 miles from seaside. Contact: MRS A. SKINNER, TY GWYN, RHYDUCHAF, BALA LL23 7SD (01678 521267). [🐾]
e-mail: anntygwyn@hotmail.co.uk

Bangor

Cathedral city and resort on Menai Strait. One of the smallest cities in Britain.

TREBORTH LEISURE LTD, THE OLD BARN, TREBORTH HALL FARM, BANGOR LL57 2RX (01248 364399; Fax: 01248 364333). In a beautiful part of Wales, our leisure complex encompasses beautifully appointed holiday cottages, challenging 18-hole golf course, well-stocked fishing lake, superb camping and touring caravan facilities. [🐾]
e-mail: enquiries@treborthleisure.co.uk   website: www.treborthleisure.co.uk

Barmouth

Modern seaside resort with two miles of sandy beaches. Surrounding hills full of interesting archaeological remains.

ISLAWRFFORDD CARAVAN PARK, TAL-Y-BONT, GWYNEDD LL43 2BQ (01341 247269; Fax: 01341 242639). On the Snowdonia coastline, just north of Barmouth, our park offers a limited number of caravans for hire; touring caravan field and camping also available. Facilities include: shop, laundry, indoor heated pool, jacuzzi, sauna, bar, amusements, food bars. [Pets £2 per night].
e-mail: info@islawrffordd.co.uk   website: www.islawrffordd.co.uk

LAWRENNY LODGE, BARMOUTH LL42 1SU (01341 280466). Seven bedroom guest accommodation overlooking the harbour and estuary. Perfect area for long walkies. Evening meal available. Residential licence and private car park. [🐾]
e-mail: enquiries@lawrennylodge.co.uk   website: www.lawrennylodge.co.uk

MRS PAULA THOMPSON, LLWYNDU FARMHOUSE, LLANABER, BARMOUTH LL42 1RR (01341 280144). Converted 16th century farmhouse retaining many original features. Cosy lounge and character dining room. Bedrooms are modern and well equipped, some with four-poster beds. WTB ★★★★ [🐾]
e-mail: intouch@llwyndu-farmhouse.co.uk   website: www.llwyndu-farmhouse.co.uk

Beaumaris

Elegant little town dominated by castle built by Edward I in 13th century. Museum of Childhood has Victorian toys and music boxes.

BISHOPSGATE HOUSE HOTEL & RESTAURANT, 54 CASTLE STREET, BEAUMARIS, ANGLESEY LL58 8BB (01248 810302). Nine en suite bedrooms with TV and tea/coffee facilities. Award-winning restaurant, relaxing residents' lounge. Ideal base for touring. AA ★★ and Rosette.
e-mail: enquiries@bishopsgatehotel.co.uk   website: www.bishopsgatehotel.co.uk

'QUALITY COTTAGES', CERBID, SOLVA, HAVERFORDWEST, PEMBROKESHIRE SA62 6YE (01348 837871). Cottages set in all coastal areas, enjoy unashamed luxury, highest residential standards. Log fires. Linen supplied. Pets welcome, free. [pw! 🐾]
website: www.qualitycottages.co.uk

Bodorgan

A rural area in South West Anglesey.

CROESO. Comfortable three-bedroomed house. Enclosed garden. Near beaches, common, forest. Fully equipped, bedding and electricity inclusive. Colour TV/DVD player, microwave. Dogs and children welcome. £240-£450 per week. WTB ★★★ [🐾] Contact: MRS J. GUNDRY, FARMYARD LODGE, BODORGAN, ANGLESEY LL62 5LW (01407 840977).

Caernarfon

Historic walled town and resort, ideal for touring Snowdonia. Museums, Segontium Roman Fort, magnificent 13th century castle. Old harbour, sailing trips.

PLAS-Y-BRYN CHALET PARK, BONTNEWYDD, NEAR CAERNARFON LL54 7YE (01286 672811). Two miles from Caernarfon. It offers safety, seclusion and beautiful views of Snowdonia. Ideally positioned for touring. Well behaved pets always welcome. WTB ★★★★ [Pets £20 per week].
e-mail: philplasybryn@aol.com   website: www.plasybryn.co.uk

CAERNARFON BAY CARAVAN PARK AND HOLIDAY BUNGALOWS, DINAS DINLLE, CAERNARFON LL54 5TW (01286 830492). Quiet, peaceful static Caravan Park with Holiday Bungalows in beautiful North Wales. 50 yards from an award-winning beach. Picturesque views from the foothills of Snowdonia's National Park. Caernarfon 7 miles. WTB ★★★★.
e-mail: info@caernarfonbaycaravanpark.com   website: www.caernarfonbaycaravanpark.com

TY'N RHOS 5★ COUNTRY HOUSE, RESTAURANT & COTTAGES, SEION, LLANDDEINIOLEN, NEAR CAERNARFON LL55 3AE (01248 670489). A special place set in a beautiful location between Snowdonia and the Isle of Anglesey. Bedrooms are en suite, with flat screen TV, luxury bathrobes and toiletries. Menus feature fresh local ingredients prepared to the highest standards. Pets are welcome by arrangement. AA/VisitWales ★★★★★ [Pets £5-£10 per night, depending on room]
e-mail: enquiries@tynrhos.co.uk   website: www.tynrhos.co.uk

BACH WEN FARM & COTTAGES, CLYNNOG FAWR, CAERNARFON LL54 5NH (01286 660336). 9 unique high quality self-catering Holiday Cottages overlooking Caernarfon Bay. Sleep 2-8. All have private gardens. Village within walking distance. Short Breaks out of season. [🐾]
e-mail: bachwen@aol.com   website: www.bachwen.co.uk

Criccieth

Popular family resort with safe beaches divided by ruins of 13th century castle. Salmon and sea trout fishing. Festival of Music and Arts in the summer.

'QUALITY COTTAGES', CERBID, SOLVA, HAVERFORDWEST, PEMBROKESHIRE SA62 6YE (01348 837871). Cottages set in all coastal areas, enjoy unashamed luxury, highest residential standards. Log fires. Linen supplied. Pets welcome, free. [pw! 🐾]
website: www.qualitycottages.co.uk

A warm welcome awaits you in comfortable self-catering cottages. Easily accessible to numerous attractions, or enjoy tranquillity of countryside. Short breaks available. Pets welcome. MRS M. WILLIAMS, GAERWEN FARM, YNYS, CRICCIETH LL52 0NU (01766 810324).[🐾]
e-mail: gaerwen@btopenworld.com   website: www.gaerwenfarmcottages.co.uk

S A. M. JONES, RHOS COUNTRY COTTAGES, CRICCIETH, PORTHMADOG LL52 0PB (01758 720047 or 0776 986 4642). Superb collection of secluded country cottages with private gardens. Private fishing and rough shooting by arrangement. Open all year. VisitWales ★★★★★ [🐾]
e-mail: cottages@rhos.freeserve.co.uk   website: www.rhos-cottages.co.uk

PARC WERNOL PARK, CHWILOG, PWLLHELI LL53 6SW (01766 810506). Peaceful and quiet, ideal for touring. Self-catering holidays – 1,2 & 3 bedroom cottages, 2 and 3 bedroom caravans and chalets. Colour brochure. [Pets £15 per dog per week.]
e-mail: catherine@wernol.co.uk   website: www.wernol.co.uk

MRS ANN WILLIAMS, TYDDYN HEILYN, CHWILOG, CRICCIETH LL53 6SW (01766 810441). Comfortably renovated Welsh stone cottage near Snowdonia National Park. Double-glazed, centrally heated and enjoying mild Gulf Stream climate. Ample grounds and doggy walks. Two-mile tree-lined walk to beach. [Pets £7 per week]
e-mail: tyddyn.heilyn@tiscali.co.uk

MIN Y GAER, PORTHMADOG ROAD, CRICCIETH LL52 0HP (01766 522151). Family-run guest house conveniently situated close to amenities and overlooking Esplanade. Warm friendly atmosphere. Good food and comfortable accommodation at a reasonable price. Walkers and Cyclists Welcome. WTB/AA ★★★★ [Pets £2.50 per night; £15 per week]
e-mail: enquiry@minygaer.co.uk   website: www.minygaer.co.uk

Dolgellau

Market town lying on the River Wyion, a tributary of the River Mawddach.

MRS HELEN ROWLANDS, LLWYN-YR-HELM FARM, BRITHDIR, DOLGELLAU LL40 2SA (01341 450254). Quiet, small working farm site, four miles from Dolgellau in beautiful countryside. Caravans, Dormobiles and tents; electric hook-ups. Facilities for the disabled. Toilet block. Laundry. Self-catering camping lodge available. Pets welcome. [🐕]
e-mail: info@llwynyrhelmcaravanpark.co.uk   website:www.llwynyrhelmcaravanpark.co.uk

Dulas Bay

On north-east coast of Anglesey, between Amlwch and Moelfre.

MRS G. McCREADIE, DERI ISAF, DULAS BAY, ANGLESEY LL70 9DX (01248 410536; Mobile: 07721 374471). Award winning Country House in 20 acres of woodland, gardens and fields. Family, twin and double rooms, all en suite. Pets welcome. Stabling/grazing available. WTB ★★★★ Country House [Dogs £3.00 per night, £20 per week]
e-mail: mccreadie@deriisaf.freeserve.co.uk   website: www.angleseyfarms.com/deri.htm

Dyffryn Ardudwy

Situated on the coastal road between Harlech and Barmouth.

SUE OWEN, PENTRE MAWR FARM, DYFFRYN ARDUDWY LL44 2ES (01341 247413). Working farm between Barmouth and Harlech. Inglenook fireplaces, spacious en suite bedrooms, and a homely atmosphere.Village shops, pubs, beach all within walking distance. Ample parking. No children under 12. WTB ★★★★ Farmhouse. Self catering also available. [Pets £10 per stay].
website: www.pentre-mawr.co.uk

Harlech

Small stone-built town dominated by remains of 13th century castle. Golf, theatre, swimming pool, fine stretch of sands

'QUALITY COTTAGES', CERBID, SOLVA, HAVERFORDWEST, PEMBROKESHIRE SA62 6YE (01348 837871). Cottages set in all coastal areas, enjoy unashamed luxury, highest residential standards. Log fires. Linen supplied. Pets welcome, free. [pw! 🐕]
website: www.qualitycottages.co.uk

Llanbedr

Ideal base for exploring mountains and coast of Snowdonia, just 3 miles from Harlech.

TAN-Y-RHIW HOLIDAY COTTAGE. A detatched secluded stone cottage set in its own grounds, offering a comfortable holiday whilst retaining its 18th century character. Sleeps up to eight people comfortably plus cot. Contact: CAROL & PAUL RICHARDSON,15 CHESWARDINE LANE, NORTON, NEAR SHIFNAL TF11 9EQ (Tel/Fax 01952 730212). WTB ★★★★.[🐕]
e-mail: tan.y.rhiw@btinternet.com   website: www.tan-y-rhiw.co.uk

Llanddona

Village on Anglesey 3 miles north west of Beaumaris

'QUALITY COTTAGES', CERBID, SOLVA, HAVERFORDWEST, PEMBROKESHIRE SA62 6YE (01348 837871). Cottages set in all coastal areas, enjoy unashamed luxury, highest residential standards. Log fires. Linen supplied. Pets welcome, free. [pw! 🐕]
website: www.qualitycottages.co.uk

Morfa Nefyn

Picturesque village 2 miles west of Nefyn.

'QUALITY COTTAGES', CERBID, SOLVA, HAVERFORDWEST, PEMBROKESHIRE SA62 6YE (01348 837871). Cottages set in all coastal areas, enjoy unashamed luxury, highest residential standards. Log fires. Linen supplied. Pets welcome, free. [pw! 🐕]
website: www.qualitycottages.co.uk

Pentraeth

Village on Anglesey, near Red Wharf Bay.

PEN-Y-GARNEDD FARM COTTAGE, PENTRAETH (01248 450580). Cosy cottage on friendly working smallholding. Sleeps 5, log burner and heating. Well behaved children and pets welcome. Close to beaches and coastal Wales. Low Season Short Breaks. Caravan Club Approved Site. WTB ★★★ [🐕].

Porthmadog

Harbour town with mile-long Cob embankment, along which runs Ffestiniog Narrow Gauge Steam Railway to Blaenau Ffestiniog. Pottery, maritime museum, car museum. Good beaches nearby.

'QUALITY COTTAGES', CERBID, SOLVA, HAVERFORDWEST, PEMBROKESHIRE SA62 6YE (01348 837871). Cottages set in all coastal areas, enjoy unashamed luxury, highest residential standards. Log fires. Linen supplied. Pets welcome, free. [pw! 🐕]
website: www.qualitycottages.co.uk

Pwllheli

Market town with harbour, 8 miles west of Criccieth

MRS RHIAN PARRY, CRUGERAN, SARN MELLTEYRN, PWLLHELI LL53 8DT (01758 730 375). Self catering holiday accommodation in large farmhouse (sleeps 12). Beaches, walking, golf, sea fishing trips and plenty of water sport facilities are available. Pets welcome at a charge.
e-mail: post@crugeran.com   website: www.crugeran.com

CEFN COED HOLIDAY COTTAGES, CEFN COED, CHWILOG, PWLLHELI LL53 6NX. (01766 810259) Three holiday cottages to let, sleep 4/6. On the south coast of the Lleyn Peninsula with sweeping panoramic views of Snowdonia, Cardigan Bay and the Meirionnydd Mountains. WTB ★★★/★★★★. [Pets £20 per week]
e-mail: enquiries@cefncoedholidays.co.uk   website: www.cefncoedholidays.co.uk

Red Wharf Bay

Deep curving bay with vast expanse of sand, very popular for sailing and swimming.

'QUALITY COTTAGES', CERBID, SOLVA, HAVERFORDWEST, PEMBROKESHIRE SA62 6YE (01348 837871). Cottages set in all coastal areas, enjoy unashamed luxury, highest residential standards. Log fires. Linen supplied. Pets welcome, free. [pw! 🐕]
website: www.qualitycottages.co.uk

Trearddur Bay

Attractive holiday spot set amongst low cliffs on Holy Island, near Holyhead. Golf, sailing, fishing and swimming.

BLACKTHORN FARM, PENRHOS FEILW, TREARDDUR BAY LL65 2LT (01407 765262). Family-run Bed and Breakfast, Self-catering, Camping and Touring site in an idyllic spot on Holy Island in North Wales. Set in 18 acres of outstanding unspoilt beauty with panoramic views. VisitWales ★★★★. [Pets £5 per night B&B, £2 per night in caravan/campsite.]
e-mail: enquiries@blackthornfarm.co.uk   website: www.blackthornleisure.co.uk

TREARDDUR HOLIDAY BUNGALOWS, LON ISALLT, TREARDDUR BAY, ANGLESEY LL65 2UP (01407 860494). Comfortable self-catering holiday bungalows sleeping 2-7 near Trearddur's lovely beaches. Locally, beautiful headland walks, fishing, golf and horse riding. Ideal location to explore Anglesey and the North Wales coast. Terms from £100-£580 per week.
e-mail: trearholiday@btconnect.com   website: www.holiday-bungalows.co.uk

Tywyn

Pleasant seaside resort, start of Talyllyn Narrow Gauge Railway. Sea and river fishing, golf.

'QUALITY COTTAGES', CERBID, SOLVA, HAVERFORDWEST, PEMBROKESHIRE SA62 6YE (01348 837871). Cottages set in all coastal areas, enjoy unashamed luxury, highest residential standards. Log fires. Linen supplied. Pets welcome, free. [pw! 🐕]
website: www.qualitycottages.co.uk

Please mention PETS WELCOME!
when making enquiries about accommodation featured in this guide

Conwy

Tal-y-Fan Cottage and Alltwen Cottage

We have two luxurious self-catering country cottages for rental. Newly developed and well appointed, these properties can accommodate up to four people comfortably. They are located nearby the sleepy village of Dwygyfylchi, with spectacular views. Ideal touring centre for Snowdonia, two and a half miles to Conwy, five to Llandudno and Colwyn Bay; three minutes' walk to the village. Pony trekking, golf and fishing locally.

Terms from £395. Suitable for disabled access.
Pets and children welcome. Short Breaks available.
Non-smoking.

Mr John Baxter, Glyn Uchaf,
Conwy Old Road, Dwygyfylchi,
Penmaenmawr, Conwy LL34 6YS
Tel & Fax: 01492 623737/622053

Cymru Wales
★★★★★

www.glyn-uchaf.co.uk

Sychnant Pass House

Sychnant Pass Road, Conwy LL32 8BJ
Tel: 01492 596868
e-mail: office@sychnant-pass-house.co.uk
www.sychnant-pass-house.co.uk

We would love to welcome your four-legged friends to our home in the hills above Conwy. Sychnant Pass House is a lovely Victorian House set in two acres with a little pond and stream running through it. Step out of our garden and straight onto Snowdonia National Park land where you can walk for miles with your dogs. Just over two miles from the beach and one-and-a-half miles from Conwy, it is an ideal base from which to tour Wales. All our rooms are en suite, our garden rooms have French windows opening into the garden which are ideal for pets. We have a lovely sitting room that you can share with your best friends after dinner which is served in our informal, friendly restaurant, doggie bags are always available. Your four-legged friends and their folk are most welcome here. **Bed & Breakfast from £50 per person**

AA
★★★★★

Tyn-y-Groes, Near Conwy

Homely Victorian stone cottage in picturesque Conwy valley. Mountain views. Enjoy walking, mountains, beaches, bird watching. Bodnant Gardens, RSPB reserve and Conwy castle, harbour and marina close by. Victorian Llandudno, Betws-y-Coed, Anglesey, Caernarfon and Snowdon easy distance. Good local food and pubs. Enclosed garden, patio, furniture. Parking. Gas fired central heating. Lounge with gas fire, dining room, kitchen, utility.

Brongain

Two double bedded rooms, one small single; blankets/duvet provided. Bathroom with bath, shower, toilet and basin. Colour TV, electric cooker, fridge, microwave, washing machine and tumbler dryer. Terms £265-£350; heating, electricity included. Linen extra. Pets welcome. Open all year. No children under five years.

Mrs G. Simpole, 105 Hay Green
Road, Terrington-St-Clement,
King's Lynn, Norfolk PE34 4PU
Tel: 01553 828897
Mobile: 0798 9080665
e-mail: gill@simpole.rlshost.net

Visit the FHG website
www.holidayguides.com
for pet-friendly acccommodation around Britain

TREFRIW • CONWY VALLEY SNOWDONIA

Secluded cottages, log fire and beams
Dogs will love it – a place of their dreams
Plenty of walks around mountains and lakes
Cosy and tranquil – it's got what it takes.
It's really a perfect holiday let
For up to 2-7 people, plus their pet(s).

Apply: Mrs Williams
Tel: 01724 733990 or 07711 217 448 (week lets only)

PENTRE MAWR
COUNTRY HOUSE

**5 Star Luxury Hotel-style Guest House
with Swimming Pool and Hot Tubs.**

PENTRE MAWR COUNTRY HOUSE • NORTH WALES

Dinner Award **AA**

When looking for something more luxurious than a bed and breakfast, why not choose a country house-style guest house which has the luxurious accommodation of a 5 star hotel?

Molly and Millie, our lovely collies, would love to welcome your four-legged friends to their family's ancestral home of 400 years with woodland, park and riverside meadows. The en suite bedrooms have all the little extras to make your stay special. Two suites have hot tubs. There is a heated swimming pool in the walled garden and lovely sittingrooms where you can sit with your best friends after dinner.

Accommodation also available in luxury Canvas Lodges with hot tubs, super king-sized beds, full bathrooms – all with an African feel.

We are also ideally located giving easy access to many places of interest including Chester, Snowdonia, Conwy, the Welsh coast and the Horseshoe Pass in Llangollen; famous Welsh castles, cities, cathedrals are all on the doorstep, or perhaps a steam railway trip or a ghost walking tour of nearby Ruthin might appeal.

Llandyrnog, Denbigh, North Wales LL16 4LA

Tel: 01824 790732

e-mail: info@pentremawrcountryhouse.co.uk

www.pentremawrcountryhouse.co.uk

A useful index of towns/counties appears on pages 455-461

FHG Guides publish a large range of well-known
accommodation guides. We will be happy to send you details or
you can use the order form at the back of this book.

'QUALITY COTTAGES', CERBID, SOLVA, HAVERFORDWEST, PEMBROKESHIRE SA62 6YE (01348 837871). Cottages set in all coastal areas, enjoy unashamed luxury, highest residential standards. Log fires. Linen supplied. Pets welcome, free. [pw! 🐕]
website: www.qualitycottages.co.uk

NORTH WALES HOLIDAY COTTAGES. Self-catering cottages and farmhouses in the beautiful regions of the Conwy Valley, coastal resorts, Vale of Clwyd, Northern and Southern Snowdonia, Lleyn Peninsula and Anglesey. Phone 01492 582 492. [🐕]
e-mail: info@nwhc.co.uk   website: www.pw.nwhc.co.uk

SEASIDE COTTAGES. MANN'S, SHAW'S AND SNOWDONIA TOURIST SERVICES (0844 448 5639). Large selection of self-catering seaside and country cottages, bungalows, farmhouses, caravans etc. offering superb, reasonably priced accommodation for owners and their pets. Please telephone for brochure.
websites: www.mannsholidays.com   www.shawsholidays.com   www.snowdoniatourist.com

Betws-y-Coed

Popular mountain resort in picturesque setting where three rivers meet. Trout fishing, craft shops, golf, railway and motor museums, Snowdonia National Park Visitor Centre. Nearby Swallow Falls are famous beauty spot.

MISS MORRIS, TY COCH FARM-TREKKING CENTRE, PENMACHNO, BETWS-Y-COED LL25 0HJ (01690 760248). Hill farm in Wales. TV, teamaking, en suite. Set in National Park/Snowdonia. Very quiet and well off the beaten track. A great welcome and good food. Many return visits. £25 B&B. [🐕]
e-mail: cindymorris@tiscali.co.uk

Colwyn Bay

Lively seaside resort with promenade amusements. Attractions include Mountain Zoo, Eirias Park; golf, tennis, riding and other sports. Good touring centre for Snowdonia. The quieter resort of Rhos-on-Sea lies at the western end of the bay.

NORTH WALES HOLIDAYS, BRON-Y-WENDON AND NANT-Y-GLYN HOLIDAY PARKS, WERN ROAD, LLANDDULAS, COLWYN BAY LL22 8HG (01492 512903/512282). Cottages with sea views at Bron-Y-Wendon or chalets, cottages and coach house in picturesque valley at Nant-Y-Glyn. 16 units in total. VisitWales 2-5 Stars [Pets £10 per week].
e-mail: stay@northwales-holidays.co.uk   website: www.northwales-holidays.co.uk

Conwy

One of the best preserved medieval fortified towns in Britain on dramatic estuary setting. Telford Suspension Bridge, many historic buildings, lively quayside (site of smallest house in Britain). Golf, pony trekking, pleasure cruises.

TAL-Y-FAN COTTAGE AND ALLTWEN COTTAGE. Two luxurious self-catering country cottages accommodating up to four people. Spectacular views. Ideal touring centre for Snowdonia. Pony trekking, golf and fishing locally. Pets and children welcome. Short Breaks available. Non-smoking. Contact: MR JOHN BAXTER, GLYN UCHAF, CONWY OLD ROAD, DWYGYFYLCHI, PENMAENMAWR, CONWY LL34 6YS (Tel & Fax: 01492 623737/622053) WTB ★★★★★. [🐾]
website: www.glyn-uchaf.co.uk

SYCHNANT PASS HOUSE, SYCHNANT PASS ROAD, CONWY LL32 8BJ (01492 596868). A lovely Victorian House set in two acres with a little pond and stream. Step out of our garden and straight onto Snowdonia National Park land. Walk for miles with your dogs. All rooms en suite. B&B from £50. AA ★★★★★ and Rosette. [🐾]
e-mail: office@sychnant-pass-house.co.uk   website: www.sychnant-pass-house.co.uk

BRONGAIN, TYN-Y-GROES, CONWY. Homely Victorian stone cottage, picturesque Conwy Valley. Snowdonia Mountain views. Enjoy lakes, mountains, walking, bird watching, beaches, Bodnant, RSPB, Conwy Castle. £265-£350. Contact: MRS G. M. SIMPOLE, 105 HAYGREEN ROAD, TERRINGTON ST CLEMENT, KINGS LYNN, NORFOLK PE34 4PU (01553 828897; Mobile: 0798 9080 665) [pw! 🐾]
e-mail: gill@simpole.rlshost.net

Conwy Valley

Fertile valley with wood and moor rising on both sides. Many places of interest in the area.

Secluded cottages with log fire and beams. Dogs will love it. Plenty of walks around mountains and lakes. For 2 - 7 people plus their pet(s). MRS WILLIAMS (01724 733990 or 07711 217 448) week lets only. [🐾]

Denbigh (Llandyrnog)

Market town 13 miles from the seaside resort of Rhyl.

PENTRE MAWR COUNTRY HOUSE, LLANDYRNOG LL16 4LA (01824 790732) Ancestral home of 400 years with woodland, park and riverside meadows, within easy reach of Chester and coast. Heated swimming pool. All rooms en suite. Pets most welcome. AA ★★★★★ and Dinner Award [🐾]
e-mail: info@pentremawrcountryhouse.co.uk   www.pentremawrcountryhouse.co.uk

Llanarmon

Village situated on River Ceriog, 7 miles south west of Llangollen.

THE WEST ARMS, LLANARMON DYFFRYN CEIRIOG, NEAR LLANGOLLEN LL20 7LD (01691 600 665; Fax: 01691 600 622). 16th century hotel full of charm and character in a tranquil picturesque setting with unpretentious hospitality and superb cuisine. Inglenook log fires, low ceilings and undulating floors. VisitWales/AA ★★★★ Two Rosettes. [Pets £6 per night]
e-mail: gowestarms@aol.com   website: www.thewestarms.co.uk

Please mention PETS WELCOME!
when making enquiries about accommodation featured in this guide

Llandudno

Coastal resort at base of peninsula running out to Great Ormes Head.

WARWICK HOUSE, 56 CHURCH WALKS, LLANDUDNO LL30 2HL (01492 876823; Fax: 01492 877908). Comfortable, relaxing and family friendly. 14 tastefully decorated en suite bedrooms with colour TV and tea and coffee making facilities. 5 minutes' walk to beach and town centre. WTB ★★★ e-mail info@thewarwickhotel.net   website: www.thewarwickhotel.net

DUNOON HOTEL, GLODDAETH STREET, LLANDUDNO LL30 2DW (01492 860787) An elegant family-run hotel with a well deserved reputation for friendly, efficient service, wonderful food and wine, and comfortable well appointed bedrooms. Small dogs by arrangement. AA/WTB ★★★. website: www.dunoonhotel.co.uk

THE MOORINGS, 3 ABBEY ROAD, LLANDUDNO LL30 2EA (01492 8767750) Offering you a range of accommodation to suit all, with great parking facilities and easy access to beautiful beaches, coastline and an assortment of attractions. Available all year round with a choice from 8 different Apartments to suit your needs. VisitWales ★★★ [🐾] e-mail: stay@themooringsholidays.co.uk   website: www.themooringsholidays.co.uk

Llangollen

Famous for International Music Eisteddfod held in July. Plas Newydd, Valle Crucis Abbey nearby. Standard gauge steam railway; canal cruises; ideal for golf and walking.

THE HAND AT LLANARMON, LLANARMON D.C., CEIRIOG VALLEY, NEAR LLANGOLLEN LL20 7LD (01691 600666). Standing in the glorious Ceiriog Valley, The Hand at Llanarmon radiates charm and character. 13 comfortable en suite bedrooms, log fires, and fabulous food, a wonderful base for most country pursuits. [🐾] e-mail: reception@thehandhotel.co.uk   website: www.TheHandHotel.co.uk

GOLDEN PHEASANT COUNTRY HOTEL, GLYN CEIROG, NEAR LLANGOLLEN LL20 7BB (01691 718281; Fax: 01691 718479). Situated in the beautiful Ceiriog Valley. All 19 rooms en suite, colour TV and tea/coffee making facilities. Pets welcome in all rooms (except restaurant and lounge). WTB/AA ★★★ [pw! £5 per night per pet, £35 per week] e-mail: info@goldenpheasanthotel.co.uk   website: www.goldenpheasanthotel.co.uk

Llanrwst (Conwy Valley)

Small town and community on the River Conwy. 11 miles south of Colwyn Bay.

MAENAN ABBEY HOTEL, MAENAN, LLANRWST LL26 0UL (01492 660247). All modern facilities. 14 bedrooms, all en suite, single, double, twin, family and four-poster bridal suite available. Spectacular views. Restaurant and bar. Small, well behaved dogs welcome. e-mail: info@manab.co.uk   website: www.manab.co.uk

BODNANT CARAVAN PARK, NEBO ROAD, LLANRWST, CONWY VALLEY LL26 OSD (01492 640248). Picturesque location 10 minutes' walking distance from town. 35 caravan and motor-caravan pitches available, 14 tent pitches. Toilet blocks with free hot water and showers. Two well equipped caravans for hire also available. AA 4 Pennants, WTB ★★★★ [Pets 50p per night] e-mail: ermin@bodnant-caravan-park.co.uk   website: www.bodnant-caravan-park.co.uk

Rhos-on-Sea (Conwy)

Popular resort at east end of Penrhyn Bay, adjoining Colwyn Bay to the north-west.

SUNNYDOWNS HOTEL, 66 ABBEY ROAD, RHOS-ON-SEA, CONWY LL28 4NU (01492 544256). A 3 star luxury family hotel just two minutes' walk to beach and shops. All rooms en suite with digital TV and approximately 40 channels, tea/coffee facilities and central heating. Hotel has bar, pool room and car park. A non-smoking hotel. [Pets £3 per night] e-mail: sunnydowns@tiscali.co.uk   website: www.sunnydownshotel.co.uk

THE NORTHWOOD, 47 RHOS ROAD, RHOS-ON-SEA, COLWYN BAY LL28 4RS (08450 533105). Family-run guesthouse in the heart of Rhos-on-Sea 175 yards from high class shops, promenade and sea. Tastefully furnished bedrooms. Vegetarian meals and special dietary needs are available. AA ★★★. [🐾] e-mail: welcome@thenorthwood.co.uk   website: www.thenorthwood.co.uk

Bronwydd Arms, Ferryside, Laugharne, Llandeilo, Llandysul

CWMDWYFRAN FARM HOLIDAY COTTAGE

Swallow View has recently been refurbished to a high standard.
Open-plan kitchen/dining/living areas; fully equipped kitchen; lounge with digital Freeview TV.
Sleeps 4. Centrally located for exploring coast and countryside.
Cwmdwyfran Farm Holiday Cottage,
Cwmdwyfran, Bronwydd Arms, Carmarthenshire SA33 6JF
Tel: 01267 281419 • e-mail: info@cwmdwyfran.co.uk • www.cwmdwyfran.co.uk

---

Three Rivers Hotel, Spa & Cottages • Ferryside
T: 01267 267270 • Carmarthenshire SA17 5TU
www.threerivershotel.co.uk

SIR JOHN'S HILL FARM HOLIDAY COTTAGES
Laugharne, Carmarthenshire SA33 4TD
The Old Stables Cottage • Tel: 01994 427001

In one of the finest locations in West Wales with spectacular views of coast and countryside, The Old Stables Cottage is the perfect place for a relaxing break. Here at Sir Johns Hill Farm we specialise in dog-friendly holidays and aim to make their holiday just as good as yours. They will have a great time at the farm which is well away from the main road, and there are lots of great country walks and long sandy beaches nearby too.

www.sirjohnshillfarm.co.uk

Relax at The Maerdy in one of six traditional cottages set within two acres of secure gardens at **MAERDY COTTAGES**. From this idyllic centre enjoy local walks and famous gardens and discover the beautiful coast and countryside of Carmarthenshire. Each cottage is equipped to give maximum comfort...two cottages are fully wheelchair accessible, and all are ideal for families of all ages. Home cooked evening meals available. Open all year.

WTB ★★★★

Maerdy Cottages, Taliaris, Llandeilo, Carmarthenshire SA19 7DA • Tel: 01550 777448
e-mail: enquiries@maerdyholidaycottages.co.uk • www.maerdyholidaycottages.co.uk

---

Typoeth Cottage

For a wonderful holiday in West Wales

18th century listed cottage. Central for the Pembrokeshire and Ceredigion coasts, the Brecon Beacons and Gower. Surrounded by fields and woodland with good walks.
Quiet location, yet only 1.5 miles from Llandysul.
Pets and horses welcome. Dog training available.

Typoeth Cottage, Llandysul, Carmarthenshire SA44 4RS
Tel: 01559 384483 • email: tourism@typoethcottage.co.uk
www.typoethcottage.co.uk

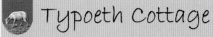

Visit **www.holidayguides.com**
for pet-friendly accommodation in Britain

Bronwydd Arms

Village 2 miles north of Carmarthen.

CWMDWYFRAN FARM HOLIDAY COTTAGE, CWMDWYFRAN, BRONWYDD ARMS SA33 6JF (01267 281419) A beautiful holiday cottage in a secluded and peaceful location. Refurbished to a high standard. Sleeps 4. Ideal for exploring coast and countryside. WTB ★★★★. [Pets £15 per week].
e-mail: info@cwmdwyfran.co.uk   website: www.cwmdwyfran.co.uk

Ferryside

Seaside village 8 miles south of Carmarthen near to the mouth of the River Tywi.

THREE RIVERS HOTEL & SPA, FERRYSIDE, CARMARTHEN SA17 5TU (01267 267270). A quiet hotel nestling on the Three Rivers estuary. All bedrooms en suite, spacious and tastefully furnished. Health Suite with heated pool. Three self-catering cottages also available. WTB ★★★.
e-mail: enquiries@threerivershotel.co.uk   website:www.threerivershotel.co.uk

Laugharne

Village on the River Taf estuary, 4 miles south of St Clears, burial place of Dylan Thomas.

SIR JOHN'S HILL FARM HOLIDAY COTTAGES, LAUGHARNE SA33 4TD (01994 427001). THE OLD STABLES COTTAGE. Specialising in dog-friendly holidays, a very comfortable cottage in one of the finest locations in West Wales, with spectacular views, lots of great country walks, and long sandy beaches nearby. [pw! £15 per week.]
website: www.sirjohnshillfarm.co.uk

Llandeilo

Town on River Towy, 14 miles east of Carmarthen.

MAERDY COTTAGES, TALIARIS, LLANDEILO SA19 7DA (01550 777448). Six traditional cottages set within two acres of secure gardens. Each cottage is equipped to give maximum comfort, two cottages are fully wheelchair accessible, and all are ideal for families of all ages. Home cooked evening meals available. Open all year. WTB ★★★★. [First pet free, others £5 per night, £20 per week].
e-mail: enquiries@maerdyholidaycottages.co.uk   website: www.maerdyholidaycottages.co.uk

Llandysul

Small town in the valley of the River Teifi.

TYPOETH COTTAGE, LLANDYSUL SA44 4RS (01559 384483). 18th century Listed cottage in an ideal location. Kitchen, sunny living/dining room with multi-fuel stove, twin bedroom and shower room. Llandysul less than 10 minutes drive. Dogs welcome. For details please contact Suzanna.[🐾]
email: tourism@typoethcottage.co.uk   website: www.typoethcottage.co.uk

Llanelli

Village on the River Taf estuary, 10 mile north-west of Swansea.

THE DIPLOMAT HOTEL, FELINFOEL ROAD, AELYBRYN, LLANELLI SA15 3PJ (01554 756156; Fax: 01554 751649). Privately owned and operated with warmth and generous hospitality. The Diplomat Hotel offers a rare combination of charm and character with excellent well appointed facilities to ensure your comfort and convenience. WTB/AA ★★★ [Pets £5 per night]
e-mail: reservations@diplomat-hotel-wales.com   website: www.bw-diplomathotel.co.uk

Llanpumsaint

Small village 7 miles north of Carmarthen.

ANNE RYDER OWEN, FFERM-Y-FELIN, LLANPUMSAINT SA33 6DA (01267 253 498). A warm welcome awaits you at this carefully restored farmhouse with log fires. B&B and two self-catering Cottages. Excellent home cooking, peace and tranquillity, a haven for conservationists. Fish for trout in the lake. [First pet free, charge for second pet]
e-mail: anneryderowen@hotmail.com   website: http://ferm-y-felin-cottages.wales.info

Llansteffan

Picturesque village overlooked by Norman castle on the headland.

MRS LIZ DUTCH, BRIG Y DON HOLIDAYS, LLANSTEFFAN SA33 5LW (01267 241585). Escape to our quality apartment beside a sandy beach. Sleeps 2, dog-friendly. Estuary views, glorious coastal and woodland walks. Friendly village. Truly, a dog's paradise! WTB ★★★★. [pw! 🐾]
e-mail: enquiries@brigydon-holidays.co.uk   website: www.brigydon-holidays.co.uk

---

🐾   Pets are welcome free of charge.

£   A charge is made for pets: nightly or weekly.

pw!   Special provision for pets; exercise facility, feeding or accommodation arrangement.

⌂   Separate pets accommodation.

Classified Symbols

Aberaeron

Attractive little town on Cardigan Bay, good touring centre for coast and inland. The Aeron Express Aerial ferry offers an exciting trip across the harbour. Marine aquarium; Aberarth Leisure Park nearby.

GILFACH HOLIDAY VILLAGE, LLWYNCELYN, NEAR ABERAERON SA46 OHN (01545 580288). Choice of modern Bungalows (up to 6 persons) or luxury 2/3 person apartments. Fully equipped, linen available, colour TV. Horse and pony riding. Tennis. Write or phone for brochure pack to the Manager. [Pets £15 per week.]
e-mail: info@stratfordcaravans.co.uk   website: www.selfcateringinwales.com
                                        or www.stratfordcaravans.co.uk

Aberporth

Popular seaside village offering safe swimming and good sea fishing. Good base for exploring Cardigan Bay coastline.

'QUALITY COTTAGES', CERBID, SOLVA, HAVERFORDWEST, PEMBROKESHIRE SA62 6YE (01348 837871). Cottages set in all coastal areas, enjoy unashamed luxury, highest residential standards. Log fires. Linen supplied. Pets welcome, free. [pw! 🐕]
website: www.qualitycottages.co.uk

Cardigan

Historic town on the banks of the Teifi estuary, with excellent leisure facilities.

PENBONTBREN, GLYNARTHEN, LLANDYSUL, NEAR CARDIGAN SA44 6PE (01239 810248). Luxury Bed & Breakfast in West Wales in 32 acres of grounds, only two miles from wonderful National Trust beaches. 5 suites each with spacious sitting room, own garden, king-size bed and sumptuous décor and furnishings. Pets by prior arrangement. [🐕]
e-mail: contact@penbontbren.com   website: www.penbontbren.com

PENWERN FACH COTTAGES, PONTHIRWAUN, NEAR CENARTH, CARDIGAN SA43 2RL (01239 710694). Character stone cottages. Peaceful setting with lovely views. Beautiful coastline. Indoor swimming pool nearby. Log fires. WTB ★★★★.[Pets £20 per week]
e-mail: info@penwernfach.co.uk   website: www.penwernfach.co.uk

Ciliau Aeron

Village in undulating country just inland from the charming Cardigan Bay resorts of New Quay and Aberaeron. New Quay 12 miles, Aberaeron 6

'QUALITY COTTAGES', CERBID, SOLVA, HAVERFORDWEST, PEMBROKESHIRE SA62 6YE (01348 837871). Cottages set in all coastal areas, enjoy unashamed luxury, highest residential standards. Log fires. Linen supplied. Pets welcome, free. [pw! 🐕]
website: www.qualitycottages.co.uk

Llangrannog

Pretty little seaside village overlooking a sandy beach. Superb cliff walk to NT Ynys Lochtyn, a secluded promontory.

'QUALITY COTTAGES', CERBID, SOLVA, HAVERFORDWEST, PEMBROKESHIRE SA62 6YE (01348 837871). Cottages set in all coastal areas, enjoy unashamed luxury, highest residential standards. Log fires. Linen supplied. Pets welcome, free. [pw! 🐕]
website: www.qualitycottages.co.uk

Please note...

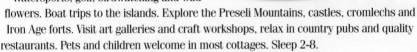
Broad Haven, Croft

A useful index of towns/counties appears on pages 455-461

'QUALITY COTTAGES', CERBID, SOLVA, HAVERFORDWEST, PEMBROKESHIRE SA62 6YE (01348 837871). Cottages set in all coastal areas, enjoy unashamed luxury, highest residential standards. Log fires. Linen supplied. Pets welcome, free. [pw! 🐾]
website: www.qualitycottages.co.uk

Pembrokeshire Coast - Newport to St Davids. Charming, individual cottages situated near sandy beaches, rocky bays and spectacular cliff walks. All comfortably furnished and fully equipped. Pets and children welcome. Sleep 2-8. Details from CAROLE ROGERS, COTTAGE RETREATS IN PEMBROKESHIRE, 29 HEOL GLYNDWR, FISHGUARD SA65 9LN (01348 875318). [🐾]
e-mail: carole.rogers@talktalk.net   website: www.cottageretreats.net

Bosherton

Village 4 miles south of Pembroke, bordered by 3 man-made lakes, a haven for wildlife and covered in water lilies in early summer.

'QUALITY COTTAGES', CERBID, SOLVA, HAVERFORDWEST, PEMBROKESHIRE SA62 6YE (01348 837871). Cottages set in all coastal areas, enjoy unashamed luxury, highest residential standards. Log fires. Linen supplied. Pets welcome, free. [pw! 🐾]
website: www.qualitycottages.co.uk

Broad Haven

Village on St Bride's Bay, 6 miles west of Haverfordwest.

PEMBROKESHIRE NATIONAL PARK. Sleeps 6 + cot. Three-bedroom fully furnished Holiday Lodge. Walking distance sandy beaches and coastal footpath. £150 to £390 per week. MRS L.P. ASHTON, 10 ST LEONARDS ROAD, THAMES DITTON, SURREY KT7 0RJ (020-8398 6349). [🐾]
e-mail: lejash@aol.com   website: www.33timberhill.com

Croes Goch

Hamlet 6 miles north east of St Davids

'QUALITY COTTAGES', CERBID, SOLVA, HAVERFORDWEST, PEMBROKESHIRE SA62 6YE (01348 837871). Cottages set in all coastal areas, enjoy unashamed luxury, highest residential standards. Log fires. Linen supplied. Pets welcome, free. [pw! 🐾]
website: www.qualitycottages.co.uk

Croft

Located 2 miles SW of Cardigan.

CROFT FARM & CELTIC COTTAGES, CROFT, NEAR CARDIGAN SA43 3NT (01239 615179). Featured in Daily Mail. Stone barn conversions with luxury indoor heated pool, sauna, spa pool and gym. Colourful gardens, indoor and outdoor play areas. VisitWales ★★★★★/★★★★ SELF CATERING. Pets welcome. [Pets £4 per night, £28 per week, pw!]
e-mail: info@croft-holiday-cottages.co.uk   website: www.croft-holiday-cottages.co.uk

Fishguard

Small town at end of Fishguard Bay

IVYBRIDGE GUEST HOUSE, DRIM MILL, DYFFRYN, GOODWICK SA64 0JT (01348 875366). Stay at Ivybridge, all rooms en suite. Evening meals served. Small heated indoor pool. Private car park. Pets welcome! [Pets £7 per stay].
e-mail: info@ivybridgefishguard.co.uk   website: www.ivybridgefishguard.co.uk

CARTREF HOTEL, 15-19 HIGH STREET, FISHGUARD SA65 9AW (01348 872430; Fax: 01348 873664). A friendly, family-run hotel in the centre of Fishguard with licensed restaurant and residential bar. En suite rooms. Only 5 minutes' drive to the ferry port for Ireland. AA ★★. [Pets £5 per night; £20 per week]
e-mail: cartrefhotel@btconnect.com   website: www.cartrefhotel.co.uk

FISHGUARD HOLIDAY PARK, PEMBROKESHIRE (01348 872462). Superb holiday park near town, shops and sandy beach. Club. Free nightly entertainment. Swimming pool. [Pets £12 per week]
website: www.howellsleisure.co.uk

Goodwick

Coastal town on west side of Fishguard Bay. Terminal for rail and car ferry services to Ireland.

MRS ROSEMARY JOHNS, CARNE FARM, GOODWICK SA64 0LB (01348 891665). Stone cottage adjoining farmhouse on 350-acre working dairy and sheep farm, sleeps 6. Easy reach of beaches. Three miles to sea. Children welcome. Caravan (sleeps 6) also available. [🐾]

Haverfordwest

Administrative and shopping centre for the area; ideal base for exploring National Park. Historic town of narrow streets; museum in castle grounds; many fine buildings.

CLARE HALLETT, KEESTON HILL COTTAGE, KEESTON, HAVERFORDWEST SA62 6EJ (01437 710440). Two apartments sleeping 4/5 each in cottage with garden. Open all year. From £240 to £450 per week. Heating, electricity and linen included. [🐾]
e-mail: enquiries@keestonhillcottage.co.uk   website: www.keestonhillcottage.co.uk

GARN ISAF, ABERCASTLE, HAVERFORDWEST SA62 5HJ (Tel & Fax: 01348 831838; Mobile: 07969 529929). Within the Pembrokeshire National Park, surrounded by stunning scenery. 4★ B&B and 5★ self catering accommodation. Secluded campsite, picnic benches. [One pet free s/c, in B&B £5 per night]. website: www.garnisaf.com

SCAMFORD CARAVAN PARK, KEESTON, HAVERFORDWEST SA62 6HN (Tel & Fax: 01437 710304). 25 luxurious caravans (shower, fridge, microwave, colour TV). Peaceful park near lovely sandy beaches. Playground. Launderette. Pets welcome. WTB ★★★★ Holiday Park.
e-mail: holidays@scamford.com   website: www.scamford.com

NOLTON HAVEN QUALITY COTTAGES. Ideal for out of season breaks. Most with sea view. 30 yards from safe, sandy beach. Sleep 2-20. 8-bedroom farmhouse sleeps 20. WTB ★★★/★★★★/★★★★★ Self-Catering. Contact: JIM & JOYCE CANTON, NOLTON HAVEN FARMHOUSE, NOLTON HAVEN, HAVERFORDWEST SA62 6NH (01437 710263).
e-mail: PW8@noltonhaven.com   website: www.noltonhaven.com

HAVEN COTTAGES. Quality beachfront cottages, sleep 2-8, adjacent sandy beach. Well equipped. Open all year. Winter breaks. Contact: SYCAMORE LODGE, NOLTON HAVEN SA62 3NH (01437 710200). [Pets £10 per week].
e-mail: info@havencottages.co.uk   website: www.havencottages.co.uk

Llanteg

Hamlet 4 miles south of Whitland.

TONY & JANE BARON, LLANTEGLOS ESTATE, LLANTEG, NEAR AMROTH SA67 8PU (01834 831677 /831371). Self-contained Woodland Lodges. Sleep 6. Children's play area. Licensed bar. Visitor attractions. Open all year. Call for brochure. VisitWales ★★★/★★★★ Self Catering [Pets £6 per night, £36 per week.]
e-mail: llanteglosestate@supanet.com   website: www.llanteglos-estate.com

Llechryd

Village on the A484 3 miles from Cardigan.

CASTELL MALGWYN COUNTRY HOUSE HOTEL, LLECHRYD, CARDIGAN SA43 2QA (01239 682382) Well behaved dogs welcome. Set on the banks of the River Teifi in large grounds. Excellent local food prepared by our superb chefs. [Pets £10 per night]
e-mail: reception@malgwyn.co.uk   website: www.castellmalgwyn.co.uk

---

🐾   Pets are welcome free of charge.

£   A charge is made for pets: nightly or weekly.

pw! Special provision for pets; exercise facility, feeding or accommodation arrangement.

⌂   Separate pets accommodation.

Classified Symbols

Lydstep

Small hamlet 3 miles south west of Tenby.

CELTIC HAVEN, LYDSTEP, NEAR TENBY SA70 7SG (01834 870000). Escape, relax, unwind, explore at Wales most complete resort. Exhilarating cliff-top walks, stunning scenery and several dog-friendly beaches. Luxury cottages; superb leisure facilities; spa and restaurant. [Pets £20 per stay]. e-mail: welcome@celtichaven.com   website: www.celtichaven.co.uk

Moylegrove

Village 4 miles west of Cardigan.

NORTH PEMBROKESHIRE COAST. 3 WELSH COTTAGES with enclosed gardens. Paddock for exercise. Dog-friendly bay and beaches within walking distance, with spectacular views. Bed linen included. (01239 881 280). [🐾]

CWM CONNELL COASTAL COTTAGES, MOYLEGROVE SA43 3BX (01239 881691) Six luxury self-catering cottages within the Pembrokeshire Coastal National Park. Sleep 2/4/7. A rural retreat to relax and unwind. Dogs with responsible owners welcome. WTB ★★★★ e-mail: info@cwmconnell.co.uk   website: www.cwmconnell.co.uk

Newgale

On St Bride's Bay 3 miles east of Solva. Long beach where at exceptionally low tide the stumps of a submerged forest may be seen.

'QUALITY COTTAGES', CERBID, SOLVA, HAVERFORDWEST, PEMBROKESHIRE SA62 6YE (01348 837871). Cottages set in all coastal areas, enjoy unashamed luxury, highest residential standards. Log fires. Linen supplied. Pets welcome, free. [pw! 🐾] website: www.qualitycottages.co.uk

Newport

Small town at mouth of the River Nyfer, 9 miles south west of Cardigan. Remains of 13th-century castle.

'QUALITY COTTAGES', CERBID, SOLVA, HAVERFORDWEST, PEMBROKESHIRE SA62 6YE (01348 837871). Cottages set in all coastal areas, enjoy unashamed luxury, highest residential standards. Log fires. Linen supplied. Pets welcome, free. [pw! 🐾] website: www.qualitycottages.co.uk

St Davids

Smallest cathedral city in Britain, shrine of Wales' patron saint. Magnificent ruins of Bishop's Palace. Craft shops, farm parks and museums; boat trips to Ramsey Island.

'QUALITY COTTAGES', CERBID, SOLVA, HAVERFORDWEST, PEMBROKESHIRE SA62 6YE (01348 837871). Cottages set in all coastal areas, enjoy unashamed luxury, highest residential standards. Log fires. Linen supplied. Pets welcome, free. [pw! 🐾] website: www.qualitycottages.co.uk

CAERHAFOD LODGE, LLANRHIAN, NEAR ST DAVIDS, HAVERFORDWEST SA62 5BD (01348 837859). Situated close to Coastal Path, between Fishguard and St Davids. Purpose-built hostel accommodation; all rooms en suite. Fully equipped kitchen/diner. Cycle hire. Dog-friendly. Walkers and Cyclists Welcome. WTB ★★★★ [🐾] e-mail: caerhafod@aol.com   website: www.caerhafod.co.uk

ST DAVIDS HOLIDAY COTTAGES. Superbly appointed self-catering cottages (sleep 2-6) situated on the spectacular North Pembrokeshire coast. Available all year round. Dogs welcome in most. For details contact: PETER DAVIES, 6 HAMILTON STREET, FISHGUARD SA65 9HL (01348 872266). [🐾] e-mail: peter@stdavidsholidays.co.uk   website: www.stdavidsholidays.co.uk

PEMBROKESHIRE SHEEPDOGS, TREMYNYDD FACH, ST DAVIDS SA62 6DB (01437 721677). B&B (in cosy cottages) and Self-catering (in farmhouse and chalet) on working sheep farm. Spectacular and unspoilt stretch of coastal path with plants and wildlife. [🐕 ⌂]
e-mail: info@sheepdogtraining.co.uk website: www.sheepdogtraining.co.uk

TRETIO COTTAGES, ST DAVIDS SA62 6DE (01437 720269). Unwind in high quality, comfortable, well-equipped cottages located three miles from St Davids, near to beautiful sandy beaches and the Pembrokeshire Coastal Path. Owner-run – personal and friendly service. Short breaks available. Pets welcome. WTB ★★★★/★★★★★ [Pets £10 per week]
e-mail: stay@tretiocottages.co.uk website: www.tretiocottages.co.uk

FFYNNON DDOFN, LLANON, LLANRHIAN, NEAR ST DAVIDS. Comfortable, well-equipped cottage with panoramic coastal views. Sleeps six in three bedrooms. Central heating. Large games room. Open all year. Pets welcome free of charge. Brochure on request from: MRS B. REES WHITE, BRICKHOUSE FARM, BURNHAM RD, WOODHAM MORTIMER, MALDON, ESSEX CM9 6SR (01245 224611). [🐕]
website: www.ffynnonddofn.co.uk

FELINDRE COTTAGES, PORTHGAIN, ST DAVIDS SA62 5BH (01348 831220). Self-catering cottages with panoramic sea and country views. Five minutes' walk from Coastal Path, picturesque fishing village of Porthgain and a great pub! Peaceful location. Short breaks available. One well-behaved dog welcome, except school holidays. WTB graded. [pw! £10 per week]
e-mail: sheilacraft@supanet.com website: www.felindrecottages.co.uk

MRS MARGO EVANS, LOCHMEYLER FARM GUEST HOUSE, LLANDELOY, NEAR SOLVA, ST DAVIDS SA62 6LL (01348 837724; Fax: 01348 837622). Welcome Host Gold Award. 7 en suite luxury bedrooms. B&B from £35pppn. Evening dinner available. WTB ★★★★★, AA ★★★★★ [pw! 🐕]
e-mail: stay@lochmeyler.co.uk website: www.lochmeyler.co.uk

Saundersfoot

Popular resort and sailing centre with picturesque harbour and sandy beach. Tenby 3 miles

VINE COTTAGE GUEST HOUSE, THE RIDGEWAY, SAUNDERSFOOT SA69 9LA (01834 814422). Coastal village outskirts. Sandy beaches and coast path nearby. Award-winning garden for guests' and dogs' relaxation and exercise. Non-smoking throughout. AA ★★★★ [pw! Pets £5 per stay.]
e-mail: enquiries@vinecottageguesthouse.co.uk website: www.vinecottageguesthouse.co.uk

Solva

Picturesque coastal village with sheltered harbour and excellent craft shops. Sailing and watersports; sea fishing, long sandy beach.

'QUALITY COTTAGES', CERBID, SOLVA, HAVERFORDWEST, PEMBROKESHIRE SA62 6YE (01348 837871). Cottages set in all coastal areas, enjoy unashamed luxury, highest residential standards. Log fires. Linen supplied. Pets welcome, free. [pw! 🐕]
website: www.qualitycottages.co.uk

Tenby

Popular resort with two wide beaches. Fishing trips, craft shops, museum. Medieval castle ruins, 13th-century church. Golf, fishing and watersports; boat trips to nearby Caldy Island with monastery and medieval church.

'QUALITY COTTAGES', CERBID, SOLVA, HAVERFORDWEST, PEMBROKESHIRE SA62 6YE (01348 837871). Cottages set in all coastal areas, enjoy unashamed luxury, highest residential standards. Log fires. Linen supplied. Pets welcome, free. [pw! 🐕]
website: www.qualitycottages.co.uk

Whitland

Village 6 miles east of Narberth. Whitland Abbey 2 km.

MRS ANGELA COLLEDGE, GWARMACWYDD FARM, LLANFALLTEG, WHITLAND SA34 0XH (0800 321 3699). Country estate with six character stone cottages, fully furnished and equipped. All linen and electricity included; heated for year-round use. WTB ★★★★ [pw! Pets £10 per pet per week]
website: www.davidsfarm.com

Builth Wells

Old country town in lovely setting on River Wye amid beautiful hills. Lively markets; host to Royal Welsh Agricultural Show

MRS LINDA WILLIAMS, OLD VICARAGE, ERWOOD, BUILTH WELLS LD2 3SZ (01982 560680).
Superior views from elevated position in Wye Valley. Comfortable ornate beds, one en suite room,
two sharing guests' own bathroom. Drinks tray, TV, washbasin. Bacon and sausage from our own
pigs, farm eggs, home baked bread and preserves. VisitWales ★★★ Farm, FHG Diploma Winner
2004.[🐾]
e-mail: linda@oldvicwyevalley.co.uk   website: www.oldvicwyevalley.co.uk

MRS KATHARINE SMITH, CAER BERIS MANOR, BUILTH WELLS LD2 3NP (01982 552601; Fax: 01982
552586). Family-owned country house hotel set in 27 acres of parkland. Free salmon and trout fishing; golf
nearby, superb walking and touring. All rooms en suite. AA ★★★ [Pets £5 per night, £30 per week].
e-mail: caerberis@btconnect.com   website: www.caerberis.com

Cilmery

Village 2½ miles west of Builth Wells.

PWLLGWILYM HOLIDAY COTTAGES, PWLLGWILYM, LLANAFAN ROAD, CILMERY, BUILTH WELLS
LD2 3NY (01982-552140/ 07909-681881). A large barn tastefully converted into 3 spacious 4-star
cottages with hardwood stairs, flagstone floors. Surrounded by a 60 acre farm with lovely views,
two miles from Builth Wells. Sleep 4-8. WTB ★★★★ [Pets £12 per week].
e-mail: bookings@pwllgwilym-cottages.co.uk   website: www.pwllgwilym-cottages.co.uk

Hay-on-Wye

Small market town at north end of Black Mountains, 15 miles north-east of Brecon.

MRS E. BALLY, LANE FARM, PAINSCASTLE, BUILTH WELLS LD2 3JS (Tel & Fax: 01497 851605). 17th
century farm in rural Radnorshire, five miles Hay-on-Wye. Wonderful walking country. Self-catering
apartments sleeping 2-14. A warm welcome for you and your pet(s). WTB ★★★ [🐾]
e-mail: lanefarm@onetel.com

BASKERVILLE ARMS HOTEL, CLYRO, NEAR HAY-ON-WYE HR3 5RZ (01497 820670). Delightfully
placed comfortable retreat with well appointed en suite bedrooms. Tasty, home-cooked food in bar
and restaurant, using the best local produce. Special break rates. WTB ★★★.
e-mail: info@baskervillearms.co.uk   website: www.baskervillearms.co.uk

Please mention PETS WELCOME!
when making enquiries about accommodation featured in this guide

Kington

Market town near the English Welsh border. Hereford 21 miles.

THE ROCK COTTAGE, HUNTINGTON, KINGTON. Secluded, stone-built cottage near Offa's Dyke footpath. Ideal for touring, birdwatching, golf and pony trekking. Sleeps 4/6. Fully equipped kitchen, lounge with wood-burner. Central Heating. Spacious garden. Children and pets welcome. Details from MRS C. WILLIAMS, RADNOR'S END, HUNTINGTON, KINGTON HR5 3NZ (01544 370289). [🐴] website: www.the-rock-cottage.co.uk

Llandrindod Wells

Popular inland resort, Victorian spa town, excellent touring centre. Golf, fishing, bowling, boating and tennis. Visitors can still take the waters at Rock Park Gardens.

THE PARK HOUSE, CROSSGATES, LLANDRINDOD WELLS LD1 6RF (01597 851201; 07918 660647). In three acres, amidst beautiful countryside near Elan Valley. Static caravans, touring pitches and fully equipped bungalows and cottages. Restaurant. Pets welcome. [Pets £3 per night, £20 per week. Guide dogs free).
e-mail: ian_barr@btconnect.com   website: www.barrscountryparks.com

Llangurig

Village on River Wye, 4 miles south-west of Llanidloes. Ideal walking countryside.

MRS J. BAILEY, GLANGWY, LLANGURIG, LLANIDLOES SY18 6RS (01686 440697). Bed, breakfast and evening meals in the countryside. Plenty of walking locally. Also caravan and campsite. Prices on request. [🐴]

THE OLD VICARAGE, LLANGURIG SY18 6RN (Tel & Fax: 01686 440280). A late Victorian property tastefully converted to a cosy Guest House. All bedrooms are well furnished and have full en suite facilities, plus little extras for your comfort. WTB/AA ★★★★.
e-mail: info@theoldvicaragellangurig.co.uk   website:www.theoldvicaragellangurig.co.uk

Machynlleth

Attractive old town with half-timbered houses. Ideal for hillside rambles.

THE WYNNSTAY HOTEL, MAENGWYN STREET, MACHYNLLETH SY20 8AE (01654 702941). Award-winning food, wine and beer. Glorious countryside and miles of sandy beaches. Masses to do and see. WTB ★★★. Good Food Guide & Good Beer Guide Recommended, Les Routiers "Best Wine List in Britain". [Pets free in kennels, £5 one-off charge in rooms]
e-mail: info@wynnstay-hotel.com   website: www.wynnstay-hotel.com

Newtown

Situated on the banks of the River Severn. Birthplace of Robert Owen.

PAUL & MICHELLE MARTIN, FOREST COTTAGE, KERRY, NEWTOWN SY16 4DW (01686 621821). Four pretty self-catering cottages and a B&B in secluded setting. Cottages sleep 2-5. Period features, tennis court, games room, play area. Owner is a veterinarian. [Pets £15 per week]
e-mail: info@forestcottageskerry.co.uk   website: www.holidaycottagesmidwales.co.uk

---

🐴   Pets are welcome free of charge.

£   A charge is made for pets: nightly or weekly.

pw! Special provision for pets; exercise facility, feeding or accommodation arrangement.

⌂   Separate pets accommodation.

Classified Symbols

Pen-y-Cae

Village 6 miles north east of Ystalyfera.

CRAIG-Y-NOS CASTLE, PEN-Y-CAE SA9 1GL (01639 731167 / 730205; Fax: 01639 731077) Fantastic location in the lovely Upper Swansea Valley. Character en suite bedrooms. Ghost Tours. Beacons Spa Facilities. Mid-week breaks. Dog-friendly accommodation.
e-mail: info@craigynoscastle.com   website: www.craigynoscastle.com

Presteigne

Attractive old town with half timbered houses. Ideal for hillside rambles and pony trekking.

WHITEHALL COTTAGE. Cosy cottage two miles from Offa's Dyke. Central heating, washing machine, dishwasher, microwave, colour TV, inglenook, woodburner, linen included. Power shower over bath. Sleeps 4 plus cot. Children and pets welcome. MRS R. L. JONES, UPPER HOUSE, KINNERTON, NEAR PRESTEIGNE LD8 2PE (01547 560207).[🐾].

Rhayader

Small market town on River Wye north of Builth Wells. Popular for angling and pony trekking

OAK WOOD LODGES, LLWYNBAEDD, RHAYADER LD6 5NT (01597 811422). Luxurious self-catering log cabins with spectacular views of the Elan Valley and Cambrian Mountains. Walking, pony trekking, mountain biking, fishing and bird watching in idyllic surroundings. Phone for brochure. [Dog £20 per week, £13 per short break; additional dogs half price].
website: www.oakwoodlodges.co.uk

TYN-Y-CASTELL SELF-CATERING CHALET. Spectacular scenery and magical walks; around the lakes, through the woods, up on the hills. A doggy paradise and the folks will love it too! Our delightful chalet is warm and comfortable and in a lovely rural location. JOAN MORGAN (07816 229235) [🐾]
e-mail: oldbedw@lineone.net   website: www.rhayader.net/tynycastell

Abergavenny, Gower Peninsula, Monmouth, Neath, Swansea

Swansea

THE
WHITE HOUSE
SWANSEA
★★★★

4 Nyanza Terrace, SWANSEA SA1 4QQ
Tel: 01792 473856 Fax: 01792 455300 Mob: 07974 695821
www.thewhitehousehotel.co.uk
reception@thewhitehousehotel.co.uk

Ranked 'best city centre hotel' by visitors, this fine Victorian Villa is situated just one mile from Swansea City Centre and is on the main road to the Gower peninsula. We've combined everything great that we'd expect ourselves & added even more, we think you'll appreciate it!

SUPERIOR BEDROOMS
GREAT HOSPITALITY
FINE DINING

CASTLE NARROWBOATS CHURCH ROAD WHARF, GILWERN NP7 0EP (01873 830001). The Monmouthshire & Brecon Canal in South Wales. Discover the beauty of Wales onboard one of our excellent narrowboats. 2-8 berth boats, short breaks available. Pets welcome.For a free colour brochure call Castle Narrowboats:
website: www.castlenarrowboats.co.uk

Abergavenny

Historic market town at south-eastern gateway to Brecon Beacons National Park. Pony trekking, leisure centre; excellent touring base for Vale of Usk.

HALF MOON INN, LLANTHONY, NEAR ABERGAVENNY NP7 7NN (01873 890611). B&B, good food and real ale in 17thC inn. Wonderful scenery of Black Mountains. Good base for walking, pony trekking, birdwatching. Dogs welcome.[Pets £1.50 per night]
e-mail: halfmoon@llanthony.wanadoo.co.uk   website: www.halfmoon-llanthony.co.uk

Pet-Friendly
Pubs, Inns& Hotels
on pages 448-453

These establishments may not feature in the main section of the book

Gower Peninsula

Britain's first designated Area of Outstanding Natural Beauty with numerous sandy beaches and lovely countryside to explore.

CULVER HOUSE HOTEL, PORT EYNON, GOWER SA3 1NN (01792 390755). One and two bedroom apartments offer modern fully equipped accommodation, stunning accessible Blue Flag beach location. Continental breakfast included. Prices from £90 per night. website: www.culverhousehotel.co.uk

HOME FROM HOME offers a wide variety of pet friendly holiday accommodation in the seaside village of Mumbles and on the beautiful Gower Peninsula. Whether you prefer a countryside walk or a stroll on one of the many stunning beaches, the area offers something for everyone. Contact: 01792 360624. [Pets £15 per week]
e-mail: enquiries@homefromhome.com   website: www.homefromhome.com

OLDWALLS LEISURE (01792 391468). Luxury 5-star dog-friendly B&B and cottages in Area of Outstanding Natural Beauty. 50 acres of land with private lakes and streams. Dog-friendly pub and restaurant. Tennis court and trout fishing on site. Numerous unspoilt beaches welcome dogs AND horses.
website: www.oldwallsleisure.com

Monmouth

Market town at confluence of Rivers Wye and Monnow 20 miles north-east of Newport.

ROSEMARY AND DEREK RINGER, CHURCH FARM GUEST HOUSE, MITCHEL TROY, MONMOUTH NP25 4HZ (01600 712176). A spacious 16th century (Grade II Listed) former farmhouse set in large garden with stream. Easy access to A40. All bedrooms en suite or with private facilities. B&B from £32pp. Evening meals by arrangement. Non-smoking. AA ★★★ [🐾].
e-mail: info@churchfarmguesthouse.eclipse.co.uk   website: www.churchfarmmitcheltroy.co.uk

Neath

Town on River Neath 8 miles NE of Swansea.

MRS C. JONES, GREEN LANTERNS GUEST HOUSE, HAWDREF GANOL FARM, CIMLA, NEATH SA12 9SL (01639 631884). 18th Century luxury Guest House with spacious en suite rooms, all with views over the Vale of Neath. Licensed bar and restaurant. Vegetarian & other diets catered for. Pets welcome by arrangement. WTB ★★★★.
website: www.greenlanterns.co.uk

Swansea

Second largest city in Wales with a wide variety of leisure activities and excellent shopping.

BEST WESTERN ABERAVON BEACH HOTEL, NEATH PORT TALBOT, SWANSEA BAY SA12 6QP (01639 884949). Modern seafront hotel. A warm Welsh welcome awaits you and your pets. 2 miles of flat promenade and a pet friendly beach. Pets Paradise!! And for you... newly refurbished rooms, fine cuisine, leisure centre and many local attractions. AA ★★★ [🐾]
e-mail: sales@aberavonbeach.com   website: www.aberavonbeachhotel.com

THE WHITE HOUSE HOTEL, 4 NYANZA TERRACE, SWANSEA SA1 4QQ. (01792 473856; Fax: 01792 455300; Mob: 07974 695821). Ranked 'best city centre hotel' by visitors, this fine Victorian Villa is situated just one mile from Swansea City Centre on the main road to the Gower peninsula. VisitWales/AA ★★★★. [🐾]
email: reception @thewhitehousehotel.co.uk   website:www.thewhitehousehotel.co.uk

Please mention PETS WELCOME!

when making enquiries about accommodation featured in this guide

IMAGINE IRELAND, HOLIDAY COTTAGES (01756 707787). 1500 inspected Holiday Cottages; many welcome pets. Half-price deals; ferry travel and car hire available. Free brochure.
website: www.imagineireland.com

Co Kerry

Lauragh

Creveen Lodge

Immaculately run small hill farm overlooking Kenmare Bay in a striking area of County Kerry. Reception is found at the Lodge, which also offers guests a comfortable sitting room, while a separate block has well-equipped and immaculately maintained toilets and showers, plus a communal room with a large fridge, freezer and ironing facilities. The park is carefully tended, with bins and picnic tables informally placed, plus a children's play area with slides and swings.

There are 20 pitches in total, 16 for tents and 4 for caravans, with an area of hardstanding for motor caravans. Electrical connections are available. Fishing, bicycle hire, water sports and horse riding available nearby. SAE please, for replies.

Mrs M. Moriarty, Creveen Lodge, Healy Pass Road, Lauragh
Tel: 00 353 64 66 83131
e-mail: info@creveenlodge.com • www.creveenlodge.com

Lauragh

Rural location on Ring of Beara.

MRS M. MORIARTY, CREVEEN LODGE, HEALY PASS ROAD, LAURAGH (00 353 64 66 83131). Small, carefully tended, well equipped park, 16 pitches for tents, 4 for caravans, with hardstanding for motor caravans. Fishing, bicycle hire, water sports and horse riding available nearby. [🐕]
e-mail: info@creveenlodge.com   website: www.creveenlodge.com

Visit the FHG website
www.holidayguides.com
for pet-friendly
acccommodation
around Britain

ooking for Holiday Accommodation?
hen visit our website:
www.holidayguides.com

arch for holiday accommodation
region, location, type of accommodation
&B, Self-Catering, Hotel etc)

**Special requirements –
Are you looking for accommodation
where children and pets are welcome,
or maybe you want to be
close to a golf course...**

details of hundreds of properties throughout the UK

Holidays with Horses

A selection of accommodation where horse and owner/rider can be put up at the same address – if not actually under the same roof!
We would be grateful if readers making enquiries and/or bookings from this supplement would mention Pets Welcome!

WESTERMILL FARM
EXFORD, MINEHEAD TA24 7NJ
(01643 831238; Fax: 01643 831216)
e-mail: pw@westermill.com   website: www.westermill.com

Cottages (Disabled Category 2) in grass paddocks. Ideal for children. Stabling and fields for horses. Wonderful for dogs and owners. Separate campsite by river.

TODDY AND CLIVE HAMILTON-GOULD
TOWER FIELDS, TUSMORE ROAD, NEAR SOULDERN, BICESTER OX27 7HY
(01869 346554)
e-mail: toddyclive@towerfields.com   website: www.towerfields.com

Ground floor en suite rooms, all with own entrance and ample parking. Breakfast using local produce. Easy reach of Oxford, Stratford-upon-Avon, many National Trust houses. Silverstone, Towcester. Dogs and horses welcome by arrangement.

PAWS-A-WHILE
KILNWICK PERCY, POCKLINGTON YO42 1UF
(01759 301168; Mobile: 07711 866869)
e-mail: paws.a.while@lineone.net • website: www.pawsawhile.net
www.dickyphotos.com

Small family B & B set in forty acres of parkland twixt York and Beverley. Golf, walking, riding. Pets and horses most welcome. Brochure available. ETC ★★★★

LYNNEY HOLDEN,
CROOKHOUSE, KIRKNEWTON, WOOLER NE71 6TN
(Tel: 01668 216113)
e-mail: stay@crookhousecottages.co.uk   • website: www.crookhousecottages.co.uk

Superior self catering accommodation in a traditional Northumbrian steading, Secluded and tranquil. Sleeps 2-12. Horses and dogs welcome. VisitBritain ★★★★.

RUSKO HOLIDAYS,
GATEHOUSE OF FLEET, CASTLE DOUGLAS DG7 2BS
(01557 814215)
e-mail: info@ruskoholidays.co.uk • website: www.ruskoholidays.co.uk

Spacious, traditional farmhouse and three charming, cosy cottages near beaches, hills and forest park. Lots of off-road riding amid stunning scenery. Stabling and grazing available for your own horse. Beautiful walking and riding country, fishing and tennis. BHS Horses Welcome Award, STB ★★ to ★★★★

MISS MORRIS
TY COCH FARM-TREKKING CENTRE
PENMACHNO, BETWS-Y-COED
NORTH WALES LL25 0HJ
(Tel: 01690 760248)
e-mail: cindymorris@tiscali.co.uk

Hill farm in Wales. TV, teamaking, en suite. Set in National Park/Snowdonia. Very quiet and well off the beaten track. A great welcome and good food. Many return visits. £25 B&B.

SIR JOHN'S HILL FARM HOLIDAY COTTAGES
LAUGHARNE
CARMARTHENSHIRE SA33 4TD
The Old Stables Cottage (Tel: 01994 427001)
website:www.sirjohnshillfarm.co.uk

A great place to come if you want to get away from it all with your horse(s) and your dog(s). Beautiful scenery, relaxing rides, including beach rides, and great accommodation.

WINALOT® Puppy
With Vitamin D and minerals

Winalot® Puppy food is full of the vitamins and minerals your puppy needs for strong bones and healthy teeth. Optimal nutrition during a dog's first years of growth helps set him up for many years to come. It also gives him the energy and strength he needs to grow into an active member of the family!

For more information about how to feed your puppy, go to

www.winalot-dog.co.uk

SINCE 1927

Winalot®
iron for vitality & protein for muscles

WINALOT® Adult
With Iron for Vitality and protein for muscles

A key ingredient in **Winalot®** Adult food is iron. Your dog needs this to carry oxygen around his body and help him release the energy from the food he needs to get the most out of life.

Winalot® Adult also contains quality protein which is the key building block of muscle. It also helps his coat stay shiny and healthy.

For more information about how to feed your dog, go to
www.winalot-dog.co.uk

PURINA

Pet-Friendly Pubs
A selection of Pubs and Inns where pets are especially welcome!

The Beehive
Waltham Road, White Waltham, Maidenhead SL6 3SH
01628 822877 • e-mail: beehivepub@aol.com • www.thebeehive-pub.com

Large front and back gardens. Bar and restaurant. Wheelchair facilities. Food served all day Saturday and Sunday. Pets welcome in gardens and bar area. Water bowls and treats for well behaved dogs.
Pet Regulars: Coco (Staffie), Bubbles and Ufano (the Guinness- drinking dog).

The Springer Spaniel
Treburley, near Launceston, Cornwall PL15 9NS
Tel: 01579 370424 • e-mail: enquiries@thespringerspaniel.org.uk
www.thespringerspaniel.org.uk

Country pub providing a warm welcome and specialising in home cooked, fresh, locally sourced food. Emphasis upon game, with beef and lamb from the owner's organic farm. Dogs can snooze by the fire or lounge in the beer garden - water provided
Pet Regulars: some very regular customers and their accompanying owners.

Cumberland Inn   Tel: 01434 381875
Townfoot, Alston, Cumbria CA9 3HX
stay@cumberlandinnalston.com • www.cumberlandinnalston.com

A comfy retreat in the secluded North Pennines. Real beer, real fires and real hospitality await your arrival. Home-made hearty fare available all day to revive flagging spirits. Our 5 recently refurbished rooms are all en suite. Muddy dogs and boots welcome.
Dog bowls filled with water (or even beer).
Pets welcome in bedrooms and bar. No charge for pets.

The Kings Arms Hotel
The Square, Hawkshead, Ambleside LA22 0NZ
Tel: 015394 36372
info@kingsarmshawkshead.co.uk • www.kingsarmshawkshead.co.uk

Family run, traditional Lakeland inn offering AA ★★★ Bed & Breakfast accommodation. Special mid-week rates. Quality home cooked food. Free fishing and 2 for 1 golf deals for guests. Children welcome.
Pets allowed in all areas except the dining room and kitchen.

Woolpack Inn
Eskdale, Cumbria CA19 1TH • 019467 23230
e-mail: office@greendoor.me • www.woolpack.co.uk

Free House situated in the heart of the breathtaking Eskdale Valley. B&B from £35pppn. Wide selection of real ales. Delicious food served all day.
Pets Facilities: Pets welcome throughout, including bedrooms.

The Fisherman's Haunt

Salisbury Road, Winkton, Christchurch, Dorset BH23 7AS
Tel: 01202 477283

Traditional coaching inn with 12 stylishly furnished bedrooms, some adapted for disabled access. Good food, wine and Fuller's cask ales. Close to Bournemouth Airport and many places of interest. Pets welcome.

Pets allowed in main bar and lounge for dining.
Two pet-friendly rooms in accommodation block.

www.fullershotels.com

The Brewers Arms

Martinstown, Dorchester, Dorset DT2 9LB • 01305 889361
e-mail: jackie_smith54@hotmail.com • www.thebrewersarms.com

Country pub with a lovely garden. Pub food. Amenities include a skittle alley, big car park and a large grassed area (which may be suitable for tents).
Chews, water bowls and areas out of the sun
Area in the pub where customers can eat and sit with their dogs.
Pet residents: Jodie and Poppy (both lurchers)

The Gaggle of Geese

Buckland Newton, Dorchester, Dorset DT2 7BS
01300 345249 • www.thegaggle.co.uk

Large pub with skittle alley, five acres of land including an orchard. Everything on our menu we make ourselves and as much of it is as locally sourced and seasonal as possible.

Pets welcome throughout • Water/food; fire in winter

The White Swan

The Square, 31 High Street, Swanage, Dorset BH19 2LJ • 01929 423804
e-mail: info@whiteswanswanage.co.uk • www.whiteswanswanage.co.uk

A pub with a warm and friendly atmosphere, three minutes from the beach. Traditional pub food, Sunday roasts. Large beer garden. En suite accommodation with parking. Free wifi and internet access. TV and pool table. Children and dogs welcome.
Water, treats • Dogs allowed in beer garden, bar area and accommodation.
Pet resident: Farley (Labradoodle). Regulars: Liddy and Em (Black Labradors), Sally and Sophie (Jack Russells), Patch (Jack Russell), Prince (King Charles Spaniel), Shadow (Boxer x Lab).

The Silent Woman Inn

Bere Road, Coldharbour, Wareham, Dorset BH20 7PA
Tel: 01929 552909 • www.thesilentwoman.co.uk

Traditional country inn nestling in the heart of Wareham Forest. Beautiful gardens, log fires in winter. All fresh ingredients, wonderful food. Real ales, good wines. Adults-only inside.
Water bowls and treats - and affection • Dogs allowed in bar areas and all outside areas except children's play areas.

http://whaleboneinn.sm4.biz/

The Whalebone *Freehouse*

Chapel Road, Fingringhoe, Colchester, Essex CO5 7BG
Tel/Fax: 01206 729307 • vicki@thewhaleboneinn.co.uk

Only minutes from Colchester, the Whalebone offers a wide range of excellent food and real ales. Pets are most welcome inside the pub and in the beer garden. Excellent dog-walking trails in and around Fingringhoe. Water bowls provided on request.
Pet Residents: Rosie and Poppy (Basset Hounds)

The White Buck • 01425 402264
Bisterne Close, Burley, Ringwood, Hampshire BH24 4AZ
Victorian Inn blending tradition with modern comfort,
located in the heart of the New Forest, with 7 stylish
bedrooms, excellent restaurant and bar. Play area and
log trail available for children. Pets welcome.
Dogs are permitted in the bar area
and bedrooms 1,3 and 8 only.

www.fullershotels.com

BLACK HORSE INN
Pilgrims Way, Thurnham, Maidstone ME14 3LD
Tel: 01622 737185 • info@wellieboot.net • www.wellieboot.net
A homely and welcoming inn with its origins in the 18thC, The Black Horse
is adorned with hops and beams, and has an open log fireplace to welcome
you in winter. A separate annexe has 30 beautiful en suite bedrooms.
Pets can stay in B&B rooms • Welcome in bar on lead
Dog bin and poop bags provided • Maps of local walks available.

The Inn at Whitewell • Forest of Bowland
Near Clitheroe, Lancs BB7 3AT • Tel: 01200 448222
reception@innatwhitewell.com • www.innatwhitewell.com
14thC inn in the beautiful Forest of Bowland.
7 miles fishing from our doorstep - trout, sea trout and salmon.
23 glamorous bedrooms, award-winning kitchen.
Voted by *The Independent* "One of the 50 Best UK Hotels"
Pets welcome in all areas except the kitchen!

Horse and Jockey
9 Chorlton Green, Manchester M21 9HS • 0161 860 7794
info@horseandjockeychorlton.com • www.horseandjockeychorlton.com
Traditional pub in village green setting. 6 cask ales, 50 bin wine cellar.
Disabled access. Traditional pub menu served all day, every day. Sunday
lunch. Separate restaurant and function room.
Pets Facilities: all dogs get a biscuit, water bowl and lots of attention.
Pet Regulars: resident dog Eddie, Golden Labrador.

Stiffkey Red Lion
Tel: 01328 830552
44 Wells Road, Stiffkey, Norfolk NR23 1AJ
e-mail: redlion@stiffkey.com • www.stiffkey.com
5 ground floor en suite bedrooms, 5 on first floor;
all with their own external door.
Pets warmly welcomed

THE ROYAL OAK
Chart Lane South, Stonebridge, Dorking, Surrey RH5 4DJ
Tel: 01306 886420
Friendly country pub with traditional appeal. Range of food from quick
bar snacks to full meals, using fresh local produce where possible.
Pets Facilities: enclosed garden at rear.
Pet Regulars: resident pub dog - Ho, Ziggy.

The Bat and Ball

15 Bat and Ball Lane, Boundstone, Farnham GU10 4SA
Tel: 01252 792108
info@thebatandball.co.uk • www.thebatandball.co.uk

Traditional village pub. • Selection of 6 ales. • Extensive home made menu. • Garden and patio area. • Situated on five converging footpaths - ideal drop-in place for walkers. • Children's play area. • Pets on leads allowed in the pub.

Pet Regulars: Mac (Assistant Landlord)

Old Ship Inn

Uckfield Road, Ringmer, East Sussex BN8 5RP • 01273 814223
e-mail: info@oldshippub.co.uk • www.oldshippub.co.uk

On the A26 between Lewes and Uckfield, this family-run 17thC inn is the perfect place to relax, with food served from 12 to 9.30pm daily. The charming oak-beamed bar and restaurant is set in one acre of well tended, enclosed gardens. Well behaved dogs welcome inside.

Pet Resident: Marley (Bernese Mountain Dog)

The Oak

Coventry Road, Baginton, Coventry CV8 3AU
Tel: 02476 518855 • Fax: 02476 518866
e-mail: thebagintonoak@aol.com • www.thebagintonoak.co.uk

Bed & Breakfast accommodation. 13 en suite bedrooms. Quality home-cooked food - 2 meals for £10 available all day. Pets welcome.

Extensive exercise area. Water bowls and waste bags available. Dog treats for sale. Pet Residents: Beau and Jasper (Border Collies)

The Lamb Inn

High Street, Hindon, Wiltshire SP3 6DP
Tel: 01747 820573 • Fax: 01747 820605
www.lambathindon.co.uk

12th Century historic inn with bedrooms full of character. Outstanding food and great wine selection. Pets welcome in the bar and bedrooms. ETC/AA ★★★★

The Harrogate Arms

Crag Lane, Harrogate HG3 1QA
Tel: 01423 567950
e-mail: info@theharrogatearms.com • www.theharrogatearms.com

An 18th century listed building set amid tranquil woodland. Restaurant and bar. Ideal for walkers. Children welcome. Pets welcome and permitted in bar and dining area. Dog bowl permanently available.

The Castle Inn

7 Wistowgate, Cawood
Selby, North Yorkshire YO8 3SH   **Tel: 01757 268324**
info@castleinncawood.co.uk • www.castleinncawood.co.uk

18thC village pub with a 60-seat restaurant and an 18-pitch caravan site. All food is local and fresh.

Pets Welcome • Water bowls outside.

THE NEW INN MOTEL

Main Street, Huby, York YO61 1HQ • Tel: 01347 810219
enquiries@newinnmotel.freeserve.co.uk • www.newinnmotel.co.uk

Modern, motel-style accommodation in quiet location 9 miles from York. Comfortable en suite bedrooms are spacious and neatly furnished. Breakfast from locally sourced produce is served in the dining room.

Pets Facilities: Pets welcome by arrangement

The Green Dragon

High Row, Exelby, Bedale DL8 2HA • 01677 422233
www.thegreendragonexelby.com

A family run, independent country inn taking pride in its friendly welcoming service, an excellent restaurant, comfortable, well appointed accommodation and a large car park. There are four tastefully decorated rooms all en suite, with colour television and hospitality tray.

Old Hall Inn

Tel: 01756 752441

Main Street, Threshfield, Grassington, N. Yorks BD23 5HB
oldhallinn@fsmail.net • www.oldhallinnandcottages.co.uk

18thC Inn, renowned for fine ales and award-winning cuisine. Large beer garden. Children's outdoor play area. B&B in four en suite bedrooms; quality self-catering available in adjacent cottages. *Well behaved dogs welcome.*

ANNANDALE ARMS HOTEL

HIGH STREET, MOFFAT DG10 9HF
Tel: 01683 220013 • Fax: 01683 221395

A warm welcome is offered to dogs with well-mannered and house-trained owners. There are all the comforts and facilities that owners enjoy such as an excellent restaurant and a relaxing panelled bar. STB ★★★ Hotel.

www.annandalearmshotel.co.uk • pw@annandalearmshotel.co.uk

SINCE 1927

Winalot®
iron for vitality & protein for muscles

WINALOT® Senior
With key nutrients to help maintain mobility

Dogs over approximately 7 years of age (depending on breed and body size), have different nutrional requirements from growing and adult dogs. To help keep him enjoying life, we use a different formula with quality protein and carefully adjusted proportions of vitamin D and minerals to help maintain strong muscles and bones and help support mobility.

For more information about how to feed your senior dog, go to

www.winalot-dog.co.uk

PURINA

Index of Towns and Counties

© FHG Guides Ltd, 2011
ISBN 978-1-85055-440-0

Typeset by FHG Guides Ltd, Paisley.
Printed and bound in China by Imago.

Distribution. Book Trade: ORCA Book Services, Stanley House,
3 Fleets Lane, Poole, Dorset BH15 3AJ
(Tel: 01202 665432; Fax: 01202 666219)
e-mail: mail@orcabookservices.co.uk
Published by FHG Guides Ltd., Abbey Mill Business Centre,
Seedhill, Paisley PA1 ITJ (Tel: 0141-887 0428 Fax: 0141-889 7204).
e-mail: admin@fhguides.co.uk

Pets Welcome! is published by FHG Guides Ltd,
part of Kuperard Group.

Cover design: FHG Guides
Cover Picture: 'Blade' and family, photo courtesy of Winalot®

All the advertisers in **PETS WELCOME!** have an entry in the appropriate classified section and each classified entry may carry one or more of the following symbols:

🐕   This symbol indicates that pets are welcome free of charge.

£   The £ indicates that a charge is made for pets. We quote the amount where possible, either per night or per week.

pw!   This symbol shows that the establishment has some special provision for pets; perhaps an exercise facility or some special feeding or accommodation arrangements.

⌂   Indicates separate pets' accommodation.

PLEASE NOTE that all the advertisers in **PETS WELCOME!** extend a welcome to pets and their owners but they may attach conditions. The interests of other guests have to be considered and it is usually assumed that pets will be well trained, obedient and under the control of their owner.

FHG Guides Ltd have been publishing an attractive range of day accommodation guides for over 50 years. For all kinds of holiday opportunities, they make useful gifts at any time of year. guides are available in most bookshops and larger newsagents but e will be happy to post you a copy direct if you have any difficulty. POST FREE for addresses in the UK. will also post abroad but have to charge separately for post or freight.

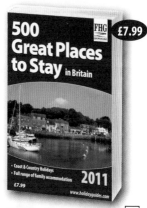

500
Great Places to Stay
in Britain
- Coast & Country Holidays
- Full range of family accommodation

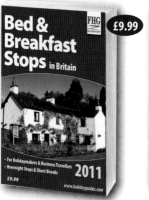

Bed &
Breakfast Stops
in Britain
- For holidaymakers and business travellers
- Overnight stops and Short Breaks

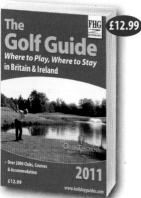

The Golf Guide
Where to Play, Where to Stay
- Approximately 2800 golf courses in Britain and Ireland plus details of convenient accommodation.

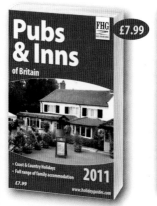

Pubs & Inns
of Britain
- Including Dog-friendly Pubs
- Accommodation, food and traditional good cheer

300
Great Hotels
of Britain
- Hotels with Conference, Leisure and Wedding Facilities

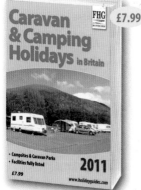

Caravan
& Camping Holidays
in Britain
- Campsites and Caravan parks
- Facilities fully listed

  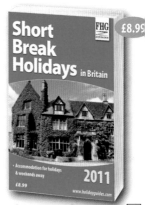

Family Breaks
in Britain
- Accommodation, attractions and resorts
- Suitable for those with children and babies

Self-Catering Holidays
in Britain
- Cottages, farms, apartments and chalets
- Over 400 places to stay
- Pet-Friendly accommodation

Short Break Holidays
in Britain
- Accommodation for holidays and weekends away

Tick your choice above and send your order and payment to

FHG Guides Ltd. Abbey Mill Business Centre
Seedhill, Paisley, Scotland PA1 1TJ
TEL: 0141- 887 0428 • FAX: 0141- 889 7204
e-mail: admin@fhguides.co.uk

Deduct 10% for 2/3 titles or copies; 20% for 4 or more.

Send to: NAME ....

             ADDRESS ....

                  ....

                  ....

             POST CODE ....

enclose Cheque/Postal Order for £ ....

             SIGNATURE ....DATE ....

Please complete the following to help us improve the service we provide.

How did you find out about our guides?:

☐ Press   ☐ Magazines   ☐ TV/Radio   ☐ Family/Friend   ☐ Other